Tarot Fundamentals

TAROT FUNDAMENTALS

Authors:
Giordano Berti,
Tali Goodwin,
Sasha Graham,
Marcus Katz,
Mark McElroy,
Riccardo Minetti,
Barbara Moore

Edited and compiled by
Sasha Graham

LO SCARABEO

Tarot Fundamentals

Edited and compiled by Sasha Graham

Authors:

Giordano Berti, Tali Goodwin, Sasha Graham, Marcus Katz, Mark McElroy, Riccardo Minetti, Barbara Moore

Graphic project:
Pietro Alligo, Santo Alligo

Editorial staff:
Riccardo Minetti, Alessandro Starrantino, Manfredi Toraldo

Editing:
Debbie Lake, Liz O'Neill, Jessica Noach

Marketing:
Mario Pignatiello, Andrea Chiarvesio

This book was printed with the contribution of:
Regione Piemonte - Direzione Cultura, Turismo e Sport
Settore Biblioteche, Archivi ed Istituti Culturali
L.R. 18/2008 "Interventi a sostegno dell'Editoria Piemontese e dell'Informazione Locale"

Volume realizzato con il contributo della Regione Piemonte
Direzione Cultura, Turismo e Sport
Settore Biblioteche, Archivi ed Istituti Culturali
L.R. 18/2008 "Interventi a sostegno dell'Editoria Piemontese e dell'Informazione Locale"

© 2015 by Lo Scarabeo srl
Via Cigna 110 – 10155 Torino – Italy
www.loscarabeo.com - www.facebook.com/LoScarabeoTarot

© images: Shutterstock.com ; Lo Scarabeo ; Right owners

First edition - September 2015.

Printed by Maple Printing

About the Authors

Sasha Graham sees Tarot as life, knows magic is alive and believes *signs are everywhere* if you know how to look.

Sasha received her Bachelor of Arts in Literature and Religion at Hunter College in New York City. Sasha maintains a thriving private Tarot reading practice. She has produced Tarot events at the Metropolitan Museum of Art and the Morgan Library.

Sasha's books titles include; *Tarot Diva, 365 Tarot Spreads,* and the forthcoming *365 Tarot Spells.* Sasha has been featured in various media outlets such as Sirius XM Radio, The Wall Street Journal, The Daily News and appeared on the cover of Crain's New York Business. She appeared regularly as a guest on the WPIX Channel 11 Morning News, reading Tarot for pop culture topics and celebrities.

Giordano Berti is an Italian writer, and one of the greatest international experts on the connection between art and esotericism. A highly respected authority on the history of Tarot, his many books have been translated into English, French, Spanish, German, Dutch, Polish and Japanese. He is also the President of the Graf Institute in Bologna, Italy.

Tali Goodwin created Tarosophy Tarot Association, Tarot Professionals, and Tarot Town with Marcus Katz. Together, Marcus and Tali have co-authored many books including; *Secrets of the Waite Smith Tarot, Around the Tarot in 78 Days* and *Tarot Face to Face, Easy Lenormand.*

Marcus Katz created the Tarosophy Tarot Association, Tarot Professionals, and Tarot Town with Tali Goodwin. Together, Tali and Marcus have co-authored many books including: *Tarot Face to Face, Secrets of the Waite Smith Tarot,* and *Around the Tarot in 78 Days.*

Mark McElroy is the author of *Putting the Tarot to Work, Taking the Tarot to Heart, What's in the Cards for You?, I Ching for Beginners* and *The Absolute Beginner's Guide to Tarot.* He calls Tarot "the ultimate visual brainstorming tool," and shares techniques designed to help others ask better questions, see more options, and achieve their goals. He holds a B.A. and M.A. in creative writing and composition from the Center for Writers at the University of Southern Mississippi. He has more than two decades of experience as a public speaker and corporate trainer. Today, he works as a writer, voice actor, and creativity consultant.

Riccardo Minetti is the Chief Editor of Lo Scarabeo for Tarot. Riccardo has a hand in the conception, design and direction of new Tarot decks and books and acts a mediator between writers, deck designers, artists and Lo Scarabeo. He has been involved in the creation of over 100 Tarot decks and books. Standouts include *Gothic Tarot of the Vampire, Etruscan Tarot, Manga Tarot, Fey Tarot* and the forthcoming *Epic Tarot.*

Barbara Moore a leading expert in the field of Tarot has published a number of Tarot books and decks, including; *Tarot for Beginners, Tarot Spreads, The Steampunk Tarot, The Gilded Tarot, The Mystic Dreamer,* and *Tarot of the Hidden Realm.* Writing is solitary work and is relieved by teaching Tarot at conferences around the world. Barbara also loves working with clients, using the Tarot to provide guidance and insight.

Letter from the Publisher

Dear reader,

The Tarot Fundamentals project was born in 2004 with the idea of creating a comprehensive book about Tarot: a guide that could accompany the reader from the very basics to the most advanced readings and techniques.

Lo Scarabeo has published for years in Europe part-works Encyclopedias about Tarot, so we already had countless material, articles and illustrations available. Our challenge was to reorganize and integrate all the information in a way that was easy to understand for the beginner and interesting enough for the Tarot expert.

After more than 10 years of development, this book is finally here. It took a lot of effort, time and energy, knowledge, competence, patience and research. As with most labors of love, it seemed too big, too ambitious and too special to hit the market. But, thanks to our Kickstarter pledgers, it is now a reality, and we're proud to introduce it to you.

The book you're holding, Tarot Fundamentals, is the first in a series of three. This book is the founding stone of the whole project. This volume has, of course, a lot of information useful to beginners, but it's also filled with interesting content for Tarot experts. The three volumes combine in a natural progression, that we have summarized in the diagram on the left.

As you will discover reading, Tarot Fundamentals doesn't just cover the basics: on its own it is already one of the more complete books ever published about Tarot. The following two volumes, Experience and Compendium, will soon be available too, after their own Kickstarter campaign, and build on the content you will find in the following pages and will travel even deeper and wider into Tarot knowledge.

Welcome to a journey through many different and fascinating aspects of Tarot.

Welcome to Tarot Fundamentals.

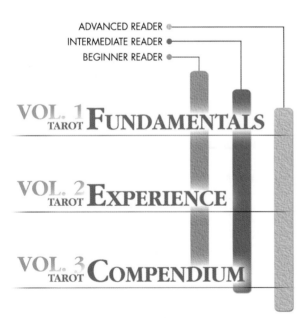

ADVANCED READER
INTERMEDIATE READER
BEGINNER READER

VOL. 1 TAROT FUNDAMENTALS

VOL. 2 TAROT EXPERIENCE

VOL. 3 TAROT COMPENDIUM

Table of Contents

Foreword by Sasha Graham

Many years ago, I sat in Manhattan on the other end of the phone with friend and colleague Barbara Moore who was calling from Minneapolis. There are those uncanny moments when you know something big is about to unfold. A phone call, in the age of email, usually signifies something important. I held my breath as I listened to Barbara's voice. She inquired if I would be interested in a project. A BIG project. Her colleagues in Italy at Lo Scarabeo had, over time, acquired years worth of Tarot texts, articles and information written in both Italian and English. They wanted to create a masterwork with their treasure trove. She asked if I would be willing to compile it into something useful. I was. The book you hold and the subsequent books that are coming are the result of that phone call.

Tarot books usually fall into one of three categories. The first kind is thick and heavy. They are encyclopedic, full of historical information but hard to read. The second kind are hardcover, illustrated books. They are put out by large publishing houses, are pretty to look at but are either light on content or loaded with esoteric material. The third and most prolific kind, are the wide variety of soft cover how-to Tarot books. Each of these contains different slants on learning and using Tarot. Each kind of Tarot books has their place in the Tarot world. All are useful. However, I had yet to see a Tarot book that was both beautiful to look at, a pleasure to peruse, yet full of essential information.

It also seemed quite daring to publish a giant book on Tarot in an age where naysayers claim that physical books have gone the way of the dinosaur. Publishing a hardcover book in a time where the current generation of children may not have the pleasure of looking for books in an actual bookstore because Internet shopping has forced the closing of exquisite brick and mortar bookstores seemed courageous. There also seemed something very special about creating essential Tarot books for serious students of Tarot or collectors of cards, in the technological age. After all, vast systems of information exist online, in the age of the instant gratification immediate download, and was it practical to create a book of this nature? Would anyone want it?

Lo Scarabeo took this question to the Tarot community via Kickstarter. The community responded with a resounding YES! You wanted a beautiful book that could be held in hand alongside your cards. You want to fall inside the nature of possibility that exists between covers that will never exist on a computer screen. The psychic imprint of the Reader congeals with a book the same way it does with a deck of Tarot cards. This is why a grandmother's treasured cookbook, complete with notes in the margin, stained with drips of oil and scattered with sugar and heavy with the weight of decades of cooking, will always win out over an electronic file of recipes. And why anyone can comb through the thousands of web pages regarding Tarot but why it is a unique and different experience to hold a physical book in your hand. It is the very same reason that even with all technological innovations, the physical deck of Tarot cards cannot be replaced. Not via apps, computer screens or video. Nothing replaces the physicality, the pleasure or the absorption of holding a physical book or deck of cards in your hand. Especially a book designed and illustrated with the extraordinary talents of Lo Scarabeo.

I also found the tackling of Tarot history an interesting challenge. Tarot is over-whelmingly, a woman's art. The history of Tarot, the way women used Tarot (and regular playing cards) for divination and fortune telling, healing or entertainment, is untold. We instinctively know that cards, palms and tealeaves have been used for divination for hundreds of years because it is a well-known cross-cultural practice. Every culture has their "wise folk," and no matter what country you are reading this book in, you know where to find them. But folk magic, fortune telling and divina-tory practices pass orally from teacher to student, from grandmother to granddaugh-ter, mother to child. And because, by and large, history is written by men, vast troves of information and divinatory systems regarding Tarot simply do not exist.

The men who interfaced with Tarot and published their findings and created decks were the great occultists. Because Tarot's nature is "arcane" or "secret" and much of the history is intertwined with secret societies and mysterious practices. This can lead to confusion and misunder-standing when trying to understand the occult history of the cards or attempting to understand the connection between Hermes Trismegistus, the Rosicrucians and how does this connect to the Knight of Cups? Great care was taken with the historical portion of Tarot Fundamentals. It attempts to unravel exactly who and what these mystics and occultists were and what they were doing in a simple and transparent way. It attempts to explain how and why the deck you are holding and questioning got there in the first place.

Tarot Fundamentals is just as its title states. A centralized beginning and the building blocks of what is collected and known about Tarot. And there is much more to come…

It is my greatest hope that through this book, through the volumes of informa-tion, you will allow the world to slip away, taken away with the magic of Tar-ot. That you will discover something new or become inspired in your Tarot practice. That your children might discover this book on a rainy day and tumble headfirst into the magic of Bonifacio Bembo's illuminated cards, become intrigued by the idea of a Mystery School or gaze into the image of the High Priestess and see something of themselves reflected back. Books are like Tarot decks. They provide answers and guidance but more import-ant, they are doorways and portals to the otherworld and the imagination. And they leave their imprint and keep whispering to us, long after we close the pages or shuffle the deck.

Sasha Graham
New York City 2015

INTRODUCTION

WELCOME TO THE CARDS

Welcome to the enchanting, beguiling, and utterly addictive world of Tarot. Hang your coat, wipe your shoes, and sit down. I guarantee you will stay a while. When did Tarot first capture your attention? Did you grow up with the cards or have them read by a mysterious gypsy? Did you come across a pack of cards on a dusty bookshelf or dabble in the cards when in college?

The first experience of having a Tarot deck in hand can be curiously enchanting, utterly fascinating, and a bit confusing. Perusing Tarot is like visiting a foreign city for the first time. A new city can feel familiar, yet strange. Overwhelmed with new smells and sensations, random streets, dark alleys, foreign transportation systems, a new metropolis can feel as if it stretches on forever with no limits or boundaries. Tarot can feel the same way.

To enter Tarot is to enter a new world. It is the territory of the subconscious, intuitive and psychic senses, dreamscapes, and the imagination. There is no roadmap. But there is a solid structure. Thankfully, Tarot contains a beautifully constructed underlying system. The cards, each containing their own specific magic, symbolism, iconography, and meanings, are easily connected to one another. They do not exist in a confusing vacuum but in a sensible and orderly fashion.

Lo Scarabeo's Tarot Fundamentals will act as your guide. It will bring you through the highways, byways, and all the marvelous places Tarot allows one to go. If you stay open, the Arcana will touch you, open you, like a budding flower. You may have plenty of experience with Tarot and know its streets like the palm of your hand. But like Paris, New York, or Rome, there is always more to explore, always a sidewalk you haven't meandered down, a scrumptious new restaurant, or an attractive stranger who changes your world in a single, sultry glance.

Authoring this volume, we have brought many schools of Tarot knowledge to your fingertips. As the editor of this book, I have but one simple request for you. Do not kick back and quietly read about Tarot. If you merely read the information contained in these volumes, without physical application, it would be like memorizing and studying the city map without actually exploring it. Make the effort to bring Tarot into your life as an active practice. Let the Arcana leap to life beneath your fingers. Allow them to provoke you, inspire you, and challenge you. Should you get confused, be brave. When the cards point out something that makes you squirm, persevere through it. If you actively use the cards, the work spent creating these comprehensive volumes will have been worth it. And you will have expanded the limits of Tarot just a bit further, changing, evolving not only yourself but the very art of cartomancy.

Let's continue with the metaphor of Tarot as a mysterious foreign city because in many ways it truly is. People, the general public, perhaps even you, approach Tarot with many preconceived notions and ideas of what Tarot is. People believe they know exactly how Tarot should be used or believe there are strict rules and regulations regarding Tarot's use. Sadly, many people are afraid of getting Tarot wrong when they begin using it. They stop themselves before allowing and inviting the space in which to play and explore the cards.

Everything you have heard about the cards is likely right. It is also mostly wrong. How can this be? Tarot is a human device, created and used by people for hundreds of years for everything from gambling to magic to fortune telling and everything else in between. If you can imagine doing something with the cards, it has probably been done. Tarot is ultimately what we make of it. But you have to jump in and begin using the cards. So, open those decks and let's begin.

I'm leaping ahead quickly but for now, indulge me. Take my hand, and together we will enter this strange city of Tarot. Let's begin afresh with your cards. Let's wander through certain twisting, half forgotten streets and slip through the ages of time. Let's get a quick glimpse of ways Tarot has been employed in these last few hundred years. Each section, every spot, I reveal is grounded in historic fact. Each place based in truth. Nothing has been made up, although plenty of facts, stories, and lore have invented about Tarot. Are you ready?

The Tarot City

"Welcome to this beautiful city. Let's begin with the regal royal way. Do you see that looming castle up ahead?" I ask.
"This main cobblestone street leads to court where the Kings, Queens, Knights, and Pages live and play. Their royal lives are spent dancing, laughing, and ruling from within the great halls

overlooking this city. Girls go mad for the Knight of Swords, the dangerous bad boy hero of the deck. Women seek to embody the Queen of Wands, famous for her beauty and magnetic charisma. Children laugh and chase the Page of Cups who exudes the dreamy fun of youth with every summersault. Men revere the King of Pentacles, financial genius. You will quickly discover the regal ones represent aspects of your very own personality. They are you. They can also represent other people in your life." I say.

A sharp sound catches your attention. A parade is snailing its way through town. We run over to watch the commotion. Smiling townspeople wave to the passing floats. A red float carries a handsome, young man and woman. They gaze at each other while a soft pudgy fellow, wearing what looks to be a makeshift diaper, and glitter wings dances around the couple. The man baby slings fake arrows into the crows. The onlookers go crazy.

"That is the Triumph of Love, and that is the angel Cupid," I explain. "Here comes the Devil."

A black float creeps forward. Dancers in scarlet costumes leap and twirl, representing the Devil's flames. The great demon is topless, horrific looking, his bat wings bobbing. Making gnarled faces at the crowd, he invites them to join him in the empty seat next to his. Boos and hisses echo from the townspeople.

An colorful jester runs between the floats, stops to cartwheel and dance a jig. A group of children collapse in giggles.

"There's the Fool. He rides on no float, he goes where he likes," I explain.

A massive glowing ball, attached by strings like a hot air balloon brings up the last float. Glittering aerialists, adorned as sparkling angels, swing through the air next to it.

"This is the World, also known as Fame and it triumphs everything that has come before. This is the arch of triumph, the parade of triumphs, and the standard parade of the Middle Ages. It had its start in ancient Rome. These parades likely influenced our modern Tarot Trumps, each allegory 'trumping' the next," I explain while grabbing your hand.

"The parade is done. Come this way. Here is Museum Mile," I point out.

We walk through past granite Corinthian columns into stunning art gallery. People speak in hushed tones and gaze up the art adorning the walls.

"Here we find the very first Tarot decks. These are the Visconti-Sforza cards, brilliant miniatures painted with real gold.

Renaissance artist Bonifacio Bembo made them for a noble family. Must be nice to have that kind of money, huh? He painted next to Leonardo Da Vinci. Tarot comes to us from the Renaissance but we have it all here. All the variations Tarot has taken over the years. The only real requirement to make a Tarot deck is that the cards contain the Major Arcana, but look here. Here is the mysterious Minchiatte deck with an additional 25 Major Arcana cards! There is not one true Tarot but many shapes and forms and they hang before you."

Taking you by the hand, we slip through a side door. In a moment, the grand gallery makes way to exposed wood floors. Fresh air blows across your skin from the open windows. The hallway is lined with doors, some open affording a peek. Poking your head inside, the pungent smell of oil paints and solvents hit your nose. A brooding artist slaps paint across his canvas.

"He is finding his expression of the Five of Cups," I whisper. "These are the artists who are creating new decks."

The next studio brings us to artist bent over a table. The cool glow of a computer screen illuminates her face while she carefully digitizes her art, creating a new set of 78 cards. You peek into the next room and the stillness of an empty studio greets you.

"Perhaps one day you will take a seat in that space?" I suggest. You hear the closing of a door and look up to see the brooding artist, wiping the sweat from his brow and locking up. He brushes through you, as if you were nothing more than a ghostly apparition. Feeling compelled to trail him, we follow his rapid gate.

The sun sets against the stark outline of this strange city. Lamps blaze to life. Each enclosure is comforting, enchanting. The artist stops and throws open a door, the sound of chaos escapes, the acrid smell of smoke hits your nose. A palatable heat emanates from inside the room and compared to the sudden chill filling the streets, you are drawn deeper into the tavern. Inside, men, their rosy, red cheeks betraying the amount of drink they have consumed, sprawl. A fight erupts. A man crashes into a table. Drinks and food fly through the air and he's swiftly thrown out the door. Oblivious tavern men remain bent in game, playing cards, betting money, laughing, and drinking.

"These the taverns are where Tarot games were played once Tarot left the courts. In this tavern, alleys, and game rooms of the past, Tarot was used for nothing more than games of chance and skill. No fortune telling here." I say taking a deep swig of cold beer.

"Now, I need you to be brave. Don't freak out." I say.

I lead you out the back door. The roar of the pub subsides in the lonely alley and a lone rat scurries away. The lights are dim as we move together. All is silent but for only our echoing foot-steps. A face emerges from shadow. Beautiful, sparkling eyes, and cherry lips draw you in. Looking closer at the dimness from which she emerged, you shrink back in horror. Her lively eyes are now cloudy white and lips bare revealing a row of rotting teeth. You sense more movement in the shadows, slithering like cockroaches. This alley is filled with shadow people, some blatantly showing themselves, others content to lurk.

"These are charlatans who use their trickery and deception to gain people's trust. They trick people out of money. They'll read a client's cards, gain their trust, then lie. They claim to see bad mojo in the cards, dark energies around their client's life. They claim to see disaster and then for a price they will fix the disaster. For money they provide prayers, candles, and spells to scare the evil away. Stop and ponder these liars. Examine how they operate. Decide for yourself, should you pursue the reading of cards for cash, what boundaries you will place for yourself and your clients. Think of your intentions the moment a person puts their trust in your hands. C'mon, let's go," we head around a corner.

An old theater with a glowing marquis lights up the street ahead. A cold knob turns in the palm of your hand, you pull open the heavy glass doors, enter the theater, no ticket required. Red velvet carpet lines the walls and floor, the sweet scent of sugar mixed with the fluffy scent of fresh popped popcorn. Walking down an aisle, you take a seat. A gentleman stands before you on stage. He wears a headdress, cloak and stands above a table, magical implements glimmering before him. He is surrounded by a group of robed people and initiates these people through a strange ceremony. They repeat after him in curious words

"You have just entered the arena of the ceremonial magician," I whisper, munching on a hand full of popcorn. "These magicians use Tarot to conjure magic, contact angelic beings, travel between worlds, and manipulate reality. They operate in a world of symbol and poetry, they change shape, travel shamanistically; use Tarot as their doorway. They had their heyday in the 19th century. Some remain in our modern times."

You are about to grab some popcorn when we are off once again. Out the backstage door, you see rows and rows of offices on the street.

"This is the therapeutic section of town. It is bustling with Jungians and psychotherapists. These professionals connect each and every point of Tarot with the human psyche. They use Tarot to analyze thoughts, motivations and urges. They operate in a world of symbol and uphold the idea of the archetype. An archetype is the great structure of shared human experience and it thrives in our collective unconscious. This is the basis of Tarot. They will interpret the theme of a dream with their cards and tell you what your subconscious wants you to know when you can't hear it.

I want to show you the witches!" We head toward a river and the air becomes humid, thick and full of the scent of honeysuckle and roses. We peek through a rusty window and discover a small, raven haired, solitary witch. She places cards before her, the Magician, the Star, and the Moon.

"She is using the Tarot for her magic spell. Each card contains a specific energy. Her magic and subconscious will pick up on it in order to manifest her wish."

Outside a hut there is an older woman, she utters Spanish words and stabs the heart of a white dove. You realize the dark stain spreading across the bird's snow white feathers is blood. Looking closer you see her dripping the animal's blood over something. It is a card. The Devil card.

"She is breaking a spell cast on her by another witch." I say as I clasp your hand and pull you away.

"There's lots more I could show you, gypsies, alchemists, myth makers, but I think this is enough for now. You know there's a reason bookstores often keep Tarot decks and Tarot books behind their counters. They are the most shoplifted items in the store. These are grimoires of wisdom and books of knowledge. Tarot contains the breadth of human experience, it reflects of our souls, the scope of our humanity. What we are, what we desire, what we strive to be, is all there in seventy-eight cards. Amazing how pictures on flimsy little cards could contain so much meaning, philosophy, art history and psychology, yet it does. Tarot books and decks are your gateway to a shimmering city of possibility. Only one question matters. How far are you willing to go?"

Sasha Graham

WELCOME TO THE ARCANA

Tarot is made up of 78 mysterious Arcanum. This key unlocks the Arcana and acts as an open door into each image.

It is impossible for any one person to know everything about the Arcana. The Arcana is an imperfectly knowable subject. The Arcana cannot be pulled apart, examined and learned precisely as one might dissect a butterfly in a scientific lab. The Arcana reveal themselves to the observer visually through symbol and archetype. Symbols and archetypes express the knowable and the unknowable, the seen and unseen, the visible and invisible.

Each card is a point of departure. Each Arcana contains seeds of possibility. A symbol of importance, which arises in the collective human consciousness or symbols that capture attention, will always be partially unknown. This unknown, this "x factor," leads to new meanings and manifestations. This is precisely why Tarot has continued to evolve for over 400 years.

The first chapter opens the Major Arcana; the twenty-two cards whose very existence defines a deck as Tarot. The second chapter considers the Minor Arcana and brings the Reader inside the cards describing daily life. The third chapter reveals the Court Cards, the human personalities and people who populate the world of the Tarot.

In order to lead the Reader inside the Arcana, Tarot Fundamentals has provided a specific formula to bring each card to life and is described in detail in the following pages. Our formula begins with language and quickly moves through the array of symbols populating the Arcana. It embraces Tarot imagery, compares and contrasts historical renderings and brings traditional meanings from the earliest Tarot texts and scholars to the fore. Examples from modern decks beg a new examination of old ideals. Metaphysical doors are opened as the Arcana "speaks" to the Reader and offers "lessons." This fundamental formula is a first step in the journey of the Arcana.

Selected reference decks

Ten decks have been selected as a reference for examples of the Arcana in various decks.

Lo Scarabeo Tarot
The unique Lo Scarabeo Tarot is chosen because it combines images and symbols from three essential Tarot prototypes, the Marseille, the Rider Waite Smith and the Thoth deck.
By Mark McElroy, artwork by Anna Lazzarini.

Nefertari's Tarot
The Nefertari's Tarot was chosen as the Arcana reflect the mystery and magic of Egyptian symbols and myth. Two-dimensional Egyptian artwork adorns these stunning Arcana whose gold foil background emits the radiance of the sun.
By Silvana Alasia.

Pagan Tarot
The Pagan Tarot's Arcana reflects the modern experience of Wiccan and Pagan traditions and lifestyle. It was chosen because it reflects the journey of a young witch in 78 cards. The sacred and the profane intermingle in her life as she proceeds upon a path of inner spiritual growth that transforms all aspects of her reality.
By Gina M. Pace, artwork by Luca Raimondo, colors by Cristiano Spadoni.

Dark Angels
The dark and gloomy Dark Angels Tarot was chosen because the Arcana plunges the Reader inside the delightfully deviant netherworld of the vampire. The shadow self of the Reader is embraced by the Dark Angels who witness humanity as it spirals into darkness.
By Luca Russo.

Universal Fantasy Tarot

Tarot reflects the landscape of the imagination and The Universal Fantasy Arcana was chosen as it reflects the literature of the fantastical. This wild deck is illustrated with beasts, witches, heroes, heroines, gods and demons. *By Paolo Martinello.*

Fey Tarot

Light and happy, positive and playful, the Fey Tarot sparkles with Fey creatures, reinventing each Arcana in order to open a gateway to a world of wonder, magic and deep meaning. *By Riccardo Minetti, artwork by Mara Aghem.*

Shaman Tarot

The Arcana may be treated as a shamanistic gateway. A multi-cultural Shamanistic experience is reflected in the Shaman Tarot. The Arcana in the Shamanic Tarot are bonded in archetypal reality and recover a connection between reality, nature and the spirit world. *By Massimiliano Filadoro, artwork by Sabrina Ariganello and Alessia Pastorello.*

Tarot of the Pagan Cats

Tarot of the Pagan Cats was chosen for its unique blend of feline essence and Pagan symbolism. It is the cat which inspires myth, is a witch's familiar and walks the boundaries of the magic and mysterious. *By Barbara Moore, artwork by Lola Airaghi.*

Tarot of the Dark Grimoire

The Dark Grimoire was chosen to exemplify an Arcana where magick is real and dwells in a shadow land full of sorcerers and strange creatures. The Arcana of this deck are inspired by magical texts and grimoires of fiction and lore, in particular, the Necronomicon. This dark deck speaks of hope shining through darkness and tears away the masks that defend us from the harsh currents of reality. *By Michele Penco.*

Manga Tarot

The Manga Tarot was chosen because it reflects the artistic style of Manga, and because it relates an immediately youthful experience. A powerful deck, very close to traditional meanings, the Manga Tarot plays upon the Eastern ideal of ying/yang, offers a gender inversion of the cards where masculine cards are cast as feminine and vice versa. It also uses dominant colors in the Arcana to intuitively relate the elemental correspondences. *By Riccardo Minetti, artwork by Anna Lazzarini.*

Key to Major Arcana

1   **Essential Meanings**

2   **Symbols**

3   **Illustration**

0 THE FOOL

Innocence – Madness

② Symbols

1 – Bag on shoulder: represents the experiences and lessons, both positive and negative, that each individual carries with them into the future.

2 – His clothing: symbolizes an extravagant and unconventional personality shining through any situation or encounter.

3 – Animal: the instinct. An irrational impulse sometimes helping to overcome obstacles and dangers, but other times appears as a sullen or self-defeating voice. It can represent forces attempting to hold you back, forces pushing you into the unknown, or the deep loyalty of another.

4 – Feather: a red feather indicating passion, vitality, but also lightness of mind and innocence.

4   **Inside the Card**

5   **When the Card Speaks to You She Says**

6   **Traditional Interpretation** *(upright and reversed)*

④ The Fool

The Fool is a free spirit. Tarot games play the Fool as the wild card, who could be played at any time. He has no need of discipline, conventions, or habits. The Fool plunges headfirst into situations with no respect for limits or boundaries. Usually, he appears in cards as a beggar. Look closer. Perhaps, underneath lays an handsome prince who has left to make his own fortune, invisible to the crowd. His weapons are spontaneity, joy and enthusiasm. He does not care about his appearance or what other people think of him. The Fool represents freedom of all things: free love, free travel, free to think. He is pure potential.

The Fool mirrors the misery of the human condition. Acting as the ultimate outsider who enters and exits on his own terms, he represents total freedom. The Fool is the first card in a Tarot deck and numbered zero.

⑤ When the Fool speaks to you he says …

"I am the essence of your spirit before you came to be. I am your complete potential in the material world and contain all your seeds of talent, your unique gifts and qualities. There are no limits except those that you place upon yourself. Every moment is a chance to begin anew. Fear not where you step. You will always be protected. Do not fear my wild recklessness. Embrace that which ushers in fresh air, new chances and unimagined possibility. Take my hand and together we shall leap. Do not be afraid."

⑥ Traditional Interpretation

Upright: A completely fresh start. The beginning of something brand new. Sheer and utter potential. You have the ability to begin again. Traveling new roads, highways and byways. There is detachment from worry and responsibility.
Reversed: Thoughtless action, negative choices. Being stuck in the same place. Stuck with an unwillingness to move or try new things. Fear and entrapment becomes paralyzing. A denial of the truth.

1 Essential Meanings

Essential Meanings are the starting points of your interpretation of the card. They are two words that try to express the core meanings of the Arcana. The two words are often similar, but they also contain subtle differences to provide a greater understanding for the card.

Use these two words as a starting point in your Tarot journal, use them for Tarot meditation, contemplation, or simply memorize them. Even if you know only the Essential meanings of an Arcana, you will be able to Read the cards.

2 Symbols

Symbols will help you understand the illustration of the card. They will show you the major elements in the image, along with their meaning and their interpretation.

Use the symbols as a gateway to a deeper understanding of the card, and a leaping off point for further study of the Arcana.

3 Illustration

The large Tarot image is from the Universal Tarot, based on the concept by A. E. Waite, with artwork by Roberto De Angelis. This deck takes familiar Tarot images and scenes and reflects them in extraordinary color in a simple and uncomplicated manner. The Universal Tarot can be an excellent reference point for traditional meanings, and it's perfect to begin your study into Tarot.

4 Inside the Card

This is the basic story of each Arcanum, as passed down through generations of Readers, esoteric scholars and mystics. The card is described in detail so no element escapes the Reader's attention.

5 When the Card Speaks to You She Says

It is important to allow Tarot to speak and communicate with to you. This section jumpstarts a Tarot communication practice as the Reader literally reads what the card would say if it were to speak.

6 Traditional Interpretation
(upright and reversed)

The traditional interpretations, both upright and reversed, are simple keys unlocking the meaning of each card. These meanings are derived from some of the oldest Tarot texts, which sought to use Tarot as a means of divination. They can be used directly to provide an interpretation if a card appears in a Reading.

Key to Major Arcana

7   **Keywords**

8   **Description**

---

⑦ Keywords

Folly, Inexperience, Potential, Beginning, Adventure, Playful, Freedom, Action, Travel, Beginning, Wandering, Essence, Madness, Visionary, Innocence, Naive, Originality, Incomprehensible Action, Strangeness, Carelessness, Journey, Hike, Pilgrimage, Thoughtlessness, Touched by Spirit, Trickster

⑧ Description

Historically, the Fool is depicted in one of two iconographic traditions, either as a ragged beggar or a jester.

Visconti
The Visconti card shows the Fool as a ragged beggar. His clothing is tattered and feet are bare. The feathers in his hair may bear a connection to the season of Lent. A look of madness plays across his face.

Marseille
Marseille shows us a strangely dressed jester. He walks with an odd look and is leaning on a stick. He and Waite's Fool both carry bags. A wild dog or cat, scratches at the Fool's pants and thigh.

Pictorial Key
The Fool looks optimistic. His upturned face soaks in the sun. He walks toward a gaping peak and shows no signs of nervousness. The real secret of Waite's card is the magical regeneration of the cliff before him. There is no danger. The Fool will never fall from the peak as he continually moves forward.

---

9   **Lesson**

10   **Aspects of the Arcana as Expressed in Various Decks**

11   **Alternate Names**

12   **To Learn More About this Archetype explore**

---

⑨ Lesson

The Arcana of the Fool will teach me to look at the world as children do, with innocent eyes, an open heart and an attitude welcoming adventure and play.

Aspects of the Arcana expressed in various decks

⑩

Les Scarabées   *Nefertari's Tarot*   *Pagan Tarot*   *Dark Angels Tarot*   *Universal Fantasy Tarot*

Innocence   Foolishness   Journey into the Unknown   Freedom   Playfulness and Opening to Dreams

Fey Tarot   *Shaman Tarot*   *Tarot of the Pagan Cats*   *Tarot of the Dark Grimoire*   *Manga Tarot*

Asking questions   The Sacred Fool touched by the Spirit World   Potential   Madness   The White Slab

⑪ Alternate Names

The Joker, The Jester, Madman, The Fugitive, The Entertainer, The Lunatic, The Innocent

⑫ Learn more about this Archetype explore:

Jester, Joker, Folly, April Fool's Day, Spirit of Lent, Wild Cards, Shakespeare's Falstaff, Clowns

7 Keywords

Keywords are an expansion of the Essential Meanings found at the beginning of each Arcana. Immersing yourself in these words is like swimming through a refreshing pool of water where you can stop and observe what is around you. The best way to use the keywords is to see them as an association of ideas, connected to the meaning of the Arcana.

8 Description

A quick examination of how each Arcana has been portrayed through history in the most impactful decks of all time. The decks move in historical order with the Visconti-Sforza Deck, the Marseille and the Pictorial Key Deck, which follows the Waite-Smith tradition.

9 Lesson

The Lesson provides valuable insight into how the Arcana could teach you to look at the world, relate to others, and learn more about yourself.

10 Aspects of the Arcana as Expressed in Various Decks

Every Tarot deck is only able to bring certain facets of the Arcana to the forefront. Like different points of view on the same subject, it is essential for the Reader to understand the Arcana through the windows of different decks and images. Explore the visuals and look to the captions below each image for complete understanding.

11 Alternate Names

Many Arcana may be listed under different names in various decks. This list is included to be sure you do not lose your way when exploring new and original Tarot decks.

12 To Learn More About this Archetype explore

New ideas to explore in order to have a full understanding of the Archetype within the Arcana.

Key to the Numerals

1	**Essential Meanings**
2	**Keywords**
3	**Image**
4	**Illustration**
5	**Correlations**

(1) **1 ACE OF WANDS**

Creativity – Initiative

(2) Keywords

Creation, Enterprise, Bud, Originality, Brilliance, Spark, Vision, Adventure, Primary, Lively, Flickering, Phallic, Energy, Surge, Invention, Origin, Potential, Strength, Potency

(3) The Image

A glowing hand emerges from swirling clouds. It holds a wooden stick, sprouting with green leaves. Leaves shed and fall to the ground as if the stick is humming with energy. A scenic landscape extends beyond with a quaint castle sitting upon a hill over a winding river.

(5) Correlations

Number: 1
Element: Fire
Sephirot: Kether (Crown)
Season: Autumn
Disposition: Melancholic

Esoteric Name: the Root of the Powers of Fire

(4)

6	**Inside the Card**
7	**Aspects of the Arcana as Expressed in Various Decks**

(6) To be inspired is to be alive

The Ace of Wands is a symbol of strength, vitality, and energy. It allows us to take action and transform the world through our desires. It can become the representation of strength, material, and physical vigor. The Ace of Wands also indicates desire, passion, and determination. The growing leaves are symbolic of life and fertility renewed by the energy of the wand.

The Ace of Wands indicates the human capacity for desire. It translates desire from a pure wanting into practical action and becomes the ability to manifest destiny through action. The Ace of Wands, more than any other card, reminds us that individuals are defined by their intentions. It is only by having the courage and strength to pursue desire can one be truly alive. Like all Aces, this card represents potential and possibilities yet to be achieved.

Aspects of the Arcana expressed in various decks

(7)

Fiery energy

Fertility

Altar of Earth

1 Essential Meanings

Essential Meanings are the starting points of your interpretation of the card. They are two words that try to express the core meanings of the Arcana. The two words are often similar, but they also contain subtle differences to provide a greater understanding for the card. Use these two words as a starting point in your Tarot journal, use them for Tarot meditation, contemplation, or simply memorize them. Even if you know only the Essential meanings of an Arcana, you will be able to Read the cards.

2 Keywords

Keywords are an expansion of the Essential Meanings found at the beginning of each Arcana. Immersing yourself in these words is like swimming through a refreshing pool of water where you can stop and observe what is around you. The best way to use the keywords is to see them as an association of ideas, connected to the meaning of the Arcana.

3 Image

The symbols of the Minor Arcana and Court Cards are less impactful than in the Major Arcana. A description of the card as a whole replaces the single symbolic elements. This description should help studying the illustration of the Arcana to get a deeper understanding of its meaning and interpretation.

4 Illustration

The large Tarot image is from the Universal Tarot, based on the concept by A. E. Waite, with artwork by Roberto De Angelis. This deck takes familiar Tarot images and scenes and reflects them in extraordinary color in a simple and uncomplicated manner. The Universal Tarot can be an excellent reference point for traditional meanings, and it's perfect to begin your study into Tarot.

5 Correlations

The Correlation box holds a quick reference key to some advanced terms you will be learning about in future volumes and is meant to prep you for advanced Tarot work. The Esoteric Name given the card will provide powerful insight on the nature of the card and its interpretation.

6 Inside the Card

This is the basic story of each Arcanum, as passed down through generations of Readers, esoteric scholars and mystics. The card is described in detail so no element escapes the Reader's attention.

7 Aspects of the Arcana as Expressed in Various Decks

Every Tarot deck is only able to bring certain facets of the Arcana to the forefront. Like different points of view on the same subject, it is essential for the Reader to understand the Arcana through the windows of different decks and images. Explore the visuals and look to the captions below each image for complete understanding.

Key to the Numerals

8 **Traditional Interpretations**

Upright: Creation, invention, enterprise and all the powers arising from this principle. The onset, the origin, birth, family and the virility behind them. A starting point for any activity, achievement, or goal.

Reversed: Efforts made in vain. Fall, decadence, ruin, damnation.

Decay and even a joy obscured. Sexual problems. Brutality.

9 **Lessons**

A strong creative energy and a source of power thrive inside every human being.

- Recognize personal power and know it when you feel it.
- You are the hand that holds this wand of passion.
- Let your passion become your beacon and illuminate the path before you.
- Embody creativity, inspire others and feed initial desire.

Aspects of the Arcana expressed in various decks

A seed growing

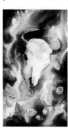
A reason to fight.

Book of Creation

8 Traditional Interpretation
(upright and reversed)

The traditional interpretations, both upright
and reversed, are simple keys unlocking
the meaning of each card. These meanings
are derived from some of the oldest Tarot
texts, which sought to use Tarot as a means
of divination. They can be used directly to
provide an interpretation if a card appears in
a Reading.

9 Lessons

The Lessons provide valuable insight into how
the Arcana could teach you to look at the
world, relate to others, and learn more about
yourself.

Key to Court Cards

1. **Essential Meanings**
2. **Keywords**
3. **Alternate Names**
4. **Image**
5. **Illustration**

6. **Inside the Card**
7. **Reflected in You**
8. **Traditional Interpretation**
   (upright and reversed)
9. **The Physical Persona**

① PAGE OF WANDS

Initiative – Vitality

② Keywords

Vitality, Creativity, Mate, Love, Loyalty, Travel, Support, Friendship, Commitment, Fidelity, Messenger, Confidence, Insights, Energetic, Adaptable, Curious, Adventurous, Playful, Outgoing, Risky, Candid, Ambitious, Impetuous.

③ Alternate names

Knave, Princess, The Inventor

④ The Image

A young person is dressed in fiery colorful clothing. He stands in profile and gazes intently at the horizon. The staff he holds is planted on the ground. The Page holds it with two hands while keenly observing green sprouts emerging from it. The Page stands in a hot desert landscape, echoing the element of Fire. In the background, mountain peaks point toward the heavens.

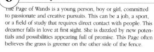

⑥ Passionate pursuit

The Page of Wands is a young person, boy or girl, committed to passionate and creative pursuits. This can be a job, a sport, or a field of study that requires direct contact with people. This dreamer falls in love at first sight. She is dazzled by new potentials and possibilities appearing full of promise. This Page often believes the grass is greener on the other side of the fence.

She becomes rather obsessed with creation, commitment and participation and forgets to take necessary caution. A Page can be quite impressionable and suggestible. She grows and matures by becoming involved in her passions. Her talent is to rework all experiences by translating them into something personal. Independent, she needs no guide to direct her, but needs stimulus for her creativity. The Page of Wands is endless, boundless enthusiasm.

⑦ Reflected in You

When was the last time you jumped up and down with cheeks red with excitement? This was the Page of Wands operating within you. When you experience the thrill of the moment, with no thought to long terms plans, this is the Page of Wands.

⑧ Additional Interpretations

Upright: Unexpectedly exciting news. A messenger. The creativity and enthusiasm of youth. An opportunity to begin afresh. Courage waiting to reveal itself. Young person with a zest for life. Travel.
Reversed: Gossip, advice and bad news. Indecision and the instability that accompanies it. Stifled.

⑨ The Physical Persona

Occupations: Student, Creative Works, Athlete, Telemarketing, Sales, Journalist, Administrative Assistant, Intern, Investigator, Travel Writer, Pilot, Boatman, Stuntman/woman, Freelancer
Appearance: Young girl, red hair, fair skin and light eyes.

1 Essential Meanings

Essential Meanings are the starting points of your interpretation of the card. They are two words that try to express the core meanings of the Arcana. The two words are often similar, but they also contain subtle differences to provide a greater understanding for the card.

Use these two words as a starting point in your Tarot journal, use them for Tarot meditation, contemplation, or simply memorize them. Even if you know only the Essential meanings of an Arcana, you will be able to Read the cards.

2 Keywords

Keywords are an expansion of the Essential Meanings found at the beginning of each Arcana. Immersing yourself in these words is like swimming through a refreshing pool of water where you can stop and observe what is around you. The best way to use the keywords is to see them as an association of ideas, connected to the meaning of the Arcana.

3 Alternate Names

Many Arcana may be listed under different names in various decks. This list is included to be sure you do not lose your way when exploring new and original Tarot decks.

4 Image

In the Minor Arcana and in the Court Cards the symbols are less important than in the Major Arcana. A description of the card as a whole replaces the single symbolic elements. This description should help studying the illustration of the Arcana to get a deeper understanding of its meaning and interpretation.

5 Illustration

The large Tarot image is from the Universal Tarot, based on the concept by A. E. Waite, with artwork by Roberto De Angelis. This deck takes familiar Tarot images and scenes and reflects them in extraordinary color in a simple and uncomplicated manner. The Universal Tarot can be an excellent reference point for traditional meanings, and it's perfect to begin your study into Tarot.

6 Inside the Card

This is the basic story of each Arcanum, as passed down through generations of Readers, esoteric scholars and mystics. The card is described in detail so no element escapes the Reader's attention.

7 Reflected in You

The Courts, while sometimes representing people in your life, often represent aspects of your core personality. This section aims to show you how an individual Court Card is operating inside of your psychology at different moments of daily life. These are the moments where you express and live inside the essence of each card.

8 Traditional Interpretation
(upright and reversed)

The traditional interpretations, both upright and reversed, are simple keys unlocking the meaning of each card. These meanings are derived from some of the oldest Tarot texts, which sought to use Tarot as a means of divination. They can be used directly to provide an interpretation if a card appears in a Reading.

Key to Court Cards

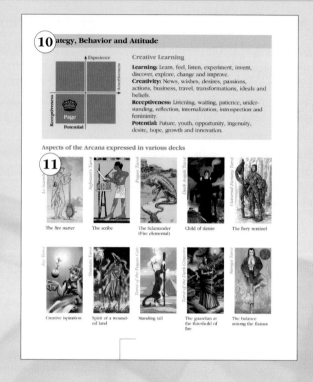

10 Strategy, Behavior and Attitude

Creative Learning

Learning: Learn, feel, listen, experiment, invent, discover, explore, change and improve.

Creativity: News, wishes, desires, passions, actions, business, travel, transformations, ideals and beliefs.

Receptiveness: Listening, waiting, patience, understanding, reflection, internalization, introspection and femininity.

Potential: Future, youth, opportunity, ingenuity, desire, hope, growth and innovation.

Aspects of the Arcana expressed in various decks

11

The fire starter

The scribe

The Salamander (Fire elemental)

Child of desire

The fiery sentinel

Creative inspiration

Spirit of a wounded land

Standing tall

The guardian at the threshold of fire

The balance among the flames

9 The Physical Persona

The Courts represent yourself and other people. For this reason, the Physical Persona reflects the Occupations suiting each Court Card and the general Appearance history has bestowed upon each Court Card.

10 Strategy, Behavior and Attitude

This section, along with the Court Diagram, expresses the meanings of the Court Cards as strategies, behaviors and attitudes. The Techniques section fully explains how to interpret the Court Cards in this way.

The diagram is also useful in comparing Court Cards to each other and to understanding the complicated relationship between them.

11 Aspects of the Arcana as Expressed in Various Decks

Every Tarot deck is only able to bring certain facets of the Arcana to the forefront. Like different points of view on the same subject, it is essential for the Reader to understand the Arcana through the windows of different decks and images. Explore the visuals and look to the captions below each image for complete understanding.

0 | THE FOOL

Innocence – Madness

Symbols

1 – Bag on shoulder: represents the experiences and lessons, both positive and negative, that each individual carries with them into the future.

2 – His clothing: symbolizes an extravagant and unconventional personality shining through any situation or encounter.

3 – Animal: the instinct. An irrational impulse sometimes helping to overcome obstacles and dangers, but other times appears as a sullen or self-defeating voice. It can represent forces attempting to hold you back, forces pushing you into the unknown, or the deep loyalty of another.

4 – Feather: a red feather indicating passion, vitality, but also lightness of mind and innocence.

The Fool

The Fool is a free spirit. Tarot games play the Fool as the wild card, who could be played at any time. He has no need of discipline, conventions, or habits. The Fool plunges headfirst into situations with no respect for limits or boundaries. Usually, he appears in cards as a beggar. Look closer. Perhaps, underneath lays an handsome prince who has left to make his own fortune, invisible to the crowd. His weapons are spontaneity, joy and enthusiasm. He does not care about his appearance or what other people think of him. The Fool represents freedom of all things: free love, free travel, free to think. He is pure potential.

The Fool mirrors the misery of the human condition. Acting as the ultimate outsider who enters and exits on his own terms, he represents total freedom. The Fool is the first card in a Tarot deck and numbered zero.

When the Fool speaks to you he says ...

"I am the essence of your spirit before you came to be. I am your complete potential in the material world and contain all your seeds of talent, your unique gifts and qualities. There are no limits except those that you place upon yourself. Every moment is a chance to begin anew. Fear not where you step. You will always be protected. Do not fear my wild recklessness. Embrace that which ushers in fresh air, new chances and unimagined possibility. Take my hand and together we shall leap. Do not be afraid."

Traditional Interpretation

Upright: A completely fresh start. The beginning of something brand new. Sheer and utter potential. You have the ability to begin again. Traveling new roads, highways and byways. There is detachment from worry and responsibility.
Reversed: Thoughtless action, negative choices. Being stuck in the same place. Stuck with an unwillingness to move or try new things. Fear and entrapment becomes paralyzing. A denial of the truth.

Keywords

Folly, Inexperience, Potential, Beginning, Adventure, Playful, Freedom, Action, Travel, Beginning, Wandering, Essence, Madness, Visionary, Innocence, Naïve, Originality, Incomprehensible Action, Strangeness, Carelessness, Journey, Hike, Pilgrimage, Thoughtlessness, Touched by Spirit, Trickster

Description

Historically, the Fool is depicted in one of two iconographic traditions, either as a ragged beggar or a jester.

Visconti
The Visconti card shows the Fool as a ragged beggar. His clothing is tattered and feet are bare. The feathers in his hair may bear a connection to the season of Lent. A look of madness plays across his face.

Marseille
Marseille shows us a strangely dressed jester. He walks with an odd look and is leaning on a stick. He and Waite's Fool both carry bags. A wild dog or cat, scratches at the Fool's pants and thigh.

Pictorial Key
The Fool looks optimistic. His upturned face soaks in the sun. He walks toward a gaping peak and shows no signs of nervousness. The real secret of Waite's card is the magical regeneration of the cliff before him. There is no danger. The Fool will never fall from the peak as he continually moves forward.

Lesson

The Arcana of the Fool will teach me to look at the world as children do, with innocent eyes, an open heart and an attitude welcoming adventure and play.

Aspects of the Arcana expressed in various decks

Lo Scarabeo Tarot

Nefertari's Tarot

Pagan Tarot

Dark Angels Tarot

Universal Fantasy Tarot

Innocence   Foolishness   Journey into the Unknown   Freedom   Playfulness and Opening to Dreams

Fey Tarot

Shaman Tarot

Tarot of the Pagan Cats

Tarot of the Dark Grimoire

Manga Tarot

Asking questions   The Sacred Fool touched by the Spirit World   Potential   Madness   The Blank Slate

Alternate Names

The Joker, The Jester, Madman, The Fugitive, The Entertainer, The Lunatic, The Innocent

To learn more about this Archetype explore:

Trickster, Joker, Folly, April Fool's Day, Spirit of Lent, Wild Cards, Shakespeare's Falstaff, Clowns

I | THE MAGICIAN

Will – Ability

Symbols

1 – Lemniscate: a sideways eight shape representing infinity. The ability to turn thought in each direction.

2 – Wand: shaped like a candle burning from two sides, it is linked to the element of Fire. A symbol of desire and power. An instrument of Magic allowing the Magician to channel energy from Above to the Earth Below.

3 – Tools: the cup symbolizes the element of Water, or knowledge; the knife is the symbol of Air, or courage; the pentacle is the element of Earth, or secrets of nature. They stand as a reminder that you always have what you need in front of you.

4 – Table: is the plane of reality the Magician is about to manipulate using his tools. The legs indicate the three worlds in which he acts: physical, intellectual and spiritual.

The Magician

The Magician is a craftsman, a talented young man and artist. This card holds a morally ambiguous tone. On the one hand, the Magician is admired for his extraordinary mental abilities, his physical coordination and the great confidence he retains in himself. At the same time, is hard to trust the Magician, the quick-change artist, who may confuse truth with falsities. The real strength of the Magician is his ability to tackle any situation lightly thanks to his extensive wealth of resources, guided imagination and improvisation.

The Magician is rooted in seemingly playful ambition, willingness and spirit of adaptation. Waite's Magician creates a posture channeling energy, grace, virtue and light. He directs this energy to the ground and into the material realm, echoing the occult phrase, "As above, so below." His table usually contains the four symbols of the tarot suits/elements: a wand (Batons, Fire), a cup (Cups, Water), a disk (Pentacles, Earth) and a knife (Swords, Air). These elements are at his disposal as he works. The symbol of infinity hangs above is head and is echoed in his snake belt. The flowers and foliage represent the Magician's growing ambition and his ability to manifest magic quickly.

When the Magician speaks to you he says …

"I am the power through which you make yourself known to the universe. You and I are conduits who bridge the spiritual to the material. We manifest together, we change the world by igniting, challenging and manipulating it. We have everything we need before us. We will always receive what is required. I am your power of intention. You are unstoppable when you claim your power. I am here to show you how. Let's make magic together."

Traditional Interpretation

Upright: The energetic creation of something new and the ability to make things happen. Charisma and mastery. The divine motive of man reflected by the union of that which is above and that which is below. Superior power and energy.
Reversed: Thwarted energy. Weakness and inability to make a decision. Listless and depressed. Shy and quiet. Blocked energy. Hiding and suppressing natural talent.

Keywords

Capability, Power, Deception, Shrewdness, Initiation, Talent, Concentration, Energy, Precision, Manipulation, Focus, Determination, Action, Mastery, Ambition, Finesse, Ability, Skill, Initiative, Diplomacy, Communication, Will, Desire, Conduit, Vessel

Description

Historically, the Magician is shown at his table. He dresses in marvelously luxurious clothing. One hand holds a wand while the elements are spread on the table before him.

Visconti
The Visconti Magician sits behind his table on a golden box. He wears sumptuous red and green clothing and carries an air of seriousness and contemplation while he works with a delicate touch.

Marseille
The Marseille Magician takes an active standing stance behind his table. His clothing is colorful and a lemniscate appears on the brim of his hat. He works outside with nature springing at his feet.

Pictorial Key
The Magician stands in a position of complete mastery. The Magician has become the energetic channel. Roses and lilies leap to life around him. The Suits symbols await his touch and he is dressed in ceremonial robes.

Lesson

The Arcana of the Magician will teach me to take action. I will discover and cultivate new talents and abilities I didn't know I had.

Aspects of the Arcana expressed in various decks

Lo Scarabeo Tarot

Mastery of Forces

Nefertari's Tarot

Skill

Pagan Tarot

Conduit of Energy

Dark Angels Tarot

Power

Universal Fantasy Tarot

Ruler of the Four Elements

Fey Tarot

Creation

Shaman Tarot

Initiation

Tarot of the Pagan Cats

Using Skills and Resources

Tarot of the Dark Grimoire

Concentration

Manga Tarot

Potential in Action

Alternate Names

The Juggler, Magus, Shaman, Diviner, Wizard, Conjurer, Prophet, Exorcist, Warlock, Alchemist, Occultist, Guru

To learn more about this Archetype explore:

Trickster Energy, Shakespeare's Prospero, Hermes, Apollo, Merlin

II | THE HIGH PRIESTESS

Knowledge – Wisdom

Symbols

1 – Veil: the fabric - embroidered with palms and pomegranates - preventing what is seen beyond, inaccessible knowledge guarded by the High Priestess. The threshold of hidden knowledge.

2 – Headwear: the papal tiara symbolizes contact with the three levels of existence, physical, intellectual and spiritual. The crown is symbolic of the three phases of the moon.

3 – Columns: the pillars at the gate of the Temple of Solomon, indicating Boaz (B) and Jakin (J): Strength and Foundation.

4 – Moon: feminine mystery, change and illusion.

5 – Book/Scroll: the book of knowledge, neither closed nor open.

6 – Cross: the focal point where the energies from Above and Below and those from Black (yin) and White (yang) meet.

The High Priestess

The High Priestess is the custodian of all knowledge, represented by the scroll upon her lap. Her crown represents her ability to understand the secrets of the scroll. The High Priestess is the symbol of research, study and analysis. Her gifts lay in abstraction and theory rather than in practical application. Knowledge can be used in a variety of ways: to seduce, attack, defend, teach, or find solutions. Too much knowledge can isolate the High Priestess on her island. When embarking on a personal search for answers, it is the Priestess's choice whether or not to share what she knows. She graces the most deserving with her secrets; to others, she remains silent.

The evolution of Tarot has linked the High Priestess to all feminine aspects of the Divine. She represents sensitivity and complete understanding of spiritual mysteries. She is indicative of all of the knowledge resting inside you, your intuition and inner truth. She holds these secrets and reminds you that someday, you will know them too.

When the High Priestess speaks to you she says ...

"I spring from the deep, damp wells of knowledge residing inside you. I contain the secrets and truths of your past, present and future. I am the book of you. When you seek an answer, I am the inner voice who responds. You operate on instinct but I steer your course. Learn my language. I communicate through symbol, synchronicity and impulse, often only making sense after events have run their course. I will not always be literal. Listen to my murmurs, whispers and inklings. Learn to trust my voice. You will never be led astray. I am your intuition and subconscious."

Traditional Interpretation

Upright: Hidden secrets and occult knowledge. Keeper of feminine mysteries and moon magic. Unrevealed future and hidden influences at work. Platonic love. Eternal truth.
Reversed: Ignoring your instincts. A person deceives you. Conceited, frantic and irrational behavior. Avoiding the truth of the situation. Fear and entrapment.

Keywords

Secrecy, Mystery, The Unknown, Virgin, Intuition, Female, Subconscious, Darkness, Secret Keeper, Knowingness, Serenity, Introspection, Mystical Vision, Secrets, Silence, Gestation, Resignation, Faith, Severity, Privacy, Study, Wisdom, Confidentiality, Self Control, Threshold, Duality, Wise Woman, Knowledge

Description

Historically, the High Priestess sits on a throne with a book in her lap.

Visconti
The Visconti deck's High Priestess, or Popess, contains an interesting history. She is called the female Pope but wears a nun's clothing. It is historically supported and suggested that she is Sister Manfreda, first cousin to Matteo Visconti. More likely she was a representation of Faith.

Marseille
The Marseille card shows a woman sitting on a throne. She is dressed with religious garments and wears the three-tiered papal tiara on her head. She holds an open book on her knees.

Pictorial Key
The High Priestess wears a regal crown. It displays the three stages of the moon. She holds a scroll containing the word TORA, meaning Jewish Law. She is nestled between two pillars containing the letters B and J. The letters reference Boaz and Jakin, the two pillars that stood of the porch of King Solomon's temple in Jerusalem. A veil with pomegranates and palms hangs behind her.

Lesson

The Arcana of The High Priestess will teach me to recognize signs and hidden meanings in the events of my life.

Aspects of the Arcana expressed in various decks

Lo Scarabeo Tarot

Intuition

Nefertari's Tarot

Occult Wisdom

Pagan Tarot

Wise Woman

Dark Angels Tarot

Secrecy

Universal Fantasy Tarot

The Unknown

Fey Tarot

Threshold
(The Seer)

Shaman Tarot

Keeper of
Knowledge

Tarot of the Pagan Cats

Knowingness

Tarot of the Dark Grimoire

Mystery and
Darkness

Manga Tarot

Sacred Mistery

Alternate Names

Papess, Popess, Wise One, Female Pope

To learn more about this Archetype explore:

Pope Joan, Sister Manfreda, Virgin Mary, Isis, Mystery Schools, Female Clergy, Female Mysteries

Nurturing – Fertility

Symbols

1 – Crown: symbol of intellectual supremacy. The Empress is said to be "crowned by the sun" with her golden tiara. At other times her crown is made of stars.

2 – Throne: expresses stability and the Empress's intellectual capacity rising above common thoughts.

3 – Scepter: expresses the power over the material world. It also indicates the combination of sense and sensibility.

4 – Heart and Venus sign: indicates the female nature of the Empress and her ability to rule and nurture without strife and violence. It also expresses her qualities as a mother.

5 – Nature, water and plants: indicates her intimate connection to the power of life and to vital energies.

The Empress

The Empress is complete intelligence expressing itself in every creative aspect. She is the epitome and embodiment of female essence in all forms. The Empress is the mother archetype who provides and creates life and also protects, supports, educates and cares for others. She reflects strength, conviction and authority. The Empress represents the transformation of knowledge into action. While the High Priestess held onto this knowledge, the Empress expresses and utilizes it.

The Empress reflects a pregnancy of the body and mind. She symbolizes the feminine aspect complementary to the Emperor, who symbolizes the male aspect. The Empress is the more emotional and nurturing of the two sovereigns.

When the Empress speaks to you she says …

"I am the essence of creativity and femininity thriving within you. Never doubt your power to manifest and transform the material world as you have imagined it. I am your greatest champion and encourage you on every step of your journey. You are safe within my nurturing arms and you will always feel my touch. I will listen to you and love you forever. I see the potential within. You and I are entwined in the eternal fabric of life. Let's create extraordinary possibilities together."

Traditional Interpretation

Upright: A creative and protective woman. Wealth, marriage and fertility. Often indicates great luxury. Anything is possible. Creativity and growth abounds. Pregnancy and sensuality. The answer is yes.
Mother and mother figures. A passionate approach to life, love and family.
Reversed: A stifled artist. Scattering of resources. Infertility of all things. Psychological problems leading to instability. Less passionate and more rational.

Keywords

Fertility, Productivity, Creativity, Nature, Abundance, Material Prosperity, Pleasure, Joy, Comfort, Sexuality, Sensuality, Beauty, Satisfaction, Expression, Desire, Power, Elegance, Harvest, The Great Mother, Maternal, Feminine, Intelligence, Protection, Receptivity, Beneficial Influence

Description

Historically, the Empress is glorious and perched on a throne, scepter in hand and crown atop her head.

Visconti
The Empress wears a regal gown bearing the emblem of Francesco Sforza, three sets of three interlacing rings.

Marseille
The tips of the Empress's crown reflect the sun's rays. This crown is a symbol of her creative and destructive power.

Pictorial Key
The Empress wears a crown of twelve stars, one for each sign of the zodiac. She reclines in a pastoral field of wheat and represents universal fecundity. The sign of Venus is inscribed on her shield.

Lesson

The Arcana of the Empress will teach me to apply infinite creativity, nurturing and passion to everything I do.

Aspects of the Arcana expressed in various decks

Lo Scarabeo Tarot
Fertility and Pregnancy

Nefertari's Tarot
Benefical Intelligence

Pagan Tarot
Maiden, Mother and Crone

Dark Angels Tarot
Allure

Universal Fantasy Tarot
Creativity

Fey Tarot
Maternal Caring

Shaman Tarot
Love of Nature (Mother of Worlds)

Tarot of the Pagan Cats
Abundance

Tarot of the Dark Grimoire
Power

Manga Tarot
Stalwart Protection

Alternate Names

The Mother, the High Queen

To learn more about this Archetype explore:

Venus/Aphrodite, Demeter, Creator, Nurturer, Fairy Godmother, Corn Mother, Mother Earth, Great Mother, Motherhood

IV | THE EMPEROR

Domain – Authority

Symbols

1 – Scepter: the globe and cross symbolize power over the material world.

2 – Crown: the will and dominion over the emotions and the instincts.

3 – Throne: solidity, stability and concrete authority.

4 – Ram's heads: connection with the Sign of Aries, representing power of creation and strong will.

5 – Mountains and desert: the weight of power and the strength, will and authority that will change physical and mental landscapes.

The Emperor

The Emperor represents the idea of government, the presence of authority and a beneficial higher power. He suggests forcible acts through intermediaries and subordinates. He expresses male qualities of assertiveness, creative energy, directed action and troubleshooting. The Emperor is the ultimate paternal figure and the father archetype. In society, he is a civil or military authority, an administrator, a guardian or a guarantor.

The Emperor reflects patriarchal discipline while lacking the passion exhibited in the Empress. He reflects solid, swift action aimed at organizational and rational activities. He is a stable reference point, enjoys rules and the setting and reaching of concrete goals. The Emperor's authority will express itself through intermediaries, rather than in person, thus echoing his detachment. His is rarely personally involved in a situation but dictates from afar. The Emperor is impartial. He is the pure expression of masculinity. His authority extends through the material realm, while the spiritual realm belongs to the Pope/Hierophant.

When the Emperor speaks to you he says ...

"I am the part of you creating habits, patterns and learned behavior. Together, we form opinions of the world and express our knowledge. I power your decisions, values and judgments. I am the part of you that orders the world. I give shape and form to an otherwise unruly existence. I am you. Together, we manifest solid change."

Traditional Interpretation

Upright: Leadership, a strict disciplinarian and rigid control. Concrete stability. Results in action and the fruits of your labor. Powerful ally.
Father or father figure. Setting boundaries and defending them.
Reversed: Sudden shock. Relinquishing power. Loss of control and temper. Loss of possessions.
Confusion on how to proceed forward. An authority figure spinning out of control.

Keywords

Authority, Rigidity, Precision, Leadership, Arrogant, Domination, Dominion, Responsibility, Solidity, Order, Power, Government, Father, Rationalism, Discipline, Command, Egocentrism, Experience, Organization, Law, Conservative, Inflexible, Tradition, Advantage, Sovereignty, Supremacy, Constriction, Administration, Requirement, Overlord, Skill

Description

Historically, the Emperor has changed little throughout the centuries. He is normally depicted sitting on a royal throne with beard and mustache.

Visconti
The Emperor, like the Empress, bears on his robes the three-ringed symbol of the Sforza family. His left hand holds an orb.

Marseille
The Emperor is seen in complete profile in a pastoral landscape and wears an austere and mature expression.
His crossed legs connect him to the Hanged Man and the World.

Pictorial Key
The card shows the Emperor in a suit of silver armor fully covered by royal robes. His throne is decorated with rams, the symbol of Aries.

Lesson

The Arcana of the Emperor will teach me to regulate my emotions in order to become effective, stable and a strong source of support for myself and others.

Aspects of the Arcana expressed in various decks

Lo Scarabeo Tarot

Rigidity

Nefertari's Tarot

Powerful Generous Protector

Pagan Tarot

Organization

Dark Angels Tarot

Overlord and Dominion

Universal Fantasy Tarot

Power

Fey Tarot

Directive

Shaman Tarot

Mental and Material Stability (Master of the Drum)

Tarot of the Pagan Cats

Efficiency, Prosperity, Stability

Tarot of the Dark Grimoire

Authoritative Judgment

Manga Tarot

Generative Force

Alternate Names

The Father, the High King

To learn more about this Archetype explore:

Father, Zeus, Mars, Monarch, Czar, Chief, Mogul, God, Creator, Giant, Tyrant

V | THE HIEROPHANT

Guidance – Dogmatism

Symbols

1 – Columns: symbolize rigor and mercy and represent the two pillars of King Solomon's Temple.

2 – Processional three tiered cross: represents three theological virtues: Faith (dogma), Hope (prayer) and Charity (benevolent actions).

3 – Three tiered tiara: triplicities; the ability to direct one's thought in the material, intellectual and spiritual worlds.

4 – Papal coat: the authority of the Hierophant regarding spiritual matters.

5 – Clerics: addressing spiritual authority via prayer and earnest request.

6 – Naked feet: humility and distance from material concerns.

7 – Keys: the ability to guide others and holding the keys to knowledge and wisdom.

The Hierophant

The High Priestess is the guardian of mysteries, while the Hierophant is the popularizer who brings the mysteries to the people, en mass. In everyday life, the Pope is a guide, teacher, mentor, or a figure of moral reference. He transmits knowledge, wisdom and counsel. He is guardian and guarantor of the dogmas of tradition, conventions and habits. These stiff qualities can give the card an aura of rigidity and intolerance. These qualities can be softened by his substantial goodness, kindness and extraordinary ability to understand others.

The Pope is a spiritual guide, a point of contact between the human and divine. He acts as mediator and translator. He represents the religious vocation, as a life choice or as a career. These meanings can become negative if his severity is not accompanied by clemency. Above all things, the Hierophant represents the gateway to learned knowledge.

When the Hierophant speaks to you he says ...

"I am the gateway to spiritual and material knowledge. All information regarding the outside world rests with me. I offer an objective point of view and help you to learn. In return, I ask you to do the same for others. I am your mentor, director, friend and benefactor. Ask me anything, experiment how you like and I will encourage you. My answers often come in the form of questions."

Traditional Interpretation

Upright: Adhering to traditional rules, regulations and ethics. The role of mentor and student. Wanting to fit into society. Gateway to knowledge. Superstitions. Great ceremony, pomp and circumstance. More than meets the eye. The wise one. Speeches and good advice. Attention to detail.
Reversed: Ignoring advice. Unwillingness to learn. Refusing to fit into the social norm. Tossing rules aside. Disrespect for elders. Unconventionality. Disillusionment with organized religion and traditional social values.

Keywords

Religion, Faith, Guidance, Education, Instruction, Mentor, Teaching, Knowledge, Institution, Belief Systems, Tradition, Dogmatism, Conformity, Blessing, Mediator, Bridge, Guide, Saintliness, Communication, Ideal, Wisdom, Discipline, Inspiration, Advice, Forgiveness, Ritual, Peace, Help, Mercy, Hierarchy, Spiritual Truth

Description

Historically, the highest spiritual authority is depicted on a papal throne, wearing the three-tiered crown and cloak while his hand forms the sign of blessing.

Visconti
The four arms of the Pope's Greek cross represent harmony between the elements.

Marseille
The Marseille and Waite cards each display two clerics kneeling beneath the Hierophant.

Pictorial Key
Spiritual keys lay at the foot of the Hierophant while the clerics wear black cloaks on a white dress.

Lesson

The Arcana of the Hierophant will teach me to lead by example and become a guide for others with my actions.

Aspects of the Arcana expressed in various decks

Lo Scarabeo Tarot

Spiritual Authority

Nefertari's Tarot

Religion (Osiris)

Pagan Tarot

Religious Intolerance

Dark Angels Tarot

Instruction

Universal Fantasy Tarot

Dogmatism

Fey Tarot

Wisdom of Time

Shaman Tarot

Spiritual Power

Tarot of the Pagan Cats

Teacher and Storyteller

Tarot of the Dark Grimoire

Indoctrination

Manga Tarot

Spiritual Legacy

Alternate Names

The Pope, High Priest, Shaman, Medicine Man, Pontiff, Holy Father, Wise One

To learn more about this Archetype explore:

The Papacy, Religious Leaders, Spiritual Advisors, Gurus, Confession, Clerics, Patriarch, Philosopher, Savior

VI | THE LOVERS

Choice – Love

Symbols

1 – Angel: sanctity of a higher power and blessings.

2 – Snake: the nature of choice and ramification of duality. On one side temptation and rebellion, on the other wisdom to be gained and growth.

3 – Nudity: the ability to be completely vulnerable in the presence of another.

4 – Tree of Knowledge: knowledge that brings awareness, but also responsibility.

5 – Tree of Life: symbol of human nature, drive and ambition.

6 – Mountain: the solitude of choice and the weight and reward of personal responsibility.

7 – Eve: the yin polarity and female, receptive nature.

8 – Adam: the yang polarity and male, creative nature.

The Lovers

The Arcanum of the Lovers depicts free will and the human ability to choose. The Lovers never suggests the correct choice. Each option carries its own advantages and disadvantages. Sometimes, the Lovers represent a rite of passage or an initiatory ordeal. Others times, it indicates a test or a temptation to be resisted.

The Lovers carries a strong emotional and sexual component. It indicates romantic relationships, physical attraction, or love at first sight. It refers to the relationship and union between lovers who have vowed and promised loyalty, even when they find themselves naked and exposed to the dangers of temptation and jealousy.

When the Lovers speak to you they say ...

"We embody the choices you make in your life, the union of opposites and what you attract. We represent the wave of desire and attraction you feel toward people and objects. We are the bridge of opposites. Our energy keeps humanity moving forward. Your erotic desires, wants and needs feed creativity. Choose wisely, yearn passionately, feel everything."

Traditional Interpretation

Upright: Choice to be made. Love, sensuality and passion. A new love comes into your life. Excitement and pleasure. Temptation and attraction. Harmony between the inner and outer aspects of life.
Reversed: An affair or relationship gone sour. A break up. Quarrels and a need to stabilize your emotions. A choice made out of haste or fear.

Keywords

Passion, Sexuality, Sensuality, Choice, Union, Pleasure, Desire, Attraction, Affinity, Bonding, Temptation, Romance, Love, Heart, Body, Tension, Infatuation, Eros, Joy, Lust, Eroticism, Oath, Alliance, Decision, Pact, Alliance, Feelings, Affection

Description

Historically, the Lovers card is depicted in the form of a triad with an angel floating above.

Visconti
The Visconti card reflects a winged, naked and blindfolded Cupid atop a pedestal, holding a bow and arrow. A regal couple clasps hands below the blindfolded angel of love.

Marseille
Cupid flies over three figures, a gentleman and two women. The man must choose. The figures embody the concept of selection and decision and the doubts and uncertainties arising when making a choice. The two women represent two different ways of being and are symbolic of the dualistic quality of choice.

Pictorial Key
The symbolism of this card is entirely Christian in nature. It is the story of Adam and Eve. Two naked figures stand in the Garden of Eden. The snake lurks behind Eve, echoing the choice she will soon make. The Tree of Life, bearing twelve fruits, stands behind Adam.

Lesson

The Arcana of the Lovers will teach me that I will find and attract other people with whom I can share my passion and find full expression with.

Aspects of the Arcana expressed in various decks

Lo Scarabeo Tarot

Union

Nefertari's Tarot

Bonding

Pagan Tarot

Choice

Dark Angels Tarot

Alliance

Universal Fantasy Tarot

Desire and Heartache

Fey Tarot

Complementarity

Shaman Tarot

Falling in Love

Tarot of the Pagan Cats

Pact

Tarot of the Dark Grimoire

Trust

Manga Tarot

Romance

Alternate Names

Love, Amour, Garden of Eden

To learn more about this Archetype explore:

Romeo and Juliet, Adam and Eve, Vice and Virtue, Cupid and Psyche

VII | THE CHARIOT

Triumph – Arrogance

Symbols

1 – Curtains: celestial symbols of Heaven protecting and monitoring the driver.

2 – Crown: the nobility of the spiritual dignity.

3 – Armor: engraved with alchemical symbols representing solar and lunar power. Indicates that the power of the Chariot came from strength and conquest.

4 – Winged solar disk and shield: balance of the yin and yang natures, as well as symbol of the inner drive.

5 – Sphinxes: two opposing natures of choice and direction, both under the rule of the charioteer but driving him forward into the unknown.

6 – Walled city: indicates how the power and domain of the charioteer is limited to the Realm of Man.

The Chariot

The Arcanum of the Chariot represents an individual who is reaching and enjoying success due to his own labors and ingenuity. The Chariot indicates a sense of forward motion. It stresses the need to take the reins of a situation. It requests you guide your will and actions, sometimes those of others, toward a direction or goal. The Chariot represents a person who knows what they want and how to get it.

The Chariot's character is dynamic, strong-willed, resourceful, self-confident, adventurous and aggressive. The Horses and Sphinxes who draw the Chariot represent outside influence. These forces may be inside the charioteer's character or they can be external, such as people who have influenced him. Strength will be used to overcome any obstacle, passing over any barriers standing in the way.

When the Chariot speaks to you he says ...

"I am the essence of knowing what you want and reaching out for it. My strength is the motion, action and activity powering you to the places you want to go. Chart your course and begin your journey. Do not allow me to languish. Take action in your life and I will be your wheels, road and engine. You steer the course and I will provide your required energy. You are unstoppable. You know what must be done."

Traditional Interpretation

Upright: Being in the driver's seat. Taking action and knowing exactly where you are going. Setting in the direction of choice. Assured success and victory. Racing toward a goal.
Reversed: Too controlling. Thinking only of oneself. Blockage and the inability to gain control. Difficulty making correct choice. Finding oneself off track. Stuck or frozen.

Keywords

Progress, Dedication, Commitment, Victory, Energy, Confidence, Discipline, Success, Bravery, Pride, Command, Willpower, Self-assertion, Action, Triumph, Travel, Warrior, Greatness, Movement, Conquest, Ambition, Directive, Progress, Movement

Description

Historically, the Chariot is depicted as a vehicle carried by two animals, one white and one black.

Visconti
A queen rides in a cart pulled by two horses, holding a golden globe. The image pays homage to triumphal processions common in ancient Rome and Renaissance Italy. These allegorical parades may be the very basis of Tarot imagery. Each float triumphs over the next, becoming larger and more important like the Major Arcana.

Marseille
The Marseille and Waite card depict a man standing on a golden chariot drawn by two creatures, one black, one white. The young man is crowned and holds a scepter. His breastplate contains shoulder straps fashioned into shape of human faces above crescent moons. The wagon is topped with a square shaped canopy supported by four columns.

Pictorial Key
The Pictorial Key card takes Marseille imagery further by turning the beasts into sphinxes and making the posture of the conqueror even more commanding.

Lesson

The Arcana of The Chariot will teach me to attain my objectives with the help of new and original ideas and will give me the drive to overcome obstacles and proceed forward.

Aspects of the Arcana expressed in various decks

Lo Scarabeo Tarot

Driver's Seat

Nefertari's Tarot

Spiritual and Material Evolution

Pagan Tarot

Travel

Dark Angels Tarot

Angel of Victory

Universal Fantasy Tarot

Progress and Dedication

Fey Tarot

Movement towards a Goal

Shaman Tarot

Successful Action (The Spinning Shield)

Tarot of the Pagan Cats

Triumph

Tarot of the Dark Grimoire

Speed

Manga Tarot

Victory

Alternate Names

Speed, Triumphal Chariot, Charioteer, Victory, Centurion, Hearse

To learn more about this Archetype explore:

Inciting action, Triumph of Spirit, Goal Setting, Voyage

VIII | STRENGTH

Power – Fortitude

Symbols

1 – Lemniscate: the symbol of infinity indicates the quiet fortitude that stems from the union of moral and physical strength.

2 – Hands: the gentle movement of Strength's hands reflects a soft touch that is simultaneously assertive and humble. The hands hold the lion's jaws indicating the ability to control rage and anger.

3 – Maiden: indicates moral and righteous strength, as well as the strength of reason.

4 – Lion: indicates physical and wild strength, as well as the strength of instinct and passion.

5 – Walled castle: indicates how true strength exists outside common manifestations of power.

Strength

The Arcanum of Strength expresses energy, conflict and struggle in a non-violent way. Strength reflects a delicate girl taming a wild, dangerous lion. She reflects the quality of reason dominating instinct, calmness trumping brutality and order reigning over chaos. Strength represents the ability to accomplish the task at hand. Your energy, resources and capabilities are placed at the service of a goal. The Arcana represents strength of character, moral rectitude and even physical stamina and health.

This Arcanum is understood as the symbol of conflict between oppositional desires and motivations. One must be defeated, allowing a new possibility to emerge. It could be the very force enabling you to overcome and face your fears. It is the energy not to surrender or succumb even to the greatest pressure. It represents the intelligence that allows one to overcome insurmountable obstacles without the use of violence. The female who tames the beast is the best part of us, able to triumph over all things.

When Strength speaks to you she says ...

"I am the reserves of power thriving within you to get things done, to help you overcome all obstacles, to help you to forge your way in the world. You need never act rashly. Style, charm, grace and clever wit is your greatest weapon. Put down swords, guns and biting words. I remind you that you are stronger than you ever thought possible. Look how far you've come. You have only scratched the surface of what you are capable of. Let's conquer the world together."

Traditional Interpretation

Upright: Spiritual power overcoming material power. Using finesse and a soft touch to get what you want. Higher nature over carnal desires. The ability to channel great power. Strength of character. Good health. Softness.
Reversed: Feeling a loss of control. Discord and fear. An abuse of power. Cruelty and immaturity. Giving into base instincts.

Keywords

Strength, Power, Force, Kindness, Self Control, Self Discipline, Moderation, Patience, Compassion, Composure, Fortitude, Endurance, Sturdiness, Vigor, Potency, Durability, Health, Ascendancy, Serenity, Kindness, Energy, Relief, Opposites

Description

Strength is numbered Arcanum VIII, but many older decks have it as the number XI.

Visconti
Fortitude is usually painted with a lion or a broken column. The Visconti deck shows Hercules attacking the Nemean lion, a vicious creature of Greek mythology. The figure on the card may be based on Sforza himself and the card would reflect the allegories of Sforza's military victories in Milan and surrounding areas.

Marseille
The Marseilles and Waite cards show an elegantly dressed woman opening the jaws of a lion with her bare hands. The lion's teeth are bared to demonstrate the animal's fierceness.

Pictorial Key
The Waite and Marseille females both have the mathematic symbol of infinity, called lemniscate, above their head. In the Pictorial Key deck the symbol floats above the maiden's head.

Lesson

The Arcana of Strength will teach me to improve my self-control, fight my weaknesses and to understand what truly motivates me.

Aspects of the Arcana expressed in various decks

Lo Scarabeo Tarot

Gentleness

Nefertari's Tarot

Composure

Pagan Tarot

Harmony

Dark Angels Tarot

Energy

Universal Fantasy Tarot

Self Discipline

Fey Tarot

Conquest

Shaman Tarot

Integration

Tarot of the Pagan Cats

Grace

Tarot of the Dark Grimoire

Fearlessness

Manga Tarot

Endurance

Alternate Names

Fortitude, Lust

To learn more about this Archetype explore:

Virtue of Fortitude, Nemean lion, Cardinal Virtues, Hercules

IX | THE HERMIT

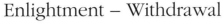

Enlightment – Withdrawal

Symbols

1 – Beard: indicates both wisdom of the age and the renunciation of all forms of vanity.

2 – Hood: expresses the ability to maintain secret thoughts and the renunciation of his own identity.

3 – Cloak: expresses the humility of the Hermit and his focus on what's inside, rather than outward appearances.

4 – Sandals: indicate the hardship of the road and the sacrifices needed to seek enlightenment.

5 – Staff: similar to a shepherd's staff, indicates the willingness of the Hermit to lead others.

6 – Lantern: symbolizes the inner light illuminating the road ahead. It is also the continuous quest for knowledge and enlightenment.

7 – Desert: indicates the solitude of the Hermit.

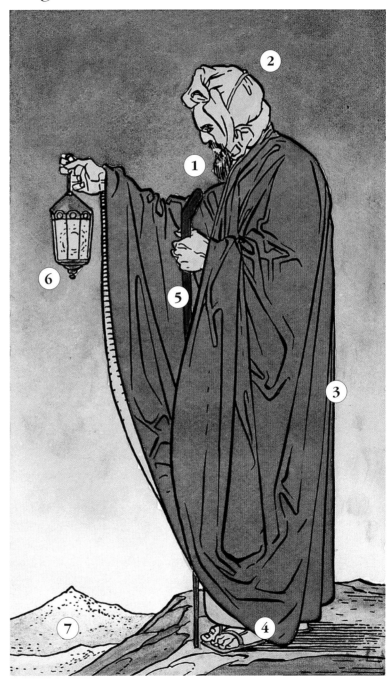

The Hermit

The Hermit is conservative, moves with caution, weighs options carefully and does not jump to make judgments or hasty decisions. He abandons all forms of vanity. He has no interest in dress or appearance, wealth or power. He is totally focused on the substance of things, contemplating peace in his isolation. Those who look to him respect his silence and regard him as a master.

The Hermit's self-imposed solitude is not fear based or antisocial. The Hermit uses isolation as an element of re-search. How can one listen without first seeking the silence? How can you know another, if you do not know yourself? The Hermit moves away from the noise of the world to look within himself. The Hermit does not merely collect facts. He strives to understand and internalize everything before him.

When the Hermit speaks to you he says ...

"I am the place where you examine and cultivate spiritual truth, where you study and analyze knowledge. You become so distracted that you forget yourself. Only you can know you. Renew yourself through reflection and observation. Once you are aware of inner truths, you bring the light of your inner knowledge to others. You lead and teach others by example. I am the ancient master. I am always here to guide you."

Traditional Interpretation

Upright: Looking inward, searching for the truth and retreat from distractions. Withdrawal from the opinion of others, detachment from material things, search for spirituality, light of truth. Arriving at answers for yourself. A need for quiet, solitary time.
Reversed: Running away from fears or responsibilities. Excess in need of others. Ignoring the truth. Sense of isolation or loneliness holding you back. Exhaustive socializing.

Keywords

Isolation, Withdrawal, Retreat, Introversion, Solitude, Experience, Ancient, Guide, Quest, Pilgrimage, Silence, Reflection, Retreat, Philosophy, Self-reflection, Self-Sufficiency, Sagacity, Prudence, Austerity, Humility, Prudence, Meditation, Search, Old Master

Description

Historically, the Hermit is drawn as an old man with white beard bearing a lantern and a walking stick.

Visconti
The Visconti card portrays the Hermit holding a timekeeping hourglass. The concept of Father Time was popular when this card was created. Time was considered to be a conquering element.

Marseille
The Marseille and Waite's Hermit holds a lantern out before them representing the light of wisdom.

Pictorial Key
The Hermit is placed atop a plateau. near the mountains and a six pointed star glows inside his lantern.

Lesson

The Arcana of the Hermit will teach me to rediscover the joy of tranquility, meditation, prayer and gratitude.

Aspects of the Arcana expressed in various decks

Lo Scarabeo Tarot

Introspection

Nefertari's Tarot

Austerity

Pagan Tarot

Study

Dark Angels Tarot

Seek through Darkness

Universal Fantasy Tarot

Individual Philosophy

Fey Tarot

Quest

Shaman Tarot

Seeker of Souls

Tarot of the Pagan Cats

Pilgrimage to Truth

Tarot of the Dark Grimoire

Solitude of Study

Manga Tarot

Eternal Wisdom

Alternate Names

Hunchback, Old Man Time, Father Time

To learn more about this Archetype explore:

Cronus, Father Time, Sage, Yoda, Ben Kenobi, Sophos, Philosopher, Senex, Odin, Yogi

X | THE WHEEL OF FORTUNE

Revolution – Repetition

Symbols

1 – Sphinx: represents the "fateful" force of the unconscious and perpetual change.

2 – Raising figure: Anubis, Egyptian god of the dead, indicates the mastery of fate over death and the mastery of death over fortune.

3 – Falling figure: Typhon, the Snake, embodies destruction and indicates the balance of creative and destructive forces.

4 – Figures in the corners: the Tetramorph, guardians of the four directions of space and defenders against a return to chaos.

5 – Wheel and Alchemical symbols: Mercury, Sulphur, Salt and Aquarius symbols can be recognized. The Wheel indicates the cyclic nature of fate and fortune.

6 – T.A.R.O.: can be read as TARO (Tarot), TORA (Truth) or ROTA (Wheel).

7 – Hebrew letters: four Hebrew letters form the Tetragrammaton (the name of God): Yod, Heh, Vau, Heh.

The Wheel of Fortune

Fortune spins her wheel and the fates of all those attached rise and fall. The Wheel of Fortune symbol is older than any Tarot deck. It is found in medieval manuscripts and upon the walls of ancient European churches. The allegory of the revolving Wheel of Fate, reflects how power is ephemeral and what has come will easily disappear. The Wheel teaches all things in the world are transitory: happiness or sadness, success or failure.

The Wheel represents the incessant flow of time. The Wheel's revolutions mark cycles, events and continuity. This card pinpoints a transitional shift in the Major Arcana. At the Wheel, the cards transform from personality types to experiential forces. The Wheel reflects the forces over which we have no control. On a simple level, it represents a change in one's luck for the better. On a deep level, it reminds one to cultivate that which lies within.

When the Wheel speaks to you he says ...

"I am the eternal force of time. My essence revolves solar systems, stars and suns in endless revolution and expansion. I am the flowing nature of life. Like tidal currents and seasonal changes, sometimes you ride high, sometimes you feel low. The only way to maintain equilibrium is to remain centered in my middle. I am you in the throws of destiny."

Traditional Interpretation

Upright: The beginning of a new cycle. The call of destiny. A reminder of life's ups and downs. Changing fortune. Luck changes for the better. Passing time. Nothing lasts forever. Karmic destiny. Mercy of external forces. Unforeseen events.
Reversed: Blockages in energy. A run of bad luck. Something must be removed. Disruption of natural cycle.

Keywords

Circularity, Fate, Flux, Cycles, Change, Revolution, Possibilities, Opportunities, Destiny, Development, Activity, Expansion, Fortune, Karma, Kismet, Alternating, Outside Forces

Description

Surrounded by the symbols of the four Evangelists, the Wheel expresses the ascending and descending fortunes of man. Inside the Wheel, the letters T, A, R and O are engraved.

Visconti
The Visconti scrolls read "Regnabo, Regno, Regnavi, Sum sine regno." This translates to, "I shall reign, I am reigning, I have reigned and I am without reign." Traditional for its time period, we see Father Time and Justice on the card.

Marseille
The Marseille deck contains beastly creatures. Whoever spins the wheel is mysteriously absent.

Pictorial Key
The card is packed with occult symbolism. The Wheel itself contains the word "Taro." It reads "Rota" or royal road. Four Hebrew letters represent the name of god. The four suits of Tarot and four elements are symbolized in the four corners. A sphinx represents balance on the wheel. Waite's card offers the Reader a specific center focal point on the Wheel.

Lesson

The Arcanum of the Wheel of Fortune teaches me to adapt to the role fate has offered me. It allows me to change my luck, influence my future and alter my fortune.

Aspects of the Arcana expressed in various decks

Revolution

Natural Cycle

Circularity

Everything falls Beneath

Eternal Time

Spinning Fate

Call of Destiny

Karmic Accounting

Central Point

Continuity through Change

Alternate Names

Wheel of Fortune, Wheel of Fate

To learn more about this Archetype explore:

Providence, Kismet, Divine Will, Karma, Fate, Fortuna, Bhavacakra

XI JUSTICE

Justice – Law

Symbols

1 – Crown: symbolizes sunlight, clarified ideas and illuminated existence.

2 – Columns: indicates the sacrality of the Temple of Justice.

3 – Sword: symbolizes rationality, logic, decision and impartial judgment.

4 – Scales: indicates care, attention, equilibrium and careful balancing.

5 – Veil: it hides what lies beyond Justice, as sometimes the reasons and ways of Justice are mysterious. The veil refers back to the High Priestess card and the essence of hidden knowledge.

Justice

Justice embodies the search for balance between all conflicting and contradictory forces animating the human soul. It is the independence of mind, the ability to express opinion, to seek answers and to act in a consistent manner. This can be found within oneself by harmonizing different needs, wishes and possibilities.

Justice points out that laws and morals do not depend solely on the subjective opinion of an individual. They stem from a greater universal or karmic source. The scale indicates the balance of opposites: head versus heart, matter versus spirit and consciousness versus unconsciousness. The scale reflects the ability to assess and distinguish right from wrong. Her sword points toward higher thinking and symbolizes the ability to act and separate just from unjust actions.

When Justice speaks to you she says ...

"I am the reminder that you get what you give. Keep an open mind and be fair in all situations. Consider others when you make choices and judgments. Look to me for answers, I shall reveal them to you. I represent your effort, your life's work and your moral center."

Traditional Interpretation

Upright: A positive outcome to legal matters. Sowing future seeds. Doing the right thing, no matter how challenging. Being objective and considering other points of view. Work, career and calling. Restoring balance.
Reversed: Negative outcome in a legal situation. Wearing blinders. You do not see the whole truth. Hidden facts. Unfair advantages against you.

Keywords

Legalism, Decision Making, Adjustment, Impartiality, Fairness, Equality, Insensitivity, Severity, Intellect, Logic, Balance, Court, Judging, Valor, Presence, Authorize, Exactitude, Legalese, Stiffness, Rules, Division, Work, Law

Description

Justice retains her traditional attributes of sword and scales on all three cards. Several modern decks have switched the placement of Justice and Strength.

Visconti
Female representations of the four cardinal virtues (Temperance, Fortitude, Prudence and Justice) were common in fifteenth and sixteenth century.

Marseille
Justice, in the Marseille and Waite cards sits on a throne, the back of which is supported by two small columns. She wears a crown on her head, her dress is bright and the look on her face is immobile.

Pictorial Key
The draping of the card reminds of the High Priestess whose veil hides profound secret knowledge. The Empress' red clothes are a symbol of the spiritual consequence of earthly actions. The square shape of her crown represents a solid mind and structured thoughts.

Lesson

The Arcanum of Justice will teach me to balance opinions, be open and fair in all situations. Justice guides me on my pursuit of truth and holds me accountable for all my actions.

Aspects of the Arcana expressed in various decks

Lo Scarabeo Tarot
Balance

Nefertari's Tarot
Merciful Judgment (Isis)

Pagan Tarot
Oaths

Dark Angels Tarot
Clever Decision

Universal Fantasy Tarot
Fairness

Fey Tarot
Vision of Truth

Shaman Tarot
Balance above Human Law

Tarot of the Pagan Cats
Karmic Accounting

Tarot of the Dark Grimoire
Insensitivity

Manga Tarot
Valor

Alternate Names

Balance, Impartiality

To learn more about this Archetype explore:

Law, Karmic Law, Law of Return, Reciprocity, Golden Rule, Hall of Justice, Athena, Jurisprudence, Maat, Themis

XII | HANGED MAN

Transcendence – Punishment

Symbols

1 – Hanging Beam: the boundary line between two opinions or two states of existence. A reference to a three-way crossroad and choices to be made.

2 – Crossed Legs and Arms: the punishment may be a voluntary sacrifice while arms behind the back are a symbol of power-lessness. The legs' posture foreshadows the World card.

3 – Tree Branch: trees are symbols of life, knowledge and express the union between heaven and earth.

4 – Upside Down: the reversal of a point of view and seeing the world with new eyes.

5 – Halo: indicates the enlightenment and wisdom that comes through suffering and perseverance. Ancient symbol reflecting the sacred, powerful and heroic.

The Hanged Man

The Hanged Man expresses a moment of difficulty, pain and the inability to act. The difficulty of action is temporary. The Hanged Man seems to have offered himself up for this testing voluntarily. Through this card, sacrifice leads to growth, progress and understanding. His folded, crossed legs are a reference to the crucifixion and martyrdom. This is the first card in the Major Arcana sequence that references suffering but the discomfort is a necessary step for growth and evolution.

Upside down suspension is symbolic of initiatory rites. The Hanged Man represents the transition from one state of consciousness to another. He hangs between two different levels of awareness. The Hanged Man is symbolic of a change of perspective and ability to empathize with a different the point of view.

When the Hanged Man speaks to you he says ...

"I come alive when you approach the world from a new point of view and see it with a new set of eyes. I am what comes from the sacrifice of oneself, what happens when we push ourselves past comfortable limits. Though I am not always a comfortable space to inhabit, I am essential to your growth. You should not dwell in my space for too long, lest you become static and stuck. Check in with me on a regular basis. I reveal new perspectives."

Traditional Interpretation

Upright: Necessary moment of pause. A new vision of yourself and the world. The time has come for self-sacrifice. Pause, limbo and stasis. Visions of wonder. Surrender to a situation. Waiting for the right moment to act. Rite of passage.
Reversed: Sudden burst of action. "Ah ha!" moment. Change in direction. Flash of brilliance. Struggling in a fruitless situation. An excellent decision. Moving forward with speed.

Keywords

Inversion, Reversals, Insight, Halt, Meditation, Sacrifice, Gestation, Fetus, Delay, Suspicion, Rest, Limbo, Surrendering, Passivity, Acceptance, Contemplation, Waiting, Detachment, Idealism, Transition, Initiation, Disinterestedness, Utopia, Punishment

Description

The Hanged Man remains upside down. His posture is relaxed and his legs crossed.

Visconti
A well-dressed young man hangs by one foot from a beam. In the Visconti's time, criminals and thieves on the run were often painted hanging upside down by one foot. Occasionally, executed bodies would be displayed but it was far more common to paint crooks in this fashion rather than actually hang them at the road.

Marseille
All three cards depict the Hanged Man's his free leg bent behind the suspended leg in the shape of a cross. The hands seem to be tied behind his back.

Pictorial Key
The card shows gallows in the form of a Tau cross. This tree of sacrifice is alive and leaves are seen leaves growing on it. The face is composed and a golden halo glows around the head like a Christian martyr.

Lesson

The Arcana of the Hanged Man will teach me to challenge myself, deal with discomfort and to view the world and my own experience from other points of view.

Aspects of the Arcana expressed in various decks

Lo Scarabeo Tarot

Nefertari's Tarot

Pagan Tarot

Dark Angels Tarot

Universal Fantasy Tarot

Insight   Punishment   Transition   Self Sacrifice   Surrender

Fey Tarot

Shaman Tarot

Tarot of the Pagan Cats

Tarot of the Dark Grimoire

Manga Tarot

Reversal of Perceptions   Initiation   Waiting   Limbo   Self Discipline

Alternate Names

The Traitor

To learn more about this Archetype explore:

The Crucifixion, Odin and the World Tree, Sacrifice, Inversion

XIII DEATH

Transformation – Ending

Symbols

1 – Armored skeleton: the Reaper or the Black Knight is the embodiment of death.

2 – Black Banner with the Mystic Rose: indicates life. And represents how death and life are connected.

3 – Rising Sun: indicates hope, immortality and how the death of the flesh is a new beginning for the spirit.

4 – Fallen King: represents how everything in the Material World is fated to pass. King, child and maiden, all are alike before Death.

5 – Bishop: surrenders in prayer to Death's arrival.

6 – Knocked crown: the old ways are overthrown.

7 – Ship on river: life continues onward in the midst of change.

Death

Death is a universal symbol. The skeleton is the base structure of our bodies, the essence of physical life itself. In ancient times this Arcanum was held as the representation of the end of all things, a veil of darkness blotting out everything. An allegorical death was the end of human vanity, the inevitable end of man who was finally free to rise above material concerns and turn to the spiritual world because of his immortal soul.

The Death card is now understood as the beginning. Everything new springs forth from an ending. It is not death in the literal sense, but in regard to change and evolution. Death is continuously happening, though sometimes it is radical, unexpected and unstoppable. The symbol separates what is frivolous and ephemeral, from what is important, eternal and true.

Looking at the Death card it is normal to sense a feeling of loss. This card destroys security and forces one to venture beyond. Fear arises from not being able to predict what comes next. Only by facing this fear directly and moving through it do we evolve. If we are sensitive and allow it, Death offers the greatest gift. It teaches us how to live.

When Death speaks to you she says …

"I stand behind you, in front of you and next to you, watching you and those you love. I am the force you may fear but will never deny. You can no more stop my bony fingers than stop the seasons from changing. I am the ending that brings about all new beginnings. Embrace me, do not fear. Look me in the face and accept the consequences. It is easier if you do not struggle."

Traditional Interpretation

Upright: An ending that brings a period of grief and loss. Sudden change and disruption leading to new growth. Uncomfortable revolution. Gateway to another plane of existence, threshold to another reality. Sudden and radical change. Release.
Reversed: Something needs to change. Putting off the inevitable. Fear of the unknown. You need to become brave. You are avoiding an issue. Stifled by fear.

Keywords

Expiration, Transition, Transformation, Evolution, Passage, Progress, Conclusion, Regeneration, Loss, Release, Mutation, Cleansing, Elimination, Revolution, Irreversible, Threshold, Radical, Gateway to Another World, Fatality

Description

Death is unrelenting in her steady pace. Everyone falls before her, no matter their station, power, or nature.

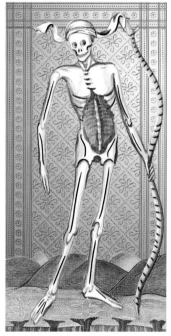

Visconti
A skeleton stands casually with a bow. His anatomy is thin, he stands before a jagged landscape.

Marseille
Death is on the move. He carries a sharp scythe, an agricultural hand tool used for mowing and reaping crops. A scythe often accompanies Death due to the Christian conception of Death as "harvester of souls." Human heads, feet, hands and bones are scattered on the ground. One head wears a crown representing authority destroyed.

Pictorial Key
Death is dressed like a judge in black robes, sitting on a throne of bones. A golden dawn literally rises as a sun in the background between two towers. Your interpretation of this card depends greatly on whether you believe the sun is rising or if you believe the sun to be setting.

Lesson

The Arcanum of Death will teach me to let go of attachments to the past and to appreciate the affairs of the present. Change is to be embraced when it arrives.

Aspects of the Arcana expressed in various decks

Lo Scarabeo Tarot

Grim Reaper

Nefertari's Tarot

Fatality (Anubis)

Pagan Tarot

Transformation via Ritual

Dark Angels Tarot

Ultimate Transformation

Universal Fantasy Tarot

Elimination

Fey Tarot

End of the Game

Shaman Tarot

Passage

Tarot of the Pagan Cats

Expiration

Tarot of the Dark Grimoire

Doorway

Manga Tarot

Threshold

Alternate Names

The Unnamed Arcana, End

To learn more about this Archetype explore:

Death, Dying Rites, Nature's Cycles, Gardening, Grim Reaper, Angel of Death, Hades, Saint Death, Angel of Light and Dark, Danse Macabre

XIV | TEMPERANCE

Mediation – Compromise

Symbols

1 – White wings: the winged angel expresses the benevolent healing and soothing intention of the Universe.

2 – Path: the journey between rational and spiritual understanding.

3 – Sun and Mountain: ascension to a spiritual realm, unburdened by the limits of the material and intellectual world.

4 – Water: indicates life, emotion and purification. A foot on water and a foot on earth represent the ability to balance psychic and material energies.

5 – Sun symbol: an alchemical sun that indicates the power of transmutation.

6 – Flower: represents peace, diplomacy, patience.

7 – Transmutation: indicates gentle change and removal of any excess.

Temperance

Temperance is a figure of peace and can indicate meekness, innocence and pacifism. Every gesture reflects infinite sweetness and the elegance of an angel. The angel is often interpreted as turning water into wine. Mixing and energetic exchanges are the essence of Temperance. Passions are controlled and expressed without violence or excesses. Opposites live, communicate and thrive in relation to one another. Temperance represents healing and recovery.

Many interpret the literal meaning of "Temperance," the social movement that prohibited alcohol. This interpretation is useful in regard to reducing what is unhealthy, a theme faced as we approach the Arcanum of the Devil.

This Arcanum includes the implication of "tempering" an object. This reflects the active work to refine a talent or skill. For example, one tempers a sword to make it sharper. Diligence in work is an interesting contrast to the Devil who patiently waits for the viewer in the next card.

When Temperance speaks to you she says ...

"I am where you find the balance of desire and need, where you discover the stability within your mental and emotional nature. I am also here when you need to hone a skill and improve a task or talent. I am the part of you able to find moderation in all things. I remind you to find your calm center. I help you to hold uncomfortable opposites until a third option appears. Acting with me, the path remains clear and true. You carry the grace of an angel."

Traditional Interpretation

Upright: Synergy, balance and equilibrium. Adaptation and the ability to combine opposites. Regeneration and practice. Harmonious blending. Care, recovery and healing.
Reversed: Imbalance and feeling out of whack. Infection or exposure to illness. Compromising in too many areas. Stop trying to please everyone.

Keywords

Tempering, Rejuvenation, Blend, Circulate, Harmony, Healing, Benevolence, Health, Recovery, Synthesis, Equilibrium, Symmetry, Moderation, Adaptation, Regeneration, Mixture, Patience, Alchemical Process

Description

Temperance, one of the four cardinal virtues, is a popular iconic image since Classical Antiquity. Depictions of Temperance are remarkably similar.

Visconti
The Visconti Temperance is placed near the sharp drop of a vertical cliff. Renaissance Virtues were always painted as women, never angels, so Temperance bears no wings.

Marseille
The Marseille and Waite cards both reflect Temperance with angel wings and the magical stream of energy between her pitchers as if defying the laws of gravity.

Pictorial Key
Temperance wears a long dress with a golden symbol on his/her chest. One foot is on land, the other in a pool of water. A path winds from the pool to a distant mountain peak, imagery repeated in the Moon card. A sparkling yellow crown glitters in the distance.

Lesson

The Arcanum of Temperance will teach me to combine various aspects of life in a harmonious manner and to move without urgency and anxiety.

Aspects of the Arcana expressed in various decks

Lo Scarabeo Tarot

Blending

Nefertari's Tarot

Moderation

Pagan Tarot

Synthesis of Spirit and Work

Dark Angels Tarot

Creating Something from Nothing

Universal Fantasy Tarot

Patience

Fey Tarot

Coexistence

Shaman Tarot

Spiritual Healing

Tarot of the Pagan Cats

Recovery

Tarot of the Dark Grimoire

Healing

Manga Tarot

Purification

Alternate Names

The Healer, Mercy

To learn more about this Archetype explore:

Cardinal Virtues, Hindu Dharma, Forgiveness, Humility

XV | THE DEVIL

Passion – Excess

Symbols

1 – Devil: represents lack of enlightenment, evil intentions and slavery to the darkest desires.

2 – Reversed star: symbol of Lucifer, indicates corruption of power or virtue.

3 – Chains: represents how our own desires and fears can become an addiction and limit freedom.

4 – Upside down torch: ignorance and lack of knowledge are tools for enslavement.

5 – Human figures: mirrors of the figures appearing in the Lovers card.

6 – Stone block: symbolizes how concerns for the material world are what prevent man to reach enlightenment and spiritual awareness.

The Devil

The Devil represents the fallen figure of human vices: anger, sloth, lust, avarice, envy and pride. The Devil is the embodiment of vice and of the bad teacher leading one to destruction. He advocates complacency, neglecting responsibility, submitting to weakness and embracing passions without hesitation. The Devil places selfish needs above the needs of others. He represents human flaws.

The Devil's wild freedom and uncensored pursuit of pleasure leads to personal slavery and dependence. Drug, alcohol and sex addictions are echoed in this card as well as manipulative and destructive behaviors towards yourself and others. His animal magnetism is seductive and fascinating, yet blind, empty and devoid of all prospects. The Devil is a mirror reflecting the dark side of the self.

When the Devil speaks to you he says ...

"I am the hedonist within. People are obsessed with me, scapegoat me and worship me. Step closer and let me gaze at you. Yes, closer. Let me whisper in your ear. I am the most seductive creature you could ever imagine. I will make your every last dream and desire come true. Money, fame, sex, love, revenge. If you want it, I will grant it ... but for a small price. I remind you to keep all aspects of life in check but to have fun. Remember, it is both the light and darkness within us make us whole. Come closer."

Traditional Interpretation

Upright: Power and control issues. Making choices against your better interest. Doing something that turns out completely wrong. Deception from another. Addiction and submission. Cruelty to others. The inability to look inward with clarity. Moving from attraction to obsession.
Reversed: Overcoming an addiction. Moving past old stumbling blocks. You are free and no longer a slave to obsession. Proceed with caution.

Keywords

Shadow, Falsehood, Forbidden, Materialism, Obsession, Anxiety, Hedonism, Anger, Temptation, Doubt, Vice, Futility, Control, Power, Sexuality, Creativity, Attachments, Impulses, Taboo, Abuse, Unethical, Indulgence, Selfishness, Charm, Emotion, Passion, Instinct, Self-Interest, Deception, The Dark Side

Description

A cruel-looking, fiery devil, enslaves a man and a woman, who are reminiscent of Adam and Eve as seen in the Lovers card.

Visconti
The Devil card is absent from the Visconti deck, along with the Tower, Knight of Coins and Three of Swords. The Devil has been re-imagined by modern deck designers.

Marseille
The Marseille and Waite cards both reflect a demonic creature with bat-like wings on a pedestal. Two enslaved creatures stand beneath the demon. They could easily slip their bonds yet they do not. The Marseille Devil body has female breasts, male genitalia and claw feet.

Pictorial Key
The Devil sprouts two horns, bears an inverted pentagram, holds a torch and lights the fellow below on fire. Chained to the pedestal, two figures are bound, naked, sprouting animal tails. Waite's card is the dark inversion of the Lover's card.

Lesson

The Arcanum of the Devil will teach me to overcome feelings of guilt and indulge without excess. It will help me to understand the darkness within myself.

Aspects of the Arcana expressed in various decks

Lo Scarabeo Tarot

Shadow

Nefertari's Tarot

Submission

Pagan Tarot

Pressure and Control

Dark Angels Tarot

Temptation

Universal Fantasy Tarot

Lust - Lilith

Fey Tarot

Hunger and Greed

Shaman Tarot

Deception

Tarot of the Pagan Cats

Futility

Tarot of the Dark Grimoire

The Dark Side

Manga Tarot

Paralyzing Fear

Alternate Names

Satan, Lucifer, Beelzebub, Iblis, Lucifer, Leviathan, Mephistopheles, Prince of Darkness, Dark Lord, The Tempter

To learn more about this Archetype explore:

Mara, Trickster, Demons, Fallen Angels, Scapegoat, Goethe's *Faust*, Milton's *Paradise Lost*

XVI | THE TOWER

Demolition – Destruction

Symbols

1 – Lightning: the wrath from above strikes the tower of Man.

2 – Fire: a destructive force that gains power by consuming everything.

3 – Falling people: lives thrown into disarray everything they know is destroyed.

4 – Tower: akin to the Tower of Babel, the Tower is a structure of pride and selfish certainty, built by man for man. It is an artificial construction providing safety, but is actually a prison of the spirit.

5 – Windows: symbolize how our understanding of the three planes of being (mental, intellectual and physical) is collapsing.

The Tower

The Tower is identified as a prison built for ourselves. Locked behind barred windows and high walls, we are captive without realizing it. We remained inside for safety or perhaps out of ignorance. Once the Tower/prison crumbles, we crawl from the ruins and into the open. The Tower is the opening of communication and change. The collapse is therefore liberation, a catharsis.

The Tower is about leaving your certainties, your opinions and your environment and tackling uncharted territory. To reach the World, one must move through the Tower, no matter how uncomfortable it may feel. It also stands as a wake up call, a flash of insight, or life changing communication.

When the Tower speaks to you she says ...

"I am the destroyer in you who eliminates what never fit to begin with. I am unexpected, a flash of brilliance, a crack of thunder, a realization. I may not come often but when I do, I shake things up so you can rebuild what wasn't working. Do not fear me. I am essential for growth. You rebuild: better, stronger and wiser. Welcome to the new you."

Traditional Interpretation

Upright: Shocking problem. Complete, unexpected destruction followed by new growth. Abandoning a major issue that is no longer serving you. Something must change.
Reversed: Being immobilized after a tragic event. An issue or situation that is not as bad as it appears. Internal strife needs to be externalized. Beating old habits.

Keywords

Ruin, Reduction, Breakdown, Opening, Shock, Lightening, Uncork, Explosion, Divorce, Dispute, Castration, Revelation, Liberation, Catastrophe, Enlightenment, Orgasm, Overthrow, Punishment, Estrangement, Separation, Humility, Chaos, Impact, Burst, Disillusion, Exile, Prison, Removal, Crash, Tyranny

Description

The Tower has retained its original qualities even in the most modern Arcana.

Visconti
The Tower card is missing or was not included in the Visconti deck (along with the Devil, the Knight of Coins and Three of Swords). A modern artist has designed it.

Marseille
The Marseille and Waite cards show an embattled tower broken by a tongue of fire or arrow. Two people plunge from the tower to their death, three windows are seen. The sky appears to fall in different colors and drops.

Pictorial Key
The wrath of Heaven strikes the Tower, sets it on fire and plummets the King and Queen (embodiments of hubris and pride) to their death.

Lesson

The Arcanum of the Tower will help me accept loss, overcome blocks and inhibitions and free up new space for growth and manifestation.

Aspects of the Arcana expressed in various decks

Breakdown

Lo Scarabeo Tarot

Fall

Nefertari's Tarot

Refusal

Pagan Tarot

Overthrow

Dark Angels Tarot

Enlightenment

Universal Fantasy Tarot

Liberation

Fey Tarot

Removal

Shaman Tarot

Chaos

Tarot of the Pagan Cats

Catastrophe

Tarot of the Dark Grimoire

Reconstruction from Defeat

Manga Tarot

Alternate Names

House of God, The Thunderbolt, Skyscraper

To learn more about this Archetype explore:

Tower of Babel, Harrowing of Hell, Kundalini Experience, Breakthroughs, Breaking Points

XVII | THE STAR

Hope – Infinity

Symbols

1 – Eight-pointed star: represents the purity of the soul in the spiritual realm.

2 – Seven stars: represent the seven visible Planets of traditional astrology, whose influences affect the world; the Sun, Moon, Mercury, Venus, Mars, Jupiter and Saturn.

3 – Tree and bird: the connection between Earth and Heaven, with the Bird of Hermes.

4 – Water: represents un-adulterated and pristine life and spiritual energy.

5 – Jugs: water pouring in the pool and water pouring on the earth: as Above, so Below.

6 – Naked woman: the highest spiritual manifestation of the feminine, both mother and connection to all things.

The Star

The Star indicates the purest form of beauty and graceful enlightenment. This Arcanum is a symbol of truth and understanding. It is the glow of light illuminating darkness. Recall the tempestuous Devil and Tower cards preceding the delicate Star. The Star is the silence following the fury, the salve that soothes the soul, the crystal clear calm after the storm. It is ultimate peace.

The Star carries a positive interpretation. It is ideal foresight and the ability to think ahead, clearly and concisely. The card is the artist in communication with the muse, creativity flowing and a wellspring of inspiration. The gentle waters are representative of hope.

When the Star speaks to you she says ...

"I am the quiet after the storm. The calm, open and inspired feeling of serenity and healing. You find me after facing a challenge. My flowing waters refresh your soul. I show you what is possible when you have proven your strength. I am the vulnerability that is the birthplace of joy and freedom. Embrace me and bask in the cooling of my inspiration."

Traditional Interpretation

Upright: Inspired grace, faith and hope. Renewal and beauty. Excellent balance and channeling inspiration. Allowing oneself to be open. A conduit of harmony and farsighted works of goodness. A great love.
Reversed: There is a blockage. You refuse guidance and help. Need for relaxation. Allow yourself to feel vulnerable. Stifling darkness.

Keywords

Hope, Optimism, Openness, Calmness, Trust, Joy, Serenity, Essence, Regeneration, Inspiration, Harmony, Faith, Generosity, Tranquility, Understanding, Clarity, Insight, Renewal, Cosmic, Irrigate, Purity, Beauty, Farsightedness, Guide

Description

The Star card is Tarot's first celestial body. The Moon, Sun and World soon follow. They represent the universe and the influence of the planets and stars on us.

Visconti
The Visconti Star card holds her namesake in her hand. The heavens and universe are physically brought down to earth. She stands near a precipice in an elegant, blue gown.

Marseille
Marseille and Waite depict a young naked woman, hair cascading past her shoulders, who kneels as she works. She pours liquid onto the pool and the ground from two jars. A bird sits behind her in a tree. She is illuminated by a night sky lit with brilliantly shining stars. One particularly large star shines with eight spokes. Seven smaller stars dot the sky.

Pictorial Key
The water from the right jug falls in a greater pool. That from the left jug falls on the ground. A bird stands over the Tree of Life, and many stars surround a greater one, with eigth points.

Lesson

The Arcana of the Star will teach me to believe that anything is possible. It will help me look at the future with hope and energy.

Aspects of the Arcana expressed in various decks

Lo Scarabeo Tarot
Mystery of Life

Nefertari's Tarot
Brilliant Ideas

Pagan Tarot
Communication with the Divine

Dark Angels Tarot
Hope amidst Loss

Universal Fantasy Tarot
Regeneration

Fey Tarot
Hope and Serenity

Shaman Tarot
Guide from Above

Tarot of the Pagan Cats
Cleansing

Tarot of the Dark Grimoire
Light in the Darkness

Manga Tarot
Clarity and Purpose

Alternate Names

The Stars

To learn more about this Archetype explore:

Astrology, Aquarius, Muse

108

XVIII │ THE MOON

Mystery – Illusion

Symbols

1 – Moon: a symbol of femininity. Indicates monthly cycles, ebb and flow. It is the renewal of nature.

2 – Rays: a reference to the Tree of Life.

3 – Night: represents the dark side of consciousness, the sleep of reason, dreams and the unconscious.

4 – Towers: symbolize the summer and winter solstices, the "gates" dividing the year into two parts.

5 – Dogs: express the duality between illusion and intuition.

6 – Crawfish: indicates constructs of the mind taking shape and becoming real.

7 – Road: the road of initiation leading one to deeper mysteries.

The Moon

The Moon connects to female temperament, water bodies and cyclical natures. The Moon is evocative of changes and transformations (as those of werewolves or as the rising ocean tides). It comes and goes, waxes and wanes and is always in motion. The Moon provides illumination of our nightime landscapes. Things look odd, strange and supernatural in her light yet without her we would be left to fend for ourselves in the darkness. The Moon represents the dreams, secret desires and the vivid imagination of the soul.

Moonlight is a reflection and the mystery of the unknown. It illuminates our bestial nature - the dog and the wolf - and the crawfish emerging from the depths. The imagination can be illusory, sometimes proving false and ephemeral. It disappears and reappears as if made of smoke. The Moon represents the ability to create, to see hidden things by receiving information through intuition rather than rationality. The Moon indicates all the mysteries, magic and the supernatural.

When the Moon speaks to you she says ...

"I am where the subconscious speaks, the birthplace of dreams, illusion and fantasy. My landscape is deceptive and murky but it is only here we can escape the harsh light of day. Embrace me and meet what resides beneath the calm exterior you present to the world. Do not resist me. Your natural urges and feelings will find a way out whether you repress them or not. I am the shadow of your psyche."

Traditional Interpretation

Upright: Intuitive understandings. Lunacy, dreams and deception. Strangeness in events, feelings of oddness, moon madness. Strong psychic flashes and impulses. Mutable situation.
Reversed: Someone is lying. You need to listen to your instincts. Cut off from your true nature.

Keywords

Dreams, Cycles, Unconscious, Tension, Doubt, Fantasy, Illusion, Imagination, Romanticism, Strangeness, Madness, Danger, Deception, Sanity, Struggle, Superstition, Secrets, Receptivity, Subversiveness, Magnetism, Instinctual, Vision, Insight, Sensitivity, Application, Psychic Ability, Magic, Boundaries, Occultism, Shadow Self

Description

Historically, the Moon changed from being represented as a woman, to that of a moon shining over a pool of water.

Visconti
The Visconti card shows a maiden holding a crescent moon similar the woman in the Star card. She stands before a cliff and holds the strings of her belt.

Marseille
The Marseille and Waite cards show a moon shining in the night sky. It emits lunar rays upon the landscape below. The sun is reflected in moonlight. On the ground, two dogs bark and howl at the moon, while a crawfish emerges from a pond. Two towers flank the card from each side.

Pictorial Key
The dogs represent the fears of the mind in a gentler way than the monster emerging from water. The Moon is a journey extending from the darkest watery depths to the highest mountain peak. It is evocative of the identical path in the Temperance card. Its call cannot and should not be ignored.

Lesson

The Arcanum of the Moon will teach me to freely express myself and explore my desires without worrying about what others might think.

Aspects of the Arcana expressed in various decks

Lo Scarabeo Tarot

Duality

Nefertari's Tarot

Occultism

Pagan Tarot

Working Moon Magic

Dark Angels Tarot

Struggle

Universal Fantasy Tarot

Illusion vs. Reality

Fey Tarot

World of Emotion and Instinct

Shaman Tarot

Deception and Falsehood - Moon of Illusion

Tarot of the Pagan Cats

Strangeness in Moon Shadow

Tarot of the Dark Grimoire

Lunacy and Lurking Monsters

Manga Tarot

The Dream

Alternate Names

Mystery, The Goddess

To learn more about this Archetype explore:

Moon Madness, Psychic Phenomena, Insanity, Sleep, Dreams, Fantasy Play

XIX | THE SUN

Light – Truth

Symbols

1 – Sun: symbolizing masculine energy, the light defeating darkness, as well as truth and intelligence.

2 – Sunflowers: represent the willingness to seek the light and follow it.

3 – Wall: the boundary between two dimensions: between self awareness and ignorance.

4 – Child: indicates simplicity, naïveness and carefree spontaneity.

5 – Horse: the animal and material nature of man, in harmony with his higher self.

6 – Red Banner: indicates glory, power, creativity and vital energy.

The Sun

The Sun is the ruler of day. A source of light so unique, so bright it contains no darkness or shadow within it. We can gaze at the moon for hours but we must never look directly at the sun. Sunlight in Tarot is always connected with life, truth, justice and righteousness. The abundance of light is translated into wealth, happiness and health. The Sun is interpreted as the triumph of life in all its forms, the desire and joy of living. While the Moon represents feminine aspects and receptive nature, the Sun embodies male aspects, expansive and affirmative.

On an intellectual level, the Sun represents truth and the ability to communicate. On the physical plane it indicates a victory, success, recognition or glory. The Sun is the spirit and state of awareness, a rebuilt world of innocence. The Sun also indicates excellent physicality and a healthy pregnancy.

When the Sun speaks to you he says …

"I am the brilliance, joy and energy that is responsible for all life. I represent fertility and growth. I am there to power ideas in your mind and love in your heart. You can hide nothing from me. I am the energy that manifests your desires and beauty in the world. Stop to feel me throughout the day. Feel my rays upon your skin and soak in my strength. I am the warm yellow energy of summer and the bleak, white light of winter. As I am the Sun for you, you are the Sun for others. Shine with me."

Traditional Interpretation

Upright: Streaming energy. A happy time with clarity and joy. Expansion and growth. Healthy body and pregnancy. Truth and light. Transparency and celebration. Joy of childhood. Complete exuberance.

Reversed: Feeling burned out. Support system is unavailable. Depression. In danger of metaphorical blindness. Too much light, too bright.

Keywords

Growth, Energy, Clarity, Glory, Exuberance, Happiness,
Success, Marriage, Heat, Love, Awareness, Radiance,
Light, Evolution, Wealth, Summer, Childhood, Friendship,
Expansion, Splendor, Brilliance, Joy, Enthusiasm, Optimism,
Enlightenment, Harmony, Friendship, Honesty, Solidarity,
Honesty, Generosity

Description

Nudity, exuberance and youth are implied on all three
version of this card.

Visconti
The Visconti version depicts a
cherub with small wings, who
steals the sun from the sky. He
moves across the landscape
upon a cloud.

Marseille
The Marseille reflects two children
dancing. The sunrays shower upon
their bare shoulders.

Pictorial Key
The card depicts two naked boys
on a sunny field. One rides a white
horse and together they carry a red
banner.

Lesson

The Arcanum of the Sun will help me to directly address any issue, to seek clarity and to address problems rationally, without hiding from the truth or myself.

Aspects of the Arcana expressed in various decks

Lo Scarabeo Tarot

Optimism

Nefertari's Tarot

Rays of Harmony

Pagan Tarot

Summer

Dark Angels Tarot

Awareness

Universal Fantasy Tarot

Evolution and Solidarity

Fey Tarot

Basking to the Light

Shaman Tarot

Dance of the Sun

Tarot of the Pagan Cats

Harmony and Pleasure

Tarot of the Dark Grimoire

Radiance filling the Darkness

Manga Tarot

Living in the Light

Alternate Names

The Light, The God

To learn more about this Archetype explore:

Solar Energy, Apollo, Nature

XX JUDGMENT

Renewal – Awakening

Symbols

1 – Angel: a higher order and a truth that cannot be denied.

2 – Cloud: expresses the unknowability, the spiritual and the impossibility to understand everything.

3 – Cross: represents directions of space, the cosmic order and the balance of opposites.

4 – Horn: the communication of a message and the wake up call to which we must respond.

5 – People: symbolize family, humanity, but also the individual compound of body, mind and soul.

6 – Tomb: is the symbol of death and resurrection.

Judgment

Judgment is the awakening of consciousness. It reflects the soul of a person who has responded to a call issued from a higher order. Judgment explicitly references the Christian Last Judgment, in which the angel of God announces the world has come to an end. The righteous will separate from the unjust. Sorting time is at hand. This is a simple metaphor to apply to our lives through the allegory of metamorphosis or being born again via transformation.

This card sometimes indicates a messenger. The most important element is its finality. As the second to last card, this last call reflects all things reaching their conclusion. Resolution, either good or bad is here and now. This Arcanum is the end of waiting, the arrival of a reward and a door opening to a different world. A world, whose fabric and tapestry is elaborate, complicated, but richer.

When Judgment speaks to you he says ...

"I am the sign that your life has changed, you are transforming, there is no going back now. The road has crumbled behind you. Embrace me even if I feel uncomfortable. Change often invokes vulnerability. Heeding my call, you rise to new heights, do not look down and have no fear. You are safe, you are brilliant, you are reborn."·

Traditional Interpretation

Upright: Hearing and heeding the call that pulls you into a new reality. A complete internal transformation. Freeing yourself and living at a higher level. Things will never be the same. A massive wake up call.
Reversed: Not doing what should be done. Acting against your true nature. Hiding from the truth. Resistance to movement.

Keywords

Revelation, Resurrection, Examination, Rebirth, Absolution, Redemption, Hope, Reconciliation, Release, Restart, Salvation, Call, Renaissance, Transcendence, Emergence, Family, Awakening, Renewal, Above

Description

The imagery of the Judgment card remains remarkably similar throughout all older Tarot decks.

Visconti

The Visconti deck offers a card called "the Angel." It represents the angel of the Last Judgment, from which the typical Tarot name is derived. God oversees two trumpeting angels while the dead rise from their graves.

Marseille

The Marseilles and Waite image offer a single winged angel emerging from a cloud of shining light, sounding a trumpet from which flies a banner with a red cross. On earth, naked men, women and children rise from their tombs.

Pictorial Key

In the card, an entire family rises to greet the angel. They are suspended in mist and look upward to the light of Heaven.

Lesson

The Arcanum of Judgment teaches me evolution is unavoidable. Embracing change, my life becomes richer and stronger. My potential is fulfilled as my boundaries expand in unimaginable ways.

Aspects of the Arcana expressed in various decks

Lo Scarabeo Tarot

Wake Up Call

Nefertari's Tarot

Rebirth through Mummification

Pagan Tarot

Reconciliation

Dark Angels Tarot

Revelation at the End

Universal Fantasy Tarot

Emergence

Fey Tarot

Energies taking Life

Shaman Tarot

Renewal and Reawakening

Tarot of the Pagan Cats

Release

Tarot of the Dark Grimoire

The Call

Manga Tarot

Courage of Truth

Alternate Names

The Angel, The Trumpet, The Last Day

To learn more about this Archetype explore:

The End of Days, The Four Horsemen of the Apocalypse, Final Judgment, Life After Death

Completeness – Balance

Symbols

1 – Symbols of the Evangelists: represent the order and meaning of the Universe.

2 – Garland: an almond shaped crown of life and glory surrounding and protecting the Anima Mundi.

3 – Naked Woman: the Alma Mundi, or Soul of the World, dancing, represents the joy of creation and the harmony of Heaven.

4 – Wands: shaped like candles with flames burning in both directions, they express both the complexity of the Universe and the four elements.

The World

The World is the final path marked by the Major Arcana. This Arcanum represents the harmonious union of all things, happiness, completeness and manifestation. It is a representation of transcendence, the ability of man to overcome human limitations and touch the Divine.

The perfection embodied by this Arcanum is real and constant. It represents a point of arrival for each element symbolized by the tetramorph of four creatures in the four corners. They have found their location and their place within the card, within the deck, within you. The World represents success, reward, happiness and the resolution of a problem.

When the World speaks to you she says ...

"Lost in the dance of life, I represent you in a moment of transcendence. Your brilliance at work, laughing with joy, living with abandon, you following your instincts, all paid off. You embrace your uniqueness; you are the essence of yourself. What lies inside you is reflected on the outside, there is no boundary between the two. The integration is complete. Magic springs around you, the world comes to you and you have arrived. You thirst for nothing, yearn for nothing, need, want, beg, or need anything except for what is found in the moment. I am your moment of arrival."

Traditional Interpretation

Upright: Successful achievement of a goal. Euphoria, travel and integration of all things. Immersed in the dance of life. Pride in accomplishment. The world is yours.
Reversed: Not moving on. Hiding in your comfort zone. Missing the point.

Keywords

Completion, Fulfillment, Movement, Travel, Accomplishment, Success, Wholeness, Contentment, Integration, Totality, Universal, Satisfaction, Ecstasy, Accord, Perfection, Reward, Happiness, Finality, Ending

Description

Historically, the World card is depicted as either the Throne of God, or the Alma Mundi (The Soul of the World), who is reflected as a naked woman dancing in an almond shaped laurel crown.

Visconti
The Visconti card reflects two cherubs holding up a medieval city as if revealing a possibility. The city lies under the stars and is surrounded by a moat.

Marseille
The Marseille and Waite card carries a more personal and immediate meaning. We discover ourselves through these Arcana. A naked female dances in the sky while she holds two wands. An oval wreath surrounds her and in the corners are the figures of the four evangelists.

Pictorial Key
Waite's card strays little from the Marseille symbol. The female figure has a gentle and soft look as she dances with abandon across a blue sky.

Lesson

The Arcanum of the World will help me to understand happiness and to find my place independently of where I am and who is with me.

Aspects of the Arcana expressed in various decks

Lo Scarabeo Tarot

Wholeness

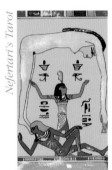
Nefertari's Tarot

The World

Pagan Tarot

Integration

Dark Angels Tarot

Ending

Universal Fantasy Tarot

World is Ours through Mastery of the Soul

Fey Tarot

Totality

Shaman Tarot

Completeness

Tarot of the Pagan Cats

Realization of Potential

Tarot of the Dark Grimoire

Fulfilling your Greatest Dream

Manga Tarot

Happy Ending

Alternate Names

The Universe

To learn more about this Archetype explore:

Anima Mundi, Nirvana, Prudence, Arrival

1 ACE OF WANDS

Creativity – Initiative

Keywords

Creation, Enterprise, Bud, Originality, Brilliance, Spark, Vision, Adventure, Primary, Lively, Flickering, Phallic, Energy, Surge, Invention, Origin, Potential, Strength, Potency

The Image

A glowing hand emerges from swirling clouds. It holds a wooden stick, sprouting with green leaves. Leaves shed and fall to the ground as if the stick is humming with energy. A scenic landscape extends beyond with a quaint castle sitting upon a hill over a winding river.

Correlations

Number: 1
Element: Fire
Sephirot: Kether (Crown)
Season: Autumn
Disposition: Melancholic

Esoteric Name: the Root of the Powers of Fire

To be inspired is to be alive

The Ace of Wands is a symbol of strength, vitality, and energy. It allows us to take action and transform the world through our desires. It can become the representation of strength, material, and physical vigor. The Ace of Wands also indicates desire, passion, and determination. The growing leaves are symbolic of life and fertility renewed by the energy of the wand.

The Ace of Wands indicates the human capacity for desire. It translates desire from a pure wanting into practical action and becomes the ability to manifest destiny through action. The Ace of Wands, more than any other card, reminds us that individuals are defined by their intentions. Only by having the courage and strength to pursue desire can one be truly alive. Like all Aces, this card represents potential and possibilities yet to be achieved.

Aspects of the Arcana expressed in various decks

Lo Scarabeo Tarot

Fiery energy

Nefertari's Tarot

Fertility

Pagan Tarot

Altar of Earth

Traditional Interpretations

Upright: Creation, invention, enterprise and all the powers arising from this principle. The onset, the origin, birth, family and the virility behind them. A starting point for any activity, achievement, or goal.

Reversed: Efforts made in vain. Fall, decadence, ruin, damnation. Decay and even a joy obscured. Sexual problems. Brutality.

Lessons

᠍— A strong creative energy and a source of power thrive inside every human being.

᠍— Recognize personal power and know it when you feel it.

᠍— You are the hand that holds this wand of passion.

᠍— Let your passion become your beacon and illuminate the path before you.

᠍— Embody creativity, inspire others and feed initial desire.

Aspects of the Arcana expressed in various decks

Fey Tarot

A seed growing

Shaman Tarot

A reason to fight

Tarot of the Dark Grimoire

Book of Creation

TWO OF WANDS

Ambition – Restlessness

Keywords

Ambition, Restlessness, Project, Desire, Risk, Plan, Design, Expectation, Appetite, Energy, Enthusiasm, Yearning, Thirst, Drive, Lust, Search, Curiosity, Duality, Flight, Arrogance

The Image

A man stands upon the battlements of a castle with a great view spread before him. He holds the world with his left hand, grasps a wand with his right. The wand sprouts ripe green leaves of potential, as does a second wand affixed to the castle at his left. Embedded in the wall is the symbol of two roses and two lilies, crossed.

Correlations

Number: 2
Sephirot: Chokmah (Wisdom)
Element: Fire
Planet: Mars
Sign: Aries

Esoteric Name: Lord of Dominion

Now is the time to make your plans

The Two of Wands is an expression, the desire to expand your horizons and to discover knowledge of the world. The man hungers to have the whole world in his hands, to know, dominate and make it his own. The battlements of the castle, placed high and strong, are the first step in facing what waits beyond. They are the security required before the adventure. The Two of Wands expresses ambition, thirst for glory, yearning for conquest and delusions of grandeur.

The man displays a cautious gesture in holding the sprouted wand. The wand represents both the material and psychological as it is securely fastened to the ramparts of the castle. It expresses vitality, growth and creative potential. The man desires the whole world, but does not yet know how to obtain it. He has come here to reflect, to organize his thoughts and make a plan so he may realize his ambitions.

Aspects of the Arcana expressed in various decks

Lo Scarabeo Tarot

Balance of opportunities

Nefertari's Tarot

Material offer

Pagan Tarot

Starting again

129

Traditional Interpretations

Upright: Making plans. The start of an exciting business venture, partnerships and planning. The first step of a long-term project put into place. Boldness and proudness. Worldly desires. Asserting yourself and showing the world you are a force to be reckoned with. Meditation over one's abilities.

Reversed: Surprise, wonder and enchantment. Great worries or even fear. Being full of yourself and exhibiting hubris. Creating excuses for yourself. Blaming others. Stifling your dreams. Not seeing the entire picture. Wearing blinders. Rushing ahead.

Lessons

- It is never too late to make a plan for the future.
- Visualize your desire before reaching for it.
- The world is your pearl.

Aspects of the Arcana expressed in various decks

Fey Tarot

Finding the courage

Shaman Tarot

Meeting your other self

Tarot of the Dark Grimoire

Planning

THREE OF WANDS

Enterprise – Delay

Keywords

Wait, Observation, Attention, Anticipation, Patience, Care, Hope, Help, Business, Motion, Action, Creation, Trade, Interdependence, Effort, Assistance, Foresight, Expansion, Contemplation, Exploration

The Image

A man adorned in elegant clothes observes the sea extending toward the horizon. Three long wands have sprouted, rooted in the soil and he holds one securely with his left hand. We cannot see his expression. There is a sense of active waiting and observing.

Correlations

Number: 3
Sephirot: Binah (Understanding)
Element: Fire
Planet: Sun
Sign: Aries

Esoteric Name: Lord of Established Strength

There is no turning back

The Three of Wands represents a moment of action. You have invested your resources to realize your ambitions. The result is not immediate. You are forced to wait. Active waiting teaches the art of patience, growing anticipation and desire for results without pushing too hard. Patience teaches self-confidence and calmness. The man waits on land while his ships are out to sea. This demonstrates the powerlessness of a plan in action. Things have been set in motion. He can do nothing other than wait for the consequences, both positive and negative.

Creativity is inherent in the Three of Wands and a third option has become available. The man in the card would do well to continue working on the project at hand or turn his attention to another passion or project while elements develop that are beyond his control.

Aspects of the Arcana expressed in various decks

Lo Scarabeo Tarot

Reaching out

Nefertari's Tarot

Sharing and exchanging

Pagan Tarot

Magic in everyday life

Traditional Interpretations

Upright: Symbolizes the assertion of force, enterprise and effort. It is the exchange, trade, discovery and launch of a passion project. It means skillful cooperation in business. Something has been set in motion and there is no going back. The Three of Wands enacts the plan hatched within the Two of Wands.
Reversed: The end of concerns or a termination of adversity. Now is not the time. More planning is required. Examine your base desires. Re-examine and reconsider your business partners and colleagues. Deception.

Lessons

⌒ Patience teaches me to wait for the proper moment and to be active while I wait.
⌒ Magical rule of three, what you put into the world returns three-fold.

Aspects of the Arcana expressed in various decks

Fey Tarot

Waiting for blooming

Shaman Tarot

Finding the hidden power

Tarot of the Dark Grimoire

Taking risks

4 | FOUR OF WANDS

Preparation – Perfectionism

Keywords

Tranquility, Celebration, Detail, Peace, Stability, Rest, Harmony, Concord, Prosperity, Peace, Achievement, Domestic Bliss, Solid, Form, Joy, Spontaneity, Freedom, Blessings

The Image

Four long wands are driven into the ground and a garland of sweet vines and grapes suspends between them. Two women prepare fruit baskets while in the background, lovely homes, a gentle bridge and a castle beckon.

Fragrant herbs dot the summer landscape.

Correlations

Number: 4
Sephirot: Chesed (Mercy)
Element: Fire
Planet: Venus
Sign: Aries

Esoteric Name: Lord of Perfected Work

Time to celebrate

The Four of Wands expresses a different form of waiting than witnessed in Three of Wands. The Four of Wands holds the expectation of a specific event and there is no doubt that the time is at hand. There is no anxiety, but rather a bustling of energy and preparation. All the checks and final details are put into place. This card reflects the moments before a party. It is a symbol of success and of a very good time.

This Arcanum encourages attention to detail and awareness of the little things. This card symbolizes the patience and meticulousness necessary to create a climate of shared joy. It can also indicate difficulties encountered when people procrastinate toward unreachable goals or chase an unrealistic ideal of perfection. There is a sense that one should be prepared but remember there is no such thing as actual perfection.

Aspects of the Arcana expressed in various decks

Lo Scarabeo Tarot

Celebration

Nefertari's Tarot

Dressing up

Pagan Tarot

Blessings

Traditional Interpretations

Upright: A place of refuge, rest and harmony. Prosperity, peace and the perfect combination of these elements. Your well-laid plans have manifested into something real. Potential marriage.

Reversed: The meaning remains unchanged. There is prosperity, reward and happiness. The beauty, however, is perhaps not as vibrant.

Lessons

◦— Your stability, joy and happiness are sweetest when shared with others.
◦— Stability breeds happiness.
◦— It's not worth doing if you can't enjoy it.
◦— Small steps have the greatest impact.

Aspects of the Arcana expressed in various decks

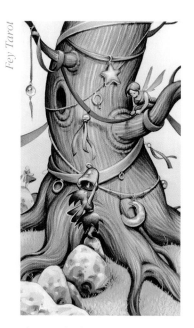

Fey Tarot

Sharing the happiness.

Shaman Tarot

A mystery in the known road

Tarot of the Dark Grimoire

Walking the long road

136

Competition – Conflict

Keywords

Imitation, Simulation, Training, Fight, Rivalry, Action, Strife, Rashness, Competition, Challenge, Struggle, Game, Skirmish, Vitality, Turmoil, Commotion

The Image

Five men are engaged in a mock battle. There is no real threat or anger, but all elements of competition are present. For some, the image represents the struggle of one man against four opponents, for others it represents the duel between two men, while the other three are incited contenders. In all cases, the adrenaline and enthusiasm for the fight are unmistakable.

Correlations

Number: 5
Sephirot: Geburah (Strength)
Element: Fire
Planet: Saturn
Sign: Leo

Esoteric Name: Lord of Strife

Passion in action

The highest aspect the Five of Wands represents training, action, or competition sports, which will improve skills for the future. It represents the growth you experience when facing and overcoming challenges and confronting peers. This confrontation brings out the best of you, without fear of losing, or not being good enough. On a more negative side, the card is a clash with no end, a conflict from out of nowhere and without purpose that leads to a depletion of energy.

Magically speaking, we can look at the Five of Wands and note how the five figures are about to step together and create the shape of a pentacle with their sticks. In this case, the agitation seen in the card is manifests itself in a combined creative collaboration.

Aspects of the Arcana expressed in various decks

Lo Scarabeo Tarot

Disagreement

Nefertari's Tarot

Challenge

Pagan Tarot

Disharmony

138

Traditional Interpretations

Upright: Simulated combat or strenuous competition. The battle for wealth and fortune. The struggle of life. A group of people worked up over drama. Competition strengthening character and preparing to face life's challenges. Period of intense action.

Reversed: Quarrels, disputes, deceit and a contradiction. Victory after conquest. Everyone is calm. Passion dissipates. The fight is over, all players have returned home. The end of struggle.

Lessons

⌒ Your passion ignites the crowd, brings out the best in others and is contagious.
⌒ Magic in creative collaboration.
⌒ Conflict breeds inspiration.
⌒ The talents of others raise your game to a new level.
⌒ Know what is worth fighting for.

Aspects of the Arcana expressed in various decks

Collaboration and competition

Listening to powerful voices

Clash of intentions

Victory – Vanity

Keywords

Fame, Limelight, Success, Award, Triumph, Eminence, Diplomacy, Accomplishment, Arrival, Send Off, Publicity, Message, News, Announcement, Parade, Cheer, Announce, Harmony, Offering

The Image

A man rides a horse victoriously wearing a laurel crown. He clutches a long wand also adorned with a second laurel. The cheering crowds around him hold sprouting wands.
The horse is completely covered in an equine parade costume and bears a knowing look in his eye.

Correlations

Number: 6
Sephirot: Tiphareth (Beauty)
Element: Fire
Planet: Jupiter
Sign: Leo

Esoteric Name: Lord of Victory

You did it

The Six of Wands captures the very meaning of victory. This victory is observed from different points of view: the man on the horseback may be the winner or he is the messenger who brings news of victory to the cheering crowd. In each case, the arrival of the knight is a sign of a transformation and the solution to a problem. The Six of Wands means that something hidden has finally become public domain.

The secondary meaning of the Arcanum relates to fame, vanity and charisma. It is the ability to attract the attention to your passions, projects and ideas. The card can act as a reminder not to be consumed by fame and adoration. Fame is an illusion but when used to carry a message, it contains great strength.

Aspects of the Arcana expressed in various decks

Lo Scarabeo Tarot

Envoy

Nefertari's Tarot

Bringing water where needed

Pagan Tarot

Harmony

Traditional Interpretations

Upright: This card represents a winner and triumph. Important news. It is the achievement of a goal and recognition of a job well done. You are celebrated. Help from friends. People are supporting you.

Reversed: Apprehension and fear. A victorious enemy at the gate. Betrayal and treachery. Your plans did not work out the way you imagined. Disappointing returns.

Lessons

- Fame is fleeting yet works endure forever.
- Bask in the glory, enjoy your success.
- Everyone loves a winner and a good comeback story.
- Don't shoot the messenger.
- Give credit where credit is due.
- When something marvelous appears, make way for it.

Aspects of the Arcana expressed in various decks

Fey Tarot

A living gift

Shaman Tarot

Meeting an ally

Tarot of the Dark Grimoire

Message

SEVEN OF WANDS

Opposition – Defense

Keywords

Inspiring, Nonconformity, Competition, Self-confidence, Opinion, Opposition, Defensiveness, Attack, Battle, Negotiation, Positioning, Contend, Fend

The Image

A warrior defends himself from a group of six unknown attackers. He uses a wand to fight off their wands. He defends himself from above, though he is outnumbered.

Correlations

Number: 7
Sephirot: Netzach (Victory)
Element: Fire
Planet: Mars
Sign: Leo

Esoteric Name: Lord of Valor

Defend at all costs

The card depicts a strong warrior opposing superior forces. Behind him, there is little room to back away and he does not lose heart. His demeanor suggests power, capacity and security. The card reflects strength and courage: courage to have an opinion different from others, to be consistent with your own choices, to think with your head and not be scared by appearances.

This Arcanum refers to the ability to say "no." It reflects the arrogance of others, the practice, customs and laws that are not written. Defending one's passions, the hardest part can be finding the courage: once courage is mastered, the strength needed will find you.

Aspects of the Arcana expressed in various decks

Lo Scarabeo Tarot

Breaking a barrier

Nefertari's Tarot

Facing danger

Pagan Tarot

Accepting assistance

Traditional Interpretations

Upright: This is a card of attack and confrontation but from a position of advantage. Intellectually, it is a card of discussion and bickering. In business it is commerce, competition, struggle and challenges. It is also a card of success, as since the fighter stands above the others his enemies are unable to reach him.

Reversed: Confusion, embarrassment and anxiety. A warning against indecisiveness. Ignorance and pretense. Waking away from confrontation and a fight.

Lessons

- Your efforts are worth it in the long run.
- To stand up for yourself is to stand for others.
- Some things are worth fighting for.
- You can't please everyone.
- Know when to walk away.

Aspects of the Arcana expressed in various decks

Fey Tarot

Protecting what is precious and defenseless

Shaman Tarot

Spiritual struggle

Tarot of the Dark Grimoire

Bringing light into the darkness

8 | EIGHT OF WANDS

Speed – Action

Keywords

Movement, Flying, Climax, Reaction, Fast, Speed, Travel, Rushing, News, Options, Fortitude, Allies, Responsiveness, Message, Advance, Flow, Evolution, Journey, Swiftness, Expedition, Headway

The Image

Eight sprouted wands stream through the sky, over a landscape of rolling hills. A castle sits in the background. The wands are symmetrical, all pointing in the same direction and moving at the same speed.

Correlations

Number: 8
Sephirot: Hod (Glory)
Element: Fire
Planet: Mercury
Sign: Sagittarius

Esoteric Name: Lord of Swiftness

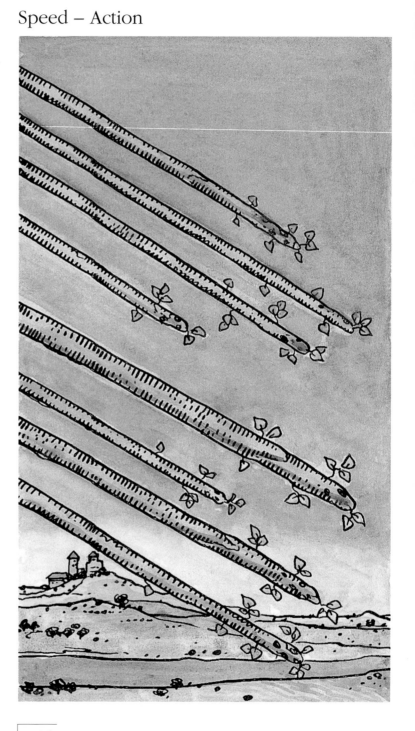

Integrity of speed

The eight wands flying across the sky offer an extremely dynamic picture of something coming suddenly. Everything in this card represents movement and action. A snapshot of motion. This moment of action allows for a future where anything is possible. Something is certain to happen but the nature of the outcome is in question.

The eight wands along the same trajectory represent a convergence of energies and events proceeding in the same direction. It represents flow. The card is the critical point of a situation; adrenaline and tension before a milestone. It is the anticipation of an outcome.

The highest aspect of this card reflects everything that is based on speed and dynamism, even in a metaphorical sense. From a lower aspect, the card represents a situation where speed takes over and leads to hasty, instinctive reactions and perhaps even panic.

Aspects of the Arcana expressed in various decks

Lo Scarabeo Tarot

Rain from the sky

Nefertari's Tarot

The long journey

Pagan Tarot

Receiving what was needed

Traditional Interpretations

Upright: Great initiative. Activities undertaken and speed of work. Effectiveness and haste. Travel across great distances. Rapid advancement. Cupid's arrows of love. A message
Reversed: Jealousy, internal disputes and stasis. Arguments and domestic debates between partners. Energy directed in negative ways. Scattered ideas and an inability to focus.

Lessons

- Thoughts become reality.
- Unseen elements are at play.
- Wheels are in motion, wait to see what develops.
- Everything moves at its own speed.
- Words and actions have consequences.
- What you are looking for is looking for you too.

Aspects of the Arcana expressed in various decks

Fey Tarot

Flowing naturally

Shaman Tarot

Meeting with the spirits

Tarot of the Dark Grimoire

Sudden developments

148

NINE OF WANDS

Protection – Tenacity

Keywords

Tenacity, Guard, Defense, Border, Risking, Vigilance, Strength Adversity, Barriers, Labor, Work, Arrival, Integration, Experience, Pragmatism, Adventurer, Threshold, Barrier, Brink

The Image

A man with a cap is holding a long wand. He waits with a cautious attitude. He stands inside a space marked by a fence of eight wands with sprouted tops behind him.

Correlations

Number: 9
Sephirot: Yesod (Foundation)
Element: Fire
Planet: Moon
Sign: Sagittarius

Esoteric Name: Lord of Great Strength

Break new ground

The character portrayed in the Nine of Wands is often identified as a guard who keeps vigil over a situation. Not knowing if and when something will happen, he must always be ready. It indicates a relationship with life marked by defense and distrust. This attitude protects oneself by keeping the world at a distance rather than opening up.

The Nine of Wands also functions as a threshold or boundary between two worlds: the sacred and profane, success and failure, or movement forward and stasis. This Arcanum, while a symbol of determination, tenacity and stubbornness, also reminds us to move past our comfort zones and into uncharted territory.

Aspects of the Arcana expressed in various decks

Lo Scarabeo Tarot

Sentinel

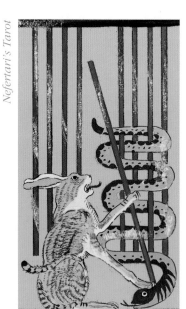

Nefertari's Tarot

Protection against evil

Pagan Tarot

Enduring adversity and changing it to opportunity

Traditional Interpretations

Upright: The power of experience. Strength in opposition. A formidable antagonist who has fought many battles. Strength in adversity. Possible delay or suspension. Breaking down barriers. Moving out into new ground and uncharted territory. A new and personal opening one has fought for.

Reversed: Remaining closed to new ideas and situations. Little effort is needed. Smooth sailing. Success too early and without the necessary experience.

Lessons

- No effort is made in vain.
- One will often find oneself when in the dark.
- Nothing risked, nothing gained.
- Mark your boundaries or others will mark them for you.

Aspects of the Arcana expressed in various decks

Fey Tarot

Avoiding needless fight

Shaman Tarot

Understanding fear

Tarot of the Dark Grimoire

Blocking the path to enemies

Fatigue – Oppression

Keywords

Toil, Duplicity, Tightness, Strength, Gathering, Finality, Emulation, Collection, Work, Burnout, Overload, Overwhelm, Completion, Termination, End

The Image

A man carries ten sprouted wands in his arms. A fortified village stands in the background. The man walks away from the viewer and makes his way toward the village. His back is bent and exhaustion is evident.

Correlations

Number: 10
Sephirot: Malkuth (Kingdom)
Element: Fire
Planet: Saturn
Sign: Sagittarius

Esoteric Name: Lord of Oppression

You have the strength to see it through

The Ten of Wands represents the effort required to achieve a goal. It is the moment of fatigue, feelings of insecurity and not knowing if you will be strong enough to reach your destination. Despite this, the village or the objective and the goals resists: it stands firm and continues to urge you forward.

The sprouting wands indicate that problems dealt with on a superficial level will grow. His grip on the wands is weak. This indicates the wands are lighter than they look. They may be heavy but you can find a different way to support your weight and deal with your issue. It also represents the conclusion of a project, passion or body of work.

Aspects of the Arcana expressed in various decks

Lo Scarabeo Tarot

Carrying the torch

Nefertari's Tarot

Making an effort until the work is done

Pagan Tarot

Doing too much at the same time

Traditional Interpretations

Upright: The state of being overburdened. Taking on too much. Excess in all things. Oppression due to fortune, gain and success. Burnout. Luck, earnings and any kind of success but the problems that come along with it.
Reversed: Something needs to end yet you refuse to let go. Painful surrender. A need to see a situation through to its conclusion. A problem will soon be solved. Ending without effort.

Lessons

- A strong creative energy and a source of power thrive inside every human being.
- Release what is no longer needed.
- Finish what you start.
- Learn to delegate, lighten your load.
- Let it go.

Aspects of the Arcana expressed in various decks

Fey Tarot

Carrying the burden of success

Shaman Tarot

The price of a Vision

Tarot of the Dark Grimoire

Entering a dark place willingly

1 ACE OF SWORDS

Power – Discipline

Keywords

Responsibility, Achievement, Conviction, Idea, Accountability, Clarity, Truth, Justice, Idea, Start, Honesty, Objectivity, Clear, Opportunity, Thought, Genesis, Intelligence, Brilliance, Determination, Discernment

The Image

A mysterious hand emerges from the cloud wielding a sword. The tip of the sword slips into a crown decorated with palm and olive branches. It is the image of victory.

Correlations

Number: 1
Element: Air
Sephirot: Kether (Crown)
Season: Spring
Disposition: Sanguine

Esoteric Name: the Root of the Powers of Air

A brilliant idea

The Ace of Swords is the symbol of strength, power and thought. It is the symbol of intelligence, the rationality of the mind and the ability to communicate well. The blade of the sword represents intelligence, language and the analytical ability to solve problems. The card expresses other forms of power: the crown as a symbol of divinity, royalty and material power. The olive tree, a symbol of peace and the palm, the symbol of spiritual triumph. These are all gained by the flash of insight this card represents.

Who has the power to assume the responsibility of their actions? The Sword does not necessarily suggest an armed conflict, but, instead, a maintained peace using psychological and mental facilities. This card is the expression of an extraordinary determination capable of going to extreme limits.

Aspects of the Arcana expressed in various decks

Lo Scarabeo Tarot

Glorious power

Nefertari's Tarot

Vigilance

Pagan Tarot

Altar of Air

Traditional Interpretations

Upright: A fabulous idea and inspired insight. Triumph. Achievement and excitement. A hole in one. A genial idea that requires implementation. The power of the mind. A flash of insight. Crowning success.

Reversed: Efforts made in vain. Fall, decadence and ruin. Damnation, decay and even a joy obscured. Sexual problems. Brutality. The mind in chains and closed thinking.

Lessons

- Ideas are the thread of reality.
- First thought, best thought.
- Trust your instincts.
- You know what to do.
- Always have an ace in the hole.
- Be your best self.

Aspects of the Arcana expressed in various decks

Fey Tarot

A seed of sorrow, pain or conflict

Shaman Tarot

Projection of the mind

Tarot of the Dark Grimoire

The Book of Rules

TWO OF SWORDS

Discussion – Arbitration

Keywords

Balance, Adaptation, Duel, Meditation, Interposition, Adjustment, Duality, Denial, Blockage, Hoodwinked, Blind, Tension, Moderator, Ponder, Stalemate, Subtlety, Grace, Compromise

The Image

A woman wears a blindfold over her eyes. She sits on the seashore, and her hands holding two swords are crossed before her. The water is still and a moon shines in the sky.

Correlations

Number: 2
Sephirot: Chokmah (Wisdom)
Element: Air
Planet: Moon
Sign: Libra

Esoteric Name: Lord of Peace Restored

Take your time

The figure in the Two of Swords holds weapons but if there are dangers, we cannot see them. She sits in the middle of the situation as an impartial observer in the role of a moderator. She has moved inside herself to seek the solution. Her purposeful retreat form the outside world provides clarity. The conflict is not necessarily linked to weapons, it is likely the discussion or comparison of ideas and priorities. It has given her the stimulus to grow but she must decide her course of action.

The figure is linked to the sea and moon, symbols of humanity and fraught with emotion. The sea and moon represent choice and the meditation of opposing forces and choices. There is a deep understanding and care of choice reflected in this card. It represents the ways two opposites can come together when choices are made carefully and from the heart.

Aspects of the Arcana expressed in various decks

Lo Scarabeo Tarot

Arbiter of a duel

Nefertari's Tarot

Twins

Pagan Tarot

Surrendering your senses

Traditional Interpretations

Upright: Adaptation and equilibrium. Balance, courage, friendship and harmony in a situation of conflict. Great tenderness, affection and confidence. It is time to move away, find privacy and debate the situation at hand.
Reversed: Fraud, deceit, duplicity and disloyalty. Release and abandon. Decisions made without thought or consideration. Rushing into a situation without proper preparation.

Lessons

∽ Taking the time to make proper decisions leads to beneficial outcomes.
∽ The truth is inside you.
∽ Initiation begins with you.
∽ Think before you speak.
∽ Cultivate inner truth.

Aspects of the Arcana expressed in various decks

Fey Tarot

Blinded by anger

Shaman Tarot

Detachment

Tarot of the Dark Grimoire

Mesmerizing cosmic melody

THREE OF SWORDS

Sorrow – Despair

Keywords

Treason, Pain, Injury, Affair, Heartbreak, Difficulty, Guilt, Regret, Suffering, Love Triangle, Analysis, Synthesis, Paranormal Experience, Introspection

The Image

A bulbous, red heart, the wellspring of human emotion floats through the sky. The sky is filled with a raging storm, clouds and rain. The heart is pierced by three symmetrical swords yet does not bleed.

Correlations

Number: 3
Sephirot: Binah (Understanding)
Element: Air
Planet: Saturn
Sign: Libra

Esoteric Name: Lord of Sorrow

What doesn't kill you makes you stronger

The Three of Swords is thought by many to be the most negative of all cards. The pierced heart and the storm are all indications of turmoil, suffering and torment. The pain is too large and fresh to be understood, accepted and passed. The pain has come from the outside world, a wound received from others. While experiencing this emotion it feel like everything is suffering and it is difficult to believe that the pain will ever end. It is actually a temporary condition.

This state of mind feels irreversible, definitive and terrible. In reality, it is not as bad as it appears. The storm will blow past and the card opens to the quiet and calm reflected in the Four of Swords. The Three of Swords indicates the lack of communication and momentary inability to find a solution. This leads to feelings of the loss of hope and tremendous heartache.

Aspects of the Arcana expressed in various decks

Lo Scarabeo Tarot

Piercing the heart

Nefertari's Tarot

Guilt and blame

Pagan Tarot

Alone with unhappy thoughts

Traditional Interpretations

Upright: Devastating heartbreak. Leakage of the human heart. A need for compassion and courage. A delay in what you want. Love triangle. Loss.

Reversed: Insanity or mistake. A lesser degree of loss, distraction and confusion. What used to affect you deeply no longer has power over you. You are free to move on.

Lessons

◦— It is better to have loved and lost than never to have loved at all.

◦— Great love risks great pain.

◦— Do not repress anguish but move through it.

◦— With the sweetness comes the sorrow.

◦— Some wounds never heal but they become less painful.

◦— Bare scars proudly, they made you who you are.

Aspects of the Arcana expressed in various decks

Fey Tarot

Seeking solace to a deep wound

Shaman Tarot

Meditation

Tarot of the Dark Grimoire

A thousand voices

FOUR OF SWORDS

Meditation – Closure

Keywords

Reflection, Waiting, Stability, Withdrawal, Sleep, Solitude, Closing, Loneliness, Repose, Retreat, Truce, Vigilance, Isolation, Retirement, Peace, Regeneration, Protection

The Image

Tucked away, inside a quiet cathedral and under a stained glass window, a monastic knight is lying on a bed. His eyes are closed and his hands are joined in prayer. His body is dressed in armor while the stained glass window portrays a religious scene. Three swords point down at his figure while one sword lies horizontally across his body.

Correlations

Number: 4
Sephirot: Chesed (Mercy)
Element: Air
Planet: Jupiter
Sign: Libra

Esoteric Name: Lord of Rest from Strife

Peace of thought leads to gentle sleep

The man who rests in the Four of Swords is often depicted in a tomb, yet he is not dead. Silence, meditation and expectation become the center of this card. After the pain of Three of Swords, full of noise and fury, this card provides immediate contrast and repose. Every feeling is thin, detached, observed and tested with the appropriate reserve. Silence, waiting and emotional detachment reflect the rebalancing of emotion. This is the relaxation before a new beginning.

The knight gathered in restful prayer focuses his free will away from anything superfluous in nature. He finds patience and is able to find the balance of mind even in difficult situations. This card bears no anxiety or hasty decisions. It reflects the need for rest that is not an indulgence but a requirement. Every accomplishment and deed requires the right preparation and resting period to regenerate itself into what it should become.

Aspects of the Arcana expressed in various decks

Lo Scarabeo Tarot

Perfection of form

Nefertari's Tarot

Prison of blood

Pagan Tarot

Waiting in arms

Traditional Interpretations

Upright: Stability of the mind and thoughts. Sleeping well. Vigilance and needed withdrawal. Exile, tomb and coffin. Regenerating darkness of the mind.

Reversed: Not trusting your decisions. Instability of the mind. An inability to reach a conclusive outcome. Confusing thoughts. A deep need for rest.

Lessons

⌇— The power of peace is cultivated in the thoughts and inner recesses of your mind.

⌇— Nothing beats a good night's sleep.

⌇— An active life requires deep relaxation.

⌇— Trust your thoughts.

⌇— Let your dreams and night visions inspire your waking life.

Aspects of the Arcana expressed in various decks

Fey Tarot

Preparing for war

Shaman Tarot

Escaping the Spirits

Tarot of the Dark Grimoire

A moment of serenity

5 FIVE OF SWORDS

Selfishness – Complacency

Keywords

Disgrace, Exile, Defeat, Revenge, Drama, Power, Conflict, Failure, Degradation, Unfairness, Slander, Cruelty, Cowardliness, Sorrow, Weakness, Domination, Uncertainty, Difficulty, Challenge

The Image

A warrior watches two contemptuous men who stand in the background. The sky is stormy, white clouds race across the sky and it is clear a violent situation has just occurred. The men in the background hold the disadvantage. The warrior in front collects the spoils of the altercation.

Correlations

Number: 5
Sephirot: Geburah (Strength)
Element: Air
Planet: Venus
Sign: Aquarius

Esoteric Name: Lord of Defeat

Something wicked this way comes

The Five of Swords is a card of extreme conflict. The victorious warrior has driven out opposing forces. They outnumbered him but could not defeat him. Swords indicate a border dispute, a competition, or intellectual rivalry. This card also reflects the inability of communication. It represents a failure to compromise.

There is no joy or enthusiastic happiness in the Five of Swords victory. The two losers have lost everything. The warrior is neither happy nor proud. The status quo and stability have been maintained but at what cost? Force or authority were used but was there another way? On a personal level, this card represents the effects of cruel words used as weapons and making yourself or others feel bad.

Aspects of the Arcana expressed in various decks

Lo Scarabeo Tarot

Disconnection from others

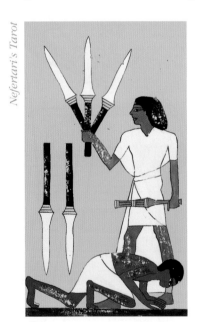

Nefertari's Tarot

Victor and defeated

Pagan Tarot

Facing challenges back to back

Traditional Interpretations

Upright: Degradation, destruction and revocation. Infamy, disgrace, loss, with its variants and analogies. This card is a call for a careful examination of how you treat others and how you allow others to treat you. A reminder to reconsider your opinions.

Reversed: Burial and funeral. A terrible situation avoided. Old conflicts do not draw you in. You have moved past old and negative habits.

Lessons

- Words can wound like weapons.
- Keep your friends close and your enemies closer.
- Others only hold power you give them.
- Let go of drama for drama's sake.
- To the victor go the spoils.

Aspects of the Arcana expressed in various decks

Fey Tarot

Understanding the transitorial nature of victory

Shaman Tarot

Taking a different role

Tarot of the Dark Grimoire

Running for salvation

Journey – Escape

Keywords

Transition, Reasoning, Curiosity, Transfer, Exploration, Obstacles, Recovery, Travel, Movement, Renunciation, Route, Expedience, Trip, Gateway, Passage, Transit, Flux, Evolution

The Image

A boat moves across watery depths. All passengers upon the boat wear hoods as if to conceal their identity. The distant shore is seen as they move closer. Swords surround the boat.

Correlations

Number: 6
Sephirot: Tiphareth (Beauty)
Element: Air
Planet: Mercury
Sign: Aquarius

Esoteric Name: Lord of Earned Success

Passage is granted

While the Five of Swords reflects an impenetrable boundary, the Six of Swords is the crossing of the border. It is the transition from one state to another, a means of traveling and also moving and leaving the past to embrace the future. The water reflects emotional states and all levels of consciousness.

This Arcanum can be seen as an escape or exile. But the card also becomes the destination. The trip becomes a discovery, an exploration and evolution. In all cases the card is the crossing of a boundary or a barrier and the siren song of a foreign land, unknown yet full of promise. The card shows the comparison of different and unfamiliar feelings of new realities, the need to forget yourself for a moment and focus on others. This journey is never taken alone. It is the need to adapt to new ways of living, thinking and communicating.

Aspects of the Arcana expressed in various decks

Lo Scarabeo Tarot

Journey to safety

Nefertari's Tarot

Mastering the way

Pagan Tarot

Fleeing ruin

Traditional Interpretations

Upright: Threshold and changing. A voyage to new possibilities. Sea trip, route, shipping, or naval command. Traversing unknown waters. Better times lie ahead.

Reversed: Stuck in a rut. Wanting to move forward but not knowing how. Inability to escape a negative situation. A refusal to be responsible for others. Hiding from a situation rather than dealing with it.

Lessons

- It's about the journey, not the destination.
- Chart your course.
- There is power in action.
- When a door opens, walk through it.
- Follow the signs.

Aspects of the Arcana expressed in various decks

Fey Tarot

Ignoring conflict through inner peace

Shaman Tarot

Mental or psychic journey

Tarot of the Dark Grimoire

Going into the unknown

SEVEN OF SWORDS

Subterfuge – Indiscretion

Keywords

Hidden, Confidentiality, Plan, Gossip, Attempt, Collection, Intrigue, Spy, Shortcut, Deception, Stealth, Isolation, Escape, Secrets, Discretion

The Image

A man wearing a cap carries five swords. He literally holds the blades in his hands. Behind him, two swords remain stuck in the ground. Large tents and flags hint at the presence of a military camp. No one seems to take notice of the man carrying swords.

Correlations

Number: 7
Sephirot: Netzach (Victory)
Element: Air
Planet: Moon
Sign: Aquarius

Esoteric Name: Lord of Unstable Effort

Take no shortcuts

The Seven of Swords embodies intelligence transformed into subterfuge. It reflects stratagems, tricks, deceptions and generally all forms of indirect action. This elaborate strategy avoids conflict at all costs. This can often reflect oratorical skill where one is able to divert the attention of others. It is a reminder to be careful, circumspect and avoid unnecessary risks.

This card reflects careful cultivation, editing and sorting as the man leaves what is not needed behind him. This is reflected in the two remaining swords. He has deemed them unnecessary. This stands as a reminder to discard the unimportant so you may move forward freely and unencumbered.

Aspects of the Arcana expressed in various decks

Lo Scarabeo Tarot

Hidden dangers

Nefertari's Tarot

Wisdom difficult to understand

Pagan Tarot

Finding unexpected refuge

Traditional Interpretations

Upright: Design, attempt and desire. Hope, confidence and fantasies may fail. The plan is not clear and well defined. Partial success. Someone close to you may be lying. Discarding what is not needed. Tiptoe escape.

Reversed: Good advice, warning and teaching. Wish fulfillment. There is no need to be covert. Lay your cards on the table. Complete disclosure.

Lessons

- Take only what you need.
- Be sure the plan is worth the trouble.
- Assess the situation before you act.
- Be clever, be fast and be smart.
- Take no chances.

Aspects of the Arcana expressed in various decks

Fey Tarot

Becoming one with the environment

Shaman Tarot

Astral journey

Tarot of the Dark Grimoire

Exploiting a moment of weakness

Limits – Paralysis

Keywords

Drowsy, Inert, Lethargic, Paralyzed, Stupefied, Stunned, Links, Trap, Fear, Difficulty, Impediment, Obstacle, Restriction, Censorship, Hoodwinked, Betrayal, Temporary Bondage

The Image

A woman is blindfolded and bound. Her expression is determined. Not scared. Eight swords surround her. They stick into the ground and form a cage-like fence.

Correlations

Number: 8
Sephirot: Hod (Glory)
Element: Air
Planet: Jupiter
Sign: Gemini

Esoteric Name: Lord of Shortened Force

The only limits are the ones you place on yourself

There are two seemingly contradictory aspects of the Eight of Swords. One point of view reflects the woman as a prisoner, blocked by external forces. She is prevented from acting or speaking. This may be due to her own thoughts and calculations that have entrapped her.

Another viewpoint reflects not a helpless victim but a willing participant. She does not give in to panic but has been placed there, as a means for transformation, like a butterfly in a cocoon. In this way, the card is seen as blindfolded initiation. Once the blindfold comes off, she sees the world with a new pair of eyes. Obstacles are transformed into opportunities and the person becomes aware of their limits. When these limits are crossed, the ties can be cut.

Aspects of the Arcana expressed in various decks

The price of freedom

The Demons inside

Finding your own strength

Traditional Interpretations

Upright: Held hostage and feeling restriction. Crisis, censorship and power of others. Conflict, slander and even disease. Rumination, metamorphosis and chrysalis. Ultimate transformation.
Reversed: Restlessness, difficulty and opposition. Unforeseen things. Nothing ties you down. You are free to do and say what you like. Unaffected by other opinions. Freedom and abandon.

Lessons

- The only bonds are the ones we place ourselves.
- To become reborn first you must venture inside.
- Empower yourself.
- Patience breeds transformation.
- Confront the inner to change the outer.
- If you don't like your situation, change it.

Aspects of the Arcana expressed in various decks

Fey Tarot

Surrendering to violence

Shaman Tarot

Never being alone

Tarot of the Dark Grimoire

Prisoners of lust and greed

178

NINE OF SWORDS

Anguish – Crisis

Keywords

Despair, Nightmare, Sleepless, Guilt, Concern, Difficulty, Bewilderment, Desperation, Deceit, Disappointment, Worry, Overwhelmed, Suffering, Loss, Misery, Desolation, Doubts, Uncertainty, Crisis, Obscurity

The Image

A woman sits up in her bed. She covers her face in a gesture of despair or fear, as if awoken from a nightmare or horrible thoughts. Above her, nine overwhelming long swords, all pointing down, hang dangerously.

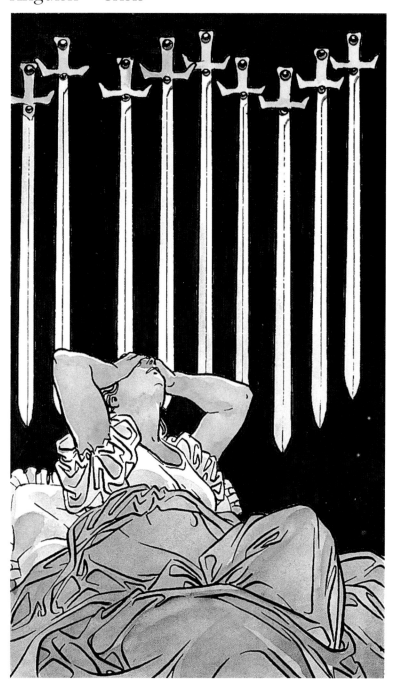

Correlations

Number: 9
Sephirot: Yesod (Foundation)
Element: Air
Planet: Mars
Sign: Gemini

Esoteric Name: Lord of Despair and Cruelty

Wide awake with worry

The Nine of Swords is the expression of fears emerging during sleep, or discomfort springing from the solitude of our thoughts. The card refers to all forms of anxiety. The sense of oppression, represented symbolically by the nine swords, is the malaise of human consciousness. The anxiety, insecurity and fear can be generated by material problems, such as economic or physical problems, but is more often caused by other fears deeply rooted in the mind.

This sense of oppression can come from the uncertainty of the future, sense of inadequacy that comes from not knowing what the future holds, or a tormented conscience causing regrets or remorse. Symbolically, nighttime anxieties indicate how we perceive our problems. How does a little noise sound like thunder? Why does a shadow look like a monster? The night plays tricks on the mind and makes difficulties look more terrible and frightening than they actually are. Do we deceive ourselves during the day?

Aspects of the Arcana expressed in various decks

Lo Scarabeo Tarot

Denial and grief

Nefertari's Tarot

Love beyond separation

Pagan Tarot

Nightmares

Traditional Interpretations

Upright: Obsessing over an issue. Death, failure and loss. Abortion, delay and disappointment. Bitter desolation. A deep feeling of guilt. Inability to relax. Distrust in one's own thoughts. Self torture.

Reversed: Patient, healing and unselfishness. Problems and habits overcome. No longer plagued by an issue.

Lessons

ᴄ— You must make peace with yourself.
ᴄ— The greatest wars are those fought in the mind.
ᴄ— Control your thoughts, control your world.
ᴄ— Thoughts alone do not have the power to wound, its what you do with them that counts.
ᴄ— What you resist, persists.

Aspects of the Arcana expressed in various decks

Fey Tarot

Grief, before finding hope

Shaman Tarot

Fear of reaching out

Tarot of the Dark Grimoire

Seeing the dark side within you

Transcendence – Ruin

Keywords

Obsession, Block, Sorrow, Tears, Desolation, Emptiness, Fear, Martyrdom, Sadness, Ending, Finish, Done, Completion, Affliction, Hidden Pain

The Image

A man lies next to a body of water. Ten swords are stuck in his body yet the man does not bleed. In the background black storm clouds seem to rise up in fury.

Correlations

Number: 10
Sephirot: Malkuth (Kingdom)
Element: Air
Planet: Sun
Sign: Gemini

Esoteric Name: Lord of Ruin

To be inspired is to be alive

Contrasting the Three Swords, where pain tore a tender heart, the Ten of Swords reveals external and obvious suffering. Pain and the difficulties represented by the swords do not murder a person or end a life but they lock progress, preventing a move forward. The card indicates stasis, paralysis, or a negative period from which it is not possible to escape.

From an intellectual point of view, the Ten of Swords shows an obsessive behavior, such as jealousy, leading a person to harm oneself or people close to them. The traditional image of the Ten of Swords reeks of the carnage of a bloody Shakespearean revenge play. In order to avoid the harshness of the traditional image, the Ten of Swords is the card most often changed and redrawn from one deck to another. Still, others connect the Ten of Swords to chakras alignment and sometimes to acupuncture.

Aspects of the Arcana expressed in various decks

Lo Scarabeo Tarot

Letting go after loss

Nefertari's Tarot

Mourning

Pagan Tarot

Breaking a vicious cycle

Traditional Interpretations

Upright: Pain, sorrow and tears. Sadness, desolation and loss. The end of a way of thinking or being. The completion of the intellectual process and old ideas laid to rest.
Reversed: Advantage, profit and success. Unfinished business. You need to wrap up loose ends before moving forward.

Lessons

- Let the process end before you begin anew.
- Let it go.
- Endings make way for new beginnings.
- Align your chakras.
- Die to be reborn.
- Things have a way of ending when they need to.

Aspects of the Arcana expressed in various decks

Fey Tarot

Losing your identity and your ego, to be reborn

Shaman Tarot

Losing yourself

Tarot of the Dark Grimoire

Becoming a monster

1

ACE OF CUPS

Feeling – Intuition

Keywords

Romance, Intuition, Emotion, Love, Opportunity, Deluge, Mental Activity, Emotional Care, Unconscious, Memory, Adaptation, Purification, Fertility, Abundance, Joy, Openness, Outpouring

The Image

A hand emerges from a cloud holding a cup. The placid surface of lily pond lies beneath the overflowing chalice and absorbs its flowing waters. Four jets of liquid stream from the cup and a white dove flies down. It holds a disk engraved with a cross in its beak.

Correlations

Number: 1
Sephirot: Kether (Crown)
Element: Water
Season: Winter
Disposition: Phlegmatic

Esoteric Name: the Root of the Powers of Water

Everything springs from life and from life springs everything

Water is life and the Ace of Cups is the universal source. It is the essence of all emotions and feelings governing the soul of humanity. Christian symbolism dictates the image of the dove as indicative of the Holy Spirit, posing as a consecrated host in the Holy Grail. The Ace of Cups, therefore, represents the sacredness and the human capacity to be inspired by the divine.

As with all other Aces, the Ace of Cups is the symbol of the entire Suit. The waters generated and contained by the cup are symbols of purity, the unconscious and dreams. The combination of these elements represents the heart and soul of every human being. In a sense, the Ace of Cups is the ability to experience the entire emotional range, from love to disgust, from joy to suffering.

Aspects of the Arcana expressed in various decks

Lo Scarabeo Tarot

Flowing water

Nefertari's Tarot

The origin of life

Pagan Tarot

Altar of Water

Traditional Interpretations

Upright: The beginning of a great love. The sign of a sincere heart, joy and happiness. Nourishment, abundance and fertility. Beauty and pleasure. Happiness beyond words. Healthy emotional outpouring.

Reversed: Emotional blockage. False love, lying heart and change. Instability, revolution and hesitancy to nurture love. An inability to express all emotions both good and bad.

Lessons

- Love is the answer to everything.
- We are the Holy Grail.
- Let emotions flow like water.
- Live large, hold nothing back.
- Let light in.
- Be the Lotus Flower.
- Let your cup run over.

Aspects of the Arcana expressed in various decks

Fey Tarot

Being one with your emotions

Shaman Tarot

An healing source

Tarot of the Dark Grimoire

The Book of visions

TWO OF CUPS

Union – Attraction

Keywords

Attraction, Gaiety, Agreement, Affinity, Understanding, Passion, Couple, Toast, Love, Friendship, Affinity, Union, Concord, Sympathy, Marriage, New Friendship, Balance, Harmony, Reciprocity

The Image

A young man and woman exchange a toast with two cups. The man makes a gesture toward the woman. Above them stands the Hermes caduceus of Greek mythology, a stick with two intertwined snakes. A winged lion's head presides over the serpentine creatures.

Correlations

Number: 2
Sephirot: Chokmah (Wisdom)
Element: Water
Planet: Venus
Sign: Cancer

Esoteric Name: Lord of Love

Two as one

The Two of Cups is the union of two water sources. They flow, mix and combine to create a new force. The two uniting forces are not necessarily similar to each other, but share commonalities and complement each other through differences.

The moment represented in the Two of Cups is the excitement, wonder and curiosity that drive each new union when two things come together in harmony. The two snakes, therefore, represent the individual's potential to grow together, while the head of the lion represents the passions and emotions that are shared and amplified from this bond.

Aspects of the Arcana expressed in various decks

Lo Scarabeo Tarot

Unity

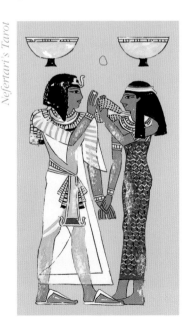

Nefertari's Tarot

Wedding union

Pagan Tarot

Relationship with your ideal self

Traditional Interpretations

Upright: Harmony of the masculine and feminine. Duality making a beautiful whole. The balance of ideas and coming together. The perfect match.

Reversed: False love, confusion and misunderstanding, missing what is right before you. Stubbornness with others. Strong dislike of another.

Lessons

◦— Open up and allow love to flourish.
◦— The greatest gifts are the ones you give.
◦— There is peace in duality.
◦— When you find what you are looking for, acknowledge it.
◦— You are loved.

Aspects of the Arcana expressed in various decks

Fey Tarot

Sharing

Shaman Tarot

Emotional sincerity

Tarot of the Dark Grimoire

A moment with your loved one

Communion – Frivolity

Keywords

Communion, Joy, Sharing, Excitement, Intoxication, Dance, Relief, Celebration of Friendship, Feast, Fruits of Love, Positive Outcome, Merriment, Victory, Comfort, Healing, Birth

The Image

Three young girls, dressed in elegant clothes, hair adorned with flowers and leaves, dance joyfully under a vine arbor. They raise a glass to each other as toast to friendship or an important event. Grapes and vegetation flourish in the field in which they celebrate.

Correlations

Number: 3
Sephirot: Binah (Understanding)
Element: Water
Planet: Mercury
Sign: Cancer

Esoteric Name: Lord of Abundance

Share yourself and love by dancing in the world

The Three of Cups expresses overall satisfaction. The cups are raised towards the sky in a gesture of thanks and celebration. The thrill is not the loss of control as in drunkenness but a threshold in which a "different" reality is reached. The dance can lead to euphoria, vertigo and dizziness, but more importantly, it is a manifestation of joy. Rejoice together in the harmony of dance, music and feelings.

Happiness creates a deep bond between those who share it with others. This is a lasting bond and an end in itself, spontaneous, free and ephemeral. This card represents the ability to grasp the present moment, without worrying about anything else and be inspired by others.

Aspects of the Arcana expressed in various decks

Lo Scarabeo Tarot

Creating joy

Nefertari's Tarot

The language of music and dance

Pagan Tarot

True friendship

Traditional Interpretations

Upright: The conclusion of abundance. Perfection and a happy ending. Victory, accomplishment and relief. Hospitality to others. Great friendship and comradery.
Reversed: Excess in food and drink. Rejecting help from friends. Pleasure turns sour as a result of overindulgence.

Lessons

◦— Friendship is the greatest gift.
◦— Be the candle or the mirror that reflects it.
◦— Community is key.
◦— Like attracts like.
◦— True friendship knows no bounds.
◦— There is music in laughter, light in love and freedom in movement.

Aspects of the Arcana expressed in various decks

Fey Tarot

Dancing with the Universe

Shaman Tarot

Harmonious concentration

Tarot of the Dark Grimoire

Meeting strangers

193

4 | FOUR OF CUPS

Omen – Disenchantment

Keywords

Expectation, Disappointment, Boredom, Discouragement, New Idea, Nausea, Saturation, Refusal, Distain, Habits, Dissatisfaction, Discontent, Distraction

The Image

A man sits at the foot of a leafy tree. He observes three cups placed on the grass before him. An arm appears out of a cloud, handing him another cup. The cup is offered despite the man's detachment and boredom. Perhaps he does not see the cup.

Correlations

Number: 4
Sephirot: Chesed (Mercy)
Element: Water
Planet: Moon
Sign: Cancer

Esoteric Name: Lord of Blended Pleasure

Life passes quickly if you don't pay attention

The detached attitude of the character sitting under the tree is interpreted in several ways. You can sense a feeling of boredom, physical and intellectual laziness. He does not seem interested in anything. The character's attitude can be disappointment leading to discouragement and distrust. The tree expresses roots in a place and also the ability to bear fruit. The figure expresses an attitude rejecting what is offered, considering it of little importance and hopes to achieve much more.

There is a glimpse of detachment from worldly pleasures, represented by the three cups. He waits for true love symbolized by the cup emerging from the cloud. The card recalls that desires and dreams are part of reality like things that are well known and already experienced. Many people refer to this card as the Buddha under the tree who awaits enlightenment.

Aspects of the Arcana expressed in various decks

Lo Scarabeo Tarot

Boredom

Nefertari's Tarot

Being burdened by habits and work

Pagan Tarot

Not noticing what's most precious

Traditional Interpretations

Upright: Disinterest in what is around you. Being distracted and therefore wearing blinders. Not seeing an opportunity before you. Meditation and repose. Boredom, disgust and aversion. Harmonious pleasure.

Reversed: Waking form a period of contentment. Reaching for opportunity. New relationship with the world around you. Goals and ambitions have been set.

Lessons

꿈— Look wider in your life.
꿈— Omens are everywhere when you begin to look.
꿈— Look for opportunity.
꿈— Make your own fun.

Aspects of the Arcana expressed in various decks

Taking things for granted

Purifying the environment

Change is in the air

Repentance – Loss

Keywords

Shortages, Difficulties, Regret, Guilt, Pessimism, Self-sacrifice, Disappointment, Disillusionment, Vain Regret, Sorrow, Sadness, Addiction, Despair, Fear, Refusal

The Image

A man wears a black cloak. He bows his head toward a river, as if watching the dry land. Not far away, three cups are upside down, their liquid seeping into the ground. Behind him, two more cups stand straight. In the right background, there is a gentle bridge, to the left, a castle.

Correlations

Number: 5
Sephirot: Geburah (Strength)
Element: Water
Planet: Mars
Sign: Scorpio

Esoteric Name: Lord of Loss in Pleasure

Do not let what you don't have divide you

The color of the man's cloak suggests sadness, distrust and gloomy thoughts. The three overturned cups beside him are vanished opportunity, lost friendships and former affections. The cups spill what is lost. This image leads to repentance and reflection on the past to understand one's mistakes, regret or remorse that stem from not having acted differently.

The two standing cups are the choices available to the individual. The man has not seen these opportunities. Perhaps, he fails to understand. Several worlds full of possibilities remain, but because they are behind the man, he does not feel or sense their presence. The acute sense of loss and his desperate need leads to pessimism or resignation. The real opportunity to overcome the situation is recognizing there is choice. Being aware of it. The bridge is a symbol of passage and possibility. It will allow the traveler the opportunity to move forward and leave the memories behind.

Aspects of the Arcana expressed in various decks

Lo Scarabeo Tarot

Being locked

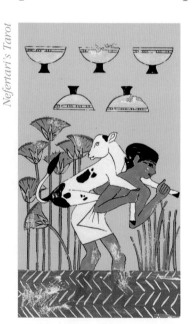

Nefertari's Tarot

A difficult possession

Pagan Tarot

Focusing too much on what is already lost

Traditional Interpretations

Upright: This card represents loss, yet something remains. Three are lost, but have been spared. It is a card of inheritance, heritage and transmission. Sorrow from that which you received. Vain regret. Addiction to thoughts, people, substance, or behaviors

Reversed: News, alliances and affinity. Lineage, kinship and nostalgia. Addiction overcome and forward movement.

Lessons

- Look with care; take what you have and move forward.
- You have options.
- Release the ego to find freedom.
- If it's not working, let it go.
- All is not lost.
- Look for bridges, they lead to new places.

Aspects of the Arcana expressed in various decks

Fey Tarot

Transforming what is bad and broken into something good or useful

Shaman Tarot

Losing connection to your Spirit

Tarot of the Dark Grimoire

Being forced to let go

199

Sharing – Nostalgia

Keywords

Gift, Offer, Message,
Peace, Remembrance, Past,
Childhood Friends, Happy
Memories, Exchange, Safety,
Home, Hearth, Sharing,
Nostalgia, Reminiscence,
Sentimentality, Longing,
Legacy, Endowment

The Image

A child extends a flower
filled cup to a young girl who
stretches her hands out to
receive it. They are tucked
away inside a Tuscan village.
In the foreground, four
flower filled cups create a wall
between the viewer and the
children. Another identical
cup is placed on the column
where the staircase ends.

Correlations

Number: 6
Sephirot: Tiphareth (Beauty)
Element: Water
Planet: Sun
Sign: Scorpio

Esoteric Name: Lord of
Pleasure

Happiness lives as long as you can remember it

After the loss represented by the Five of Cups, the Six of Cups symbolizes aspects of sweet memories and hope for the future. Children represent the future, while this idealized town represents the past. The flowers filling this Arcanum also represent the gifts of childhood: they are the moral qualities and intellectual gifts we inherit from the "family strain." Knowledge is handed down, from elders and friends. The boy who offers flowers to the girl expresses the transmission of a message and the sharing of a secret. This message is important for the development of the girl.

The five blooming cups represent the five senses and the staircase symbolizes the stages of existence. The cup placed at the column indicates new knowledge and experiences. In the Six of Cups, the old joins the new without regrets. It is full of joy and generosity.

Aspects of the Arcana expressed in various decks

Lo Scarabeo Tarot

Perfection of memory

Nefertari's Tarot

Spending time together

Pagan Tarot

Children and adults

Traditional Interpretations

Upright: Memory and the past. Reflecting on childhood, happiness and joy. New relationships, new knowledge and a new environment. A gift from an admirer. A walk down memory lane. Transmission of knowledge.

Reversed: The future and renewal. What is to be implemented? Stasis and living too much in the romance of the past. Possibility of inheritance.

Lessons

- We are the living expression of our past.
- Gifts of the heart give for a lifetime.
- Our bodies may change but our souls remain ageless.
- Love doesn't cost a thing.
- You have inherited great gifts, use them wisely.

Aspects of the Arcana expressed in various decks

Fey Tarot

A garden of possibilities you may have forgotten

Shaman Tarot

Recovering the connection with your Spirit

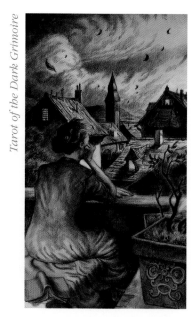

Tarot of the Dark Grimoire

A long wait

202

Fantasy – Temptation

Keywords

Choices, Fantasy, Temptation, Illusion, Desire, Vision, Envy, Deception, Dreams, Daydream, Selection, Variety, Imagination, Conjure, Vision

The Image

A man is seen in darkened silhouette. He observes seven cups suspended before him. They float as if they have been conjured from a dream. Each cup contains a specific object: a head, an idol covered by a veil, a snake, a castle, jewelry, a laurel wreath and a dragon.

Correlations

Number: 7
Sephirot: Netzach (Victory)
Element: Water
Planet: Venus
Sign: Scorpio

Esoteric Name: Lord of Illusionary Success

Dream big

The figure portrayed in the Seven of Cups is exposed. His entire interior world is visualized and looms before him. His desires and fears are symbolized by the contents of the seven cups: a face of seduction (beauty or love), a veiled idol (doubts, forebodings, worry), a snake (sexuality, desires, temptations), a castle (the family, personality), jewelry (wealth, vanity, greed), a laurel wreath (ambition for knowledge or success) and a dragon (intemperance, aggression, hatred).

The Seven Cups reflect different aspects of the unconscious trying to emerge. Meanwhile, the rational mind seeks to control, direct and sublimate it. Dreams and illusions have an essential function in your psychological equilibrium. They can transform and transcend the deeper impulses of creative stimuli without risking dangerous behavior. They show you what is possible.

Aspects of the Arcana expressed in various decks

Lo Scarabeo Tarot

Ghost rising from the unconscious

Nefertari's Tarot

Dream with open eyes

Pagan Tarot

Learning to ignore distractions

Traditional Interpretations

Upright: Dreams, feelings and imagination. Visions in a crystal ball. Realization or success, but nothing lasting and substantial. Castles in the air. Hesitancy in choice. Blinded by brilliance. Awareness of desire.

Reversed: Desire, determination and willingness to attack a project. Good resolutions. Intelligent selection. Renewed determination. Not stopping to ponder but moving straight ahead.

Lessons

◦— Beware of the easy path, because it may be using your own greed to entrap you.
◦— Do not fear that which lives inside you.
◦— Never force a choice, live with the possibility.
◦— Your options are endless.
◦— Freedom lay in choice.
◦— Reach for what you want.

Aspects of the Arcana expressed in various decks

Fey Tarot

Losing control of your perception

Shaman Tarot

Pursuing a vision

Tarot of the Dark Grimoire

Dream journey

8 | EIGHT OF CUPS

Release – Waiver

Keywords

Rejection, Journey, Restart, Freedom, Venturing, Travel, Changing Direction, Transition, Moving, Renunciation, Shyness, Farsightedness, Adventure

The Image

A man, head down, walking stick in hand, moves toward a path. The path looks as if it leads toward high mountains. A rare solar eclipse hangs in the quiet sky above him, the water of a placid inlet quietly reflecting the eclipse's strange light.

Correlations

Number: 8
Sephirot: Hod (Glory)
Element: Water
Planet: Saturn
Sign: Pisces

Esoteric Name: Lord of Abandoned Success

Life is about the journey

Eight cups are arranged one over the other in an orderly manner behind the gentleman. The man is an individual wanting to hone his skill or whose desire is the expression of his full potential. We see in this traveler the rejection of worldliness and customs. He commands the courage to leave certainties and frivolity, represented by eight cups standing behind.

The mountains are high not only in the physical sense, but also intellectually, morally and spiritually. The peak of a mountain is as high as man can go toward the ascent of their spirit. This Arcanum indicates the beginning of progress toward a better future and maturity. This may reflect the abandonment of certainties and is most definitely the beginning of a journey into the unknown.

Aspects of the Arcana expressed in various decks

Lo Scarabeo Tarot

Changing path

Nefertari's Tarot

Focalizing too much on details

Pagan Tarot

Leave

Traditional Interpretations

Upright: Moving away from what is gained in search of something greater. Joy, moderation and timidity. Shyness, honor and modesty. The beginning of a solitary adventure. Releasing the past so you can move forward. Moving to the next level.

Reversed: Joy, happiness and celebration. Spiritual abandoned for material. A stalled trip. Unwillingness to move forward.

Lessons

- You can't take it with you.
- We venture alone.
- Become the journey.
- When adventure calls, respond with action.
- Life is like hiking; full of ups and down, but worth it in the long run.
- Life is a journey.

Aspects of the Arcana expressed in various decks

Fey Tarot

Refusing a useless challenge

Shaman Tarot

Need for purification

Tarot of the Dark Grimoire

Resisting temptation

9 | NINE OF CUPS

Satisfaction – Contentment

Keywords

Satisfaction, Well-being, Pleasure, Saturation, Fulfillment, Sensuality, Success, Good Life, Granted Wish, Virtue, Affection, Admiration, Yes

The Image

A well-fed man, calm and satisfied, sits on a finely carved bench. His arms are crossed in front of his chest and behind him a tall table contains nine cups in a row.

Correlations

Number: 9
Sephirot: Yesod (Foundation)
Element: Water
Planet: Jupiter
Sign: Pisces

Esoteric Name: Lord of Material Happiness

Enjoy what you have

The Nine of Cups represents abundance and satisfaction through his physical appearance, clothing and his environment. His pleased smile indicates a purpose realized, while his relaxed pose expresses peace of mind.

His bench denotes wealth and dowry, but there is more than simple wellbeing on this card. He hides what is behind him, both with his body language and with drapery beneath the cups. He allows his nine cups to be seen. These are his materials and possessions. He is willing to share the contents of the cups but not what hides behind the curtain. What lurks is very valuable and regards emotions and feelings. This card also carries the sense that this fellow is a genie who has materialized before you. And your wish is about to come true.

Aspects of the Arcana expressed in various decks

Lo Scarabeo Tarot

Full satisfaction

Nefertari's Tarot

Wedding

Pagan Tarot

Finding a hidden treasure

Traditional Interpretations

Upright: Your wish comes true. Receiving what you want. Genie in a bottle. Harmony, joy and prosperity. Victory, success and profit. Personal satisfaction. Material success. Pleasure in life.

Reversed: False freedom, errors and imperfections. Overindulgence in food or drink. Your request not granted. Denial.

Lessons

⌒ Anything is possible.
⌒ Be careful what you wish for because you just might get it.
⌒ Accept all gifts.
⌒ Surprises await those who reach for the stars.
⌒ Acknowledge the power of "Yes."

Aspects of the Arcana expressed in various decks

Fey Tarot

Filling your body, your mind, your heart

Shaman Tarot

Achieve equilibrium

Tarot of the Dark Grimoire

Drinking something pure

211

TEN OF CUPS

Happiness – Harmony

Keywords

Happiness, Harmony, Success, Family, Conclusion, Contentment, Peacemaking, Friendship, Joy, Cycles, Fulfillment, Commitment, Familiarity, Community, Recognition, Rest

The Image

A man and woman embrace each other while gazing at the horizon. Two children spin and dance happily. A house sits on a hill and a stream flows. Ten cups shine in rainbow colors gracing the scene and the people below.

Correlations

Number: 10
Sephirot: Malkuth (Kingdom)
Element: Water
Planet: Mars
Sign: Pisces

Esoteric Name: Lord of Perfected Success

Rainbows follow the storm

The Ten of Cups reflects the appearance of marital happiness. The couple embraces one another in happiness, harmony and unity of feeling and intention. The vibrant countryside around them represents fertility. The rainbow of golden cups shining in the sky symbolizes optimism and confidence in the future. The two playing children represent what the couple has already produced, their future and also their relationship with the world. The house represents family and security.

The happiness expressed in the Arcana reflects feelings and relations and also the professional dimension, the sphere of friendship and the interior of an individual. One discovers this sense of satisfaction when they are at peace with themselves and the people around them. Senses are stimulated by positive ideas and feelings. The Ten of Cups also suggests the positive outcome of a situation and an important achievement. It is expansion and satisfaction in every area. As always, the number ten reminds us a situation has reached its finale.

Aspects of the Arcana expressed in various decks

Lo Scarabeo Tarot

Converging energies

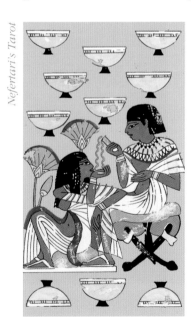

Nefertari's Tarot

Bliss

Pagan Tarot

Perfect shared harmony

Traditional Interpretations

Upright: Joy and rest in the heart. A lovely situation. The contentment of human love and friendship. Happy family. Domestic bliss. Positive flow of energy. "Happily ever after."
Reversed: Misplaced trust, anger and violence. Betrayal, loss of friendship and waste. Idealizing a situation rather than being realistic about it.

Lessons

- You deserve and can cultivate great happiness.
- If you can imagine it, you can live it.
- Write your own ending.
- Chase rainbows and believe in magic.
- It can be yours.

Aspects of the Arcana expressed in various decks

Fey Tarot

Finding that special connection

Shaman Tarot

Self-healing

Tarot of the Dark Grimoire

Journey to a blessed place

1 | ACE OF PENTACLES

Gain – Materialism

Keywords

Gain, Materialism, Acquisition, Success, Possessions, Physicality, Opportunity, Gift, Start, Chance, Genesis, Abundance, Fortune

The Image

A puff of fluffy clouds sits on the left side of the sky. A hand extends holding a golden disk. It bears a five pointed star enclosed by a circle. The hand hovers over a lush flower garden bordered by a high hedge. A path leads through an arch in the hedge. Mountain peaks are seen in the distance.

Correlations

Number: 1
Sephirot: Kether (Crown)
Element: Earth
Season: Summer
Disposition: Choleric

Esoteric Name: the Root of the Powers of Earth

Ready for business

The Ace of Pentacles is an opportunity. It symbolizes success in economic activities. This success derives from both skill in trade and the ability to seize an opportunity. Material success is the result of a positive attitude born from the awareness of possibilities and the desire to achieve a precise result. This card expresses a strong link with materiality, objects and tangible things. It is also health of the physical body.

The Ace of Pentacles is the gate to worldly success. It represents the well-being that involves financial success. While it is true that money does not buy happiness, money does offer tremendous opportunity and is the major source of security in the modern world. The Ace of Coins thus also indicates stability and a solid foundation on which to build other aspects of our lives.

Aspects of the Arcana expressed in various decks

Lo Scarabeo Tarot

Prosperity that creates prosperity

Nefertari's Tarot

Economic ideas

Pagan Tarot

Altar of Earth

Traditional Interpretations

Upright: Perfect happiness, ecstasy and intelligence. The power to acquire what you need. The beginning of wealth and material gain. Delight, prosperity and pleasure in beauty. An opportunity in the material world. A fresh start.

Reversed: The downside of wealth and having everything handed to you. Miserliness. Throwing your money away. Refusing a gift.

Lessons

- Accept the opportunities and gifts surrounding you.
- Step through the gate.
- If a magic seed appears, you must plant it.
- Life is your garden, cultivate it.
- Nature holds all the answers.

Aspects of the Arcana expressed in various decks

Fey Tarot

The soul of a maker

Shaman Tarot

Vibration

Tarot of the Dark Grimoire

The Book of Possessions

Duality – Inconstancy

Keywords

Gaiety, Dance, Rhythm, Flexibility, Indecision, Choice, Vacillation, Industrious, Juggle, Dexterity, Balance, Eternal Dance, Fluctuation, Division

The Image

A young man in festive attire dances upon a stage. He juggles two disks engraved with pentagrams and they form a symmetrical lemniscate in his hands.

Correlations

Number: 2
Sephirot: Chokmah (Wisdom)
Element: Earth
Planet: Jupiter
Sign: Capricorn

Esoteric Name: Lord of Harmonious Change

Opposites attract

The Two of Pentacles expresses playfulness, fun and carefree adolescence. It is the ignorance of the adult life of responsibility. The figure indulges in gratifying pastimes. This card also represents a person who has adapted to the rhythm of their life. They have harmonized themselves with the difficulties and the demands of life. They are able to feed both parts of the psyche and satisfy their needs with balance.

The foot raised in a hint of dance represents partial detachment. The other foot is placed on the ground and there is an expression of "lightness". The high hat upon the young man makes him look like a dreamer or a person with little practical sense. His pentacles roll from one side to the other and represent instability in moods or feelings and uncertainty in making decisions.

Aspects of the Arcana expressed in various decks

Lo Scarabeo Tarot

Infinity

Nefertari's Tarot

Energy

Pagan Tarot

Running or being late

Traditional Interpretations

Upright: Making a choice and both options are pleasant. The ability to juggle two things at once. News and messages from far away places. Lightheartedness and gaiety. Division.
Reversed: Forced gaiety and simulated joy. Inability to handle too many things at once. Remove yourself from stimulation. Options disappear. No choices left.

Lessons

- Life is a dance.
- Go with the flow.
- Stay light on your feet.
- There are two sides to every story.
- Never rush to decide.

Aspects of the Arcana expressed in various decks

Fey Tarot

Dance of opposites

Shaman Tarot

Listening

Tarot of the Dark Grimoire

Struggle

THREE OF PENTACLES

Engineering – Planning

Keywords

Creativity, Craft, Talent, Project, Installation, Inspiration, Art, Collaboration, Consulting, Trade, Skill, Work, Building, Publicity, Teamwork, Combination

The Image

An artisan is completing works inside a church. He stands on a pedestal. Above him, three pentacles are carved into the wall. Behind the sculptor, two figures discuss the building plans.

Correlations

Number: 3
Sephirot: Binah (Understanding)
Element: Earth
Planet: Mars
Sign: Capricorn

Esoteric Name: Lord of Material Works

Power of creative collaboration

The Three of Pentacles expresses collaboration and the comparison between different points of view. The building symbolizes complex business, art and collaborations utilizing many contributions, bodies of knowledge and energy.

The archway with three pentacles symbolizes an openness to the three worlds: material, intellectual and spiritual. To complete a project there must be harmony between all participants. Suggestions and ideas guide the artistic inspiration of the sculptor but do not dominate him. Not surprisingly, the sculptor turns his back to work as discussion continues.

Aspects of the Arcana expressed in various decks

Lo Scarabeo Tarot

Adding details

Nefertari's Tarot

Freedom of money

Pagan Tarot

Three in one

Traditional Interpretations

Upright: Craft, trade and masterful skills. Nobility, aristocracy and fame. Commercial transaction. This card marks Masons, guilds and secret society members. Blossoming creativity.
Reversed: Mediocrity in work. Banality, meanness and weakness. Lack of skill. Poor planning and an unwillingness to work with others.

Lessons

◦— Your work blooms, as you stay open to the opinions and constructive criticism of others.
◦— Allow others to feed your creativity.
◦— The work remains, long after you are gone.
◦— Be the gateway of creativity.
◦— Instruct others gently.

Aspects of the Arcana expressed in various decks

Clarity of inspiration

The beat of life

Giving shape to Darkness

Fey Tarot

Shaman Tarot

Tarot of the Dark Grimoire

4 | FOUR OF PENTACLES

Possessions – Greed

Keywords

Control, Gain, Thrift, Savings, Concentration, Stagnant, Stable, Solid, Possessive, Hardy, Chakras, Inheritance, Determination, Control, Realization, Investments

The Image

A man with a gloomy face sits on a square cube, holding a large pentacle. Two discs rest below his feet and a fourth pentacle balances above the crown of his head. A city looms behind him.

Correlations

Number: 4
Sephirot: Chesed (Mercy)
Element: Earth
Planet: Sun
Sign: Capricorn

Esoteric Name: Lord of Earthly Power

Nothing lasts forever

The character sits alone, looks hostile and clings tightly to his money. This card immediately expresses the idea of material attachment. His feet are resting on the money, while the disc above the crown seems to crush his thoughts and his emotions. Every aspect of this man seems to be dominated by matter and his heart appears overwhelmed by the fear of losing what he has gained. The city is the place from where he has fled. This card is a symbol of how greed and fear obscures life and its joys.

The Four of Pentacles also suggests savings, thrift and prudence in a positive light. It allows us to build wealth, overcome times of economic hardship and protects us from outside attacks. This attitude, however, must remain temporary, so we do not become closed within ourselves and lose the spice and joy of life.

Aspects of the Arcana expressed in various decks

Lo Scarabeo Tarot

Self-confinemen

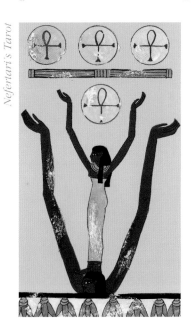

Nefertari's Tarot

Greed

Pagan Tarot

Looking for bargains

Traditional Interpretations

Upright: The security of property and attachments to what you have. Gifts, bequests and inheritance. Assured material gain. Holding too tightly to material things. Miser. Great earthly power but lacking in spiritual and moral realms. Building solid financial portfolio.

Reversed: Suspension, delay and hurdle. Instability in your financial world. Coveting things that other people have. Losing money. Instability leads to great change.

Lessons

◦— Build security yet do not cling to it so tightly that the important things fall away.

◦— You can't take it with you.

◦— Money carries it's own energy.

◦— Do not let inconsequential things bring you down.

◦— Run your money, don't let it run you.

Aspects of the Arcana expressed in various decks

Fey Tarot

Giving up your freedom

Shaman Tarot

Being one with the rhythm

Tarot of the Dark Grimoire

Forgetting to live

226

FIVE OF PENTACLES

Need – Poverty

Keywords

Need, Poverty, Lack, Deficiency, Longing, Cold, Dark, Sadness, Despair, Victim, Hardship, Struggle, Rejection, Material Worries, Obstacles, Useless Expense, Challenge

The Image

A man and woman, poorly dressed, bandaged and hobbled walk a bitter street in the rages of a blizzard. The man is lame and relies on crutches. The woman draws her shawl closer for warmth. The couple passes an illuminated window decorated with five pentacles.

Correlations

Number: 5
Sephirot: Geburah (Strength)
Element: Earth
Planet: Mercury
Sign: Taurus

Esoteric Name: Lord of Material Trouble

Money buys a house but not a home

This card is the reflection of need, hardship and poverty. The swirling snow emphasizes a difficult time. Even as everything seems to get worse, these two lost souls do not stop walking, but they do not seem to seek a solution. The stained glass window represents light, warmth and richness. This window may generate envy and provoke the characters to think the world is unfair. Perhaps, they do not see the window at all.

The window represents a source of hope, a place of help and comfort. Compassion and aid is right there. The window represents a threshold. Once breached, the cold, needs and difficulties will be behind. The snow covering the ground is also a symbol of purification. Through poverty, the couple finds themselves and the value of things. They balance against this their needs, both personal and spiritual.

Aspects of the Arcana expressed in various decks

Lo Scarabeo Tarot

A treasure in the snow

Nefertari's Tarot

Seeds of prosperity

Pagan Tarot

Patience when in need

Traditional Interpretations

Upright: Winter of discontent. Feelings of sorrow and loss. Material considerations. Love and lovers - a relationship, wife, husband, friend, or lover - and even business partnerships. It represents the ups and downs of all long-term relationships.
Reversed: Money regained after disaster. Movement forward. Getting past old habits and patterns of a couple or relationship.

Lessons

- What doesn't kill you makes you stronger.
- There is always an escape hatch.
- Adversity builds character.
- Find light in the darkness.
- Give yourself time.

Aspects of the Arcana expressed in various decks

Fey Tarot

Longing for the hearth fire

Shaman Tarot

Losing the rhythm

Tarot of the Dark Grimoire

Being on the sideline

SIX OF PENTACLES

Favor – Charity

Keywords

Generosity, Gift, Distribution, Fairness, Mercy, Justice, Aid, Alms, Gain, Altruism, Success, Sympathy, Comfort, Offerings

The Image

A richly dressed man distributes coins with one hand and balances scales with the other. Beggars kneel at his feet waiting for his charity. Six pentacles hang in the air.

Correlations

Number: 6
Sephirot: Tiphareth (Beauty)
Element: Earth
Planet: Moon
Sign: Taurus

Esoteric Name: Lord of Material Success

Giving is receiving and receiving is giving

Mercy, justice and generosity are all important elements of the Six of Pentacles. The balancing scale reflects the measurement of charity you can provide without going to the poorhouse yourself. The kneeling people symbolize reliance on generosity, fortune or events. It can reflect requesting a favor both financial and otherwise.

This card shows the ability of man to realize the needs of others. It becomes a card of adaptation, attention and sensitivity. The kneeling figures reflect the humility of requesting a favor or assistance. The hierarchy of the card stands as a reminder to help others without doing so to make you superior. All gifts should come from the heart.

Aspects of the Arcana expressed in various decks

Lo Scarabeo Tarot

Economic exchange

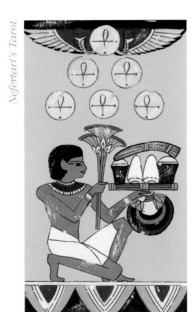

Nefertari's Tarot

A gift offering

Pagan Tarot

Finding help in a kin spirit

Traditional Interpretations

Upright: Rewards, gifts and attention. Supervision and acceptance of prosperity. You receive what you give. Potential of great generosity. Be sure your kind acts aren't truly a grasp for power.

Reversed: Desire, greed and envy. Jealousy and illusion. Bribery offered. Being cheap and unwilling to help others.

Lessons

- Law of return: you get what you give.
- Accept help when offered.
- What comes around, goes around.
- You will always have what you need.
- There is comfort in giving.

Aspects of the Arcana expressed in various decks

Fey Tarot

The Universe provides

Shaman Tarot

Melody

Tarot of the Dark Grimoire

Charity among the dispossessed

232

SEVEN OF PENTACLES

Evaluation – Dissatisfaction

Keywords

Developments, Deal, Counting, Checking, Exchange, Planning, Accomplishment, Contemplation, Charity, Civil Duty, Business, Expansion, Flowering, Ripening

The Image

A young man, perhaps a farmer, leans thoughtfully on his tool. He stands next to lush vegetation and a thriving garden. Seven gold pentacles have grown. Tendrils move through the garden indicating more is to come.

Correlations

Number: 7
Sephirot: Netzach (Victory)
Element: Earth
Planet: Saturn
Sign: Taurus

Esoteric Name: Lord of Success Unfulfilled

No rush

Seven of Pentacles reflects a person examining their possessions. They are dissatisfied with what they see. Not because they do not have enough, but rather because it has no meaning. Perhaps, achievement was too easy and did not represent enough challenge to bring satisfaction of success. Perhaps, he is considering what steps to take next or he ponders on how he will proceed.

This attitude is mistaken for arrogance when perceived by people who attach great value to wealth, property and privileges. The card relates to the old saying "Money does not bring happiness." It should not to be confused with contempt of material success. Rather, it calls us to find a balance between what you have and what you want.

Aspects of the Arcana expressed in various decks

Lo Scarabeo Tarot

Immature reaping

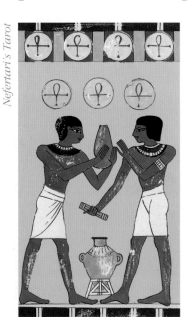

Nefertari's Tarot

Unsettled negotiation

Pagan Tarot

A spell of growth

Traditional Interpretations

Upright: A pause and moment of reflection while building an enterprise. Dissatisfaction leading to reevaluation. What you need to feel alive is something you hadn't thought of. Being very productive at what you are naturally talented at. What is easy for you may be challenging for others. What next?
Reversed: Anxiety about money. You may require a loan. You are working hard yet not seeing the right profits. Impatience and angst.

Lessons

- Growth is the natural state of the world.
- Allow things to bloom.
- Let your gifts work for you.
- There is always a second act.
- Allow yourself to be surprised.

Aspects of the Arcana expressed in various decks

Fey Tarot

Inner peace creates outer peace

Shaman Tarot

Dancing on the boundary

Tarot of the Dark Grimoire

Not seeing the darkness

Work – Habit

Keywords

Commitment, Dedication, Skill, Routine, Repetitive, Dexterity, Craftsmanship, Refinement, Finesse, Autonomy, Learning, Personal Limits, Technique, Proficiency

The Image

A craftsman hammers and chisels a pentacle made of gold. Five discs are completed and are displayed next to him. One rests at his feet, awaiting the work to be done.

Correlations

Number: 8
Sephirot: Hod (Glory)
Element: Earth
Planet: Sun
Sign: Virgo

Esoteric Name: Lord of Prudence

Create to live and live to create

The card shows how us how to fill our workdays with joy. The Arcana reflects all aspects of labor and the payoff from repetitiveness and practice. The card reminds you to find a way to make the things you do every day special. Doing so, you will derive great satisfaction. Otherwise, work becomes trudgery bringing fatigue, oppression and making you feel pessimistic.

In contrast, the pride and the will to excel are important for the balance of any person, in all areas. Every action you take can be a small challenge, leading to growing and improving should you approach it that way. This card also calls for you to examine where you are placing your efforts. Your efforts should be spent on things which truly count.

Aspects of the Arcana expressed in various decks

Lo Scarabeo Tarot

Conscious effort

Nefertari's Tarot

Reaping rewards

Pagan Tarot

Magical helping

Traditional Interpretations

Upright: Pleasure in work and employment. An excellent commission and manual dexterity. Activity, craft and trade, perhaps in a preparatory phase. Work at what you love and time will cease to exist. Integration of work and lifestyle. Training for a new skill.

Reversed: Lack of ambition, vanity and greed. Failing in one's ambitions. Cunning and sneaky behavior. Trying to pass someone else's work off as your own. Not taking pride in your work.

Lessons

- Time is precious, spend it well.
- Let your talents move through you.
- Creativity thrives in every profession.
- There is pleasure in an honest day's work.

Aspects of the Arcana expressed in various decks

Fey Tarot

A work of art

Shaman Tarot

An extended endeavor

Tarot of the Dark Grimoire

Expresing your inner fears

NINE OF PENTACLES

Richness – Education

Keywords

Discernment, Prudence, Safety, Elegance, Fabulousness, Self Assurance, Security, Enjoyment, Accomplishment, Refinement, Self Reliant, Independence, New Projects, Investments

The Image

A woman, richly dressed, stands alone in her garden and vineyard. Pentacles are attached to the bursting, ripe grape vines. Resting atop her hand is a fierce bird of prey, a falcon. His head is protected by a hood. A castle looms in the distance and two green trees frame her on either side.

Correlations

Number: 9
Sephirot: Yesod (Foundation)
Element: Earth
Planet: Venus
Sign: Virgo

Esoteric Name: Lord of Material Gain

Luxury is in the eye of the beholder

The Nine of Pentacles reflects a woman who has it all: wealth, intelligence, beauty, youth and health. She has achieved the perfect balance between her desires, ambitions and successes. She represents the harmony between what we want and what we already have. The real wealth, therefore, is the result of intelligence of the heart, which allows you value what you already have, thereby enjoying it.

The castle represents inherited wealth and the grapes create wine bringing intoxication, pleasure and abandon. The hooded falcon represents a lack of ambition and aggressiveness and can be understood as either a virtue or a defect, depending on the circumstances. The card also reminds us never to take our fortunes for granted and always to appreciate our gifts. It also reflects a person who is at perfect ease with herself and who acts out of personal and graceful authenticity.

Aspects of the Arcana expressed in various decks

Lo Scarabeo Tarot

Accomplishment

Nefertari's Tarot

Prayer

Pagan Tarot

Taking a well deserved break

Traditional Interpretations

Upright: Enjoying precious solitude. Enjoying material things not because they are expensive or status worthy but because you enjoy fine craftsmanship. Treating yourself well. The good life. Inheritance. Utilizing your inherited talents. Knowing who you are. Love of gardening and home.
Reversed: Possible loss of home or friendship. Not being happy with what you have. Projects not panning out. Not taking enough time to recuperate. Great need for solitude. Someone may try to take what you have.

Lessons

- A good life is simple and beautiful.
- Love yourself before loving another.
- Quality time.
- Discover pleasure in unlikely places.

Aspects of the Arcana expressed in various decks

Fey Tarot

Living in opulence

Shaman Tarot

Invisible richness

Tarot of the Dark Grimoire

A difficult to reach, but worthy place

10 | TEN OF PENTACLES

Wealth – Inheritance

Keywords

Wealth, Legacy, Home, Family, Passage, Links, Security, Continuity, Cycles, Safety, Material Gain, Family, Treasures, Culmination

The Image

An old man in a fanciful coat sits near a child, his parents and a pair of white dogs. The entire group is at the threshold of a town. Ten pentacles hang in the air.

Correlations

Number: 10
Sephirot: Malkuth (Kingdom)
Element: Earth
Planet: Mercury
Sign: Virgo

Esoteric Name: Lord of Wealth

The cycle of life is continual

The Ten of Pentacles represents material wealth and other forms of wealth that come from sharing what you have. The picture reflects several generations of the same family: the old man symbolizes wisdom, the young couple indicate the energy and capacity to act, while the child represents the future, growth and hope.

The family is complete, strong and resistant to time. If an element of the picture were to disappear, something else would take its place, continuity would be maintained. This card represents how the material ties and unites people. Every generation has its role and responsibility. This Arcanum is not related only to the family, but to every group evolving over time, linked by a project or shared experience.

Aspects of the Arcana expressed in various decks

Lo Scarabeo Tarot

Unity of form and purpose

Nefertari's Tarot

What is most precious

Pagan Tarot

Items linked to memories

Traditional Interpretations

Upright: income and wealth. Family matters and archives. Residence and the house of a family. Completion and success for all.

Reversed: Chance, fate and loss. Theft and gambling. A gift, endowment, or pension. A family who has come apart at the seams.

Lessons

- Find yourself in the tapestry of life.
- There is no beginning or end. It simply is.
- Accept your house of spirits, whoever they may be.
- There is richness everywhere.
- This is your time.

Aspects of the Arcana expressed in various decks

Fey Tarot

The family table

Shaman Tarot

The dance of life

Tarot of the Dark Grimoire

The light where people connect to each other

PAGE OF WANDS

Initiative – Vitality

Keywords

Vitality, Creativity, Mate, Love, Loyalty, Travel, Support, Friendship, Commitment, Fidelity, Messenger, Confidence, Insights, Energetic, Adaptable, Curious, Adventurous, Playful, Outgoing, Risky, Candid, Ambitious, Impetuous.

Alternate names

Knave, Princess, The Inventor

The Image

A young person is dressed in fiery colorful clothing. He stands in profile and gazes intently at the horizon. The staff he holds is planted on the ground. The Page holds it with two hands while keenly observing green sprouts emerging from it. The Page stands in a hot desert landscape, echoing the element of Fire. In the background, mountain peaks point toward the heavens.

Passionate pursuit

The Page of Wands is a young person, boy or girl, committed to passionate and creative pursuits. This can be a job, a sport, or a field of study that requires direct contact with people. This dreamer falls in love at first sight. She is dazzled by new potentials and possibilities appearing full of promise. This Page often believes the grass is greener on the other side of the fence.

She becomes rather obsessed with creation, commitment and participation and forgets to take necessary caution. A Page can be quite impressionable and suggestible. She grows and matures by becoming involved in her passions. Her talent is to rework all experiences by translating them into something personal. Independent, she needs no guide to direct her, but needs stimulus for her creativity. The Page of Wands is endless, boundless enthusiasm.

Reflected in You

When was the last time you jumped up and down with cheeks red with excitement? This was the Page of Wands operating within you. When you experience the thrill of the moment, with no thought to long terms plans, this is the Page of Wands.

Traditional Interpretations

Upright: Unexpectedly exciting news. A messenger. The creativity and enthusiasm of youth. An opportunity to begin afresh. Courage waiting to reveal itself. Young person with a zest for life. Travel.
Reversed: Gossip, advice and bad news. Indecision and the instability that accompanies it. Stifled.

The Physical Persona

Occupations: Student, Creative Works, Athlete, Telemarketing, Sales, Journalist, Administrative Assistant, Intern, Investigator, Travel Writer, Pilot, Boatman, Stuntman/woman, Freelancer
Appearance: Young girl, red hair, fair skin and light eyes.

Strategy, Behavior and Attitude

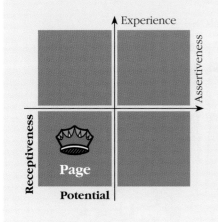

Creative Learning

Learning: Learn, feel, listen, experiment, invent, discover, explore, change and improve.

Creativity: News, wishes, desires, passions, actions, business, travel, transformations, ideals and beliefs.

Receptiveness: Listening, waiting, patience, understanding, reflection, internalization, introspection and femininity.

Potential: Future, youth, opportunity, ingenuity, desire, hope, growth and innovation.

Aspects of the Arcana expressed in various decks

The fire starter

The scribe

The Salamander (Fire elemental)

Child of desire

The fiery sentinel

Creative ispiration

Spirit of a wounded land

Standing tall

The guardian at the threshold of fire

The balance among the flames

247

KNIGHT OF WANDS

Courage – Recklessness

Keywords

Courage, Recklessness, Traveling, Distance, Adventure, Idealism, Exploration, Impetuous, Daring, Impatient, Passionate, Foresight, Protective, Dramatic, Capable, Chivalrous, Optimism, Outgoing, Enterprising, Brilliance.

Alternate names

Prince, The Traveler

The Image

The Knight of Wands rides on a horse that leaps into action. The horse's sudden movement is anticipated by the Knight who remains in complete control while traveling over hot desert sands. Holding a sprouted wand in his right hand, he grasps the rein with his left. He wears a suit of armor under a tunic decorated with salamanders, symbolic of fire. A red plume extends from his helmet and a yellow cape flaps behind him like racing flames. Three pyramids, tomb of kings and doorways to the otherworld, loom in the distance.

Fearless exploring

The Knight of Wands stands for pride and initiative. This leads him to unpredictable actions and decisions. He often launches into ventures that seem impossible. His extreme courage and self-reliance are fundamental elements of his character. He often begins an undertaking without necessary means, or without a clear goal, but his strength of spirit and vitality of soul make up for any deficiencies. His innate curiosity often leads him to far away places, not just for the sake of discovery, but also for the desire to obtain tangible and new rewards.

His qualities mean the Knight of Wands resists strong roots, yet he always brings something along that reminds him of the place where he comes from. He may not always travel just for himself and often opens the way for others who follow and imitate him. The Knight of Wands is fearless.

Reflected in You

When you are flirting, charismatic and outgoing you are operating within the field of the Knight of Wands. Feeling impetuous? Do you desire to break free? That's this Knight as well. His behavior is alive in you when you are on the prowl, traveling and satisfying your thirst for adventure.

Traditional Interpretations

Upright: Travel, departure and absence. Flight and emigration. A rescue is at hand. Speed is of importance. Change of residence. Expect company.
Reversed: Fear and stasis. Break, separation and disruption. Discord and wasted effort. Moving backwards when you should move forward. Deadly passion.

The Physical Persona

Occupations: Athlete, Social Service Worker, Firefighter, Actor, Comedian, Writer, Construction Worker, Promoter, Manager, All Professions of the Arts
Appearance: Young man, red-haired, fair-skinned and light eyes.

Strategy, Behavior and Attitude

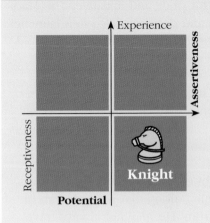

Experience ↑

Assertiveness →

← Receptiveness

Potential

Knight

Creative Action

Action: Decide, move, do, believe, conclude, risk, exposure, progress, choose, fight and break up.
Creativity: News, wishes, desires, passions, actions, business, travel, transformations, ideals and beliefs.
Assertiveness: Business, initiative, aggressiveness, belief, confidence, extroversion, determination and masculinity.
Potential: Future, youth, opportunity, ingenuity, desire, hope, growth and innovation.

Aspects of the Arcana expressed in various decks

Lo Scarabeo Tarot

The Traveler

Nefertari's Tarot

Pride of the stallion

Pagan Tarot

Apprentice of Fire

Dark Angels Tarot

The relentless hunter

Universal Fantasy Tarot

The king of the hill

Fey Tarot

The joy of the journey

Shaman Tarot

Seeking the children within

Tarot of the Pagan Cats

Jumping forward

Tarot of the Dark Grimoire

The Protector of Fire

Manga Tarot

The quiet center in the firestorm

250

QUEEN OF WANDS

Attention – Inspiration

Keywords

Magnetism, Dignity, Sensuality, Passion, Power, Attractive, Fertility, Self-Assured, Charisma, Autonomous, Vivacious, Upbeat, Magnetic.

Alternate names

The Muse

The Image

The Queen of Wands sits in a comfortable yet commanding posture on her throne. Her throne is carved, decorated with leaves and regal lions. She holds a sunflower in her left hand. A sprouted wand, whose buds represent life and activity, is grasped by her right hand. Her gaze is set in the distance over a kingdom extending across dunes and deserts. A loyal black cat sits at her feet and gazes at you.

Magnetic inspiration

The Queen of Wands has a very strong personality and an equally strong morality. Under her appearance she masks instinctive aggression and a fiery character, ready to unleash it against those who would disturb the quiet that animates her world. She carries the elegant qualities of a cat, an aristocratic bearing, a magnetic look and elusive charm. Like the flowers and trees, she renews herself every season while remaining true to herself.

She is attentive to everything that surrounds her, stays firm to her purpose, is friendly and generous with those she comes into contact with. Should conflict arise, she quickly becomes hard and vindictive, a viable enemy. Both the wand and the flower symbolize the Queen's vitality and beauty. Her power is through inspiration. The Queen of Wands prefers to be direct about things, encourages people and stimulates creativity in subtle and patient ways, making full use of her charisma.

Reflected in You

The Queen of Wands is in you when you feel alive, awake and up for any challenge the world might toss your way. She is there when you are feeling deliciously at home in your body, confident and sexy, exuding vibrancy and spirit. Emulations of fiery power accompany this Queen wherever she goes so when you are energized she is inside you.

Traditional Interpretations

Upright: Success in business. Attracting exactly what you want. A fruitful mind and body. Love of passion and success. Kindness and generosity. Sexuality and sensuality.
Reversed: Indulgent and obliging. Signifies opposition, jealousy, or even deceit and infidelity. A person who is inauthentic to themselves and their passions.

The Physical Persona

Occupations: Business, Performing Artist, Actress, Dancer, Politician, Television Personality, Advertising Executive, Activist
Appearance: Blonde hair with blue or hazel eyes.

Strategy, Behavior and Attitude

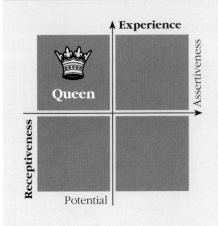

Experience

Assertiveness

Queen

Receptiveness

Potential

Creative Perception

Perception: Receive, understand, listen, think, adapt, accept, embrace, tolerate, convert and endure.

Creativity: News, wishes, desires, passions, actions, business, travel, transformations, ideals and beliefs.

Receptiveness: Listening, waiting, patience, understanding, reflection, internalization, introspection and femininity.

Experience: Competence, skill, knowledge, customs, security, calm, lucid, certainty and habit.

Aspects of the Arcana expressed in various decks

Lo Scarabeo Tarot — The source of inspiration

Nefertari's Tarot — Dwelling in beauty

Pagan Tarot — Practitioner of Fire

Dark Angels Tarot — Waiting for unfulfilled promises

Universal Fantasy Tarot — The Queen of the wild

Fey Tarot — Anger replaced by life

Shaman Tarot — Changing skin

Tarot of the Pagan Cats — Encouraging curiosity

Tarot of the Dark Grimoire — Dynamic stability

Manga Tarot — Fire that warms, but never burn

KING OF WANDS

Leadership – Experience

Keywords

Security, Presumption, Entrepreneur, Experience, Initiative, Sponsorship, Explosive, Bold, Vitality, Inspiring, Boss, Motivator, Courageous, Persuasive, Dominating, Witty, Respected, Bold, Persuasive, Loyal, Enthusiasm, Dynamic.

Alternate names

The Leader

The Image

The King sits in profile holding a sprouting wand in his right hand. His feet are firmly planted, legs apart on a simple throne decorated with regal lions and salamanders eating their tail as a symbol of eternal life. An actual salamander is seen at his side. His crown is crafted in the shape of flames flickering upward while the green of his costume and slippers match the color of the sprouts from his wand. He sits in his domain of savannah, a landscape most directly related to the element of fire.

Leading by example

The King of Wands carries a distinct security and you can see it manifesting itself in his posture. His strength lies in his physical character, he has a mental attitude that checks every detail, leaves no stone unturned. Like the lizards often seen on and around his throne, he is in tune with the rhythms of nature, symbolized by a sprouting wand. The King of Wands reminds one of an old lion that does not need to fight. His authority and expertise are recognized by all.

His carries integrity and the attitude of a good-natured person when he faces the world. Yet, behind this veneer are traits severely judging and punishing those who are dishonest. The King of Wands, therefore, acts as the arbiter of conflicts among the people around him. He can show shades of a benevolent dictator in his own way, but never for his own personal advantage. He is, above all things, passionate about his life and works.

Reflected in You

The King of Wands operates within you when you act with passion, self-belief and personal fire. Effecting the needed change that you wished to see, leading by example, you can't help but be charismatic when you express the passion of your soul. Your performance has everyone stopped and staring.

Traditional Interpretations

Upright: Friendly, passionate man and honest. Conscientious. A man who stands up for others. Needs to do the right thing. News concerning unexpected inheritance. Massive charisma and appeal. A forceful presence. Risk taker.
Reversed: Severe, austere and intolerant. Passion taken to extremes. A powder keg ready to explode.

The Physical Persona

Occupations: Politician, Agent, Host, Actor, Dancer, Performer, Non-profit Organizer, Rock Star, Salesman, Inventor, Activist, Athlete
Appearance: Mature man with red or blonde hair, fair-skinned and bright-eyed.

Strategy, Behavior and Attitude

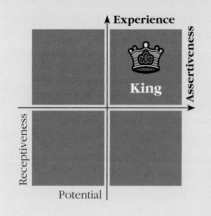

Creative Control

Control: Deciding, drive, knowledge, educate, evaluate, judge, arrange, plan, select and manage.

Creativity: News, wishes, desires, passions, actions, business, travel, transformations, ideals and beliefs.

Assertiveness: Business, initiative, aggressiveness, belief, confidence, extraversion, determination and masculinity.

Experience: Competence, skill, knowledge, customs, security, calm, lucid, certainty and habit.

Aspects of the Arcana expressed in various decks

Lo Scarabeo Tarot

The Fire King

Nefertari's Tarot

The King surrounded by life

Pagan Tarot

Elder of Fire

Dark Angels Tarot

Lost in memories

Universal Fantasy Tarot

Pride in power and conquest

Fey Tarot

The ever young king

Shaman Tarot

The master of the underworld river

Tarot of the Pagan Cats

Perfect stability is not stasis

Tarot of the Dark Grimoire

Dynamic rulership

Manga Tarot

Empowering wisdom

PAGE OF SWORDS

Apprenticeship – Eagerness

Keywords

Attention, Circumspection, Genius, Insightful, Spy, Helper, Vigilant, Daring, Detached, Clever, Precise, Cunning, Acuteness, Espionage, Secrecy, Scholar, Calculation, Vigilance, Dexterity, Logic.

Alternate names

Knave, Princess, The Student

The Image

An agile, active young person raises a sword with both hands. Dressed in fine clothes, exhibiting a pointed posture, he moves over rocky terrain not distant from a country house. Clouds race across the sky pulled by a strong wind. This Page is alert and ready. He looks here and there, as if expecting something or someone to appear at any moment.

Endless curiosity

The Page of Swords represents a young person, boy or girl, engaged in study, research, analysis and investigation. Her character is extremely curious, dynamic and impetuous. Her thinking is fast, emotional and passionate. However, this Page is also an introvert and tends to act discreetly. She makes use of strategy and subterfuge. She prefers to move without being noticed.

Curiosity and cultivated fascination leads her to great knowledge. She reads, studies and travels. When she seeks outside help she tends to be cautious. She can be wary of teachers, instructors and authority figures until they have proven themselves to her. She seeks the deeper meaning of any situation. She believes in the underlying truth of any situation and actively searches for confirmations and insights offering greater understanding.

Reflected in You

This daring Page is reflected in you when you finesse the truth of any situation. You embody this Page when you are determined to solve a mystery or problem and nothing stands in your way. Your intellectual fires rev up and the world bends to your will when you engage the inner Page of Swords.

Traditional Interpretations

Upright: Surveillance, authority and attention. Privacy, espionage and stealth. Intrigue is afoot. Games are at play. Diplomacy in attracting what you need. Read between the lines.
Reversed: Loss of insight. Inability to see and predict. Unpreparedness. Jumping to conclusions. No need to read between the lines. Things are just as they appear.

The Physical Persona

Occupations: Spy, Diplomat, Mathematician, Writer, Technical Assistance, Designer, Secret Service, Lawyer, Student, Novelist, Scientist
Appearance: Young female, black-haired, fair complexion and dark eyes.

Strategy, Behavior and Attitude

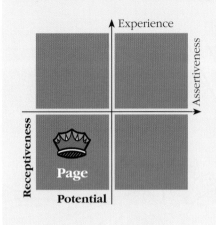

Experience
Assertiveness
Receptiveness
Page
Potential

Mental Learning

Learning: Learn, feel, listen, experiment, invent, discover, explore, change, improve.

Mind: Thoughts, concepts, words, studies, theories, definitions, questions, concerns, conflict analysis.

Receptiveness: Listening, waiting, patience, understanding, reflection, internalization, introspection, femininity.

Potential: Talent, future, youth, ability, ingenuity, desire, hope, growth and innovation.

Aspects of the Arcana expressed in various decks

Lo Scarabeo Tarot

The wind starter

Nefertari's Tarot

The student

Pagan Tarot

The Sylph (Air elemental)

Dark Angels Tarot

Child of reason

Universal Fantasy Tarot

The focused hunter

Fey Tarot

Juggling logic and emotion

Shaman Tarot

Seeking freedom

Tarot of the Pagan Cats

Always watchful

Tarot of the Dark Grimoire

The guardian at the threshold of air

Manga Tarot

Rising up to the storm

259

KNIGHT OF SWORDS

Bravery – Aggression

Keywords

Warrior, Momentum, Courage, Bravery, Anger, Hostility, Rage, Temper, Hasty, Skillful, Wit, Clever, Sharp, Heroic, Rebel, Fury, Valor, Champion, Self-assured, Impatient, Brusque, Powerful, Single minded, Impetuous, Frank, Extremes.

Alternate names

Prince, The Fighter

The Image

A Knight rides full speed ahead, as if in pursuit. He is the essential prototype of the ideal romantic hero of chivalric times. Like Sir Galahad, hero of Grail romances, whose sword is fast and safe, he is a pure heart. Dressed in light armor with a red cape flapping in the wind, the sky is filled with racing clouds as he gallops across the barren desolate landscape.

Never turning back

The Knight of Swords blows into your life like a hurricane with his fiery personality. Upon reaching his goal, the Knight of Swords moves on quickly. He is an overwhelming vortex, stopping only when he has exhausted his energy. His actions in the world depend on where they stem, a force of either extreme and pure good or containing violent and lasting fury. He cannot be stopped by reason alone and will not be satisfied until his goals are met.

He is action and thought woven into a single gesture of pure motion. There is no hesitation, no contemplation, except his pure focus on going forward. He holds nothing back.

Reflected in You

The Knight of Swords is reflected in you when you snap quickly into action or verbally or physically snap at another person without thinking. He is your gut reaction and is an instant defense. The Knight of Swords rushes through your blood in moments of heightened awareness when nothing stops you from accomplishing the task at hand.

Traditional Interpretations

Upright: Skill, courage and ability. Defense and dexterity. Hostility, anger and opposition. Rushing into a situation without thinking about it. A need to defend others, no matter the cost. Rapid movement.
Reversed: Carelessness, incapacity and extravagance. A trapped essence needing to surge forward. Repression of expression.

The Physical Persona

Occupations: Soldier, Bodyguard, Assassin, Executive, Judge, Scientist, Writer, Stockbroker, Computer Programmer, Lawyer, Attorney, Mathematician, Consultant, Teacher, Litigator, Speech writer.
Appearance: Young male, black hair, fair complexion and dark eyes.

Strategy, Behavior and Attitude

Experience ↑

Assertiveness →

← Receptiveness

Potential |

Knight

Mental Action

Action: Decide, move, do, believe, conclude, risk, exposure, progress, choose, fight and break up.
Mind: Thoughts, concepts, words, studies, theories, definitions, questions, concerns and conflict analysis.
Assertiveness: Business, initiative, aggressiveness, belief, confidence, extroversion, determination and masculinity.
Potential: Talent, future, youth, ability, ingenuity, desire, hope, growth and innovation.

Aspects of the Arcana expressed in various decks

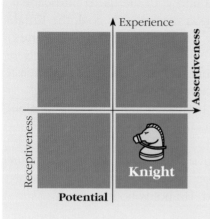

Lo Scarabeo Tarot

The warrior

Nefertari's Tarot

Aggressive action

Pagan Tarot

Apprentice of Air

Dark Angels Tarot

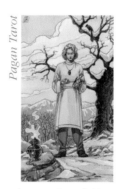

The unmerciful slayer

Universal Fantasy Tarot

The king of armies

Fey Tarot

The joy of battle

Shaman Tarot

Fueled by anger

Tarot of the Pagan Cats

Courage and ambition

Tarot of the Dark Grimoire

The hunter in nightmares

Manga Tarot

The quiet mistress of the tumbling clouds

QUEEN OF SWORDS

Honesty – Abruptness

Keywords

Honesty, Strength, Ruthlessness, Direct, Concise, Precise, Widow, Decision, Astute, Realistic, Straightforward, Unpretentious, Strategist, Rigorous, Discriminating, Self-disciplined, Organized, Clinical, Impartial, Keen, Sharp, Clever, Logical, Delegator

Alternate names

The Critic

The Image

The Queen sits in her regal attire. Her right hand holds a long, high sword pointing upwards to the sky and higher truth. She wears a crown on her head and butterflies themes, symbols of air, decorate her throne. A red cloak is draped over her green dress. Calm water is behind her throne, yet the trees are shaken by an invisible wind. Her left hand extends outward. Does she extend a ruling or welcoming hand?

The violence of truth

The Queen of Swords is an intensely, perceptive figure with great sensitivity and sense of observation. She is subtle in her reasoning, ready to respond and persevering in her actions. She is profoundly honest and tends to react quickly to any given situation. She responds with unprecedented violence against those who wrong her. The best way to reason with the Queen of Swords is to calm your emotions and stay balanced. She will provide an opportunity for dialogue and confrontation. However, if she perceives deception or bad faith, conflict will probably ensue.

Her sense of justice is often excessive, even for those who are closest to her. The Queen of Swords always acts justly with no interest in her own advantage. The Queen of Swords is hard on others only because she is so hard on herself.

Reflected in You

The Queen of Swords is reflected in you when you find the precise expression of your thoughts. Conducting your business, delegating responsibilities and communicating honestly are at the heart of this Queen. You embody her when you react in an intelligent way without the slightest hesitation.

Traditional Interpretations

Upright: A subtle, keen and quick-witted woman. Kindness yet firmness. Widowhood, sadness and plight of women. Ability to articulate all ideas with precise language. Fierce expression and intelligence. A woman to be reckoned with. Powerful delegator.
Reversed: Malice, bigotry and deception. Modesty and quiet nature. Falsehood. Not speaking your truth.

The Physical Persona

Occupations: Lawyer, Architect, Physicist, Academic, Pharmacist, Economist, Surgeon, Venture Capitalist, Researcher, Writer, Editor, Chief Executive Officer, Strategist, Politician, Producer, Director, Graphic Designer
Appearance: Dark haired woman, dark eyes and fair complexion.

Strategy, Behavior and Attitude

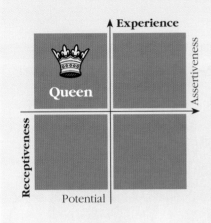

Experience

Assertiveness

Receptiveness

Queen

Potential

Mental Perception

Perception: Receive, understand, listen, think, adapt, accept, embrace, tolerate, convert and endure.

Mind: Thoughts, concepts, words, studies, theories, definitions, questions, concerns and conflict analysis.

Receptiveness: Listening, waiting, patience, understanding, reflection, internalization, introspection, femininity.

Experience: Competence, skill, knowledge, customs, security, calm, lucid, certainty and habit.

Aspects of the Arcana expressed in various decks

Lo Scarabeo Tarot

The source of unforgiveness

Nefertari's Tarot

Dwelling in power

Pagan Tarot

Practitioner of Air

Dark Angels Tarot

Unwillingness to wait

Universal Fantasy Tarot

The Queen of the unattainable peak

Fey Tarot

Living onward even if scarred by pain

Shaman Tarot

Changing shape, from one to many

Tarot of the Pagan Cats

Encouraging thinking and observation

Tarot of the Dark Grimoire

Cruel stability

Manga Tarot

Breaking the chain of conflict

KING OF SWORDS

Analysis – Judgement

Keywords

Analysis, Judge, Power, Authority, Charisma, Order, Decisive, Clear, Analytical, Impartiality, rationality, diplomatic, Precise, Tactical, Logic, Intellectual, Focused, Articulate, Authoritative, Guide, Just, Father, Brilliance.

Alternate names

The Judge

The Image

A King sits on a throne, holding an unsheathed sword in his right hand. It points diagonally to the heavens. He rules and passes judgement dressed in full armor. His throne is surrounded by bushes and the fallen leaves show how a strong wind just stopped. The King's throne is carved in relief with wings and fairies, symbolic of air. His expression is stern yet calm. His beard is white and his eyes are tired by his constant watchfullness.

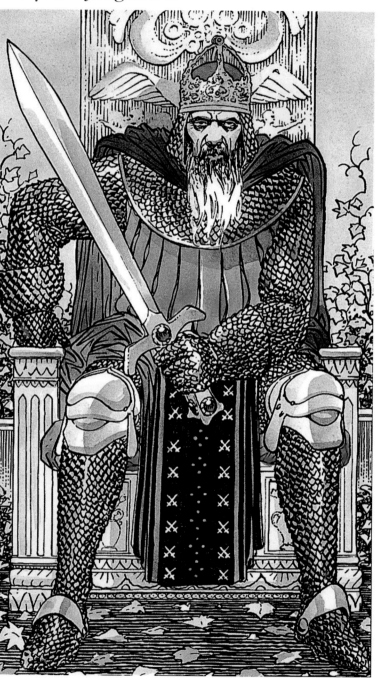

The burden of responsibility

The King of Swords is a complex character. His appearance may display qualities appearing gruff, scary and awesome. Once he establishes a sincere relationship with you, you realize behind the breastplate of the warrior rests a sensitive, noble and sociable soul. This man loves justice and order. He tends to take authority and power over all things. He is a fine thinker, brought by rational analysis and is able to devote time to study.

Examining his negative qualities, this sovereign tends to be distrustful and suspicious, especially with those he does not know. He can become bitter, even sour. His sword is an integral part of his way of being. He is not to be taken lightly as he will not suffer fools gladly. He is the most direct Tarot card in the deck. He is a man of great knowledge, who gives more importance to principle than he gives to himself or to the people he loves.

Reflected in You

The King of Swords is activated within you when you are speaking, writing, ordering, or clearly stating how you feel, what you want and how things should be. He is within you when you judge and evaluate a situation and desire your effect upon it. This extremely active King is within you when you effectively change your world and circumstances.

Traditional Interpretations

Upright: All things associated with the idea of Judgment and all its connections. Power, control and authority. Political attitudes, law and the prerogatives of the crown.
Reversed: Cruelty, perversion and barbarism. Malice and bad intentions.

The Physical Persona

Occupations: Boss, Judge, Police Officer, Academic, Principle, Government, Lawyer, Military Officer, Executive, Dictator, Doctor, Public Speaker, Analyst, Advisor, Scientist, Novelist
Appearance: Man, dark haired, dark eyes and fair complexion.

Strategy, Behavior and Attitude

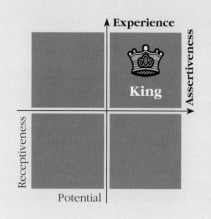

Experience

Assertiveness

Receptiveness

King

Potential

Mental Control

Control: Deciding, drive, knowledge, educate, evaluate, judge, arrange, plan, select and manage.

Mind: Thoughts, concepts, words, studies, theories, definitions, questions, concerns and conflict analysis.

Assertiveness: Business, initiative, aggressiveness, belief, confidence, extraversion, determination and masculinity.

Experience: Competence, skill, knowledge, customs, security, calm, lucid, certainty and habit.

Aspects of the Arcana expressed in various decks

Lo Scarabeo Tarot

The Air King

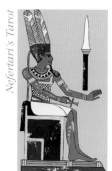

Nefertari's Tarot

The judge King

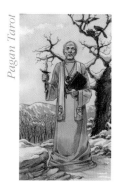

Pagan Tarot

Elder of Air

Dark Angels Tarot

Lost in regret

Universal Fantasy Tarot

Pride in strength and justice

Fey Tarot

The king who sacrificed all and still has hope

Shaman Tarot

The master of the arrow

Tarot of the Pagan Cats

Perfect understanding is not knowing all

Tarot of the Dark Grimoire

Cruel rulership

Manga Tarot

Stern but fair wisdom

PAGE OF CUPS

Enthusiasm – Superficiality

Keywords

Enthusiasm, Messenger, News, Intuition, Psychic, Purpose, Idea, Receptivity, Catalyst, Friend, Romantic, Gracious, Joyful, Emotional, Contemplative, Gentle, Sweet, Open, Insightful, Devoted, Instinctive, Emotive, Perceptual, Visceral, Noncognitive.

Alternate names

Knave, Princess, The Dreamer

The Image

A young Page stands upon flat ground dressed in a colorful costume. A backdrop of rolling water is displayed behind him. He holds a cup in his right hand, his left hand is pointing to the sandy ground with the fingers outstretched. The cup is simple and golden. A fish emerges from within. The Page seems to listen closely to the message the fish brings forth.

Falling in love

The Page of Cups represents a young person, boy or girl, of great sensitivity, culture and beauty. She reflects wellness and peace. She carries profound psychic ability. She may seem superficial and even frivolous due to her eccentric attitudes expressing herself via clothing, language, or other forms of communication.

She expresses a gentle and poetic personality. Her goal is not necessarily seductive, but her relationship to abstract dimensions of beauty, to a utopian vision of life and human relationships is beguiling. She is an idealistic and generous person capable of intense dedication to those she loves. This translates into a spirit of sacrifice. At times, the Page of Cups will disappear but never completely. Romance is the essential element of her existence.

Reflected in You

The Page of Cups is reflected in you when you feel dreamy and are lost in the worlds of the imagination. Beautiful emotions, like falling in love with people, places, or the arts awaken the Page within you. She is always whispering psychic information to you; simply listen carefully to hear her.

Traditional Interpretations

Upright: Psychic activity. Person open to inner guidance. A young artist or poet. Signifies news, message and application Reflection and meditation. Vivid response to beauty and art.
Reversed: Disappointment and artifice. Ignoring and suppressing emotions within. Ignoring messages.

The Physical Persona

Occupations: Psychic, Medium, All Creative Arts, Dancer, Performer, Writing, Photography, Visionary, Therapist, Service Industries, Clergy, Guidance Counselor
Appearance: Young girl, light brown hair, fair skin and light eyes.

270

Strategy, Behavior and Attitude

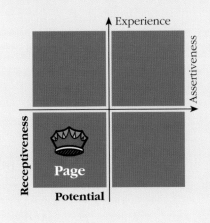

Experience

Assertiveness

Receptiveness

Page

Potential

Emotional Learning

Learning: Learn, feel, listen, experiment, invent, discover, explore, change and improve.

Emotions: Sensations, feelings, spirituality, emotions, dreams, passions, intuitions and unconscious memories.

Receptiveness: Listening, waiting, patience, understanding, reflection, internalization, introspection and femininity.

Potential: future, youth, opportunity, ingenuity, desire, hope, growth and innovation.

Aspects of the Arcana expressed in various decks

Lo Scarabeo Tarot

The water lover

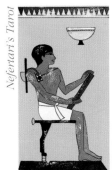
Nefertari's Tarot

The dreamer

Pagan Tarot

The Undine (Water elemental)

Dark Angels Tarot

Child of love

Universal Fantasy Tarot

The daydreamer

Fey Tarot

Kinship and affection, independent of form or race

Shaman Tarot

Healing spirit

Tarot of the Pagan Cats

Standing in peace

Tarot of the Dark Grimoire

The guardian at the threshold of water

Manga Tarot

Harmony in the flowing waters

271

KNIGHT OF CUPS

Feeling - Attraction

Keywords

Seduction, Flattery, Seducer, Approach, Invitation, Encouragement, Praise, Chivalrous, Pleasure-Loving, Imagination, Compassionate, Reflective, Introspection, Sensitive, Warm, Idealization, Temperamental.

Alternate names

Prince, The Lover

The Image

The knight and his horse pause before a lake, near a waterfall. The knight is dressed in full armor but the visor of his helmet is open. The metal of his armor shines blue, symbolic of the element of water. He holds a simple golden cup in his right hand while holding the reins in his left. His gaze is directed on or above his cup.

The seducer seduced

The Knight of Cups reflects an interestingly contradictory personality. He can be calm and serene like water, but also rumbling and volatile like a wave. He has the qualities of both a warrior and a pacifist.

His sensitive soul leads him to understand and help neighbors and friends. He is equally known to be hard and inflexible toward those he perceives as cruel. He loves art, nature and is tied to the family and the people he cares about. However, he is often the first to violate or betray them. He enjoys seduction for the sake of conquest, then struggles through the bonds he has created. He neither respects nor cares for rules or limitations and is extremely vain. He is a rather irresistible heartbreaker.

Reflected in You

When you are cultivating the art of seduction to have your way with someone, expressing your feelings toward another in a romantic way, or pulsing with emotion, this Knight is activated within you. All of your charming and artistic qualities stem from the Knight of Cups.

Traditional Interpretations

Upright: The arrival and approach of a message. A messenger. Advances, intentions and seductive attitude. Invitations and encouragement. Haunted by one's dreams. Dreamy, poetic behavior. Lightening fast speed of emotion but a lack of action. Love at first sight.
Reversed: Deceit, artifice and subtlety. Fraud and duplicity. Overactive imagination. Delusions of grandeur.

The Physical Persona

Occupations: Salesman, All Creative Arts Professions, Acting, Dancing, Writing, Therapist, Teacher, All Aspects of Medical Field and Patient Care, Small Business Owner, Makeup and Fashion Artist, Philosopher.
Appearance: Young male, light brown hair, fair skin and light eyes.

Strategy, Behavior and Attitude

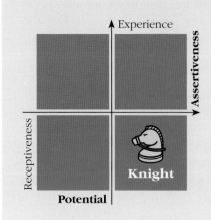

Experience ↑

Assertiveness →

Receptiveness

Potential

Knight

Emotional Action

Action: Decide, move, do, believe, conclude, risk, exposure, progress, choose, fight and break up.

Emotions: Sensations, feelings, spirituality, emotions, dreams, passions, intuitions and unconscious memories.

Assertiveness Arts, initiative, aggressiveness, belief, confidence, extroversion, determination and masculinity.

Potential: Future, youth, opportunity, ingenuity, desire, hope, growth and innovation.

Aspects of the Arcana expressed in various decks

Lo Scarabeo Tarot

The tamer of instincts

Nefertari's Tarot

Pride of innocence

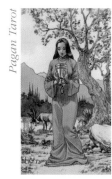
Pagan Tarot

Apprentice of Water

Dark Angels Tarot

The temptress in the mist

Universal Fantasy Tarot

The ancient centaur sage

Fey Tarot

The joy of a new meeting

Shaman Tarot

Seeking healing in life energies

Tarot of the Pagan Cats

Prudence while crossing a river

Tarot of the Dark Grimoire

The protector of dreams

Manga Tarot

The quiet surface of the bottomless power

274

QUEEN OF CUPS

Sensitivity – Emotionality

Keywords

Sensitivity, Emotionalism, Wife, Lover, Friend, Empathy, Understanding, Listening, Affectionate, Love, Joy, Responsiveness, Sympathy, Dreamer, Artist, Charming, Caring, Listener, Tranquil, Reflecting, Alluring, Maudlin, Warm, Mysterious, Kind, Sweet, Supportive, Tender-hearted, Compassionate.

Alternate names

The Friend

The Image

The Queen holds a precious golden cup in her hands while intently gazing upon it. She sits oceanside, her slippers almost touching the calm waters while resting on smooth ocean stones. Her dress echoes the ripples of the tides, as if she were made of sea foam. Her throne looks as if made by seashells. Great cliffs emulating the Rocks of Gibraltar rise behind her to greet the salty, coastal air. Has she dreamt this scene or is she the dream herself?

Listening with the heart

The Queen of Cups is a figure of great charm, capable of seducing with her grace, rather than with her beauty. Aware of her seductive powers, she can manipulate situations easily. She assumes an attitude of exaggerated romance and pretends she does not have weaknesses. In fact, her soul is perpetually poised between dream and rationality, between emotion and self-control.

The Queen of Cups is jovial but not willing to become involved with the complications of others when they are dark or negative. Sometimes she is far too sensitive to external influences, so she takes great care to arrive at decisions independently. She is a sincere friend, a loyal wife and devoted lover. She has a sweet, spontaneous and generous side but can be distracted and capricious. She is deeply empathetic to others.

Reflected in You

When you are empathetic and feel deeply for another person, truly knowing what it means to walk in their shoes, you embody the Queen of Cups. Emotional nurturing, creative support and flirtation are all activating her qualities inside of you. It is important not to take on and bring home the emotions and attitudes of others if you carry many of the Queen of Cups empathetic qualities.

Traditional Interpretations

Upright: Honest and faithful behavior. Supportive and willing. Confidant, loving temperament and the gift of clairvoyance. Success, happiness and pleasure. Wisdom, virtue and a good parent. Great empathy.
Reversed: Person who should not be trusted. Wicked, dissolution and depravity. Emotional chameleon. Deviously manipulative. Blocked emotions and suffocated needs.

The Physical Persona

Occupations: Artist, Poet, Psychic, Medium, Healer, Therapist, Crafter, Florist, All Public Service Careers, Doctor, Nurse, Midwife, Doula, Tarot Card Reader
Appearance: Blonde haired female, fair skin and light eyes.

Strategy, Behavior and Attitude

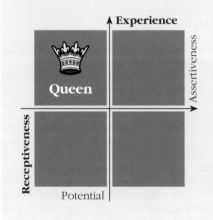

Experience

Assertiveness

Queen

Receptiveness

Potential

Emotional Perception

Perception: Receive, understand, listen, think, adapt, accept, embrace, tolerate, convert and endure.

Emotions: Sensations, feelings, spirituality, emotions, dreams, passions, intuitions and unconscious memories.

Receptiveness Listening, waiting, patience, understanding, reflection, internalization, introspection and femininity.

Experience: Competence, skill, knowledge, customs, security, calm, lucid, certainty and habit.

Aspects of the Arcana expressed in various decks

Lo Scarabeo Tarot

The source of affection

Nefertari's Tarot

Dwelling in family

Pagan Tarot

Practitioner of Water

Dark Angels Tarot

Waiting for the lovers return

Universal Fantasy Tarot

The Queen of the house

Fey Tarot

Living your dreams and giving them shape

Shaman Tarot

Healing where you walk

Tarot of the Pagan Cats

Encouraging sentiments

Tarot of the Dark Grimoire

Dreaming stability

Manga Tarot

Wonders at the underwater palace

277

KING OF CUPS

Charisma – Composure

Keywords

Charisma, Composure, Patron, Protector, Creative, Vision, Support, Charm, Sympathetic, Intuitive, Placid, Cooperation, Wise, Loving, Jovial, Loyal, Affectionate, Protective, Calm, Subtle, compassionate, Aristocratic, Cultural, Chivalrous.

Alternate names

The Artist

The Image

The King sits on his throne above a rolling ocean. The sea is churning and active, yet he remains steady and calm. He holds a simple golden cup in his right hand. His left hand grasps a short golden scepter. A necklace with a fish hangs on his chest and his throne is decorated with sea horses and seashells. His right toe almost dips into the salty ocean. A dolphin swims off to his right and a pitching ship rolls to his left.

Cultivating emotions

The King of Cups is strong and authoritative. He can successfully hide his good-natured attitudes behind this exterior. His character leads him to direct and control events around him. His strength comes from self-confidence and his ability to experience emotions without being dominated by them.

At home, within the family, his affection is sincere. His goals are long term and his future foresight moves beyond his own mortality. His fiery temper becomes belligerent if provoked. Generally, he prefers diplomacy in all matters. Artists and cultured people seek his company and protection because he is a man of the arts. He is a successful artist, able to see his creative projects through to the end, watching them flower and grow as they take on a life of their own.

Reflected in You

The King of Cups operates within you when you have a dream you see through to fruition. The King is distinguished by making the things he has imagined actually happen in the world. When you do the same, you are operating like the King of Cups.

Traditional Interpretations

Upright: Very fair person willing to help you. Success in arts, sciences, or divinity. Artistic or legal success. A person of great vision who is capable of putting this vision into action.
Reversed: Dishonesty, double-crossed and extortion. Injustice, robbery and considerable loss. A person suffering mental issues.

The Physical Persona

Occupations: Film director, Composer, Artists of All Types, All Health Professions, Counseling, Education, Aquatic Professions, Environmentalist, Sales.
Appearance: A mature man with light hair, graying or white, fair skin and light eyes.

Strategy, Behavior and Attitude

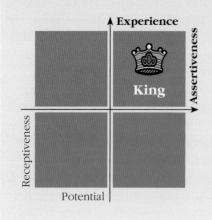

Experience ↑
Assertiveness →
Receptiveness ↓
Potential

King

Emotional Control

Control: Deciding, drive, knowledge, educate, evaluate, judge, arrange, plan, select and manage.

Emotions: Sensations, feelings, spirituality, emotions, dreams, passions, intuitions and unconscious memories.

Assertiveness: Business, initiative, aggressiveness, belief, confidence, extraversion, determination and masculinity.

Experience: Competence, skill, knowledge, customs, security, calm, lucid, certainty and habit.

Aspects of the Arcana expressed in various decks

Lo Scarabeo Tarot

The Water King

Nefertari's Tarot

The King surrounded by harmony

Pagan Tarot

Elder of Water

Dark Angels Tarot

Lost in passion

Universal Fantasy Tarot

Pride in endurance and constancy.

Fey Tarot

The generous king

Shaman Tarot

The master of healing

Tarot of the Pagan Cats

Perfect bliss is not self centered

Tarot of the Dark Grimoire

Dreaming rulership

Manga Tarot

Life changing wisdom

PAGE OF PENTACLES

Practical sense – Effort

Keywords

Student, Application, Study, Learning, Practical, Realistic, Stable, Studious, Warm, Examine, Detect, Curious, Steadfast, Dependable, Cautious, Certain, Novice, Apprentice, Schoolchild, Undergraduate.

Alternate names

Knave, Princess, The Apprentice

The Image

A young person gently balances a golden pentacle on his fingertips and gazes intently upon it. He stands in a gentle summer landscape. A plowed field waits in the distance ready to be fertilized. A group of green trees balance the rising hills in the distance.

Day to day effort

This Page represents a young person, boy or girl, committed to work and practical activities. Pages are often in search of a mentor to help them hone their skills. Their goal is to become successful on their own merits. The Page of Pentacles learns about everything around her and builds her knowledge base through day-to-day activities.

The Page of Pentacles can be absent-minded, sloppy and careless of practical problems. Her enthusiasm and vitality toward learning will sometimes leave her distracted from other responsibilities. This is only because she fully invests herself in the task at hand and the world slips away. The Page of Pentacles excels in all goals. She displays an admirable perseverance and tenacity in the direction she sets for herself. She is the perpetual student.

Reflected in You

If you find yourself caught up in the act of learning or creating and when you are lost in the fascination of the world, this is the moment the Page of Pentacles operates within you.

Traditional Interpretations

Upright: Eager student. Study, reflection and knowledge. News and the bearer of these messages. Practical application of all things. Love of learning.
Reversed: Extravagance, profligacy and generosity. Disillusionment of learning.

The Physical Persona

Occupations: Student, Farmer, Florist, Bookkeeper, Social Worker, Secretary, Librarian, Intern, Childcare Worker, Researcher, Chemist
Appearance: Young brown-haired female, dark complexion and dark eyes.

Strategy, Behavior and Attitude

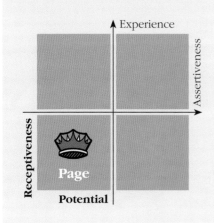

Experience

Assertiveness

Receptiveness

Page

Potential

Practical Learning

Learning: Learn, feel, listen, experiment, invent, discover, explore, change and improve.

Practicality: Physical, things, reality, objects, substance, truth, stability, robustness, reliability, perseverance and simplicity.

Receptiveness: Listening, waiting, patience, understanding, reflection, internalization, introspection and femininity.

Potential: Future, youth, opportunity, ingenuity, desire, hope, growth and innovation.

Aspects of the Arcana expressed in various decks

Lo Scarabeo Tarot

The Earth lover

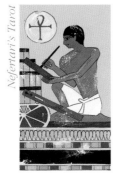

Nefertari's Tarot

The Accountant

Pagan Tarot

The Gnome (Earth elemental)

Dark Angels Tarot

Child of family

Universal Fantasy Tarot

The gilded officer

Fey Tarot

Wandering aimlessly

Shaman Tarot

Drums of creation

Tarot of the Pagan Cats

Beginning of a material adventure

Tarot of the Dark Grimoire

The guardian at the threshold of earth

Manga Tarot

Cherishing dawn in your domain

283

KNIGHT OF PENTACLES

Realism – Pragmatism

Keywords

Realism, Professionalism, Pragmatism, Dependable, Service, Traditionalist, Offering, Determined, Dogmatic, Faithful, Hardworking, Honest, Realistic, Persistent.

Alternate names

Prince, The Builder

The Image

The Knight sits on a massive, patient, workhorse. He holds a golden pentacle in his right hand while holding the reins in his left. He is covered head to toe in armor and a flaming plume springs from his helmet. He gazes at or past his pentacle. The horse stands near a tilled field. The scene is ripe for growth, the damp earth patiently waiting for a seed to be planted.

Creating prosperity

The remarkable quality of the Knight of Pentacles lies in the hard work and commitment he places on everything he turns his attention to. All situations absorb his serious and lasting attention. He treats every task as a duty assigned to him.

The Knight of Pentacles carries an ambition for improving his economic situation and he relies on his intellectual stamina. This Knight is willing to work long hours in a row, giving up rest periods or holidays in order to obtain satisfactory results. Of course, this takes a toll on his personal relationships. He is often a solitary individual, a lonely character who hides his weaknesses behind the success he has achieved. He is an honest person, responsible and trustworthy. He is always willing to help you.

Reflected in You

The moment you settle down and get to work you embody the Knight of Pentacles. This Knight can work diligently through the night, burn the midnight oil and get the job done. It may not be done quickly but it will be meticulous and well thought out.

Traditional Interpretations

Upright: Helpful, prompt and responsible person. Honesty. What you see is what you get. Hard work and thoughtfulness before action is taken.
Reversed: Inertia, laziness and rest. Stagnation, even placid, discouragement and carelessness.

The Physical Persona

Occupations: Craftsperson, Entrepreneur, Physical Trainer, Farmer, Chef, Gambler, Hunter, Veterinarian, Retail Worker
Appearance: Young man with dark hair, dark complexion and dark eyes.

Strategy, Behavior and Attitude

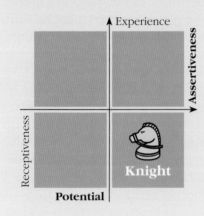

Practical Action

Action: Decide, move, do, believe, conclude, risk, exposure, progress, choose, fight and break up.

Practicality: Physical, things, reality, objects, substance, truth, stability, robustness, reliability, perseverance and simplicity.

Assertiveness: Business, initiative, aggressiveness, belief, confidence, extroversion, determination and masculinity.

Potential: Future, youth, opportunity, ingenuity, desire, hope, growth and innovation.

Aspects of the Arcana expressed in various decks

The Plower

Pride of prosperity

Apprentice of Earth

The shadow mourner

The King of the little world

The joy of returning home

The powerful energy of the Earth

Careful positioning

The Protector of the dwelling

The quiet center, aside from conflict

QUEEN OF PENTACLES

Abundance – Conservation

Keywords

Heiress, Wealth, Comfort, Domesticity, Protection, Conservation, Sensuous, Generous, Warmhearted, Caretaker, Decorator, Practical, Capable, Traditional, Systematic, Orderly, Caring, Conscious, Sensual, Nurture, Nurse

Alternate names

The Preserver

The Image

The Queen holds a golden pentacle in her hands and she gazes down upon it. Her throne is heavy, carved with cherubs, flora and rams - symbols of Earth. Her crown covers her entire head. Her veil protects her entire body, which is covered. The landscape around her is lush and fragrant as if at the height of summer. She has naked feet and her toes connect to the earth. Flowers of many kinds blossom and bloom in her grove and mountains are visible in the distance.

Taking care of little things

The Queen of Pentacles is a woman able to take full advantage of what she has acquired. She recognizes the value of everything from people to objects. She carries the unique ability to exploit her own talents and the talents of those around her in the most advantageous way possible. Her strong practical sense does not hinder her ability to see nuances or details. She is careful and wise not to fall into the trap of excessive behavior.

The Queen of Pentacles will prove to be bullish and protective if she or someone she loves is provoked. This will lead to over cautious behavior, especially with regards to children. Even if she sees a possible advantage, she will never take a risk if she doesn't have to. She prefers the safer route to a risky option. She tends toward the predictable and is an excellent administrator. She is the goddess of house and home.

Reflected in You

The Queen of Pentacles thrives within you when you are creating a beautiful environment around yourself. The Queen of Pentacles is the master manipulator of physical things and makes the world an easier and more beautiful place to be in.

Traditional Interpretations

Upright: Opulence, generosity and magnificence. Security and freedom. Nurturing the house and home. Availability to others. Sensuality in all things. Great trust and warm heart.
Reversed: Evil and suspicion. Fear, mistrust and coldness.

The Physical Persona

Occupations: Gardener, Caretaker, Teacher, Nurse, Finance, Healer, Chef, Business Owner, Decorator, Designer, Sculptor, Restaurateur
Appearance: Dark haired woman, dark skin and brown eyes.

288

Strategy, Behavior and Attitude

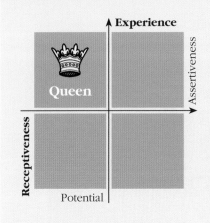

Practical Perception

Perception: Receive, understand, listen, think, adapt, accept, embrace, tolerate, convert and endure.

Practicality: Physical, things, reality, objects, substance, truth, stability, robustness, reliability, perseverance and simplicity.

Receptiveness: Listening, waiting, patience, understanding, reflection, internalization, introspection and femininity.

Experience: Competence, skill, knowledge, customs, security, calm and lucid.

Aspects of the Arcana expressed in various decks

Lo Scarabeo Tarot

The source of contemplation

Nefertari's Tarot

Dwelling in opulence

Pagan Tarot

Practitioner of Earth

Dark Angels Tarot

Waiting for things to pass

Universal Fantasy Tarot

The Queen of the castle

Fey Tarot

Music builds harmony between body and spirit

Shaman Tarot

Maternal instinct

Tarot of the Pagan Cats

Encouraging relaxation

Tarot of the Dark Grimoire

Possessive stability

Manga Tarot

Sharing bountiful things with a welcome

289

KING OF PENTACLES

Administration – Trade

Keywords

Businessman, Ambition, Money, Practical Intelligence, Success, Materialistic, Enterprising, Security, Successful, Concrete, Stable, Commerce, Administration, Practical, Dependable, Maturation, Germination.

Alternate names

The Provider

The Image

The King sits amidst the essence and beauty of growth, abundance and prosperity. The King of Pentacles represents complete harvest and abundance. His throne is decorated with rams and foliage, his clothing with grapes and flora. A pentacle is balanced between his left knee and hand while a scepter is in his right hand. A concrete wall rises behind him. Further still, the rising towers of a city.

Sharing abundance

The King of Pentacles is an able administrator. He makes his money through good investments and concrete projects. He will, at times, be reckless with speculations in various commercial and financial areas. Whatever the case, becoming wealthy is not his only objective. He avoids luxury but loves the wellbeing that, thanks to his parsimonious use of money, he attains not only for himself, but also for his family and business partners.

He shines in every area of his life and the King of Pentacles manages to attain a level of economic security without becoming greedy. He loves the value of things, he follows his instincts and never forgets to see the practical side. He always unites economy with practicality. He will always look for an advantage and a source of profit. It is difficult for him to let go and live in the moment. He also finds it difficult to be carried away by enthusiasm because he is grounded and practical.

Reflected in You

You access your inner King of Pentacles when you are successful and enjoying that success. You can look at the things that you have created, take pleasure in them and reach out for more. The responsibility of your finances all lay in the King of Pentacles aspect of yourself.

Traditional Interpretations

Upright: Great security and importance placed on inherent value. Practical intelligence. Excelling in all areas of business and intellectual activities. Enterprising attitude toward mathematics and culture. Great success.
Reversed: Vice, weakness and abjection. Depravity, corruption, or danger. A person overcome with greed.

The Physical Persona

Occupations: Chief Financial Officer, Banker, Venture Capitalist, Real Estate Agent, Business Owner, Restaurateur, Collector, Curator
Appearance: A mature man with dark hair, dark eyes and olive skin.

Strategy, Behavior and Attitude

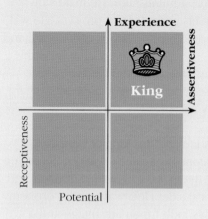

Practical Control

Control: Decide, guide, know, instruct, evaluate, judge, place, plan, select, direct.

Practicality: Physicality, things, reality, objects, substance, truth, stability, solidity, reliability, consistency, simplicity.

Assertiveness: Activity, initiative, aggression, conviction, trust in oneself, extroverted, determination and masculinity.

Experience: Competency, ability, understanding, methodical, security, calmness, lucidity, certainty and habits.

Aspects of the Arcana expressed in various decks

The Earth King

The King living in opulence

Elder of Earth

Lost in his own things

Pride in mastery and art

The king who ruled everything

The master of the visions

Perfect abundance is not greediness

Possessive rulership

Bountiful, learned wisdom

Your journey begins here. Enter the forest of symbols, myth and Tarot.

Two Essential Steps

In order to cultivate an active and empowering Tarot practice, the Reader must consider two essential steps. These two steps, as a whole, will encourage the Reader to take an active stance, experiment boldly and use the cards without fear or prejudice. The Reader will also learn to approach the Tarot with both her intuitive and sensitive side in conjunction with her logical and rational mindset.

1. Forge a Relationship

It is essential to foster a relationship with the cards. Various systems exist to do just this. *Tarot Fundamentals* and future volumes will unlock various systems that will bring Tarot's symbols and meanings to life. Personal and intuitive tarot meanings will be picked up along the way. A combination of traditional meanings and unique personal understandings offer the richest Tarot experience. Understanding and un-locking the tapestry of the cards can become a pleasurable, lifelong quest. Tarot's meanings, though systematic, are endless. Each Reader brings unique personal perspectives to their deck of cards. Card interpretations and readings are as unique as every person walking on the earth. No two people read the cards the same way. A personal relationship with the cards is the most important step a Reader will take.

2. Actively Use the Cards

Begin using Tarot immediately. Tarot practice requires just that: practice. It is not enough to know and memorize Tarot meanings and systems. To read about the Tarot but not use the Tarot would be like holding the key to a shiny new car and never firing the ignition. Start your engine and begin flipping cards, asking questions and performing readings.

TAROT USAGE

Divination and Cartomancy

Tarot cards are most commonly used for divination. Fortune-telling is what the general public usually thinks of when they think of Tarot cards. Divination is the worldwide practice of inquiry into future events and matters. The art of divination is as old as humanity itself. The word derives from the Latin *divinare* meaning, "to foresee, to be inspired by a god." Divination attempts to gain future insight via a standardized process or ritual. Divination is a blanket term and includes a variety of systems: tea leaf reading, palmistry, numerology, astrology, etc. Using Tarot as a tool of divination is referred to as Cartomancy. The person who reads the cards is called the Cartomancer or - most commonly - the Reader. The person who receives the reading is called the Querent or Client.

A Cartomancer drawing the cards for the Celtic Cross Spread.

Julian Jaynes (1920-1997),
American Psychologist.

Psychologist Julian Jaynes' Four Categories of Divination

Omens
The primitive but most enduring method of divination. It is an indication of future outcomes based on a seen event or unusual occurrence. Superstitions are often regarded as omens.

Spontaneous
Free form divination is spontaneous. The answer derives from whatever object the diviner happens to see or hear. Bibliomancy is an example of spontaneous divination with books. A question is posed and a person riffles through the text of a book. The first passage their eyes or finger fall on contains their answer. A fun example of spontaneous divination is entering a crowded space and asking a question aloud. Eavesdrop on passersby and listen to the first complete sentence overheard.

Sortilege (cleromancy)
Sortilege consists of casting lots, or sortes. It could be sticks, stones, beans, coins, dice, or any other group of items. It is an ancient form of divination and even referred to in the Bible. Modern playing cards and board games developed from sortilege.

Augury
Augury is the art of ranking a set of given possibilities. Augury includes divination by studying the flight patterns of birds and dowsing, the practice of locating ground water or other buried objects with a dowsing rod. Etruscan, Babylonian and Hittite augury included the inspection of entrails of sacrificed sheep and poultry for prophetic signs.

Reading Tarot cards to discover information on future events is a form of both Sortilege and Augury.

Multiple purposes for using Tarot

In the next page:
Let the past inform your present and the present empower your future.

While Divination is probably the most common use of Tarot, there are many other ways for which Tarot can be helpful. A practioner will eventually choose which aspect of the Tarot experience they are interested in and give other aspects less attention, if any at all.

Knowing the past and the future

Tarot is most commonly used to answer questions about the past and the future. However, the future is not written in stone. Future outcomes hinge on choice and action. Tarot works well when it helps people to build their future.

Tarot reflects options but the choice of path is yours.

Reading the Future vs. Changing Your Future

You can learn to read your future using Tarot cards and have a great deal of fun doing so. Did you know that you could also use Tarot to change your future? The same way you request information regarding a future event from a card, you can request guidance from the cards about how to cir-cumnavigate a troublesome issue. You can discover how to make the issue less burdensome. In fact, you can completely change your future by focusing on the present. Best of all, the answer stems from your own subconscious. Using the cards as a focal point and a bit of common sense, Tarot becomes an effective device promoting positive and helpful changes in life.

Why Read the Past?

People approach Tarot with a keen interest on what will happen in the immediate future. You can flip a card right now and glean some insight on what will happen tomorrow. But we often forget that what occurred in our past has a direct impact on the choices we make and actions we take. Using Tarot to recover past information and motivations does much to improve the quality of life and make better decisions.

Decision Making and Advice

A Tarot deck is helpful when feeling indecisive. Use Tarot to clarify inconsequential matters like what to prepare for dinner. Use Tarot to clarify matters of the greatest consequence like how to best express your marital dissatisfaction to your partner. Tarot will provide answers to simple or complex issues.

Self-Reflection

Self-reflection is the capacity for every human to exercise introspection about themselves and curiosity about their fundamental nature, purpose and essence. The act of self-reflection begins with an interest in oneself. It often leads to questions about humanity and expands to intriguing roads of philosophic thought. When asking, "Why am I here?" or "What is my purpose?" you have engaged in the act of self-reflection. Tough questions with no immediate answer can be helped with Tarot. A card or archetype will often serve as a signpost toward your personal truth and spirituality.

Meditation

Meditation is the practice of quieting the mind and self-inducing beneficial consciousness. Meditative practices often include a ritual object to be focused on. Tarot pictures, archetypes and images will offer the mind and eye a focal point. Meditation may be used to invoke a feeling or internal state. In such a case, the energy of a particular Tarot may be called on for inspiration. Regular and guided meditations are a technique used to explore Tarot itself. Meditation into a card will foster discovery of a deeper personal meaning within the cards. Meditation into cards can be done by yourself, using prerecorded material, with a trusted friend, or a professional hypnotherapist.

Focus

Reality can be overwhelming. Life offers an unlimited number of things to focus on and the mind can only focus on one thing at a time. Tarot's symbolic imagery offers a sanctuary. It provides a sacred space offering a chance to reflect, ponder, ask for guidance and information. Tarot slows the world down, takes us out of our head and gives us a chance to listen to ourselves.

Magic

Magic is the manipulation of natural energies to create a desired outcome. Magic is performed via ritual or spell. The spell is created and cast to manifest a desired result. Tarot is an excellent addition to spell work, magical and spiritual practice because each card contains archetypes, energies and potential scenarios.

Deck Collecting

Collectors will amass Tarot decks the same way bibliophiles collect books or stamp collectors treasure stamps. There are many decks to choose from with imagery spanning all of art history and symbolism. Self published and out of print decks can become valuable over time. Collections and collectors vary. Some collectors have every deck they can get their hands on; others focus on historical decks or art decks, while some collect themed decks.

Intuition/Psychic Building

Tarot and intuitive or psychic readings have always been intertwined. An active Tarot practice will activate intuition and natural psychic ability because reading Tarot exercises both of these facilities. Like any muscle in the body, the more it is exercised, the stronger and more valuable it becomes. Tarot is a doorway to the imagination, the supernatural self and latent power.

Entertainment

Tarot Readers are often hired as party entertainment along side henna tattoo artists, circus performers, palm readers, tea leaf readers, etc. You will also bump into Tarot Readers at certain dark and mysterious restaurants, nightclubs, festivals, street fairs and boardwalks.

Creative Endeavors from Inspiration to Installation

Artists, writers, filmmakers and poets through history have used Tarot themes and archetypes in their works.

View of Niki de Saint Phalle's Tarot Garden in Tuscany.

"Madame Sosostris, famous clairvoyant,
Had a bad cold, nevertheless
Is known to be the wisest woman in Europe,
With a wicked pack of cards. Here, said she,
Is your card, the drowned Phoenician Sailor,
(Those are pearls that were his eyes, Look!)
Here is Belladonna, the Lady of the Rocks,
The lady of situations.
Here is the man with three staves and here, the Wheel.
And here is the one-eyed merchant and this card,
Which is blank, is something he carries on his back,
Which I am forbidden to see. I do not find
The Hanged Man. Fear death by water."

T.S. Elliot's Wasteland

Tarot can be used as inspiration for an artistic project. For instance, a screenwriter may feel stuck in his screenplay. How does his hero escape the evil villain? The writer pulls a Tarot card to discover the solution.

Tarot symbols and cards are used as fine art and installation pieces. Niki de Saint Phalle's Tarot Garden in Tuscany, Italy is open to the public. It contains monumentally scaled Tarot mosaic sculptures, all twenty-two Major Arcana.

The walls of the Tarot Chapel, in the Chateau des Avenieres.

Nestled on France's Saleve mountain side, Le Chateau des Avenieres was built by Mary Wallace Schillito and her husband Assan Farid Dina. This eccentric couple had an eye for the esoteric when they built their chateau. They included a Tarot chapel. The walls of the chapel contain mosaic Marseille Tarot images blended with the occult mysteries of the Oswald Wirth Tarot.

Theatrical performances like New York City's Pattie Canova's *Souled Out* utilize Tarot as a device for audience communication. Haute Couture fashion houses use Tarot structure and themes to inspire clothing or fragrance lines. Modern artists, musicians and writers often include Tarot images. Tarot jewelry, clothing and folk art continue to evolve every day.

Games

Tarot was once played as a game in European courts and taverns. Modern people continue to play Tarot games. New and innovative Tarot board games hit the marketplace each year. Tarot games vary, some bring entertainment while others are played to access deeper Tarot card meanings and explore personal psychology.

Professional Tarot

Professional Tarot Readers around the world read the cards for clients online, one to one, in cafes and private offices. Readers are often hired for special events: product launches, bridal showers, or birthday parties. Tarot is often combined with other modalities like: life coaching, massage, reiki, astrology, hypnosis, etc. Professional readers often write, lecture and teach Tarot classes and retreats in addition to reading for a private clientele.

Gateway to the Esoteric Arts

Tarot acts as a doorway and introduction to esoteric, metaphysical arts. Astrology, Kabbalah, Magic, Numerology, Path working, Shamanic Journeying, etc., can be connected to Tarot's unique structure.

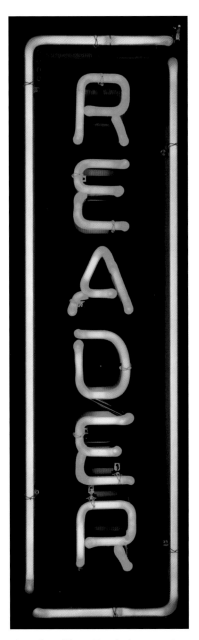

An urban Tarot Reader's neon sign glows in the darkness.

Hats a Tarot Reader Wears:

Philosopher	Occult Expert/Cabbalist
Art Historian	Alchemist
Symbologist	Astrologer
Fortune Teller	Numerologist
Therapist/Psychologist	Writer/Storyteller
Channeler	Healer
Comparative Religion Scholar	Mystic

SELECTING YOUR DECK

Hundreds of Tarot decks flood the market and Tarot diversity continues to expand. Readers may become confused when selecting a deck for study, reading and personal use. Keep your larger goals and a few tips in mind. It is easy and fun to discover a deck you will enjoy reading and studying for years to come.

Do not rush to select your deck, especially if you are new to Tarot. A deck whose images captivate you, draw you inside of them, pictures that keep you returning again and again, will help you in your learning process.

A few questions you can ask

Tarot is like cooking and each deck has a different flavor. The choice is yours. What whets your appetite?

What is your goal?
Before selecting a deck to purchase and read, ask yourself three questions:

᠀— What am I trying to achieve?"
᠀— What are my plans with for this deck?
᠀— What do I hope to accomplish?

Is your goal ownership?
Some people want a deck, any deck. These people are unlikely to read or study the Tarot; instead, they are looking for an intriguing decoration or a prop for a spooky party. When this is the case, virtually any deck will do. Decks with great artwork, or with strange and enticing names may be good choices.

Is your goal to become a Tarot Reader?

If so, the selected deck should offer a great deal of symbolic depth and rich images capable of inspiring intuitive insights. Because you will spend a great deal of time with the cards, it is important to select a deck you will find attractive and engaging. Who wants to spend hours upon hours with an unappealing or frightening deck? An intriguing deck draws you back again and again.

Is the goal to become a serious student of the Tarot?

If so, it is important to select a historical deck. Historical decks are the subject of scholarship. A popular deck will be featured in many books and reference works, making it easy to research. Many decks are packaged with a full-length companion book offering insights into the meaning of every symbol on every card.

Other Points to Consider

Fully Illustrated Decks

Many decks feature vivid images of every card while others only feature illustrations of Majors Arcana and Court Cards. It can be challenging to read a deck with nothing more than suit markers (wands, cups, swords and coins) on cards numbered Ace through Ten. For intuitive Readers, fully illustrated decks work best.

Style

Different decks have different visual styles. Some people find the heavy lines and delicate colors of older decks add an air of authenticity to the cards; others find such decks too "old fashioned." Some people prefer delicate watercolor or colored-pencil drawings; others are far more intrigued by the hypnotic clarity of computer-generated images. No one style is right or wrong. The Reader should find the style that suits him or her.

Size

If the goal is to acquire a deck for study purposes, large cards with clear illustrations may be the best choice. On the other hand, smaller cards are much easier to cut and shuffle.

A Reader with small hands may find larger decks difficult to work with over time. Before buying a deck, the Reader should try to handle a copy and determine his/her comfort with the size of the cards.

Theme

Themes add interest to Tarot decks and provide insights into the infinite number of ways Tarot's universal ideas can be expressed. Clearly, the Tarot of the Elves appeals to those especially intrigued by Elvin lore. For the right Reader, Tarot of the Elves becomes a powerful tool for divination and reflection.

When the Reader is choosing a deck exclusively for her own use, the Reader should feel free to choose any deck she finds appealing. That said, if the deck will be used for others, the Reader should consider whether or not all Querents will share her enthusiasm for elves, fairies, gnomes, Celtic culture, etc.

Themes provide a powerful frame for Tarot decks. A well-themed deck yields exquisite readings, like flowers from fertile, loamy soil.

Temperance from the Lo Scarabeo Tarot, concept by Mark McElroy and artwork by Anna Lazzarini. The Lo Scarabeo Tarot combines three essential Tarot traditions, the Rider Waite Smith, Marseille and Thoth deck. Yet, even the Lo Scarabeo Tarot is not a "perfect" deck.

Perfect Deck?

Not every deck is suitable for every purpose. A Reader's deck preference is likely to change over time as the Reader changes. Wise Readers are less likely to obsess over finding one perfect deck and more likely to experiment with a healthy selection of decks. This way, the reader may take advantage of the unique perspectives of as many decks as possible. The perfect deck may be the one that is right for you, right now. Once the need that lead you to your perfect deck is satisfied, it may be time to find a new deck.

Why More Than One Deck?

There are many reasons to own more than one Tarot deck. Efficiency with more than one style of cards will keep an experienced Reader on their toes. Multiple decks keep reading styles fresh.

You can also use different decks for different moods. For example, you may pick a particular deck to suit the mood you are in. If you are feeling melancholy you may choose a moody deck such as Dark Grimoire Tarot. Conversely, if you feel lighthearted and silly and you may choose to read with Happy Tarot. Feeling creative? Reach for New Vision Premium Tarot.

Different decks work for different purposes. You reserve one deck for magical use, another deck for meditation, another deck for healing, another deck for reading for the public, etc.

Theme The Reading

You can use different Tarot decks to theme the readings you perform for yourself or others. Different themes can suit your mood or your Querent's needs. A Querent who comes from a Christian background may enjoy working with a deck containing Christian Symbolism. Are you looking to spice up your relationship? Offer yourself and your lover a reading using the Kamasutra Tarot. Does your teenage niece have a soft spot for vampires? Give her a reading with the Gothic Tarot of the Vampires. Your Querent wants to work on issues of embracing her inner child? Use the Children Tarot. The varieties are endless.

Tarot and Children

Children will always be interested in what their parents do. If you read Tarot, be prepared to answer a lot of questions and to be surprised by their interest and skill.

Looking for a fresh definition or interpretation of a Tarot card? Ask a child what the picture means and prepare for an amazing answer. A child's perceptions and ability to risk without fear yields illuminating and surprisingly deep answers about what a particular image may mean.

Tarot is a new and unique way to communicate with children. Several Tarot board games offer questions, themes and jumping off points from the cards which lead to great discussion points. You can open new lines of communication as you talk to children about images or themes expressed in the cards.

No matter how you integrate children into your reading practice, be sure to use cards that are age appropriate and in line with your core values.

YOUR TAROT LIBRARY

You can find many ways to organize your Tarot library. Most people will organize their decks "on a hunch." However, rational organization will help to understand decks and their potential, which help you grow as a Reader. Below is a description of five Major families of decks, divided according to their nature and usage. Many decks, especially very good ones, will obviously have claims to more than one category.

Historical Decks

Historical Tarot decks are reproductions, reconstructions, or reinterpretations of the great decks of the past. They are selected from a number of history-making cards. Studying and understanding these decks leads to an excellent understanding of Tarot origins. It leads to a personal awakening of the original symbols and images on each card. Some historical decks are true reproductions, showing the old age of the original cards. Others are restorations or reconstruction, and have a more modern feeling.

The World from three different historical decks. From left to right: Marseille Tarot (Nicolas Conver in Marseille, 1760) ; Estensi Tarot (Ferrara, ca. 1470) ; Sola Busca Tarot (Venice, ca. 1491).

Esoteric Decks

Inspired by esoteric philosophy and symbolism, this category includes decks created by history's most influential occultists as well as metaphysical decks developed by modern mystery schools. The esoteric philosophy of Tarot masters leads to a temple of mystical knowledge.

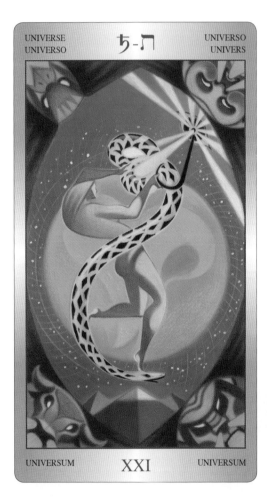
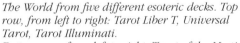

The World from five different esoteric decks. Top row, from left to right: Tarot Liber T, Universal Tarot, Tarot Illuminati.
Bottom row, from left to right: Tarot of the Mystic Spiral, Initiatory Tarot of the Golden Dawn.

Art Decks

Artistry and beauty are the keys for interpreting Art decks. They offer new emotional and intuitive insights using visual expression. Art decks lead us inside captivating worlds, the shadowy place where image intermingles with meaning. These decks explore and break emotional boundaries. They describe the indescribable.

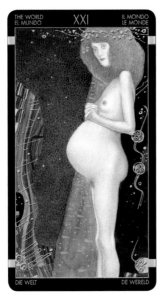

The World from five different art decks. Top row, from left to right: Tarot Art Nouveau, Klimt Tarot, Crystal Tarot.
Bottom row, from left to right: Botticelli Tarot, Impressionist Tarot.

Cultural Decks

Cultural decks bridge the gap between traditional archetypes and the collective imagination. They create a mirror that reflects the experience of the world around us. Reading with these decks brings us on an exciting journey of rediscovery, allowing us to glimpse familiar Tarot symbolism through a cultural kaleidoscope.

The World from five different cultural decks. Top row, from left to right: Universal Fantasy Tarot, Mayan Tarot, Gothic Tarot of Vampires.
Bottom row, from left to right: Tarot of the Celtic Fairies, Tarot of the Sacred Sites.

Metaphysical Decks

Modern Tarot uses cards as spiritual and meditative tools. The journey of personal understanding and enlightenment begins with the journey within. Metaphysical decks channel intuitive insights and enhance the exploration of personal, psychological and spiritual dimensions. Tarot becomes a tool to explore beyond the illusions of the Material World.

The World from five different metaphysical decks. Top row, from left to right: Tarot of the Black Cats, Yoga Tarot, Tarot of the Angels. Bottom row, from left to right: Tarot of the Spirit World, Pagan Tarot.

313

Beyond Tarot

Many decks are available for readings that are not Tarot cards. A Tarot deck is strictly defined as a set of cards containing the Major and Minor Arcana. A Tarot deck can be used an oracle/divination deck but there are many oracle/divination decks that are *not* Tarot decks. The Reader should be familiar with such cards but be careful not confuse them with Tarot. These include; Lenormand, Angel Cards, Oracle Cards, Playing Cards, Gypsy Fortune Telling Cards, etc. If a deck of cards contains no Major and Minor Arcana it is not a "proper" Tarot deck.

No boundaries exist in the Spiritual world. Tarot is a gateway to the infinite and threshold of possibility.

Detail from the Three of Swords of the Universal Fantasy Tarot, artwork by Paolo Martinello.

A short list of available Tarot Themes

Alien
Egyptian
Ancient Greek
Angel
Animal
Anime, Chinese and Eastern
Art Styled
Arthurian
Beginner
Cats
Celtic
Children
Christian
Dark and Gothic
Dragon
Dream
Eastern European
Erotic
Fairies
Fairy Tales
Fantasy
Flowers, Plants and Nature
Food
Gay and Lesbian
Goddess

Golden Dawn
Historical
Humorous
I Ching
Karma
Love
Marseilles Inspired
Medieval and Renaissance
Modern
Moon
Multicultural
Native American
Occult
Pagan and Wiccan
Kabbalah
Russian
South and Central American
Sports
Surreal
The Grail
Thoth Clones and Inspired
TV, Books and Movies
Vampires
Visconti
Women

A QUEST FOR PERFECTION

More than one Reader has heard the siren song of the perfect Tarot deck...

Does the perfect Tarot deck exist? Setting aside expectations and approaching new decks on their own terms will improve a Reader's chances of finding the right deck. The quest for perfection may lead the Reader in surprising directions.

Don't let yourself be fooled by the siren song.

What illustrations would it feature? What numbering system will it use? What titles or keywords, if any, appear in the borders? What features would it borrow from existing decks? What innovations would it introduce? What esoteric systems, books or philosophies would it use?

These questions make for engaging debates but before they can be answered, we must first answer a more pressing question. By what standard should the perfection of a specific Tarot deck be judged?

The Mental Deck

Before a Reader sets out to evaluate a deck, he or she must acknowledge the influence of an invisible and often overlooked standard: *the mental Tarot deck.*

The mind and heart of every Tarot reader contains a mental Tarot deck. For beginners, this is frequently the deck the Reader used when their Tarot study first began. For esotericists, it is often a deck reflecting the Reader's specific occult philosophies. This mental deck need not be based on any one specific deck. It may be a composite deck featuring favorite cards from dozens of decks.

The Physical Deck is what you shuffle, use, touch and refer to when performing a Reading.

The mental deck, while associated with card images, titles and keywords stored in the Reader's memory, is supported by the framework of associations and experiences that are unique to every Tarot Reader. In one Reader's practice, the Fool comes up repeatedly in association with moving from one city to another. To that particular Reader, the Fool becomes inexorably linked with moving. In your practice, the same card may be linked to any number of other experiences. Each association contributes to your unique mental deck.

The Physical Deck

A mental deck, a library of associations, expectations, insights and memories, will influence the Reader as she evaluates a new deck. Problems arise when the mental decks limit the Reader's ability to approach and appreciate new physical decks on their own terms.

Detail of the red robed Magician from the Tarot of the Pictorial Key. His belt is crafted in the image of an Ouroboros, a silver snake consuming his own tail, reflecting eternal return and the nature of recreation.

Every Tarot deck is a physical artifact: a printed, cut, laminated set of cards that reflects the efforts of writers, designers, artists and publishers. There are literally thousands of decks available, each reflecting themes, philosophies and the design decisions of their creators.

Readers who strongly prefer one deck or who ardently subscribe to one esoteric philosophy tend to disregard new decks. They may even be viewed as a source of frustration. The Reader who only accepts the red robed Magician who points to the sky and ground, might take offense to a Magician card featuring an illustration of a man in a business suit. It may seem too mundane to be inspirational. A Reader who believes the two monks at the feet of the Hierophant convey a secret doctrine might find a new deck depicting the Hierophant as an old man in a cave misguided or even offensive. Such reactions have to do with the Reader herself rather than the deck under consideration. The expectation of what a deck should be is entirely dependent on an individual's mental deck.

Setting Expectations Aside

To approach a new deck on its own terms, the Reader must resist the urge to be dogmatic. Decks need not be illustrated, structured, or organized in one certain way. It benefits every Reader to investigate and appreciate the advantages and benefits of new decks.

This may take some effort. The Reader must be willing to embrace differences and consider the potential value of a new look, new content, or new approaches. The Reader should read the little white booklet, learn more about the culture or philosophy behind the deck and understand the intention and agenda of the deck's designer.

The Reader must go beyond emotional or gut responses. They should allow themselves to become immersed in the world of the deck. Then the Reader will be able to judge a deck purely on its own merits.

To grow, you must destroy and move beyond your mental walls.

The Perfect Deck

The first step on the quest for the perfect deck is identifying and embracing personal expectations, the mental deck. The second step is allowing those expectations to inform, while never limiting, the ability to approach a new deck on its own merits.

Having taken these first two steps, the Reader may, ultimately, reach the same conclusion shared by many other collectors, scholars and students: that the perfect deck, instead of being any one deck, is whatever deck serves the Reader's purposes at any given time.

There is no single perfect tool for every job. But every job has one perfect tool.

Meeting a New Deck

The Art of Cutting Cards

The shiny box, the crackle of a cellophane wrapper, the crisp card stock, the pristine Arcana, arranged in numerical order and divided into suits; who can resist the allure of a new Tarot deck?

The arrival of a new deck is always an exciting moment. While Readers may be tempted to "jump right in" and read right away, investing even a little time in exploring, verifying and getting to know a deck makes that first reading even more effective!

Over time, most Readers develop a personal ritual for getting to know a new deck. Some thumb through the cards one by one. Others deal the new cards onto corresponding cards from an older, more familiar deck. Some dive in and begin reading. Eagerness is awesome but a little patience and preparation will help the Reader get the most out of a newly acquired deck.

Opening the Deck

Most modern decks are packaged in a cardboard box and sealed in a cellophane wrapper for additional protection. Inside the wrapper, the Reader will find both the deck and the "little white book" (or LWB). The LWB is a concise guide to the deck, offers background information and a brief commentary on the meaning of each card. Some decks have different packaging and maybe even a companion book.

When a deck is first unwrapped, the Reader may detect a mild aroma of residual ink from the printing process. This should be of no concern because odor fades quickly. To speed the process, the Reader may leave the cards spread out on a table or pass the cards through incense or sage smoke.

Many decks include two extra cards: a title card and a card advertising other titles by the same publisher. Because the backs of these cards are often identical to the backs of the cards used for divination, it is easy to mix these in with the rest of the deck. To prevent this, remove these cards immediately before shuffling and set aside.

Verifying the Cards

Once the extra cards and the LWB are set aside, the Reader should proceed through the deck card by card, examining each one. In addition to satisfying the Reader's immediate curiosity, this practice will verify that all cards in the deck are present and accounted for. If the cards are out of order, the Reader should sort them into five piles (Majors, Wands, Cups, Swords and Pentacles) and place each pile in order by number and rank.

Modern publishers print, cut, sort and package cards. Most commercially published decks will be ordered and complete right out of the wrapper. Still, because mistakes do occasionally occur, it is wise for the Reader to confirm the readiness of the deck. It is better for the Reader to discover a missing card at this point rather than noticing it during an important reading later on!

Breaking in the Deck

Many new decks are too stiff or slippery to be easily shuffled. After verifying the completeness of the deck, the Reader may wish to shuffle the cards for an extended period of time. Five minutes is usually sufficient. Use whatever method you prefer, as a means of breaking in the deck. In addition to making the cards more flexible and easier to handle, extended shuffling may also loosen and separate any sticky cards.

An Initial Reading

An initial reading provides the Reader with an opportunity to get a feel for the symbolic vocabulary and presence of a new deck. Initial readings may be awkward or difficult to interpret. The professional Reader should probably avoid performing the initial reading in the presence of a client. Many Readers enjoy asking the deck itself, "What will you

Meeting a new deck is like meeting a new friend, there is a lot to discover and it's a gradual process.

On the previous page:
Every new deck opens a new door.

teach me?" or "What do I need to know about you?" Others prefer a more structured approach and use spreads specifically designed for use with new decks.

Appreciating the Voice of the Deck

Each deck has a unique voice. It is a combination of its structure, theme, titles, keywords, illustrations and symbolic vocabulary. Some decks are based on and intend to imitate or recall other, more established decks. The term "clone decks" are used to describe decks that carefully adhere to the Rider Waite deck. Many decks are designed to deliberately depart from the norm. These explore new ground and expand the range of what Tarot is and can be.

The Reader is encouraged to suspend judgment for the first few readings of a new deck, rather than critique an artist or deck designer for their choices. This will allow the Reader to get to know the deck on its own terms before drawing comparisons. Doing so will allow the Reader to see beyond preconceived expectations and become attuned to the unique voice and viewpoint of the deck.

In the next page:
People perform ritualistic actions
every day without even realizing it.

A savvy Reader avoids the trap of insisting that every deck should follow a certain pattern or be based on a specific set of correspondences. If that were true, if every deck conformed to the standards set by earlier decks, innovation would end. There would be no reason for the Reader to explore new decks at all!

What Powers a Tarot Deck?

You do!
The theme and art will coax you in a certain direction but the ultimate advice and direction stems from you.

Simple Ways to Bring Tarot into Your Life

- Think of people in your life as tarot cards. Which card would they be?
- Think of interesting life situations. How would this situation be expressed as a card?
- Blend novels and films with Tarot. Every book/film has a clear beginning, middle, and end. Put together the three Tarot cards expressing the beginning, middle and end of your favorite book/film.
- In the morning, think of a quality you would like to bring into your life. Find that quality in a card and keep in plain sight all day.
- Read anything and everything having to do with Tarot.
- Practice reading the cards for others as often as possible.
- Throw self-doubt out the window. This is sometimes easier said than done. If you don't trust yourself, you can't move forward with the cards.

324

RITUAL AND TAROT

Deck preparation and purification rituals have fallen out of favor for many people in modern day life. In a busy, ready for gratification lifestyle, we sometimes rush to Tarot for answers. Older Tarot reading guides came with elaborate instructions on how to work with the deck. Specific information was given on preparing, purifying and storing the deck. Ultimately, the way you work with cards is up to you. Scrimp on the ritual and you may be missing out on a pleasurable, if not overlooked aspect, of working with Tarot.

What is Ritual?

A ritual is a series of actions, performed for their symbolic value. Ritual actions may be prescribed by a religion such as a Catholic Mass or Jewish Seder. A ritual can stem from the traditions of a community such as New Orlean's Mardis Gras or Rio de Janeiro's *Carnaval*. Rituals are performed by groups or individuals, in public or in private.

Sometimes a personal ritual becomes a habit and vice versa. The lines become blurred. Tooth brushing is not strictly a ritual. It carries no symbolic meaning and is done for hygienic reasons. However, if personal cleanliness is called into question, the brushing of teeth may soon become ritualistic because doing so proves you are hygienic.

Birthday celebrations are ritualistic. Each candle on the cake is symbolic of one (or ten) years of life. Annual holidays and their decorations are ritualistic. Sporting events hold pre and post game rituals. Tarot may become ritualistic if you allow it. Tarot operates in symbolic language. It is natural that ritual can go hand in hand with the symbolic language of Tarot.

Why Tarot Ritual?

Tarot rituals are not designed for the benefit of the cards but for the psychological state of the Reader. Over time, the ritual becomes a trigger for the reflective mindset of the Reader and opens a state of heightened awareness. Many Readers find their Tarot rituals quite pleasurable.

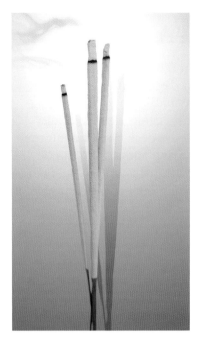

Lighning an incense stick might be a very easy and effective Tarot reading ritual.

Rituals are often simple symbolic gestures. Do not expect the magic to be visible.

Tarot rituals communicate an attitude of respect toward the deck and help to form a deeper emotional bond with the cards. The bond you share will be conveyed to the people you read for as they see you treating the cards with true reverence. Consider the difference between a Tarot Reader who pulls a disorderly deck from a disheveled purse full of receipts, tissues and coins and the Reader who keeps her deck wrapped in precious silk and in an intricately carved wooden box.

There is no right or wrong way to create a Tarot ritual as long as it is done for the benefit of yourself and your deck. Invent, adapt and change a ritual, as it feels good for you. Tarot rituals, rites and preparations vary between readers and vary widely according to personal tastes and belief systems.

A few rituals you can use

New Deck Consecration

Consecration of a new Tarot deck is done to establish a relationship and bond with new cards. The opening and blessing of a deck is important whether the deck is new or second hand. Used rare decks are sometimes acquired and they should be reviewed to ensure they are a complete set and are not missing some cards.

Fan the deck in front of you and pass your hand over each card while expressing gratitude aloud. This may be done at a table, at an altar, or on the floor as you sit inside the center of a complete circle of fanned cards.

Smudging

Smudging is the act of burning of herbs and creating ritualized smoke for emotional, psychic and spiritual cleansing and purification. Smudging is used to cleanse and energize people, places and objects. It is also used to alert compatible spirit energies. Sage is the common smudging herb but any variety of dried herbs can be used.

326

The smudging of a deck has a twofold advantage. Mystically, it consecrates the cards. Smudging also dispels the sharp odor prevailing on today's commercially printed decks. Pass each card through a cone of incense smoke or smoldering bundle of Sage smoke.

Smudging.
Smudging is a simple and effective ritual that cleanses rooms, objects and people, smoking away negative energies.

Many Tarot Readers smudge their reading space both before and after a client comes for a reading to cleanse the space. Smudging is a way to conduct spiritual housecleaning and clear the air whatever the occasion.

Basic Clearing Ritual

A basic and powerful clearing ritual is to mindfully and deliberately arrange all the cards in order. Many Readers consider this act to be an extremely effective ritual.

Full Moon/Sunlight Cleanse

Fill your cards with the energetic qualities of moonlight or sunlight. Place your Tarot cards in a pool of moonlight on the next Full Moon. Leave them to absorb the lunar rays all night. Conversely, charge your deck with solar energy by placing it in the light of the sun for an entire day. A sun cleanse is especially effective on the Summer Solstice, the longest day of the year.

White Cloth Cleanse

Whenever you feel the need to purify or cleanse your deck, simply wrap it in a white cloth for twelve to twenty-four hours.

Crystal Cleanse

Clear quartz and amethyst may be used to energize or neutralize a deck's energy. You can regularly keep the crystal on top of the deck if your deck sits out. You can keep the gem stowed inside the deck's bag or silk wrapping when you put your deck away.

Sleeping with Tarot

Place your deck under your pillow while sleeping to foster a deep unconscious connection to them. This may be done with the entire deck. It can also be done with one particular card if you wish to draw on one card's energy. For instance, if you are beginning a new job in the morning, you may stow the Magician card under your pillow to imbue yourself with his electric energy the next day.

Cleaning Your Cards

To literally clean the cards, the safest method is to gently rub each card with talcum powder. This works for greasy buildups, fingerprints and light stains. A talcum clean will do wonders to restore the cards to their original sheen.

Crystals
Stones and Crystals contain helpful properties. Use them for charging, cleansing and protecting decks and to enhancing the Reading experience.

In the next two pages:
The most useful accessories are favored items carrying strong personal and spiritual connections.

Who Can Touch?

The Reader should make the decision about who can handle their cards. Some Readers let others touch and shuffle and some don't. Mystically inclined Readers may believe every person who handles the deck leaves an energetic imprint upon the cards (though this can be cleared with a purification ritual). Others argue that allowing Querents to handle the deck builds trust and eliminates fears that the Reader has manipulated the deck. The decision rests in the Reader's hands.

Storing a Deck

Decks ship in protective cardboard cases. The Reader is interested in the value of a deck as a collector's item, he/she should consider storing the deck exclusively in this case. A second copy may be purchased so the first may remain encased in its plastic shrink wrap.

Many Readers store and transport favorite decks in specially made velvet or silk Tarot bags. Boxes, especially well-worn containers, can open in briefcases or purses, while drawstring bags will stay closed. They protect the deck and preserve its integrity.

Some Readers keep special, personal, or treasured decks in elaborately decorated wooden boxes. Mystically, boxes made of natural materials shield decks from negative energy and preserve balance. Practically, storing a deck this way expresses reverence and reflects the Reader's appreciation for their deck.

Disposing of a Deck

When a deck becomes damaged or too worn to use, it should be disposed of in a respectful manner. Readers interested in the power of ritual usually prefer burning a well-worn deck. Symbolically, burning a deck releases its stored energy back into the Universe. According to tradition, ashes should be disposed of in swift-running water. Other Readers may choose to incorporate an old deck into an arts project to be treasured for years to come.

How To Shuffle

Many Readers shuffle and handle Tarot cards the same way one might handle poker cards. Others prefer to handle a deck with a lighter touch, using gentle, overhand shuffles. "Finger painting" is mixing the cards by spreading them into a face down pile and gently rearranging them.

Symbolically, a light touch suggests more respect and reverence. Practically speaking, a gently handled deck will last longer than a man-handled one. It maintains the appearance of the cards and makes the most of the Reader's investment in them. Some decks become broken in with regular use and their worn appearance adds to the unique history of the deck.

To treat cards lightly, simply spread the cards out across table and bring them back together again. From a ritualistic standpoint, this is represents chaos and chance followed by order and knowledge. Once you have all the cards in a pile, divide the deck into small stacks and the rebuild into one pile.

Shuffling
Beside the ritual component, shuffling is subject to a practical consideration: shuffling roughly will ruin the cards sooner or later.

No matter what style of shuffling you choose, it may be useful to utter a sentence, prayer, intention, or incantation aloud while doing so. "This reading is for the Querent's highest good," or "Help them build a strong future," or "Wisdom guide me in this reading." This creates a revered state for both yourself and your Querent.

Additional Ritual Elements

Selecting Your Space

It is the psychological space you inhabit with your cards, not the physical space, that is truly important. However, if possible, select one space in your home to dedicate to card reading. Having a spot regularly dedicated to the cards adds reverence. Your reading table and space should be clean and clear at the onset of a reading. It is a act of honor and respect to the cards, your reading and to yourself.

Ritual Space.
Do not forget that space is a ritual element itself. It's not just about having many things, but how to position them and yourself.

Candles

Candles are sacred objects. Candlelight permeates darkness in a way electric light can't. Candles light space for possibility, spirituality and magic. Through history, cross-culturally and even today, candles and the element of Fire play a major ritualistic role. Lighting a candle's wick alerts your unconscious that you are preparing for a reading. The moment the flame lights, your intention is made clear.

Music and Sound

Music is powerful, mood altering, affects your heart rate, can sooth and inspire you. Technology makes it simple to listen to any genre of music and meditative channels are easy to come by. Choose any music that gets you in the mood and allows you to open you up. You may leave it on for the duration of the reading if you like. You may also use bells, chimes, drums, or singing bowls at the opening of a reading.

TAROT SYMBOLS

Books, guides and Internet sources regarding Tarot cards frequently provide conflicting meanings. What is a Reader to do? You should go directly to the cards of course, allowing the silent language of symbolism to reveal the secret meaning of every card.

Any well-stocked bookstore will contain several Tarot books. Interpretations vary, based on anything from the notes of the early Tarot readers to the modern author's own experience. As a result, one book's meanings are often dramatically different from those in the book sitting next to it. How does a Reader determine, once and for all, what a given card really means?

The Testimony of Symbols

Recognizing the limitations of books, a serious Tarot student should move beyond what others say about the cards. They must begin working with the cards themselves. As Eliphas Levi, a 19th century Tarot Reader, noted: "an imprisoned person, with no other book than the Tarot, if he knew how to use it, could in a few years acquire universal knowledge."

Levi refers to the deck itself, sans book, sans metaphysical teacher. If you allow the symbols to speak, they will spring to life. Well-designed decks contain treasure troves of information and in almost every case; this information is encoded into the visual language of symbols.

Thumb through the Major Arcana to see them. Symbols drawn from Alchemy, Astrology, religious texts and mythology are available in multitudes of decks. Using a little effort, almost anyone can decode them. Once the decoding process begins, each card transforms into a wordless guidebook, communicating its meaning to anyone willing to look and listen. Particularly sensitive individuals will even become sensitive to the symbols appearing off the cards and in their regular lives.

Basic Symbolism

Certain symbols frequently appear in deck after deck. Astute Readers use these symbols to evoke insights during the reading process. While the following list is not comprehensive, it introduces commonly used symbols. Begin to explore symbolism by looking out for:

Animals

The animal kingdom has come to represent specific qualities. The Fool is often accompanied by a dog, generally believed to represent his basic instincts. The Fool in the Wirth deck is attacked by a cat-like lynx. Wirth claimed this creature, "hastens his course" and speeds the Fool toward his destiny. You will also find imperial eagles, cautionary snakes, fierce lions and howling wolves. What might each of these animals suggest about you or your Querent's needs? Might the Moon indicate a need to get out at night and "howl?" Does the presence of the Fool's dog imply loyalty? Does a snake symbolize temptation?

Body Language

Does the character on the card look toward the left to the past or the right toward the future? Does Strength look down at her lion or away from the beast? Is the character's back facing you; perhaps the Querent has something she is hiding? Characters on the Wheel of Fortune move quickly but get nowhere; might your Querent be in a similar state of affairs? Characters on the Tower are falling down; reversed, though, they appear to be flying upward. What might this suggest?

Elements

Earth (Pentacles) is associated with practicality. A quick way to gauge a Querent's state of mind is to see how many of his cards feature well-grounded characters. Water (Cups) constantly ebbs and flows; watery illustrations may suggest emotional instability or subconscious motives. Fire (Wands) is vibrant and energetic, suggesting the need for sudden change and radical transformation. Air (Swords) connects with thoughts and perceptions; what might this say about the Hanged Man, who dangles upside-down … in mid-air?

Flesh and Clothing

In the Wirth Tarot, the Fool's bare buttocks may suggest a Querent's embarrassment or exposure. Resurrected figures on The World have returned to their newborn state — how might your Querent restore lost innocence? The Star's costume warns of naiveté, while Death's lack of flesh suggests the need to get to the "bare bones" of a situation.

Pairs

The Chariot card is pulled by two beasts, frequently of opposing colors, what might that mean? Many characters sit between two columns, suggesting their roles as mediators; others stand in pairs, suggesting the need for balance or the necessity of choice. Temperance combines the contents of two vessels; in contrast, the Star, pours her vessel out. Readers spotting this would recommend two very different courses of action as a result.

Possessions

What do the characters on the cards carry? A pack of possessions may suggest the Querent already possesses the solution for his/her problem. Sharp swords call for swift decision-making. Walking sticks can point to dependencies, veils can suggest hidden knowledge and the style of a hat may tell you, quite literally, what is on the mind of the Querent.

Symbols.
The symbol stands for an idea. A symbol transcends the mechanics of language. It works by way of relationship, association and idea. It is visible sign describing the invisible. For instance, a lion is symbolic of courage.

From Association to Application

In a well-designed Tarot card, every element in every illustration is a symbol and every symbol is there for a reason. With practice, you can learn to use the symbols on a card to amplify and enrich the meanings you've memorized over time, producing insights not found in any book.

Jump Start Your Practice

Dive into the world of symbols. Perform a reading based on each one category of Basic Symbolism. Write down or state aloud five questions. Pull three cards to answer each question. Answer the first question, using only Body Language symbolism to answer the question. For the second question, use only elements symbols to answer your question. The third question, use only the clothing and flesh to reveal your answer and so on …

Three images from the Universal Fantasy Tarot, artwork by Paolo Martinello: The Star, The Lovers, The Hanged Man.

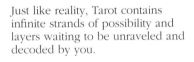

Just like reality, Tarot contains infinite strands of possibility and layers waiting to be unraveled and decoded by you.

Decode Tarot Symbols

A simple 3-step process, (Symbols, Associations and Strategies) will allow you to decode, learn and apply symbolic Tarot reading skills. Any deck can be used.

Step One: List the Symbols

Draw a card from any Tarot deck and study the illustration on the card. Move slowly from the top of the card to the bottom. Make a handwritten list of every element catching your eye. For example, a Reader working with the Justice card from the Universal Wirth deck might create a list including: crown, throne, sword, scales. Two Readers working from the same card may create different lists. This is to be expected, as each Reader will be drawn to the symbols needed to answer the question at hand.

Step Two: Make Associations

When the first step is complete, the Reader will possess a list of symbols. List in hand, the Reader can discover the

337

Doesn't this Biblical scene remind you of a King in your Tarot deck?

associations existing between the symbols and the Querent's personal question. Associations can come from several categories. The Justice card is used here as an example:

Astrological

Some cards feature astrological glyphs; others merely suggest astrological associations. The scales of Justice are associated with Libra. Is the Querent or someone associated with the question a Libra? Might the qualities of a Libra suggest a way to deal with the situation?

Biblical or Mythical

Even though Justice is often drawn as a female, an enthroned, crowned and sworded figure may suggest the Biblical King Solomon. How might wisdom or decisiveness play a role in the situation? What would King Solomon do were he facing your situation?

Emotional

What emotion does the image suggest? Justice is usually represents objectivity and evidence. This suggests emotions should be set aside in lieu of hard evidence.

Personal History

The Justice card might prompt you or the Querent to recall a previous brush with the law, a prior court case, or a time when he/she felt justice was or was not achieved. These memories may have a direct bearing on the question at hand.

Literal

Is the Querent in court or on trial? Is the law or legal system involved? Does the situation involve weight (scales) or weapons (the sword)? Is there an authority (crown) the Querent should appeal to?

Metaphorical

Could the Querent be on trial in a figurative way? For example: are you or the Querent being unfairly accused of something? Is someone at work rendering unfair verdicts?

Personal

What does Justice mean to you or the Querent? What would be a just and fair outcome? How would Justice best be served in the current situation?

Physical

Some symbols - like those appearing on Justice - refer to a universal cultural heritage and are especially easy to recognize and decode.

Is the figure on the card a reminder of someone you or the Querent knows? If not, does the physical posture of the figure on the card suggest an attitude or approach that might prove helpful?

Visual

Does the figure on this card seem to reflect or mimic the postures of figures on other cards? In terms of their composition, Justice, the High Priestess and the Pope are strikingly similar. Might these parallel cards reference themes worth exploring further?

Off the Cards and into Life

A Reader becoming competent at symbolic reading, will often find her awareness slips off the cards and manifests in real life. Symbols and signs outside of Tarot are read. As the Reader habitually looks for symbols in their deck, they start to notice symbols appearing before them in real life. Any symbol capturing attention is worth interpreting.

The sensitive Reader reads their reality like a Tarot card. The Reader who becomes captivated by Spring's budding trees contemplates the nature a tree as a symbol of life, reach, rootage, sturdiness and balance. They incorporate this symbolism into their life as they see fit. A Reader with a fondness for roses begins to incorporate the nature of the rose; love, sensuality, innocence, youth, victory into their life. The simple door of one's home becomes a sacred threshold, a place of transition, or a marker between the "inner" and the "outer" nature of life.

How will symbols speak to you?

Step Three: Suggest Strategies

Each association must be transformed into a strategy. Symbolic based solutions will represent a change the Querent can make in thoughts, feelings, actions, or environments.

In the example above, associating Justice with Libra might prompt a change of action: the suggestion to avoid conflict (as Libras are said to do). The association with objectivity might prompt a change in feelings, prompting someone to work harder at being objective. The association with the legal system might prompt a change in environment, prompting the Querent to head for court!

While time-consuming at first, the process of listing symbols, making associations and suggesting strategies soon becomes automatic. It yields far more interactive and organic readings. If you trust the process and trust yourself, you'll discover the most relevant meanings tend to be the ones you decode from the symbols that caught your eye.

In the next page:
Readings are for everyone and everyone can find a meaningful reading.

ONE CARD, MANY MEANINGS

Tarot history contains over six centuries of evolution. The modern Reader has every unique system at their fingertips. Traditional Arcana meanings, while often contradictory, are all equally correct. How can this be? The meaning of the Arcana will change depending on the questions and circumstances of the reading.

Ultimately, the interpretation of a card depends on the personality and experience of the Reader.

Reading Types

Personal Life

Common themes for readings include love, work, money, or health. Health questions are best left to a certified doctor.

Divination

When someone requests information about the future it is important to be concise and appropriate. A Reader can make a divinatory reading short and simple using only the Major Arcana. For divinatory readings, it is useful to break up your reading into three parts:

- **1.** A clue of what will happen in the future.
- **2.** Advice on how the person might/should behave.
- **3.** Timing of the event.

Soul and Psyche

Regular readings become deep and complex. They often take psychological and spiritual aspects into account. Working with your own or a Querent's spirituality leads to probing examinations of core beliefs and values.

Astrology

Astrology is a useful esoteric association with Tarot. Depending on your chosen system, each card is connected to Signs, Planets, Decans, Equinoxes, Solstices and Zodiac. Astrology is especially helpful in the timing of an event.

Alchemy

The best way to utilize Alchemy is in understanding of the four elemental suits of the deck. Earth, Air, Fire and Water.

Kabbalah

Each Tarot card connects to a place or path on the Kabbalistic Tree of Life. These meanings can be utilized in the reading.

A representation of the Tree of Life.

Which Interpretation?

Traditional Tarot meanings incorporate multiple points of view. Analyzing all possible meanings of a card would result in mass confusion. How does one select the appropriate information from Traditional, Alchemical, Kabbalistic, or Astrological meanings? Experience soon teaches you it is the ability of listening to your intuition that will point the way. Usually, your first instinct is correct.

Challenge Yourself

The best way to hone your intuition is to read Tarot with different decks. Observe the same Arcanum. Examine the High Priestess in Tarot of Marseilles. Compare her image to The Metamorphosis Tarot and The Fairies Tarot. Regardless of your intuitive interpretation, notice the fundamental symbols of the card remains similar. Never dispense with the theoretical knowledge of the Arcanum. It will give you a context to further develop your intuition.

Channel and funnel your intuitive thoughts consistently using the traditional meanings of the cards. The Hanged Man represents a painful trial to overcome. He also represents seeing things from a different perspective. He represents the meeting of two perceptions from two distinct worlds. Knowing all these meanings, a Reader can look at card and select the most appropriate meaning.

Tarot cards are like fossils packed deep under layers of dirt, sand and time. Layers of information, meanings and systems have grown over the original interpretation of these images. Each individual layer adds value, depth and richness. As you dig to discover, reveal and expose these layers, you simultaneously add your own unique imprint. This provides fresh life and vitality to your personal Tarot practice. It also adds to Tarot's collective unconscious. Each card is a prism, a distinct universe, a doorway. Open it.

There are as many possible interpretations as colors in a pencil case. Listen to your instinct and pick the right one.

TAROT STRUCTURE

Tarot is a simple stack of paper cards. The 78 cards can appear fascinating or frighteningly overwhelming. Thankfully, the 78 cards are not random. Tarot contains a solid structure. This underlying, interconnected skeletal structure is like a rack on which any system, idea or theme may be placed. You will always know where you are in a Tarot deck if you understand this structure. It is why scholars have connected Tarot to various esoteric, philosophical and magical systems. Tarot's exquisite structure is why endless themed decks and hundreds of Tarot books exist. Virtually any set of ideas, dogmas, visuals or themes can be placed on top of Tarot's structure and leap to life.

The Sun, Major Arcana number XIX, of the Dark Angels Tarot, artwork by Luca Russo. Detail.

The Major Arcana (22 cards)

The Majors are the twenty-two cards in addition to the four suits and court cards. As a rule of thumb, any deck of cards with a Major Arcana is considered a Tarot deck.

The Minor Arcana (56 cards)

The Minor Arcana contains the four suits and are numbered ace through ten. The four suits are traditionally Cups, Wands, Pentacles and Swords, but the names vary in different decks. These four suits equate to a traditional playing card deck with the ace through ten of Hearts, Clubs, Diamonds and Spades.

The 9 of Chalices, Minor Arcana and numeral card of the Dark Angels Tarot, artwork by Luca Russo. Detail.

The Court Cards (16 cards)

The Court Cards contain courtly pictures depicted on them in each of the four suits: Page, Knight, Queen and King.

What comes to mind when you think of...

... the Major Arcana
- Archetypes
- Triumphal Procession
- Hero's Journey
- Soul Themes

... the Minor Arcana
- Hero's Daily Life
- Daily Events
- Ordinary Moments

... the Tarot Suits
- Cups are Hearts
- Wands are Clubs
- Pentacles are Diamonds
- Swords are Spades

... the Court Cards
- Aspects of Yourself
- Other People
- Attitudes and Strategies

The King of Swords, Minor Arcana and Court Card of the Dark Angels Tarot, artwork by Luca Russo. Detail.

Trumps, Triumphs and Majors

Tarot contains four suits like standard playing cards. However Tarot contains a very special fifth suit. The fifth suit contains a set of 22 cards and are called *trumps*.

Trumps: Cards of Power

Gaming Tarot makes trumps the most powerful cards in the deck. When played, they trump, or outrank, other cards. Trumps eclipse each other numerically. The High Priestess (2) trumps the Fool (0), while the the Wheel of Fortune (10) trumps the High Priestess (2). The World card (21) outshines all others.

The Triumphal sequence represents a philosophical map of the world, as perceived from a Renaissance perspective. Older, historical decks use lavish illustrations and characters: beggars and magicians, emperors and empresses, devils and angels, to depict their story.

The Triumphal Procession

Tarot's images and titles were likely inspired by popular European Renaissance parades, called the *triumphal procession*. Costumed actors portrayed authorities (Emperors and Popes), Christian virtues (including Strength and Justice), life events (like Death and Resurrection) and even heavenly bodies (including the Stars, the Sun and the Moon).

As the parade progressed, each new character "triumphed over," (trumped, or outranked) the last. Given this connection, the 22 trumps of the Tarot deck can be considered a "paper parade," a series of cards depicting important truths. Europe's general public tended to read images rather than words. The first printing press was not invented until 1440. Books were rare in the Renaissance, belonging only to the wealthy and the clergy. Triumphal images were popular and familiar to the general public.

Tarot was a gambling game in the Renaissance. Trump cards held greater value than any other card and guaranteed a win.

347

From Trumps to Majors

Trump card illustrations captured the attention of Esotericists and Mystics in the 19th century. These Readers knew the trumps were more important than the other cards but were not quite sure what inspired the images.

They deduced the pictures were a visual code concealing ancient secrets. As a result, they called the trumps the *Major Arcana*, a phrase meaning "the great mysteries." They named the other cards the *Minor Arcana*, or "little mysteries."

Modern publishers issue 22-card "Majors Only" decks in addition to 78-card Tarot decks. Some Readers prefer to work exclusively with the Major Arcana. This is especially helpful for the beginning Reader.

Major vs. Minor

Shuffle and lay out any Tarot spread with a minimum of 7 cards. Interpret all of the Major Arcana cards first, ignoring the Minors. After a clear interpretation Majors, proceed to interpret the Minors. It will become clear that the meaning of the Minors are influenced by those of the Majors.

Majors Receive Meanings

Esotericists and Readers associated specific themes to each Major. Famous and iconic images already contained an obvious, implied meaning.
For example:

Strength Reflects a figure wrestling a wild beast. This became associated with physical strength and strength of character.

The Tower Reflects disaster and became associated with upheaval and unexpected events.

Death The grinning skeleton is associated with both physical death (the end of life) and symbolic death (the end of a relationship or phase of life).

Esotericists continued to build upon their Tarot associations using Astrology, Alchemy, Kabala, Myth and religious allegories. Over time, Tarot and the Majors became linked to every Western European mystical philosophy available.

Strength, the Tower and Death of the Visconti deck.

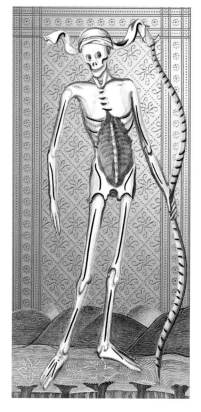

The Hero's Journey

Scholar Joseph Campbell took the idea of universal symbols a step further. He observed that the myths of all cultures repeat and reveal the same archetypal story: *The Hero's Journey.*

A Universal Story

Hero's Journey is the ultimate adventure story. The context and the protagonist or Hero may change but the story structure remains the same. *The Hero's Journey* is reflected in the Major Arcana's sequence and structure thanks to the mythological roots of Tarot. Reading cards for yourself, you become the Hero. The cards reflect your journey. Reading for a Querent or friend, they become the Hero and the cards reflect their journey.

Personal Journey

Place the Fool to the left side. Place remaining Major Arcana cards in three lines, sequentially:

The Fool:	Hero
Cards I – VII:	the earthly journey, the material world and encountered personalities.
Cards VIII – XIV:	the second stage of the journey, the spiritual world.
Cards XV – XXI:	the final stage of the journey, the heavenly world.

The Earthly Journey: Cards I – VII

At the beginning, an inexperienced young person (The Fool), sets off to find his fortune. She meets a series of terrestrial authorities, each more powerful than the previous: a street Magician, a virginal High Priestess, a maternal Empress, an authoritarian Emperor, a pontificating Hierophant. Once having found her true love (The Lovers), she becomes as powerful as is possible for a human being (The Chariot). From an earthly point of view, her journey is finished.

Earthly Journey: conquering the Material World

Spiritual Journey: finding spiritual Enlightment

Heavenly Journey: communing with the Divine

The Spiritual Journey: Cards VIII – XIV

The Fool understands that there is power beyond the mere material dominance (Strength). Removing herself from society (The Hermit), she intuits the mystical mechanics of reality (The Wheel) and learns that there is an higher purpose in the Universe (Justice). She faces a difficult test (The Hanged Man) and loses everything (Death). During the process, she learns the meaning of life (Temperance). This concludes her spiritual growth.

A dove is the archetypal image for peace, literal or figuratively and it's also the Christian symbol for the Holy Spirit.

The Heavenly Journey: Cards XV – XXI

Having overcome her profound fears (The Devil) and having broken her pride (The Tower), the Fool ascends to the heavens (the Star, the Moon, the Sun) to face one final test (Judgement). She is worthy of the greatest reward (The World).

Our Story

This is the story of every Hero and protagonist. The details change but the structure. From King Arthur to Luke Skywalker, from Katniss Everdeen to Bella Swan, the story remains the same. This storyline is a metaphor for growth, lessons and life experience. Every single life is a Hero's Journey. Through each triumph and tribulation, we grow and become closer to who we really are. It is the journey of wisdom and understanding. The Major Arcana is a symbolic representation of this voyage. The cards graciously indicate where we are in our journey with "illumination" on a daily, monthly, or yearly basis.

Archetypes

The Major Arcana is full of archetypes. An archetype is a collective human idea, an original model on which similar things are patterned. Jungian psychology was first to explain this innate universal prototype but Jung did not invent the idea. Plato's Theory of Forms stated that the essence of a thing is its underlying form or idea. An archetype is our collective body and subconscious layer of knowledge buried in our psyche. Your mind contains a collection of archetypes whether you know it or not.

"Mother" or "father" figures are examples of archetypes. We each have a biological mother and father. We share a general understanding of what the terms mother and father mean. In Tarot, the Empress card is the archetypal mother while the Emperor is the archetypal father. A "wise man" or "wise woman" is another example. The Hierophant represents a wise man while the High Priestess is the wise woman.

An archetype can be a recurring symbol, such as a cross representing the Christian idea of eternal life. An archetype

can be a recurring motif in literature or painting. Adam and Eve in the Garden of Eden or Romeo and Juliet are both examples of Lover archetypes.

Tarot archetypes foster human understanding through symbol. Tarot is an innate psychic structure allowing expression. An archetype may be understood as a stereotype. While stereotypes should be avoided in daily life due to their limiting perception of the world and others, stereotypes are quite helpful while learning what Tarot cards represent. An archetype can be understood as an epitome or a personality type exemplified by using the "greatest" example. The Star card could represent a person who carries the epitome of openness and vulnerability in their personality. The Tower is the epitome of destruction and so on.

Phoenix is the archetype for rebirth, renewals and new beginnings.
Below: A phoenix appears in a card sketch for the Epic Tarot (release in 2016, artwork by P. Martinello).

Variations in the Major Arcana
The Majors remain fairly consistent throughout Tarot history although some transformations should be noted.

Historical decks place Justice as the 8th card and Strength as the 11th. The Esotericists of the Golden Dawn preferred to reverse these two card numbers making Justice number 11 and Strength number 8. Many modern decks follow his preference.

The Papess is often called the High Priestess in modern decks and the Pope card is often called the Hierophant, Greek for "interpreter of esoteric mysteries."

The Wheel often called The Wheel of Fortune. The Lovers and The Stars will appear as singular titles, The Lover and The Star. The Fool, who is almost always the number 0, at times is associated with the number 22.

Some occult traditions have created many changes, to the Arcana, even if they are not visible at a first glance. These changes affected the meaning of the card or one of the esoteric elements associated with it (like Kabbalah or Astrology). It is best to start with a strong and simple frame of reference. Once mastered, variations and exceptions can be considered.

The Minor Arcana

The Minor Arcana reflect the mysteries of everyday life. While the Major Arcana reveals great influences at work, the Minor Arcana demonstrate how we maneuver through ordinary life and transitory events on a regular basis. The Minor Arcana breaks down into four suits, each composed of ten numerical cards and four royal court cards.

Hero's Journey in Daily Life

The Minor Arcana, like the Major Arcana, describe a process of maturation. The objective of growth and evolution remains yet the range is limited and more personal. The suits represent four sectors of life. The numbers on the cards delineate the ten phases bringing a person to maturity or accomplishment in each sector. The Ace represents the beginning while the ten represents the finale. All other numbers fall in accordance. The Court Cards represent the manner in which the person behaves and thinks or can represent other people.

Minor Arcana takes you deeply into everyday life.

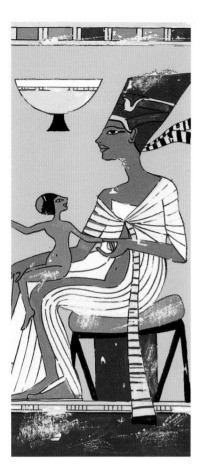

The Queen of Cups of the Nefertari Tarot, artwork by Silvana Alasia. It is much easier to connect with cards that reflect an experience we know, like that of a mother playing with her child.

The Numerals

Scale from one to ten

Each suit has ten numerical cards, Ace through Ten. Ancient decks expressed the value of a card by a number and the suit's symbols. For example, the Six of Clubs reflected six clubs. Illustrated decks combine a symbolic image with the suit. The ten cards of each suit represent the ten phases of the road to maturity, with reference to desire (Wands), emotions (Cups), thoughts (Swords) and material goods (Pentacles).

Each number is associated to one meaning.
- **Ace :** beginning or origin
- **2 :** choice
- **3 :** action
- **4 :** foundation and result
- **5 :** conflict
- **6 :** collaboration or change
- **7 :** imagining alternative
- **8 :** progress
- **9 :** challenges overcome
- **10 :** completion

The Minor Arcana combines the symbolism of each suit with the knowledge that characterizes each phase of the journey. The Two of Cups indicates the need to take into account choices (the number 2) of an emotional kind (Cups). The Three of Wands however, indicates the need to act (the number 3) following your inner energy (Wands).

- Two of Cups (2 + Emotion) = Emotional choices.
- Three of Wands (3 + Creativity) = Creative action.

Numbers and the "Hero's Journey"

The progression of Ace through Ten matches up with the Hero's Journey.
After the *beginning*, the first *choices* lead to *action*. This provides *results* but also leads to *conflict*. Once harmony is created through *collaboration or change*, it's time to *imagine new ways and alternatives*, and *progress* further, *face more challenges* and finally *reach maturity or success*.

355

The Four Paths of the Numeral Cards

The Path of Wands
Maturity of desire through passion and creativity.

1 2 3 4 5 6 7 8 9 10

The Path of Swords
Maturity of intellect through communication and adversity.

1 2 3 4 5 6 7 8 9 10

The Path of Cups
Maturity of emotion through intuition and sensibility.

1 2 3 4 5 6 7 8 9 10

The Path of Pentacles
Maturity of material concerns through physical experience and economic administration.

1 2 3 4 5 6 7 8 9 10

The Four Suits

Tarot's four suits are similar to playing cards. People incorrectly assume that Tarot evolved from standard playing cards. Historical research reveals that playing cards and Tarot evolved right alongside one another.

What do the suits represent? Various theories exist. They may have represented the four medieval classes of Europe. In this scenario, the Wands represented peasants who worked the fields and forests, Cups represented the clergy, Swords reflected nobility and Pentacles represented the merchant class. Court de Geblin, with whom Tarot finds its first recorded occult ties, claimed the four suits represented the four classes of Egyptian society. He arrived at the same conclusion about the stratified layers of society.

Alchemically, the suits relate to the four elements: Earth (Pentacles), Air (Swords), Fire (Wands) and Water (Cups). The qualities of each suit share characteristics common to their element. Pentacles manifest like gardens, Swords move fast like winds, Wands are explosive like flames and Cups are fluid like rivers. This will help you to quickly and easily decipher the meanings of the cards.

Above: Alchemical symbols for the four elements: Fire, Air, Water and Earth.

Minor Names and Suits

Minor Arcana names and suits vary according to deck variety. Regardless of name, the symbolic meaning of each suit generally retains the same essential meaning.

Wands
Clubs, Rods, Batons, Sticks, Staves, Fire, Rods, Torches

Swords
Spades, Knives, Air, Daggers, Arrows, Clouds, Athames

Cups
Chalices, Love, Water, Vessels, Hearts

Pentacles
Coins, Diamonds, Discs, Spheres, Money, Earth, Crystals

Symbols of the four Suits who usually appear on the Magician Arcanum.

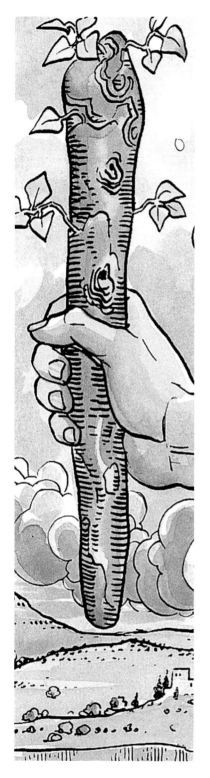

The Wands

Element
Fire

Roles
Creative
Masculine
Ascending
Explosive

Keywords
Desire, Passion, Spirituality, Work, Morals, Growth,
Action, Evolution, Sexuality, Inspiration, Intention,
Objectives, Career, Growth, Insight, Creativity, Ardor,
Excitement, Fervor, Rapture, Devotion, Calling, Pursuits,
Yearning, Appetite

"She's mad, but she's magic. There's no lie in her fire."
Charles Bukowski

Wands are the ability to identify objectives, express creativity
and fuel passions. Wands are associated with the element
of fire, the color red, the sexual sphere, business, career
affairs and season of spring. A spread where multiple Wands
cards appear indicate indicate decisive action. An absence of
Wands indicates impotence, inability to act, or restlessness.

Wands, like the full force of any element, can be destructive
because they are associated with the explosive element of
Fire. Following passion blindly can lead to disarray. But
without the spark of creation embodied by Wands, there
would be no drive, ambition, or desire.

Wands indicate what we want and why we want it. They
symbolize inspiration, intention, orientation and actions.
Wands express the emotion and intensity driving us to
action. They include all moral and traditional activities,
such as family care, education, teaching, law and religion.
Wands indicate evolution and brilliance. Wands share all the
dynamics of Fire.

Intuition

Wands provide simple and immediate insights. These arise spontaneously and unpredictably. It is important to follow these observations, especially when involved in creative and professional work.

Decision-making and Thinking

Wands illuminate with insight and impulse even in practical and intellectual matters. Used analytically, Wands can indicate control and awareness in every choice.

A Comparison of the Cards

Wands represent the ability to live in harmony with natural cycles and expansive energies. Wands connect to nature and the essence of evolution. The developmental nature of Wands is often illustrated with sticks that bear bright, sprouting green leaves.

Ace of Wands in the Fey Tarot
The Wands are drawn as live staves, with leaves and flowers. Passion, drive and desire are expressed as the growing and expanding energy of life.

Ace of Wands in the Tarot of the Zodiac
The Wands are drawn as Torches. The creative and destructive aspect of the suit's fire element is indicated.

Ace of Wands in the Pagan Tarot
The Wands drawn as literal Wands. This expresses the suit's close relationship to magic, willpower, ambition, desire and passion.

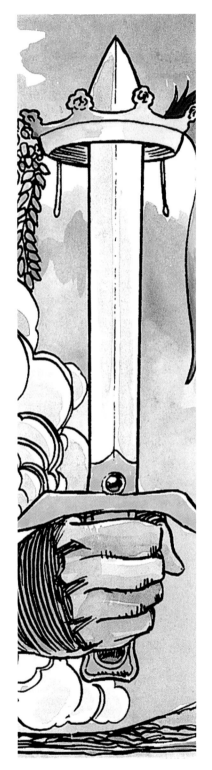

The Swords

Element
Air

Roles
Rational
Masculine
Directional
Divider

Keywords
Thoughts, Articulation, Communication, Decisions, Intellectualization, Ideas, Stories, Expression, Conflicts, Thinking, Rationalization, Analysis, Rationality, Speculation, Apprehension, Translation

"If the road is easy, you're likely going the wrong way."
Terry Goodkind

Swords represent the way we think, intellectualize and rationalize the world around us. Swords are based in pragmatism and the intellectual facility. Swords embody human communication, extend to personal responsibility and are the way we express ourselves. Our interpretation of personal reality is discovered in the suit of Swords. Swords are the stories we tell about ourselves, our history and others. Swords represent learning, integration and expression. Swords represent language, mathematics, conflicts, responsibility and trouble shooting.

Swords indicate what we are thinking and why we think it. They express logic, reason, intellect, rationality and analysis. Razor sharp swords express conflict, pain and defense. Swords are associated with the element of Air, the color yellow, human behavior and the season of autumn. A prevalence of Swords in a spread indicate decisions, accuracy and research. The absence of Swords in a spread indicates confusion, uncertainty and incomprehension.

Intuition

The intuition of Swords allows for rapid, intelligent solutions to complex and deep issues. Intuitive thinking leads to the best possible choice in the vast ocean of options. Intuitive logic, deductive and inductive reasoning can be improved by focusing on the element of Swords.

Decision-making and Thinking

Swords encourage a rational approach to choice, careful consideration of the *pros* and *cons* of each situation, understanding the bigger picture and recognizing the chance of success and failure.

A Comparison of the Cards

The Swords symbolize humanity's collective unconscious. They come to us through art, myth and literature. Symbols vary. Some decks utilize the Swords as weapons of conflict or expressions of rationality.

Ace of Swords in the Fey Tarot
Swords illustrated as Thought express the ability to analyze problems, to judge actions and act in accordance with established rules. As weapons of war, however, they also embody pain and conflict.

Ace of Sword in the Zodiac Tarot
The Swords illustrated as Clouds symbolize the will to impose ideas about reality, supporting them with determination, strength, intellectual authority and superior communication.

Ace of Sword in the Pagan Tarot
Swords illustrated as Athames (the Wiccan ritual knife) express the magical power of the Suit, ability to channel male energies, enhance communication and to focus concentration.

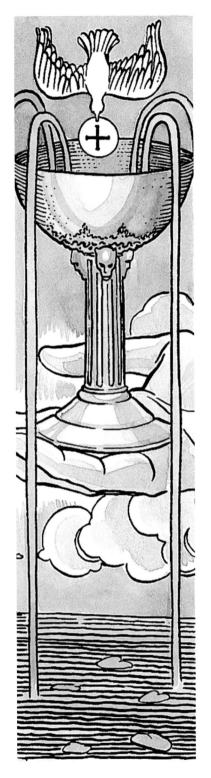

The Cups

Element
Water

Roles
Receptive
Feminine
Adaptive
Reflexive

Keywords
Emotions, Feeling, Love, Senses, Intuition, Empathy, Sentiment, Psychic Ability, Knowing, Caring, Thoughtfulness, Considerations, Sentimentality, Art, Loyalty, Affections, Sensitivity

"Any emotion, if it is sincere, is involuntary."

Mark Twain

The Cups express the spiritual and emotional reality of a person. Cups represent intuition, feelings and the deepest most evocative places in a person's soul. They represent the entire emotional span from the highest highs to the lowest lows. The suit of Cups includes art, music, vision, empathy and love.

Cups intertwine with the realm of intuition and psychic realm. Cups express the ability to communicate on an emotive level, without resorting to - and sometimes ignoring - language and reason.

Cups indicate what we feel and why we feel it. They symbolize instincts, emotions, sentiments, empathy, intuitions and perceptions. Cups are associated with the element of Water, the color blue, our emotional sphere, relationships and the season of summer. Cups prevailing in a spread indicate an introspective journey is necessary. An absence of Cups indicates separation, coldness or boredom and a need for personal connection.

Intuition

Cups provide spontaneous and sudden insight. Cups offer moments of deep clarity and understanding. They are the Suit of the inner emotional life. Cups are how we communicate without language or articulation. Sometimes, the greatest truth cannot be spoken. These truths are seen, felt and known. This truth exists in the field of Cups and why they are the Suit of arts, music and love.

Decision-making and Thinking

Cups always encourage a person to act out of instinct and follow their feelings. Cups require attention to subjective perceptions. They ask us to relate to others through empathy rather than judgment.

A Comparison of the Cards

The Cups as Chalices or Vessels clearly express the receptive ability of the Suit. As Water, the Cups express the ability to flow clearly and gently envelope all things.

Ace of Cups in the Fey Tarot
Cups illustrated as Vessels represent the ability to adapt to surroundings, understanding others at a deep level and process reality through our heart.

Ace of Cups in the Zodiac Tarot
Cups illustrated as Waves and Water express the receptive and nurturing qualities of the element. They represent the human soul and are the source of emotions.

Ace of Cups in the Pagan Tarot
Cups seen as Chalices represent psychic activity, human emotion, emotional richness and spirituality. They are connected to the element of water and to the feminine.

364

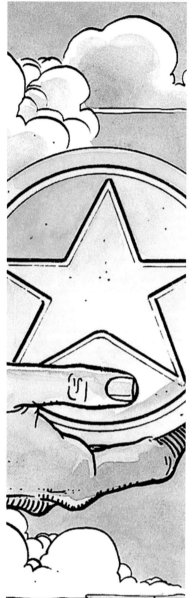

The Pentacles

Element
Earth

Roles
Stabilizer
Feminine
Material
Spatial

Keywords
Possessions, Money, Bodies, Things, Health, Value, Luxury, Finance, Objects, Nature, Commodities, Physical Forms, Property, Earth, Stability, Order, Slowness, Tradition, Endurance

"Tradition is the illusion of permanence."

Woody Allen

Pentacles express everything we can see, feel and touch. They represent bodily activities, land, property, material objects and refer to everything falling under the dominion of the senses. The relationship with the material creates a foundation for internal consistency. It fosters a deep sense of community and an emotional bond with the external environment.

Pentacles are also an expression of our relationship with objects of any kind, including technology and vehicles. Especially objects we use in our daily life.

Pentacles represent what we have and why we have it. They represent the human body, materialism, sensuality, practical issues, values, thriftiness and luxury. Pentacles are associated with the element of Earth, the color green or brown, the environment and season of winter. Pentacles prevailing in a spread will indicate obsessive thoughts relating to health or money. The absence of Pentacles indicates poverty, sickness, or privation.

365

Intuition

Pentacles relate to the tactile senses. Pentacle intuition is engaged through the five senses, the scent of a favorite homemade meal roasting in the oven provides happiness, the stroke of a cat's soft fur brings contentment, or an old song playing on the radio brings you to a happy memory.

Decision-making and Thinking

Pentacles encourage slow and deliberate thinking. There is no rush and no urgency, but once a decision is taken, it is unshakeable. A slow approach is a defense against the fleeting influence of emotion, the temptation of greed and desire and the cold arrogance proper of rationality.

A Comparison of the Cards

Pentacles represent the way in which the individual experiences their relationship with technology, objects and money.

Ace of Pentacles in the Fey Tarot
Pentacles illustrated as Coins represent our relationship to the material world, but not necessarily the material world itself. They are our ability to create constancy.

Ace of Pentacles in the Zodiac Tarot
Pentacles illustrated as Stones express the deep roots of being. Stones are what remain unchanged, even when everything else mutates, grows and transforms.

Ace of Pentacles in the Pagan Tarot
Pentacles illustrated as Pentacles represents materiality, what is practical and concrete and express our deep link with Earth itself and its nourishing energies.

The Court Cards

The traditional technique: the Court Cards indicate actual people

The Page, Knight, Queen and King possess a unique symbolic significance among the cards. There are two commonly used methods of interpretation. One, traditional, the other a modern technique.

When a Court Card appears in a Spread, this indicates a real person, her actions or her influence over a situation.
The card therefore enables the identification of the person in this manner:

- **Page** = Boy
- **Knight** = Young man
- **Queen** = Woman
- **King** = Mature man

The suit of each card dictates physical appearance:

- **Cups** = Blond hair, fair skin
- **Pentacles** = Dark hair, olive skin
- **Wands** = Red hair, fair skin
- **Swords** = Black hair, fair skin

The King of Wands, for example, represents a mature man (King) with red hair and fair skin (Wands). This is a simple system for interpreting but one that presents numerous limits.

The modern technique: the Court Cards indicate strategies for action

A more efficient technique is one that identifies each figure with a role:

- **Page** = Learning
- **Knight** = Action
- **Queen** = Perception
- **King** = Control

To interpret a Court Card the role is matched to the area represented by the suit:

- **Cups** = emotions and feelings
- **Pentacles** = objects and practical matters
- **Wands** = passion and desires
- **Swords** = thoughts and communication

King of Cups represents a need to control the emotions because:
King (control) + Cups (the emotions) = Need to control emotions.

The King of Cups of the Universal Tarot by R. de Angelis.

Knight of Pentacles represents a need to act in a pragmatic way because: Knight (action) + Pentacles (the material) =
Need to act pragmatically.

In general the court cards suggest a way or a strategy for dealing with the situation. The expressions and the meanings that can be attained using this system lack preconceived ideas regarding race, age and gender and can be applied to a wide range of people and to any situation.

Consider the Court Cards

Every Tarot deck contains sixteen Court Cards also called face cards, coat cards, or people cards. Beginning readers often become bogged down and confused when interpreting court cards but you have little to fear. At first glance a King may be confused with a Knight or even The Emperor. Queens may be confused with the Empress card due to similar depictions. Court cards, unlike the other Tarot cards portraying scenes of action or story, generally just have a figure sitting a throne or horse. Rarely is there action drawn out or taking place, until we look a bit closer.

What function do they serve? What systems exist for interpreting them? And who, ultimately, has the authority to say what these cards mean?

Fortunately, there are many systems for bringing the court cards to life. Each has its own pros and cons. Readers who choose to explore each system will find themselves empowered. As a result, you simply choose the system working best for you.

Take Time To Know The Courts

Remove and separate the Court Cards from your deck before reading any further. Examine them, play with them and place in coordinating piles. Put the Queens together, comparing and contrasting them. Do the same with the Kings, Knights and Pages. Now arrange the families according to their Suits. Place the King, Queen, Knight and Page of Pentacles next to each other.

The Page of Wands of the Crystal Tarot by E. Trevisan.
Depending on the deck, the Page may also be called Knave.

Three Cup Courts cards from the Universal Tarot by R. de Angelis. The Courts can be connected to an archetypical family. The Page is the younger son, the Knight is the elder son, the Queen is the mother and the King is the father.

Do you notice similarities? Differences? What cards are you drawn to and which do you dislike? Pick one court card to represent yourself. Who would it be?

The Traditional Method

Traditionally, the court cards represented exactly the kinds of people who appeared on the card:

- **Kings:** older, mature men
- **Queens:** older, mature women
- **Knights:** young men
- **Pages :** young boys

Suits defined individual physical characteristics:

- **Cups:** Blonde hair, fair skin
- **Pentacles:** Brown hair with dark skin
- **Wands:** Red or honey-blond hair, fair skin
- **Swords:** Black hair, fair skin

Using this system, the Page of Pentacles would represent a young man with brown hair and a nice tan.
Equation: Page(young boy) + Pentacles (brown hair) = Young boy with brown hair.

The Knave of Pentacles of the Silver Witchcraft Tarot, artwork by F. Rivolli.
In many modern decks the Knave is portrayed as a female in order to keep gender balance between the Court Cards.

This system is simple to master. Unfortunately, it severely limits the ability of the Tarot to refer to and address women and people of different races. Deservedly so, this system, while grounded in tradition, has fallen from favor.

The Balanced Court

Under this system, the age and gender of a Court Card are defined regardless of the apparent age or gender of the figure in the illustration:

- **Kings:** Older men
- **Queens:** Older women
- **Knights:** Younger men
- **Pages:** Younger women

The Suits indicate personal temperament:

- **Cups:** reflective, passive, weepy, emotional, intuitive
- **Pentacles:** grounded, physical, athletic, practical, strong
- **Wands:** fiery, passionate, romantic, active, progressive
- **Swords:** thoughtful, cerebral, calculating, talkative, analytical

Under this system, the King of Wands represents a fiery, passionate older man with progressive attitudes, while the Page of Pentacles represents a strong, pragmatic,

The King of Wands of the Silver Witchcraft Tarot, artwork by F. Rivolli.

athletic young woman even when the illustration on the card depicts a boy.

This adaptation of the traditional system is far more balanced, enhancing the court cards' ability to represent a broader range of ages, genders and nationalities.

Function and Theme

Modern systems sidestep concerns with gender and race entirely by defining the Courts according to their function (based on rank) and theme (based on Suit). Under this system:

- **Kings:** controlling or conserving
- **Queens:** consulting or questioning
- **Knights:** acting or reacting
- **Pages:** learning or trying

Suits define themes, or broad areas of concern:

- **Cups:** emotions, intuition, reflection, feeling
- **Pentacles:** physicality, finance, sensation, practicality
- **Wands:** goals, activity, achievement, passion
- **Swords:** thoughts, communication, logic, analysis

Using this system, the King of Wands could represent anyone regardless of age, race, or gender who tries to control the actions of others or limit their achievements. The Page of Pentacles would represent someone, regardless of age, race, or gender, who is learning to do some physical task or trying to be more careful with money.

While this system does not allow the Reader to describe the age or gender of the person involved, it provides a very specific portrait most Querents will have no trouble recognizing.

Aspects of Yourself and Others

The Court Represents You

You act, feel and operate in many different ways in the course of twenty-four hours. Court Cards represent different shades of your personality and even actions. The Queen of Wands will point to your outgoing, passionate side, The Page of Cups to your shy tendencies, The King of Pentacles is taking financial control and The Knight of Swords represents you racing to the defense of a friend in need.

371

The Courts Cards Represent Other People

The same way Court Cards represent aspects of your own personality, the courts will also represent people who are playing a role in your life. The Queen of Wands may represent your mother, The Knight of Pentacles may represent a handsome man who has a lot to offer you, The King of Swords your favorite philosophy professor and so on.

Easy Understanding: The Nuclear Family

The simplest way to become grounded in what the Court Cards mean is to understand them through the simple structure of the nuclear family. Who makes up a traditional nuclear family? Four people:

- **King:** Father
- **Queen:** Mother
- **Knight:** Teenage Son
- **Page:** Young Daughter

Portrait of a nuclear family: Mother, father and two children of different ages.

An illustration by L. Mattioli for the Court Cards of the Tarot of the Fairy Lights.

Choosing a System

In addition to the systems outlined here, there are dozens of ways to interpreting the Court Cards. Each has strengths and limitations. The Reader must determine the extent to which a given system fits in with his or her reading style.

Approaches to this include:

Adopting a System. The Reader embraces one system for a specific period of time, then switches to another and another. Eventually, the Reader can determine which system seems to work best and adopt it exclusively.

Comparing Systems. The Reader interprets a spread using one system, then interprets the same spread using a different system. Over time, a preference for one system may evolve or you discover that different systems work better with different clients!

Referring to the Booklet. Every deck comes with a booklet providing basic card meanings. Referring to the booklet can provide insight into the mind of the deck's designer, illuminating the system he or she used when assigning meaning to the cards.

Developing your Own System. The Reader is free to pick one system, fuse several systems, or design a system of his or her own. Ultimately, experience and experimentation will reveal what works best!

The Empress, inspired by Elizabeth Taylor. Illustration by D. Cammarano for a deck designed by C.A. Eschenazi.

Connecting the Tarot Arcana to famous personalities is an useful technique to memorize the meaning of any card in the deck.

Three Fun Exercises

Assign Legendary Personalities to The Courts

Does the Queen of Swords remind you of JK Rowling, weilding her sword like a pen? Perhaps the King of Pentacles reminds you of Donald Trump or Richard Branson? Whatever connection you can make with actual people and/or celebrities or fictional characters will help bond your understanding with the cards.

Family Portrait

Take some time to recreate a family portrait of your childhood or your current family. Use one court card and the qualities assigned to them to represent each family member. Don't forget to use reversals if you feel one member was blocked or stifled.

The Dinner Party

Imagine you are having a dinner party. Who would you like to invite? Make a list of your favorite friends, celebrities and literary or historical figures. After you've created your guest list, select a court card to match each personality. Best part? Who would you bring as your date?

The Court Diagram

The Court Diagram is a very simple way to understand and study the complex relations between the Court Cards and to interpret them during a reading.

Reading the Court Diagram

The Court Cards sometimes present contradictions and difficulties in their interpretation. The Court Cards Diagram was developed to very simply link these cards together. This diagram will help you find the appropriate meaning of the courts.

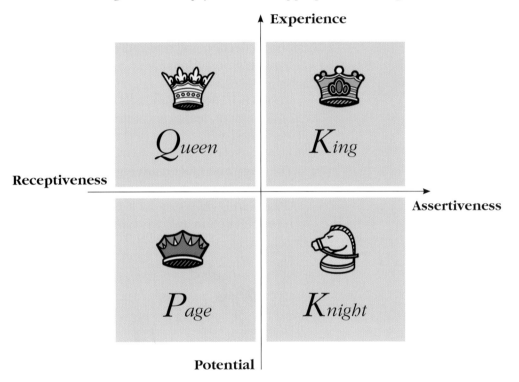

The Court Diagram

The Court Diagram is formed by two axes. The horizontal axis indicates the transition from **receptiveness** to **assertiveness**. The vertical axis indicates the passage from **potential** to **experience**.

These four qualities will help you articulate meaning of the Court Cards. The diagram is divided into four boxes, each of which is occupied by a Court Card character.

The attributes of each Court Card are summarized below:

	Potential	Receptiveness	Assertiveness	Experience
Knave	√	√		
Knight	√		√	
Queen		√		√
King			√	√

The Receptiveness of the Page and Queen

The keywords related to Receptiveness are:
Listening, waiting, patience, understanding, care, regeneration, reflection, internalization, liabilities, memory, thought, femininity, emotionality.

In practice, Receptiveness is the way one adapts to the environment, learns and listens to others. This is the attitude associated with change and transformation.

The Page and Queen are linked by this attribute: when the Receptiveness is combined with Potential you are learning (Page) and when instead it is combined with Experience you have perception and wisdom (Queen).

The Page and Queen of Wands of the Harmonious Tarot, artwork by W. Crane and E. Fitzpatrick.
Both the Page and the Queen have a receptive nature. This is their main common attribute.

Receptiveness is opposite and complementary to Assertiveness.

The Potential of the Page and Knight
The keywords related to Potential are:
Talent, inexperience, promise, future, youth, possibilities, innocence, longing, hope, expectations, growth, innovation and renewal.

In practice, Potential indicates the possibility of something happening in the future. It's energy is not yet expressed and not decided, so, from the same potential, different futures will unfold.
The Page and the Knight are linked by this attribute: when Potential is combined with Receptiveness you are learning (Page), when it is combined with Assertiveness, you are exploring and trying out (Knight).

Potential is opposite and complementary to Experience. It must be noted, however, that Potential will always evolve into Experience, but it's not possible for Experience to return back to Potential.

The Assertiveness of the Knight and King
The keywords related to Assertiveness are:
Activities, action, initiative, aggressiveness, movement, power, authority, facticity, convenience, expression, masculinity, rationality.

In practice, Assertiveness refers to the ability to impose oneself on a situation and the surroundings. This attitude leads to development and to communicate and defend one's opinions and way of being. It makes people be themselves in any case, even at the cost of forcing others to change. This way is associated with strength and determination.
The Knight and the King are connected by Assertiveness: when Assertiveness is combined with Potential there is action (Knight) and when it is combined with Experience there is control (King).

Assertiveness is opposite and complementary to Receptiveness.

The Knight and King of Wands of the Harmonious Tarot, artwork by W. Crane and E. Fitzpatrick. Knight and King are linked by the common attribute of Assertiveness.

The Experience of the King and Queen

The keywords related to Experience are:
Competence, skill, knowledge, custom, security, certainty, habit, calm, confidence.

In practice, the cards related to Experience have matured. They have completed their journey. Therefore, the appearance of these cards indicates possessing the knowledge and power to solve a problem. Experience provides strength and indicates the calm and tranquility that only self confidence can confer. This attitude suggests trusting in your own abilities and indicates a mature and experienced point view. The Queen and the King are linked by this attribute: when Experience is combined with Receptiveness you have perception and wisdom (Queen) and when it is combined with Assertiveness you have power and control (King).

Experience is opposite and complementary to Potential. It has to be noted, however, that Experience can be the expression and evolution of Potential.

From the Court Diagram to Interpretation

Once you understand the relations and connections between the Court Cards, it's very easy to find their meaning during a Reading.

The Court Cards for the Suit of Chalices in the Happy Tarot. Artwork by S. Ficca.
In many modern decks, the Court Cards are connected to each other, not just by meaning, by also graphically.

On the next page: Black and white sketch for the Suit of Pentacles Court Cards. Happy Tarot, artwork by S. Ficca.

Above: The King of Swords of the Visconti Tarot. Milan, 1450 ca.

The cards are easily interpreted as attitudes or courses of action. They indicate how a person stands in relation to a problem, a difficulty or the environment that surrounds it.

The meanings of the cards can then be summarized as follows:

↬ **Page:** learning – approaching a situation with a learning attitude, assessing things, gathering information.

↬ **Knight:** action – approaching a situation with a decisive attitude, taking action, taking initiative.

↬ **Queen:** perceiving – approaching a situation with an understanding attitude, listening to different options, being curious and empathetic.

↬ **King:** control – approaching a situation with a commanding attitude, expressing authority, making decisions, working through others.

Two Different Directions

A Tarot expert who studies the Court Diagram will realize that the two directions – Receptiveness/Assertiveness and Potential/Experience – are not equivalent to each other.

The Knight of Chalices (called the Prince of Chalices) of the Illuminati Tarot. Detail. Artwork by E. C. Dunne.

In fact, the vertical axis of the diagram (the one that connects potential and experience) seems to create a temporal relationship: the King is the adult version of the Knight and the Knight is the King in his youth. A similar relationship connects the Page to the Queen. In contrast, the horizontal axis, or assertiveness and receptivity, indicating two opposite sides of the character, which are entirely complementary between them.

Taking this into account, the Court Cards can also be defined this way:

⌒ **Page:** Receptiveness from the bottom – The Page receives information from the outside in order to grow and to better express her potential.

⌒ **Knight:** Assertiveness from the bottom – The Knight imposes himself on the outside in order to grow, to leave his mark on the world and to let others know who he is and what he wants.

⌒ **Queen:** Receptiveness from the top – The Queen receives information from the outside, to understand, advise and help others.

⌒ **King:** Assertiveness from the top – The King imposes himself on the outside with the intent to direct others and to control events. Thanks to his experience and power, he can influence the situation and then make sure it evolves in the best way.

READING REVERSALS

Open a Tarot deck and place any card on the table, face-up. Without lifting the card from the table, rotate it 180 degrees. Turn the card so the image, titles and numbers appear to be upside-down from your point of view. You've just created what Tarot Readers call a "reversal" or, more commonly, a "reversed card."

The Hermit from the Fey Tarot, artwork by Mara Aghem. Detail. A card can be seen from different direction and still make sense.

Reversals may be assigned special significance within the spread if the Reader chooses. Reading reversals is optional. However, embracing reversals adds an exciting degree of variety and clarity to your readings.

How Cards Become Reversed

Tarot cards may become reversed in any number of ways:

⌒ During shuffling, a card may fall out of the pack. It may be re-inserted upside-down relative to the rest of the cards.

⌒ Someone cuts the cards and the two halves of the deck may be reunited in such a way that half of the cards in the deck become reversed.

⌒ Someone uses the finger-painting method of shuffling the cards (spreading face-down cards on a table in a random pile, then squaring them up again). Some cards are almost certain to be turned upside down.

How to Recognize a Reversed Card

It is very easy to recognize when a card is reversed or not.
If the figure in the card appears upside down, the card is Reversed. If it appears upright, the card is not.

Upright Cards   **Reversed Cards**

Benefits of Reading Reversals

There are two primary benefits associated with reading reversals.

Variety

Over time, it becomes easy to get stuck in reading habits and ruts. Reading reversals forces the Reader to see familiar cards in a new light and avoids the same old cards in the same old way.

Clarity

Tarot cards contain a wide variety of meanings, not including your own intuitive interpretations. Reading reversals helps the entire spread become a clearer picture and a reflection of what is going on with you or the Querent.

Each Tarot card in this book carries two *Essential Meanings*. The Magician, for example, is assigned the meanings "Will" and "Ability" It is easy to associate the first (more personal) keyword with the upright Magician and the second (more pragmatical) keyword with the reversed Magician.

382

Reading Reversals is Optional

Remember that not all Tarot Readers read reversals. If you choose not to read a reversal, simply turn any reversed cards right-side-up again. This is a time-honored practice. Readers with a strong preference for upright cards should feel free to ignore reversed cards entirely.

Many Readers find that reversals add a degree of texture, depth and insight to their readings. A student Reader should experiment with reversals. If assigning special interpretations to reversed cards helps to generate more accurate or insightful readings, feel free to incorporate reversals into your reading process.

Consistency

This decision to read with reversals or ignore them entirely need not be made "once and for all." The Reader may read with reversals for a while, ignore them for a while and then embrace them again. A Reader may read reversals on one day and ignore them the next, use them only when working with specific spreads or not use them at all.

Once a reading begins, however, the Reader should be consistent. Prior to shuffling and dealing the cards, the Reader decides whether or not he/she will use reversals. Readers who elect to read reversals and then reject them after being frightened or disappointed by the number or nature of reversals that appear in a spread cheat their clients and themselves.

383

Interpreting Reversals

There are many different ways to interpret reversals. Some are simple, while others may be more complicated. It is important to understand that using Reversals adds depth and complexity to a reading, but the ultimate purpose is not to have a complicated reading, but a clear useful one, that can really help the client.

Always choose a way to use reversals that benefit the reading as a whole.

Use only one reversal system at a time.

The Opposite Meaning

The simplest reversal system involves interpreting a reversed card as having the exact opposite of its upright meaning.
For example:

— An upright Fool is associated with *Innocence* or *Madness* so the reversed Fool would be associated with *Guilt* or *Seriousness*.

— An upright Chariot is associated with *Triumph* or *Arrogence*, the reversed Chariot would be associated with *Defeat* or *Humility*.

— An upright Tower is associated with *Demolition* or *Destruction*; the reversed Tower would be associated with *Construction* and *Preservation*.

— An upright Ace of Cups is associated with an abundance of emotion or inexhaustible spiritual energy, the reversed Ace of Cups would be associated with rigidity or spiritual exhaustion.

— An upright Eight of Swords is associated with limits, fears and obstacles, the reversed Eight of Swords would be associated with freedom, fearlessness and unimpeded progress.

The Reversed Tower
Using oppositional meanings can help you to understand the meanings of the upright card. For instance, in the Tower, the essential meanings of *Demolition* and *Destruction* are often seen as synonymous. However, when turned to their opposite - *Construction* and *Preservation* - they clearly show their difference.

The World from the Manga Tarot. Concept by R. Minetti and Artwork by Anna Lazzarini. Detail.
As The World means something completed, a reversed world, may indicate that there is still something lacking before completition.

Blocked Energy

You can look at a reversed card as a blockage of the card's regular meanings. In this case the reversal suggests a course of remedy for that particular situation, in order to let the energy of a card flow freely again.

⁓ An upright Empress is interpreted as a creative woman who lets her artistic energies flow. The reversed Empress suggests she's not allowing herself creative expression and freedom she needs.

⁓ An upright Hermit indicates a person who is taking plenty of time out for himself. The reversed Hermit suggests this person is socializing to excess and needs to spend quality time alone and slow it down to regain perspective.

⁓ An upright Devil card could represent excess, debauchery and control issues while a reversed Devil card could suggest that a person has moved beyond a situation that used to hold them hostage. They are now free.

⁓ An upright Ace of Cups represents free flowing emotion. A reversed Ace of Cups suggests blocked emotions welling up. The emotion must be released in some way.

385

Reversals Scream "Look at Me!"

There are moments, especially in a spread involving a great number of cards, when reversals call attention to themselves. The reversal appears as a blinking light or red flag begging for your attention. If you choose to do this, do not change the meaning of the card, but give it more importance. Do not fret to give an interpretation, as there may be something not apparent that could be helpful to notice.

Magic in Reversing the Reversal

A reversed card appears for you or your client. You identify it as a block and discover the card signifies a problem. Perform a magical unblocking action. Create an affirmation on the spot and verbalize it. Turn the card right side up to free yourself or your client.

For example, a reversed Temperance card in the present placement of a spread indicates personal energy is out of whack. Things are out of balance and you are worrying about others rather than taking care of yourself. Create an affirmation on the spot, "From this moment forth, I bring balance to my life." Now upright the card. Voila!

For those not comfortable using literal or metaphorical magic, the reversed card still indicated a block that should to be challenged and broken by the client. Asking the client to verbalize the block and his intent to break through it can be very useful.

The Reader could ask the client to say aloud: "My personal energy is fragmented. I need to bring balance to my life". Other cards appearing in the Spread will often suggest steps on how to achieve that goal.

The Hanged Man from the Manga Tarot. Concept by R. Minetti and Artwork by Anna Lazzarini. Detail. Being upside down is not always a bad thing.

WHAT DOES READING MEAN?

Who can read Tarot?

Anyone and everyone can master the art of Tarot if they wish. No prerequisite is required other than a curious mind and willingness to learn.

Cross-culturally and for thousands of years, the divinatory arts have held a special place in human culture. Etruscans taught Romans to see the future amidst animals' entrails. The Oracles of Delphi foretold future events to the Greeks. Victorian mediums held séances in private homes and indigenous peoples interpreted flying birds and clouds in hopes of future rains. Divination, once the work of shamans and priestesses, is no longer the work of a specialized few. It can be learned and practiced by anyone with the desire to pick up a deck of cards and begin reading them.

People are usually drawn to Tarot while searching for answers. Questions are formed, a spread is used, the cards are laid out and the cards are interpreted. Certain questions will examine the future, others are aimed at introspection and others are concerned with confirmation, intuition, imagination or creativity. Tarot's answer comes in the form of storytelling. Every answer depends on the question posed. The Reader decides how to use the Tarot according to personal belief systems, philosophy, education and inspiration. Tarot is a highly personal practice and as a result becomes many different things to many people.

A Tarot Reading on a busy street.

Six Essential Components of a Reading

A Tarot reading can be divided into six different components. While they may not always have the same importance, they are all an integral part of Reading Tarot. The Tarot Reader will progress in experience and knowledge when giving proper attention to all six components.

1 **Meanings**

Each Tarot card reflects a meaning. The Reader knows these meanings and chooses the one most relative and applicable to the reading.

2 **Spreads**

Arcana meanings are not interpreted singularly. The cards are placed in a spread; a particular sequence and pattern of cards. The cards interrelate to one another when placed in a spread. This is how Tarot forms a complete discourse, narrative and story. The story changes every time the cards are flipped.

3 **Questions**

An intelligent question must be articulated when reading. It is fundamental to stay on point with each particular question. The Reader must be able to communicate what is seen in the cards in a way that relates to the question asked. If no questions are asked, it is up to the Reader to interpret the story they see in the cards.

A Reading is a complex environment and it's not done just by cards and meanings.

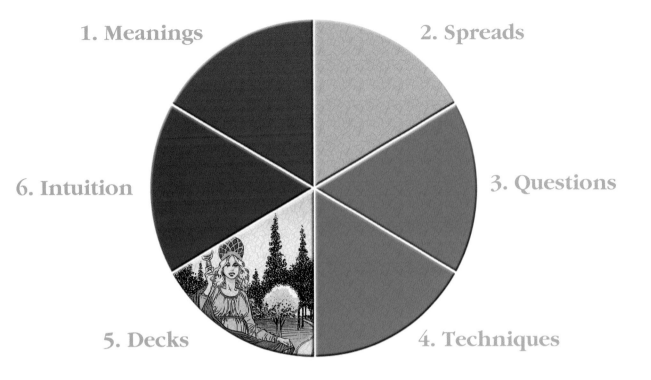

1. Meanings **2. Spreads** **3. Questions** **4. Techniques** **5. Decks** **6. Intuition**

4 Techniques

Tarot interpretation techniques are endless. Various techniques explain how to combine significance, spread and question in a way so the most useful answer is given.

5 Decks

Each and every Tarot deck is different, even two decks of the exact same style. Two copies of the same deck will contain different energies based on who owns them. Opposing themes carry opposing interpretations. A Vampire themed deck will obviously carry a different energy than a Goddess themed deck. Each Reader develops a personal link and energetic connection to their collection of decks.

6 Intuition

Once all the elements are in place, the Reader will use her/his own intuition, instinctive knowing and sensitivity to interpret the cards. He or she will also use the meanings, the spreads, the techniques and the questions, to find an answer that is more than the simple sum of the cards.

How to Begin

The first step toward learning how to read the cards is gaining confidence with them. Tarot is an important, precious and personal object. Each handling of the cards will connect you to them as they absorb the movements of your hands, the imprints of your fingers and your spiritual energy.

Even if a potential Reader has never looked through a deck of cards before, they will find the cards reveals images that are pleasingly familiar. This occurs because of the Archetypal nature of the images. These symbols are capable of evoking memories, mental associations and stimulating the imagination.

Examine the Cards
Glance over the cards one by one. Perhaps you describe them out loud, allowing your imagination to run free with an association of ideas. Keep a small book of essential meanings and key words by your side. The Little White Book inside a new deck of cards is a helpful reference point and guide in learning to interpret the cards.

Ask a Question

Ask a question. Flip a card. See what happens. If you don't know what to ask, here's a great beginning question: "What will I learn from the Arcana?"

Extract a Card

Shuffle the deck and choose a card at random. Flip it over and look at it. Be guided by personal intuition. What possible meanings does the image suggest? Look the card meaning up. Choose the meaning you feel is most suitable.

Ending Your Reading

Ask a few more questions before terminating your reading:
What have I learned?
What new meanings have come to mind?
What cards have been the most difficult to interpret?
The answers to these questions help a Reader grow.

Magical or Psychological Link?

Tarot Readers often perceive a strong link between themselves and their deck of cards. It is not so easy to explain the exact nature of this link. For some, a magical and ritualistic connection is formed. They fill the deck with their own spiritual energy, thereby imprinting the deck. Others find a psychological link developing between themselves and the cards. In this way, a psychological bond is formed. Deep bonds are formed with cards that have been used for many years.

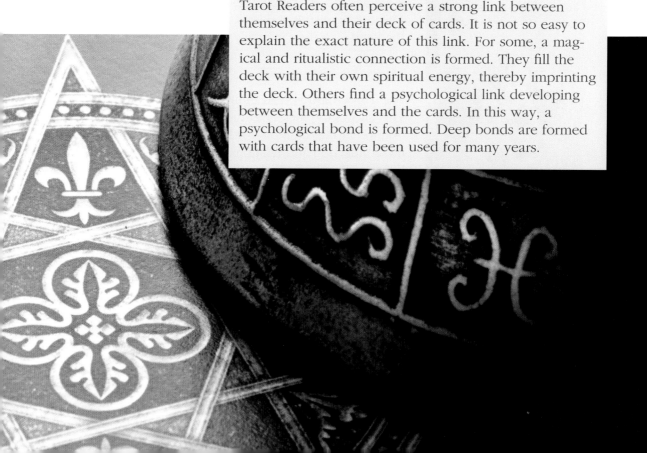

SIMPLE SPREADS

Four essential Spreads should be learned. Each of them serves a specific function and purpose and remains useful even to the most experienced Reader.

Nine of Wands from the Universal Fantasy Tarot, artwork by P. Martinello. Detail.

- **One Card Spread**
- **Three Card Spread**
- **Celtic Cross Spread**
- **Card of the Day**

One Card Spread

The single card spread is the basis of all other Tarot Spreads. A single card spread focuses on the meaning of one card. This card's meaning creates a clear and succinct answer to the Reader or the Querent's question.

Three Cards Spread

The Three Card Spread utilizes three cards placed in a row. This allows the Reader to move from a single card interpretation to reading multiple cards. This teaches the Reader about the connection and relationship between multiple cards and how the Past leads to the Present that affects the Future.

Celtic Cross Spread

This ten-card Spread is the most famous and commonly used Spread in the world. Once mastered, the Reader will be able to read on any topic and provide answers to any questions.

Card of the Day

Similar to the One Card Spread, the Card of the Day fosters a relationship between Tarot and personal, everyday life. It is also a useful Spread for personal Readings.

The Two of Wands from the Fey Tarot. Concept by R. Minetti, artwork by M. Aghem.
As a Card of the Day, it seems to say, "Hey dude, it's really time to get up".

394

ONE CARD SPREAD

1 Card
3 minutes average
a quick and to-the-point indication

A simple One Card Spread will provide all the answers needed. Even the most experienced of Readers gain knowledge from a One Card Spread. A One Card reading allows extreme specificity. This is helpful when looking for information on how to help yourself or improve in some way. Answer the question based on what you see in the card, what you know the card reflects and what you feel in your gut.

The Preparation and Positioning of the Cards

The Reader and Querent shuffle the deck. The Querent cuts the deck using their left hand and the Reader turns the card over.

Reading and Interpretation

The Reader thinks, "This card contains all the answers I need."

Example of a Reading

Card drawn: Queen of Cups
Essential Meanings: Sensitivity – Emotionality

Key Words: Sensitivity, Emotionalism, Wife, Lover, Friend, Empathy, Understanding, Listening, Affectionate, Love, Joy, Responsiveness, Sympathy, Dreamer, Artist, Charming, Caring, Listener

Reading and Interpretation
The Queen of Cups represents a person who is emotionally open and available others. She is a faithful lover, a good nurturer. If the Querent is looking for love, the answer is to maintain their current course. In relationships it is important they not lose themselves in the needs of their partner.

The interpretation is that you can trust what you feel, no matter the question.

The beauty of a One Card Spread lies in the simplicity and focus it provides. The Reader arrives at a concise answer using one card. The Reader is less likely to become distracted from the question at hand and runs less risk of confusion.

395

THREE CARD SPREAD

**3 Cards
5 minutes average
to quickly explore past,
present and future**

The Three Card Spread is a basic and most important spread for any Reader to master. It is also known as the *Time Line Spread* or the *Past, Present and Future Spread*. This spread is based on the conviction that the past informs the present and the present creates the future. The Reader uses this spread to resolve past events, understand the present situation and look into the future.

This Spread connects the Tarot cards and they are read in relation to one another. This card combination will often appear as part of more complex spreads. The ability to clearly interpret the connection between the causes of a situation (the past), the situation itself (the present) and the possible outcomes (the future) fosters the discovery of important answers.

The Reader must remind the Querent that the Future is not to be seen as an immutable destiny. We look at the Future in order to understand the direction we are currently heading, but we can still change our choices and create a different outcome.

Divination, is actually only useful when it helps people to create what they want through their choices and effort.

The Preparation and Positioning of the Cards

The Reader and Querent shuffle the deck in turn. The Querent cuts the deck using the hand he/she does not write with. The Reader places three Arcana in a straight line. The first card is placed to the left, the second in the middle and the last to the right.

Reading and Interpretation

The Reader proceeds to interpret the Arcana in each position while keeping in mind the relative meanings. Having interpreted all the cards, the Reader summarizes the entire reading in a complete discourse, known as a Synthesis.

1 The Past

The card appearing in this position represents the causes and the roots of the actual situation. The other two cards will be influenced by the interpretation of this one.
The Reader, while turning over the card of the past thinks: "This is what was before."

2 The Present

The card appearing in the second position represents the present. It is a photograph of the Querent's current situation. While turning over this card the Reader thinks:
"This is what is now."

3 The Future

The card appearing in the third position represents the possible future. The Reader, while turning the card over thinks:

The future nonetheless, is never certain. This card represents what could occur, what is most likely if the Querent does not modify the present situation.

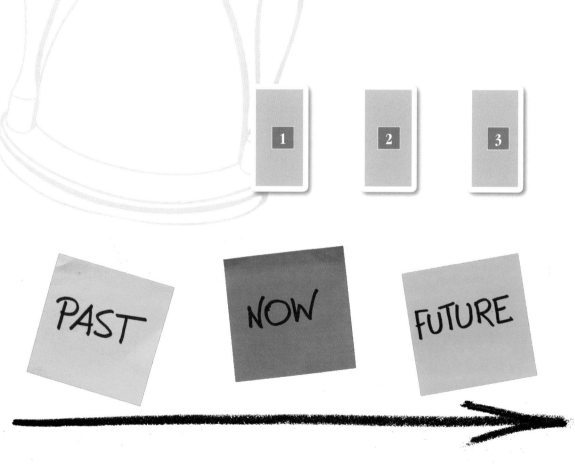

*The Fool, from the Happy Tarot.
Artwork by Serena Ficca.*

*Artwork for the Box of the Happy
Tarot, by Serena Ficca, showing
four Major Arcana walking
together on the hills. The scene is
inspired by the Seventh Seal, by
Ingmar Bergman.*

The Synthesis

The Past, Present, Future Spread is not about revealing what
will happen tomorrow. The future is a changeable entity
influenced by our actions. The Querent has most likely come
to the Reader for advice about what to do or how to better
understand a situation. Using these three cards the Reader is
able to help him/her reflect on past actions that have bought
things to this point. The Reader can demonstrate what
could possibly happen from there onwards. If the card that
indicates the future is positive, the Reader can reassure the
Querent that things are working well. If the card is negative,
the Reader should urge the Querent to change the way in
which he or she is dealing with the problem.

Example of a Reading

As the Spread is very simple, for the example we will be
using only the Major Arcana, using the Happy Tarot deck.
The cards are drawn and then turned in sequence. Depending on the Reader choice, it's possible to turn them all over
before starting the interpretation.

Cards drawn:
- **1.** Fool (past)
- **2.** Emperor (present)
- **3.** Hermit (future)

So many keywords

As every card has so many keywords associated to it, a beginner Reader may feel overwhelmed by the choice or be scared of forgetting something important by ignoring even one keyword.

In reality, keywords are supposed to help the Reader. Just reading the keywords in your mind will help focus on the Card concept and then your intuition will suggest which keyword - if any - to follow through the interpretation.
If a Reader is truly a beginner, she could just limit herself to the Essential Meaning. During interpretation, she will have only to choose between two meanings which often express the same concept with a positive and a negative light. There is not a right or wrong choice: just choose the meaning that best connects with the other cards.

With experience, the process will become easier and easier.

The Emperor, from the Happy Tarot. Artwork by Serena Ficca.

Fool
Essential Meanings: Innocence – Madness
Key Words: Folly, Inexperience, Potential, Start, Adventure, Playful, Freedom, Action, Travel, Beginning, Wandering, Essence, Madness, Visionary, Innocence, Naive, Originality, Incomprehensible Action, Strangeness, Carelessness, Journey, Hike, Pilgrimage, Thoughtlessness, Touched by Spirit, Trickster.

Emperor
Essential Meanings: Domain – Authority
Key Words: Authority, Rigidity, Precision Leadership, Arrogant, Domination, Dominion, Responsibility, Solidity, Order, Power, Government, Father, Rationalism, Discipline, Command, Egocentrism, Experience, Organization, Law, Conservative, Inflexible, Tradition, Advantage, Sovereignty, Supremacy, Constriction, Administration, Requirement, Overlord, Skill.

Hermit
Essential Meanings: Enlightenment – Withdrawal
Key Words: Isolation, Retreat, Introversion, Solitude, Experience, Ancient, Guide, Quest, Pilgrimage, Silence, Reflection, Retreat, Philosophy, Self-reflection, Self-Sufficiency, Sagacity, Prudence, Austerity, Humility, Prudence, Meditation, Search, Old Master.

The Hermit, from the Happy Tarot. Artwork by Serena Ficca.

What do you think?

How would you have interpreted the three cards?
And would the interpretation have changed if read for a different person?
Or with a different deck? Reading is not a science. This is why a Reader must follow her intuition and embrace the subjectivity of the event. Nothing metaphysical can ever be fully rational or scientific without losing it's worth.

The Fool Indicates the Past

The Querent is coming from a long, carefree, almost thoughtless period. She was happy and did not worry much about the future, taking each day as it came, without objectives or a sense of direction.

The Emperor Commands the Present

Having lived without worrying about anything or anyone, the Querent is now busy with many things to do and manages her time with attention. It could be said that she has got her head sorted out.

The Hermit Reveals the Future

There is no doubt that the Querent is becoming more mature and self-sufficient, but risks remaining alone. Without proper care, the Querent may loose past friendships and finding herself having no fun at all.

The future is a changeable entity. As a Tarot Reader, when speaking of the future, do not say, "This will be," but rather suggest "this could be". When a negative card appears in a position indicating the future, the Querent gains great benefit from the reading. She will be advised of the possible consequences of a situation she is facing in the present and, as such, she will have the chance of changing her future for the better.

Synthesis

The three cards indicate a process of maturation. From the lightheartedness of the past emerges a new sense of responsibility. The actual situation seems more constructive and the Querent seems to be happy. Nevertheless, by proceeding in this direction she could lose friends and people that were important to her. The Reader could ask the Querent how much these friendships matter. If the Querent does not mind abandoning them, then it is fair to proceed along this pathway. Alternatively, if the friendships are important, an effort can be made to remain close. This action will modify the future as indicated by the Hermit.

The Reader can also point out that the Fool and the Hermit seems to be opposite to one another, while the Emperor appears to be a balanced middle way between the two.

THE CELTIC CROSS

10 Cards
20 minutes average
to anwer any generic
question

The Celtic Cross Spread, found in almost every single Tarot book, has been popular since its introduction in the early 20th Century as it hits every possible topic with an exceptional balance of simplicity and depth.

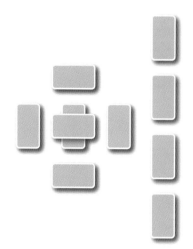

The Preparation and Positioning of the Cards

The Reader and Querent shuffle the deck in turn. The Querent cuts the deck three times with the left hand. The Reader then deals ten face down cards, arranging them in the shape of the Celtic Cross.

Reading and Interpretation

The Reader proceeds to interpret the Arcana in each position keeping in mind the relative meanings. Having interpreted all the cards, the Reader summarizes the entire reading in a complete discourse, known as a Synthesis.

1 The Cover

The cover card tells the Reader the nature of the Querent's question. Upon turning this card over, the Reader thinks: *"This card is the situation surrounding my Querent."*

2 The Cross

The crossing card represents the obstacle and influence challenging the Querent. As the Reader turns this card over, the Reader thinks: *"This card is the Querent's challenge."*

3 The Crown

The Crown represents the Querent's goal, an ideal outcome, from the Querent's perspective. Upon turning this card over, the Reader thinks: *"This card is a resolution my Querent would happily embrace."*

The Reader should not forget to examine, in addition to the individual cards, the spread as a whole. How many Major cards appear? What suits are present? What suits are absent? What numbers are represented or repeated? In what direction are the card's characters looking?

401

4 The Foundation

This card represents the foundation or root of the situation. As the Reader reveals this card, the Reader thinks: *"This card depicts an event in the more distant past that caused the present situation."*

5 The Past

The Past card represents very recent events related to the situation. As the Reader reveals this card, the Reader thinks: *"This card depicts recent events leading to the present."*

6 The Future

This card represents events in the near future. As the card is turned over, the Reader thinks: *"This card depicts what must come to pass very soon."*

The Reader will notice that the following four cards are positioned to create an ascending tower. The cards 7, 8 and 9, all contribute to the final result (card 10).

7 The Self/Attitude

This card represents the Querent's self-image. As the Reader turns the card over, the Reader thinks: *"This is how the Querent sees him/herself."*

8 The Other

This card represents how others see the consultant. As the Reader reveals this card, the Reader thinks: *"This reveals how others see the Querent."*

9 Hopes and Fears

This card represents the Querent's hopes and fears. As the Reader turns this card over, the Reader thinks: *"This card depicts what my Querent's desires or dreads."*

10 Final Result

This card represents the ultimate outcome of the situation. As the Reader reveals it, the Reader thinks: *"This is how the situation will finally be resolved."*

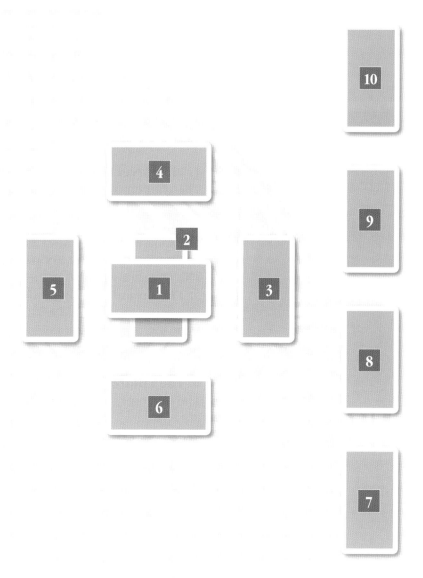

The Synthesis

The initial cross of six cards provides the Reader with a concise overview of the Querent's situation. It is a portrait of the Querent's life. The final four cards provide psychological insights that skew the Querent's ability to deal effectively with the matter at hand.

Justice reversed.
It is about the rules, but it's not about following them.

Example of a Reading

The Querent is a dark-haired, serious woman in her late forties. She is employed as a financial advisor.

1. The Cover is the Five of Pentacles
The Querent has failed to handle a financial matter appropriately.

2. The Cross is the Eight of Coins (reversed)
The Querent's job is now in jeopardy.

3. The Crown is the Six of Coins
The Querent wants to make amends.

4. The Foundation is Justice (reversed)
The situation evolved because the Querent has a history of knowing the rules but fails to follow them.

5. The Past is the Seven of Swords
Recently, the Querent has tried to hide her mistakes.

6. The Future is Judgment
The Querent's misdeeds will be revealed and cause a major life change.

7. The Self is the Hanged Man
The Querent sees herself as a persecuted victim of circumstance and is not ready to accept responsibility for her actions.

8. The Other is the Devil
Others see the Querent as dangerously selfish and dishonest.

9. Hopes and Fears are the Seven of Cups
The Querent would like to "wake up" and discover that the events of the past few months have been a dream.

10. The Final Result is the Eight of Wands
Ultimately, the Querent will face swift and sudden - but not life-altering - change.

Synthesis

In addition to the story revealed here, a skilled Reader would note the dominance of Pentacles (suggesting an emphasis on financial themes) and the scarcity of Wands, Swords and Cups (suggesting the Querent has failed to make a plan, consider alternatives, or grasp the emotional impact of the situation).

The good news: the ultimate outcome is represented by a Minor card, suggesting the Querent will likely keep her job (a card like Death, for instance, would have predicted a dismissal). The bad news: as long as the Querent continues to see herself as a victim, she is unlikely to experience the growth that would prevent similar incidents from happening in the future.

What Has Been Learned?

The Celtic Cross provides a holistic overview of a Querent's situation but may fall short in terms of providing recommendations for action. In other words: a Celtic Cross reading may leave Querents saying, "Yes, that's what's going on but now, what do I do about it?"

To make the spread more action oriented, some Readers prefer to assign very different meanings to the final four cards:

7 Advice

A frank, advantageous, or honorable action the Querent can take.

8 A First Step

A small action the Querent can take immediately to change things for the better.

9 Passive Outcome

The outcome if the Querent does nothing.

10 Active Outcome

The outcome if the Querent follows the advice offered by the spread.

Eigth of Wands of the Universal tarot. Detail.
If interpreted as "Active Outcome", the Arcanum should be seen as a strong encouragement to act, move and stop losing time.

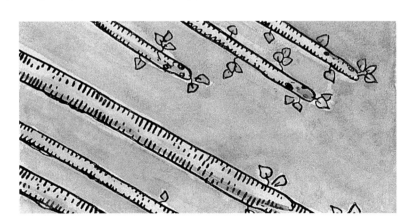

CARD OF THE DAY

The Card of the Day is a powerful daily reading ritual. It has the potential to foster immense personal growth and improve accuracy in readings. The Daily Card is a powerful transformational tool that should never be dismissed as a simple beginner's exercise.
This Spread is invaluable to connect the Reader's daily experiences to the Tarot and it's the first and most important step to use Tarot for Reading to oneself.

The Daily Card reading should be conducted once a day, every day. The Daily Card is drawn at random from any deck, placed face-up on the table and intuitively interpreted.

The Card of the Day can be used in two different and complementary ways if used at the beginning of the day (usually at morning), or at the end of it (usually at evening).
If a card is drawn at morning the Reader is asking "What will happen today?" In a different form it may be asking "What should I pay attention to today?" or "What opportunity for growth and learning I will have today?"
If a card is drawn at evening the Reader is asking "What happened today?" or "What lesson for growth and learning I can take from the events of today?"

This Spread is geared toward self-reading and contemplation. The Reader's attention should not focus on what happens, but on the interpretation of the card, its meaning and significance as an experience. The Card of the Day will help the Reader pay attention to daily events with greater participation and awareness.

The Preparation and Positioning of the Cards

The Reader shuffles the deck and cuts the cards with her non-dominant hand. The Reader pulls a single card from the top of the deck and places it, face-up, on the table.
If in the morning, it should be done immediately after waking, as the link to the subconscious is strongest when

The Reader may also draw a card of the day twice. One in the morning and one in the evening. The Spread is read normally in the morning, but in the evening it should be treated as a two card Spread, positioning the evening card close to the morning card.

406

arising from sleep. If in the evening, the interpretation should be followed by a couple of minutes of meditation, to help interiorize the events of the day, through the meaning of the card.

Reading and Interpretation

The Reader is careful to note any and all impressions that spring to mind. The chosen card could be interpreted as:

- A preview of an upcoming event
- A theme for the day
- An inspiration for a journal or diary entry
- A subject for meditation
- A challenge to overcome
- A lesson
- A potential
- A word of encouragement
- A focal point of the day

After considering these first impressions, the Reader chooses one, saying:
"I believe this is my message."

Tarot Journaling.
A journal can be a Reader's best friend.

The Reader records this interpretation, called The Synthesis, in a notebook and sets it aside for the day.

Just before bed, the Reader checks in with the Synthesis. It is examined in light of the day's events. To foster growth the Reader may choose to make notes regarding the accuracy and validity of the morning interpretation.

Alternatively, a second card may be drawn as an evening card and be interpreted close to the original card.

The Synthesis

Many Readers allow their impression of the card to shape their understanding of its meaning and message. The nature of the card may change from day to day, making it a preview of an upcoming event one day, a word of encouragement the next and a subject for meditation the next.

Alternatively, some Readers will decide what the card represents before pulling it from the deck. In this case, a Reader might say:

"This card is my lesson for the day."

The end of day check in is an often-neglected aspect of this work. The daily "self-check," looking at the journal entry at the end of the day, provides the Reader feedback in regard to precision and accuracy. It is critical for growth.

Example of a Reading

The Reader draws the Wheel of Fortune. The Reader writes in her notebook, "The Wheel: change, time, seasons, cycles, revolution, turning, returning. Today, I will accept change as a normal part of life and be on the look out for good luck."

During the day, the Reader learns that her work department has been reorganized. Many co-workers are upset, but the Reader makes it a point of looking for the potential for positive change in the situation.

The Synthesis
At the end of the day, the Reader reviews her notes to determine if that her interpretation of the card was valid, accurate and useful.

What Has Been Learned
Though the Daily Card is a simple process, its effect is cumulative. By keeping a record of this practice over time, the Reader creates a record of growth and a library of intensely personal interpretations for each card.

The Wheel from the Marseille Cat Tarot. Artwork by Severino Baraldi.

Did you learn to think positive today?

QUESTIONS

The question is an essential part of a Tarot reading. A good question is more important than the deck you select, more important than the atmosphere created and could contain more value than the final answer. The ability to ask a good question and to stay on the topic of the question is paramount.

There are no right and wrong questions. The sky is the limit!

For a Querent, understanding what is the question she really wants to ask is a fundamental and very useful part of the Reading.
This is because in order to ask a good question she will have already started to make clarity within herself.

Asking and Phrasing

Asking the best question will help guide you to the best answer. Correct formulation of the question is essential. This will lead to an answer that is as clear and precise as possible. Three simple steps will formulate excellent questions.

Each question asked, opens a different journey.

☙ 1. Acknowledge the role you play in your future.

None of us are slaves to destiny. Note the responsibility of your actions. Nothing affects your future more than you do.

☙ 2. State your desired outcome.

You wouldn't be asking about something if you weren't hoping for a specific result. Verbalize what you want and why you want it.

☙ 3. Construct your question.

You are now ready to construct a thoughtful question. Construct your question in a manner that makes you an active participant in your future.

Precise Question Equals Precise Answer

Asking a precise question and being sure to answer it with equal precision will offer an active solution of any issue or problem. Avoid questions that end in yes or no.

Say a Querent is looking for love. They want to ask the question, "Will I find my soul mate?" Help the Querent rephrase the question so they receive a practical answer. "What can I do to bring a healthy romantic relationship into my life?"

The former question answers with a yes or no. The latter question will be articulated in something the Querent can actually do.

411

Aim for Simplicity

The more concise the question, the more useful it will be. This is especially important when you are reading for yourself. Resist the temptation to concentrate all of your concerns or worries in one single reading or question. It is better to ask one simple question, then another and so on. Not only will the answers become clearer but you will likely detect a pattern in the cards.

Avoid Why and When, Embrace How and What

Asking the questions "When..?" or "Why...?" are not generally helpful in phrasing questions. Questions typically beginning with "What...?" or "How...?" will provide practical and effective answers which are full of suggestions.

Example: "When will I get a raise?" vs. "What can I do to get a the raise I deserve?" See the difference? The "What" question offers a doable solution.

Generic Questions

Sometimes, you or a Querent will sit before the cards without a clear idea of what to ask. The Querent may be nervous or confused, scared or overwhelmed. Luckily, Tarot is a patient and sensible friend. In these cases simply ask, "Tell me what I need to know right now?" This is always an appropriate and wonderful question.

Seeking the Answer

The Tarot replies to questions with cards rich in meaning. The answers will be expressed in numbers, titles, key words, images and symbols. A Reader extracts pieces of the answer from each of these elements. The Reader decodes the Arcana, creating an association between the situation, the question and what is shown in the cards. This is called the Interpretation. Interpreting Tarot requires time and patience but anyone can do it. Deep and evocative information can come from a beginning student. You must trust yourself, your instincts and intuition when interpreting the cards. This is important, no matter your skill level.

What does "staying on topic" means? It means focus.

Staying on Topic

It can be a struggle to stay on the topic of the question. A card or theme will catch the Reader's attention and suddenly you are off on a tangent. Returning to the original question is important unless you decide it is no longer relevant.

To remain on topic, simply write the final question on a piece of paper. American Tarot Reader Scott M. Martin suggests using an index card for each question. Write each question on the top of the index cards. Arrange in a spread and lay the Tarot card with the answer on top of the index card. The question will remain seen and be referred to. This is an excellent practice while learning a complicated spread like the Celtic Cross. Simply write what the card's position is on each index card until the spread is committed to memory.

In the previous page:
Seven of Pentacles from the
Manga Tarot, concept by R. Minetti,
artwork by A. Lazzarini. Detail.

Unethical Questions

Many Readers feel that inquiring about a third party without consent is unethical and improper. Tarot snooping involves questions about another person. "What is my husband's state of mind? Is he having an affair? Does he really love me?"

A helpful way to address these questions is to turn the question back to you, "Are my husband and I in the right state of mind to be together? Do I attract lovers who cheat? Is this a good long term relationship for me?"

It is better to focus on yourself and the things which you have direct control over. Don't ask a question like, "What does Tim think of me?" A better way to phrase the question is, "What can I do with regard to what Tim is thinking of me." In this case the subject of the question is the Querent, not a third party and the answer will also be more useful, as it will help the Querent take action or decide a strategy.

Each Reader will make personal judgment calls about the ethics of peeking into another person's life. That being said, it is best to keep yourself and your own life as the focus of the questions.

Serendipity always helps.

READING FOR YOURSELF

The modern practice of reading one's own Tarot is popular. But in the long history of Tarot, self-reading is a fairly recent development. Using Tarot for you has numerous wonderful advantages. It is important and sometimes challenging to not blend personal reading with your personal desires. It is challenging to be objective when we are the subject of a reading.

Objectivity of inter-pretation is the most difficult thing to master when reading for yourself.

Can you read for yourself? Certainly. Self-sufficiency is a given for the modern Tarot Reader. The cards become a dialogue between the Reader and her intuition. As such, reading Tarot for oneself becomes a form of reflection. Objectivity of interpretation is the most difficult thing to master when reading for yourself. Keep the Justice card in mind when reading for yourself to be sure your views are balanced.

Fear the Future

A number of vintage Tarot books take a fixed and predictive view of Tarot. These books may warn the Reader against reading for themselves. They never explain why one should avoid this practice. These books which often include warnings about not taking money for readings and other old wives tales are based on superstition and beliefs of the past.

These books were written at a time where people truly believed destiny was set, fixed and unchangeable. Additionally, it was thought that only those who possessed strong psychic ability could use Tarot with success.

Modern Freedom

You will meet your love

Tarot is not fortune cookies.

Modern day reading has mostly left the fatalistic culture behind. Querents are less likely to fear their own fate and come to Tarot with an open and willing mind. Querents come to Tarot with a hope of understanding more about themselves and their situations. The cards are still used to make predictions but these are understood as part of a possible (not fixed) future. The potential future is based on their actions. Rather than be at the mercy the card's predictions, they can use Tarot to see themselves and their choices with increased clarity. Tarot has evolved from darkened corners into widespread popularity.

Tarot is a tool to see more clearly.

Why You Should Read Cards for Yourself

Convenience
A good Tarot reader is not always available when you need one. Reading the cards for yourself, you will benefit from the wisdom and knowledge available to the 19th Century Reader as well as modern interpretations.

Money
Consulting a professional card reader can become an expensive practice, especially if you visit them with frequency. Reading cards for yourself becomes a great way to save all that money and become self aware without reliance on another.

Privacy
Some of your questions may be too difficult, too personal to explain to another person. If you can ask these deeply private questions of the cards, you can address them without feeling forced to share or explain to others.

Practice

Each and every time you flip a card to gain clarity, guidance, or wisdom, you are becoming more familiar with the cards themselves, the myriad of potential meanings and with yourself. You'll discover new ways of working with the cards and uncover the unique characteristics of a deck newly purchased.

Meditation

The Questions you can ask yourself may be different than those you ask another person, however gifted a Reader she may be. Asking questions to yourself may be a process more similar to meditation, introspection and self-exploration. All things that are necessarily part of a personal journey and cannot be effectively shared.

Challenges

Any and all challenges of personal readings can be alleviated with the right attitude and correct preparation.

Objectivity

We project our attitudes and views on the world around us more than we realize. Tarot is no exception. You may be tempted to interpret cards for better or worse when dealing with an emotional situation.

Meditation can benefit you in many ways, beside Tarot Readings.

To begin reading you only need yourself, a question and a Tarot deck.

417

Reading for yourself will help you
When reading for others.
Reading for others will help you
when reading for yourself.

Freshness

Tarot interpretations are based on traditional meanings. We can accidently fall into habits of understanding card meanings. Alternating your decks will help to keep your vision fresh and crisp.

Dependency

Tarot reading should offer independence and inspiration while enjoying your life. A Tarot practice can teach you how to ask new and fresh questions. Remember the magic of a properly phrased question; it will trick your brain into finding the proper answer.

Focus

Personal readings can spiral out of control with emotionally charged questions. You pull one card, then another only to find yourself swimming in a pool of fifteen cards with no clear outcome. Focus is of extreme importance, whether you are reading for yourself or another.

The best way to stay on target and focused is to write down your information with pen and paper. Form a clear, articulate and proactive question. Then, as best as you can, flip your card and write down a clear, concise answer. Writing your answer or interpretation down will slow your thoughts and coax you towards a clear, concise answer. Your mind won't run amuck when you focus on one clear stream of thought.

418

WHAT ARE TECHNIQUES?

Reading Tarot is not difficult. Each card has a meaning. You shuffle the Arcana while asking questions, draw a few cards, and place them on the table according to a Spread's positions. Each position has significance which, combined with the meaning of the card, is used to provide an answer.

Tarot techniques are not much different from Martial Arts techniques.

The process is straightforward, intuitive and, while easy, it allows for incredible depth and outstanding clarity.
And yet the art of Reading Tarot does not end here.

Different Techniques

More experienced Readers may apply different techniques to their interpretations, Spreads and Readings in order to help the Reader answer different questions or provide additional information.
The use of Reversals is considered a technique, and it's probably the most commonly known. As with the Re-

*Two of Pentacles from the Manga
Tarot. Detail.
Artwork by Anna Lazzarini.*

versals, most Techniques are definitely optional, but each of them can potentially help a Reader. Some other techniques, like keeping a Tarot journal, do not apply directly to a Reading, but are still useful for learning Tarot, interiorizing the meanings and growing as a Reader. Other Techniques are useful when the Reading is at risk of becoming stuck or stagnant. For instance, the appearance of frightening cards may scare or paralyze the Querent. A technique regarding these situation may came in handy and be extremely useful to the Reader.

Tarot Techniques come in many varieties. Some are complex like the Elemental Dignities codified by the Hermetic Order of the Golden Dawn at the beginning of the 20th Century. Others rely on Astrology and Kabbalah, and require a level of confidence and experience from the Reader that make them unsuitable for beginners.
Other techniques however, are very simple and immediate. These are a core part of Tarot Reading fundamentals.

The Techniques described in the present volume will be:
- Balance of the Spread
- Keeping a Tarot Journal
- Intuitive Reading
- Symbolic Reading
- Negative Cards
- Unmatched Illustrations
- Using Gender and Age
- Meditating with Tarot
- Tarot for Expression

BALANCE OF THE SPREAD

The Balance of the Spread Technique is particularly useful in Spreads with a large number of cards, while it gives very little informations in Spreads with few cards.

Important information can be gained from a spread without interpreting every single card. A technique called the Balance of the Spread examines the relationship between suits, numbers, Majors and Minors. This system establishes the tone of the reading and the cards are read as a single connected unit.

Compared to more advanced Techniques with a similar approach - like the Elemental Dignities - the Balance of the Spread focuses on an intuitive interpretation, and allows for a much faster Reading, even when cards have been drawn.

All Elements Under Consideration

The balance technique begins with the assumption that the images and meanings of single cards are only part of a reading. It can be used along with the normal interpretation of a spread. Important information is gained even from other elements, for example:

- Majors or Minors
- Suits
- Court Card Ranking
- Card Numbers

Major Arcana usually weight more than Minor Arcana.

Balance Between Major and Minor Arcana

The Reader counts how many Major and Minor Arcana are present in the spread. The more Major Arcana present, the stronger the impact will be on the situation described by the Querent. A greater presence of Minor Arcana means the situation will not have a great impact on the Querent's life. Despite how difficult or insurmountable the problem appears, when faced with an abundance of Minor Arcana, the situation must be viewed as transient.

However, in case of a relative abundance of Majors, the few Minors present should be looked at with greater attention. They may indicate weaknesses in the situation or things the Querent is not giving enough importance to.
If there are a significant majority of Minors, the few Majors are even more important. They often represent focal points in the situation, and are a very clear indication of where the Querent should give more attention.

Suits and questions

The information gleamed by the predominance or absence of a suit, can be particularly useful in the case of specific questions. If, for instance, the Querent had asked for a reading on work, an abundance of Wands or Pentacles may be expected. However if one of these Suits were to be under-represented it could immediately point to the heart of the problem.

Many Cups? There is likely much emotion and drama in the air.

What Suits Reveal

Important elements can be ascertained by counting the appearing suits. A balanced spread, where all suits appear in a balanced number, indicates a stable situation where things are unlikely to change dramatically. It also indicates a healthy situation where nothing has too much or too little space.

However, if one Suit is over represented against the others, we can gleam some information.

High number of Wands
Accent on work: intense passion, good intentions and frenetic activity.

High number of Swords
Accent on thought: interminable discussions, exchanges of opinion and endless analysis.

High number of Cups
Accent on emotions: inexplicable instincts, overwhelming feelings and great emotional roller coaster.

High number of Pentacles
Accent on the material: financial fixation, health issues and reorganization of home and things.

There are no Cups. Are we sure that without feelings things can really be ok?

The Absence of a Suit

It is important to note what suits are absent or barely appear in a spread.

Absence of Wands
Indicates lack of desire: intuition and passion waning, neglected projects are dissipating. It is necessary to establish new objectives.

Absence of Swords
Indicates a lack of analysis: unclear reasoning, prejudices, confusion, inability to communicate and irrational behavior. It is important to analyze and be objective.

Absence of Cups
Indicates a lack of emotion: privation, detachment or refusal to recognize emotions or unexpected intuitions. It is necessary to foster one's instincts.

Absence of Pentacles
Indicates a lack of attention: poverty, inability to provide for one's needs and a scarce interest in material goods. A pragmatic approach and commitment are required.

The Page of Bows in the Shaman Tarot. Design by M. Filadoro, artwork by S. Ariganello and A. Pastorello.
In some Tarot decks, the suits vary from traditional suits. The divinatory meanings do not change.
The Shaman Tarot represents the element of Air with a Bow instead of a Sword. The meaning of Air remains.

Court Card Strategies

Court Cards often represent a suggestion regarding a helpful strategy or behavior in regard to a situation.
Many Courts of the same rank appearing in a Spread may be interpreted as Questions to ask the Querent to help him find a strategy to cope with the current situation.

Pages

Highlight the need to learn and invite the Querent to ask:
- What type of information is needed?
- What skills are necessary?
- What information could resolve the problem?
- How can I have fun with this?

Knights

Highlight the need to act and invite the Querent to ask:
- What choices do I have?
- What is the first move I should make?
- What actions could radically change the situation?
- How can I expand this?

Queens

Highlight the need to understand and invite the Querent to ask:
- How can I look at this differently?
- What experts could be consulted?
- What aspects need to be explored deeper for resolution?
- How can I nurture this?

Kings

Highlight the need to exercise control and invite the Querent to ask:
- What limits should I impose?
- What obligations should I impose?
- What rules would make the situation easier to manage?
- How can I control this?

Repeating Numbers

Numbers appearing often in a spread reflect additional meaning.

- **Aces** indicate indecision when faced with two conflicting choices.
- **Twos** indicate the need to carefully evaluate choices.
- **Threes** suggest taking immediate action.
- **Fours** underline the need for change.
- **Fives** show the importance of the conflict.
- **Sixes** indicate the need to collaborate with others.
- **Sevens** suggest adopting a very creative approach.
- **Eights** signal the need to make an effort.
- **Nines** suggest gathering strength for a last effort to reach an objective.
- **Tens** advise avoiding excesses and exaggerations.

Numbers and Majors

Sometimes Major Arcana numbers have special significance in a Spread. For instance, the Magician, through his number 1, is connected to all the Aces in Tarot, which are also numbered 1. If a Major Arcana's number appears in other places through the Spread via Minors, it can have significance. The meaning associated with the number should be considered in the Synthesis.

Balancing the Spread

The Reader will try to balance the spread for the client once the general vision has been determined. This is usually done in the Synthesis of the spread. The Reader can point out what is dominant and what is missing. The Reader suggests a course of action that re-establishes balance.

For example, if an absence of Cups (emotions) is observed, the Reader points this out in the Synthesis. The Reader suggests the Querent should concentrate on the emotional aspects in her life. If the opposite occurs and there are only Cups present, the Reader suggests that emotions are overly influential and the Querent should focus attention also on reason (Swords), practical issues (Pentacles) or desires (Wands).

Too many Cups, or not enough of them, usually means to the same outcome: the inability to listen to oneself.

Technique and Traditional Interpretation

Balance of the Spread's strength is that it allows for an interpretation that is already very precise, even before looking at the cards actually appearing in a spread. The challange in utilizing this technique is that it should not replace the traditional card-by-card interpretation. It must accompany it. It provides the Reader with an interpretative key through which to look for the correct meaning of each single card. Applying this technique is a first step towards understanding how all the cards of a Spread are connected and developing a total vision of a spread.

KEEPING A TAROT JOURNAL

A Tarot journal, made for recording your thoughts, ideas and Tarot experience is an important and pleasurable tool for tracking the growth and accuracy of your practice. A Tarot journal's magic is its ability to collect insights and reveal patterns over time.

Many Readers keep a Tarot journal, a record of readings done for themselves and their Querents, daily meditations on the meanings of the cards, notes on favorite spreads, predictions, outcomes and lists of decks owned or desired.

Keep the Journal with you, and you will find many unexpected and peaceful moments to use it.

Tarot Journaling Benefits

- The Reader observes evidence of growth when comparing new and old entries.
- The Reader detects patterns and cycles apparent only when readings and daily cards are tracked over long periods of time.
- The Reader may add notes about the interpretations of each Arcana every time he meets it on a Spread. In time those notes will become a personal and very useful reference.
- The journal becomes a *Grimoire*, a personal divinatory textbook. In later years the journal makes a powerful gift for heirs or students.

- Writing about a personal Tarot practice assures a focused, precise point of view and interpretation of each card. This becomes especially helpful when reading cards for yourself.
- Writing about a Reading will allow you to return to it later and with a fresher mind, or in order to meditate on the answer received. This becomes especially helpful when reading cards for yourself.

Finding Your Tarot Journal

Any blank book, notebook or journal will do. Size and weight impact the portability of the journal. Paper quality is a consideration because ink bleeds through thin paper, making journal pages harder to read.

The "right choice" encourages the Reader to write freely and often. For many, a simple pocket-sized notebook (like those produced by the Moleskine or Lo Scarabeo) is the perfect choice. But thousands of journals exist in a variety of styles and colors. Some Readers find unusual designs distracting, while others find them inspiring.

Remember that your Tarot journal should just reflect you: do not choose a journal you don't like.

Don't forget to add a bit of magic to your journal!

Privacy should be considered, especially if the Reader maintains detailed notes on readings done for others. Locks on diaries and journals are too flimsy to offer real protection. Journals should be kept in a safe, secure and secret place.

Some Readers choose to keep their journals on a computer or electronic device using software (such as Microsoft OneNote or MacJournal) or apps to index the entries and protect them from prying eyes. While this is the perfect option for some, the meditative quality of putting an actual pen to paper cannot be overstated. If an electronic format is chosen, be sure to back up all information on files and external drives so the work is never lost. Consider printing and binding work in a physical journal.

Writing and Recording Process

Journal entries are extremely personal in nature. They vary significantly in length, content and format from Reader to Reader. Generally, shorter entries are better, as Readers are more apt to maintain a long-term journaling practice when writing an entry is not seen as a time-consuming chore. Make sure to reserve a couple of pages for each Arcana: in time they will fill up with notes and useful information.

Tarot Journal Section Ideas

Card of the Day

In the morning, the Reader draws a card and jots down basic impressions. That evening, the Reader writes a passage about how the energy of that card was manifested in the course of the day. An example:

Morning: Drew the Eight of Wands, which looks like speed or haste with those flying Wands. I'm wondering if I'll feel rushed or overwhelmed today?

Evening: At work today, my boss asked me to complete an assignment in three hours that should have taken three days. I did it, but felt unhappy with the work. What a perfect example of the Eight of Wands. On the happy side, my evening subway came the second I stepped on the platform and ran express to my stop. I suppose that represented the Eight of Wands too!

This day seems full of 8 of Wands energy.

434

Tarot will not only point out problems. In the hands of a skilled Reader, Tarot also suggests solutions.

Reading Record

A reading record captures the date and time of the reading, cards received, their orientation, if the Reader reads reversals, interpretation notes and any other impressions. Example:

Reading for: Myself
Date/Time: 1/3/09 at Noon
Spread: The Key Spread
Deck: 78 Doors
Cards: Lovers (Reversed), Six of Pentacles, Ace of Swords (Reversed), Page of Swords (Reversed), Nine of Cups (Reversed).

Initial impressions: Absence of Wands suggests reluctance to take action; many reversals reflect my feeling of being "stuck" in a bad situation. Laughed out loud at the image of the maze on the Ace of Swords in this deck, as I told someone just yesterday I felt trapped in a maze with no way out.

The Reader proceeds to make interpretive notes for each card, followed by a synthesis of his or her verdict on the overall message of the spread. Later, the Reader may return to this entry to add notes on its accuracy.

Record how you felt when performing readings for other people. As your reading style evolves, record keeping will quicken your path as a Reader. Make note of the rituals performed, what worked, didn't seem to work, psychic pops, did you feel energized, did you pick up on the Querent's energy, were you reading the Querent, the cards or a little of both?

435

On next page:
Just a few essential lines can give
you the essence of a card.

Page per Card

Some Readers dedicate a page (or more) of their journal to
individual cards, creating an index of notes, interpretations
and impressions. Example:

> **Nine of Pentacles**
> 4/3/09 - Never noticed the snail on the 9 of Pentacles
> before. Makes me think of the saying, "Slow and steady
> wins the race."
>
> 5/7/09 - Came up as a career card for an athletic trainer
> today; must remember this card is about more than
> money and finance!

Sketching a Card

Artistically inclined Readers may find it helpful to sketch their
Tarot cards on blank pages of the notebook. Why would you
want to sketch an image that already exists? The focus of
replicating the Tarot image via sketching is a form of meditation and observation. The sketching process brings bits
and pieces of the card to your attention you might otherwise
have overlooked. The discovery of a new aspect of a card is
exciting. Additionally, no artistic talent is required since no
one need see the sketch but you.

Probably, your sketches will not
be as good as the artwork of a
professional artist. But looking at
them, you will always recognize
what is important for you in any
card.

Synchronicities/Psychic Pops

You may notice synchronicities occur with increasing frequency as you work with Tarot. Many times, more psychic phenomena will happen as a result of working with the cards as well, depending on how you work with them. It is important to keep a record of such things for three reasons:

~ Synchronicity/psychic pops helps to confirm and strengthen our chosen path.

~ Recording these events help us to pay attention and honor our intuition.

~ It is fun and helpful to discover and cultivate these qualities in your life. Especially synchronicity ~ it means you are paying attention.

The Power of a Daily Discipline

The commitment required for keeping a Tarot journal offers an essential discipline. It encourages the Reader to work with and study the cards on a daily basis. Writing daily entries becomes a measure of the Reader's dedication to Tarot. This alone can have a radical impact on the Reader's skill and accuracy.

438

INTUITIVE READING

The Intuitive Tarot Reading technique is about the delicate and mysterious relationship between the image on the card and the meaning of the Arcana. The idea association that springs from observing a card creates a highly personal interpretation of Tarot. These meanings may be unique and not shared among other Readers. Intuitive Reading is what most modern Readers use. Intuitive Reading allows important information to rise to the top of the Reader's consciousness.

Occultists Assign Meaning

Pamela Coleman Smith was the first artist to illustrate the Minor Arcana since the Sola Busca deck. Before Smith's deck, Tarot's Minors were cards illustrated with only symbols of their suits. Pamela Coleman Smith created the Rider Waite Deck and Intuitive Tarot Reading was born.

Western Europe was undergoing a profound cultural transformation in the late nineteenth and early twentieth century while the traditional Tarot meanings became encoded. Popular thought held that the mind and human reason could categorize, explain and control everything. This conviction influenced science, art, philosophy and even magic. It was not surprising that the occultists of the early twentieth century sought to define every aspect of Tarot with a precise rule and meaning. Their work was useful and amazing but it did neglect a key feature, the value of which is impossible to quantify. The intuition of the Reader! It would be many years before Tarot would come to be understood as a tool of personal growth.

Images and Intuition

The heart of an intuitive reading is the relationship that develops between image and meaning. The power of imagery is its ability to evoke thoughts, reflections and an association of ideas. Ideas sometimes arise from a single element, like the posture of a character or from a particular symbol. More often than not, it is the image as a whole that evokes emotional definitions and intuitive feelings.

Using Intuitive Tarot Reading, care must be had not to allow yourself to be excessively influenced by cards that suggest negative emotions like the Three of Swords, the Five of Pentacles, or the Tower.

Each Arcanum contains hidden messages. Focus on the picture in the card and ask:

๑ What emotions do I feel looking at this card? Sadness or joy? Strength or weakness? Security or need? Communication or loneliness? Excitement or boredom?

๑ Can I identify with the images on this card?

๑ What scene is revealed to me?

๑ What happened before and what will happen next?

๑ How do I interpret the expression and the gestures of the characters?

The answers to the questions above alone do not define the exact meaning of the card. They help to form a series of impressions in the mind of the Reader to delineate and define their own personal intuitive meanings.

Intuition uses what you know to give shape to what you feel.

440

The Five of Pentacles in the Fey
Tarot. Design by Riccardo Minetti,
artwork by Mara Aghem.

Questions for your intuition

Just looking at the card for a few seconds and your intuition will start giving you an interpretation of what you see. Most cards, however, may be interpreted in many different ways depending on how you look at them.

 Do you think the Querent is represented by the people inside the room, in a place full of light and warmth?
Or is the Querent the creature outside, in the cold darkness?
 Is the creature outside a threat, an enemy and a menace? Or is it just a wanderer? Maybe a cozy, cute "monster" looking for friendship?

There is no right or wrong: only your intuition can give you an answer.

The Association of Ideas

Each element of the image may become a point of departure for the free association of ideas. An open flower can provoke a train of thought: flower, spring, start, dawn, awakening. The mind of the Reader is free to follow this flow of ideas beginning with the impressions of the person who drew the card.

Two Different Intuitive Moments

Intuitive Reading can be performed in two different ways:

Intuitive Deck Study

A Tarot journal becomes a handy repository of intuitive associations. What did you feel the first or the hundredth time you look at a Tarot image or symbol? What becomes aroused in you? Does the card awaken joy or sadness? Be sure to note when this happens in your journal. Over time, personal meanings will associate with the essential keyword meanings of each card. Readings will spring to life.

During an Active Reading

The second Intuitive moment comes during a reading where it is necessary to choose only one meaning among many. In this case, the associations, ideas and intuitive impressions will transform the way the cards are read. The card's narrative will spring to life beneath your eyes. The cards link, the story unfolds, the truth comes out and your intuition sings. This is the magic of working intuitively. It is exciting when everything comes together and you are able to provide helpful knowledge to yourself and others.

Intuition of the Querent

When reading intuitively, you can also engage your Querent and ask them to look carefully at the pictures. Pooling your impressions will often encourage valuable information to emerge. Ask your Querent questions:

᎐ What do they think?
᎐ Which character do they identify with on the card?
᎐ Who does the card remind them of?
᎐ What image on the card are they drawn to?
᎐ What feelings does the card evoke?

Listen to what the Querent thinks and feels.

443

This technique and tool is helpful if the Reader finds they are blanking out or at complete loss of what to say.

It is also invaluable when the Querent takes an active role in the Reading and find his own answers rather then rely on what the Reader tells him.

Differences Between Decks

Intuitive Reading is the reason a wide variety of Tarot decks exist. The Reader will prefer a deck they feel in tune with. A deck may be chosen to suit the mood of the Reader, of the Querent, or of the question asked. Sometimes the intuition feels cleaner and clearer with a certain deck. Using Intuitive Reading, you can study the differences between decks and discover whether some decks "speak" to you while others remain "silent." Some decks form associations that are close to the traditional meanings while others lead in entirely new directions.

The Fool in the Harmonious Tarot, artwork by W. Crane and E. Fitzpatrick.
Serious, quiet decks, communicate these feelings through Intuition in every reading.

The Fool in the Mibramig Magical Tarot, artwork by Mibramig.
A happy, energetic card can shed light on a dark or negative situation and thus provide lighter insights and solutions.

The Fool in the Royo Dark Tarot, artwork by Luis Royo.
Dark and gothic decks are well suited to spreads and questions dealing with fears, negative emotions and shadow work.

The Intuition can sometimes hurt and hinder readings when it is confused with personal projection or makes the Reader lose focus.

The Challenges of Reading Intuitively

Reading Intuitively presents two main challenges. These can negatively affect the outcome of the Reading and block a Reader's growth.

Projective mechanics

Our intuition is "ours". It belongs to each of us, individually. If a Reading or a card image evokes a powerful emotion or recollection in the Reader, and she is relying only on her intuition, the interpretation may seem clear and immediate. But in this case, the Reader is not really looking at the card, but projecting herself, her memories, her opinions, or her experiences on the card, overwriting it.

If you feel that a card resonates too strongly with your intuition, take a step back, breath deeply for a few seconds and look again.

Losing track of the structure

Using intuition alone, the Reader may stray quite far from the traditional meanings and interpretations. Sometimes, this is a very good thing and marks the moment a Reader is finding her own path into Tarot and her gifts. Other times, the opposite is true. The Reader is losing sight of what Tarot is. She follows intuition without anchoring it to the cards and the images. Intuition is a realm where boundaries are soft, mutable and undefined. Without boundaries, the Reader may become lost.

SYMBOLIC READING

Symbolic Reading is not a technique itself, but a set of devices you can use to read the meanings of the Arcana using symbols. You will use your expanding body of symbolic knowledge to interpret the cards and find set meanings.

Difference Between Symbolic and Intuitive Reading

Intuitive and Symbolic readings may be confused. Both techniques have several elements in common and are based on the study of the images in the Arcana. However they are actually opposed and complementary approaches. Intuitive Reading encourages a subjective interpretation of the cards by acting and reading on impulse and captures the emotional essence of the cards. The Symbolic Reading creates a symbolic alphabet allowing a rational interpretation for each Arcana.

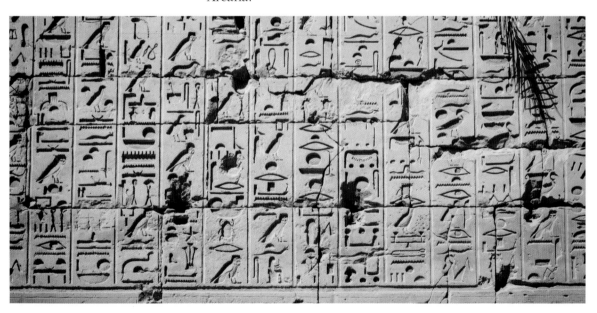

All symbols have a meaning.

Meaning Within a Symbol

Some Tarot decks are particularly useful for Symbolic Reading because the authors and artists include a precise symbolic alphabet. These decks are often the most esoteric. Symbolic Reading was developed within the esoteric orders

Symbols inform every aspect of our life. In doubt? Simply look to the screen of your cell phone or computer.

in the late nineteenth and early twentieth century. This technique is easily incorporated without reading the original esoteric texts. Such texts explain the rise of the symbolic decks. Reading them, while sometimes challenging, is often enlightening and fun.

However the technique can be used with all decks, independently of the original intention of the author or artist.

Reading Symbols

Symbols always carry the same meaning while an Intuitive interpretation will change. A symbol in Tarot can be an object like the Cup appearing on the Magician's table. A symbol can be a gesture like the blessing hand of the Hierophant. A symbol can even be a generic image such as the veil hanging behind The High Priestess.

You may already have a good deal of knowledge about certain symbols and you will enjoy learning about new ones. A pleasurable aspect of acquiring symbolic knowledge is the discovery that these same symbols repeat in other areas of life. Symbolism repeats in artwork, architecture, advertising, literature, etc. Suddenly, the world opens wider and becomes rich with symbolic meaning.

Symbolic Connections

Here is a brief list of connections that can be done with the symbols appearing on a card:

- Astrological
- Color
- Mythological
- Alchemical
- Masonic
- Spiritual/Religious
- Numerical

The more the Reader is familiar with the symbols, the more it will be easy for her to notice them and remember their meaning.

Breaking Apart the Symbols on a Card

An example on how the Symbols on a card can be broken down: the High Priestess.

A List of Symbols

1. Black and white columns
2. Veil
3. Cross necklace
4. TORA scroll
5. Moon
6. B & J
7. Palms and Pomegranates
8. Moon-shaped Headwear

Associations

1. Yin and Yang
2. Blocked vision or passage
3. Convergence
4. Knowledge
5. Mystery
6. Strength & Solidity
7. Male and female spiritual fruits
8. Spiritual authority

Combining the Symbols

A stable and unshakable keeper of knowledge, capable of harmonizing different energies. While she possesses knowledge, she also understand mystery and protects what is hidden behind her seat. She dwells between the Spiritual and the Material realms.

Even without knowledge of the High Priestess, the Symbolic Reading technique allows anyone to reach her meaning with surprising accuracy.

Symbols are not the enemy of intuition. Intuition is an essential tool to put all the symbols together, and find the meaning of the card during a Reading.

Put it To Use

How to work with symbols:

1. Examine and make a list of the symbols appearing on the card.

Remember that everything can be considered a symbol: a gesture, an object, a color, an expression, a figure...
As you look at the image, you can break it into the single elements that create her. Each element could be a symbol on your list.

2. Make your associations.

Each symbol can be associated with a specific meaning. For example, the scales of Justice may easily be connected to the zodiac's sign of Libra. The Sword may represent power or logic. The bare feet may be an indication of humbleness.

3. Combine the symbols together.

After dividing the image into individual components, it is time to reassemble and draw your symbolic meanings together to form an interpretation. Sometimes each symbol in the card can express a different facet of the Arcana meaning, These facets are so different they cannot be synthesized together. And yet, they make perfect sense. For example, in the Death card, you will have a skeleton (symbol of end) and the sun rising (symbol of beginning). This is because the Death Arcana embodies neither end or beginning, but the complex relationship between the two concepts.

NEGATIVE CARDS

Readers must come to terms with cards they find trouble-some or uncomfortable. The Reader must understand and comprehend their emotional reaction to an uncomfortable card and know how to utilize these cards when they appear for themselves. It is important as well to know how to deal with a Querent's negative reaction to any card or image they find troublesome.

Dealing with Negative Cards for Yourself

Ideally, as you learn Tarot, you will fearlessly accept and face everything Tarot has to teach you about yourself, good and bad. You will learn the Death card need not be interpreted literally, the Five of Swords means more than defeat at the hands of another and The Eight of Swords represents the ability to break free. But ultimately some Readers will find these and other cards tricky and they cause strong, frighten-ing or negative reactions.

Death, The Devil and the Tower from the Universal Wirth Tarot, design by Oswald Wirth and artwork by Stefano Palumbo.

Codename: Spooky Cards

Most Readers will not want to use the term "negative", as each Arcana contains both a negative and a positive aspect. With a certain practical sense and a lack of ceremony, Readers prefer the term "spooky cards".

The most common Spooky Cards are:
- Death
- The Devil
- The Tower
- Three of Swords
- Nine of Swords
- Ten of Swords

Oddly enough, a card which has a negative (mostly undeserved) reputation is the Hierophant. While not a spooky card, many Readers or Querents will have an intuitive dislike of the card for its association with organized Religion. A Technique of dealing with Negative Cards is useful in these circumstances.

The Ten of Swords of the Universal Tarot, concept by A. E. Waite and artwork by R. De Angelis

During the learning process of reading Tarot, it is perfectly acceptable to remove any card that makes you uncomfortable. It is also appropriate to remove these cards during certain procedures like the Card a Day practice. A beginner Tarot reader might not want to face the Death card first thing, Tuesday morning. However, the faster you embrace and work with challenging Tarot images, the faster your practice will evolve. Time and study integrates every card into your practice. As you learn the deck, give yourself time and take it easy if you find certain images troubling.

Why You Must to Deal with Negative Cards Eventually

Challenges in Tarot are like challenges in life. They exist to provoke growth. The best way to integrate Tarot is as 78 reflections of you. Tarot is the human experience of life. No challenge equals no change. An acceptance of challenging or negative cards will encourage strength in life. Receive challenges as gifts that provoke your evolution. Welcome rather than reject them.

Dealing with Negative Cards for a Querent

Querents are often nervous or scared about the future. A Querent may project personal fears onto the cards. The Reader must be ready to deal with the following problematic cards:

Death: Generally associated with a literal death, physical illness or the realization of a Querent's worst fears.
The Tower: Suggests ruin, destruction and despair.
The Devil: Due to the Devil's legendary reputation, he is often conceived of as pure evil and a symbol of destruction, darkness and negativity.
Five of Pentacles: Displays poverty and defeat.
Three of Swords: Displays heartache, betrayal and the image of a broken heart.
Nine of Swords: Usually indicates distress, nightmares, remorse, regret and grief.
Ten of Swords: Often depicts a person pierced by ten swords, suggesting death, violence, betrayal and cruelty.
Queen of Swords: She is often connected to concepts of widowhood, mourning, revenge, malice and sterility.

Recall that different decks will portray the same card in different ways. Sometimes it's not the cards that are overly negative, but the image on it. An example includes the Queen and King of Swords who are sometimes portrayed holding a severed head in their hand. While this made perfect sense as an esoteric symbol in the early 20th century, it should not be surprising if it calls forth powerful negative feeling in a Reader or in a Querent.

The Five of Pentacles of the Universal Tarot, concept by A. E. Waite and artwork by R. De Angelis.

Negative cards often portray images with a strong negative feeling, dark colors, and scary symbols. However, the message of the card may end up being positive.

The Three, Nine and Queen of Swords of the Initiatory Tarot of the Golden Dawn, artwork by Patrizio Evangelisti.

Reset the Course

Do not allow the negativity of the cards to take precedence over all other aspects of the reading. This makes the entire interpretation pessimistic and anxious.

The first step to handling a potentially negative situation is understanding and explaining that the cards are symbols. Symbols should not be taken literally. Often, despite the image on the card suggesting negativity, the reality of the deeper meaning is positive.

Examples:
Death: Indicates the end of something but the transformation sets you free.
The Tower: Indicated the destruction of a mental or physical prison. It also suggests learning an important lesson. Viewing it sexually, the Tower represents the ultimate male orgasm.
Devil: Represents the passions, instincts and hidden parts of oneself. The Devil also represents a rip roaring good time.
Five of Pentacles: Indicates need but also prudence and economy. Can also represent the ups and downs of a married couple and their ability to get themselves through tough times.

Three of Swords: Represents the ardent ability to overcome pain and suffering and become stronger as a result of them.

Nine of Swords: Indicates the ability to communicate with the conscience and take one's responsibilities seriously. Also indicates that issues are worse in one's head and mind than in reality.

Ten of Swords: Represents catharsis, liberation and the resolution and ending of a difficult problem.

Queen of Swords: Indicates the ability to do what feels right even against the opinions of others and a superior intellect.

Understand negativity and hardships for you and your Querents as instruments of growth and harbingers of change that can transform an ordinary life into an extraordinary life.

Fun Exercise

Look for the dark side of even the most optimistic cards. Select your favorite card and discover what could be the most challenging issue it provokes.

UNMATCHED ILLUSTRATIONS

Working with a variety of decks, the Reader discovers the same Tarot cards are illustrated differently in different decks. Why do illustrations differ from deck to deck? What should a Reader do when confronted with cards that dramatically differ from meanings already committed to memory?

Readers tend to associate one meaning or a range of closely related meanings with each card inside a deck. These meanings may be drawn from tradition. A trusted teacher may have handed down meanings. They may be based on months or years of personal experience. These meanings become an integral, heartfelt part of how the Reader interprets the cards.

There are days when different decks may look like this.

The Fool from Klimt Tarot, artwork by A. A. Atanassov.
The posture and the extreme thinnes of the figure in this card make it hard to match the illustration with the brightest meanings usually associated to the Fool, like *Playfulness, Innocence* or *Carelessness.*

Readers who read with more than one deck will stumble on versions of a card appearing to contradict traditional, learned or personal meanings. When this happens, the Reader struggles to relate the unfamiliar illustration to the meanings she has committed to memory. Worse, a Querent may interrupt the reading claiming, "You keep saying this card means happiness. So, why does it show a sneaky-looking man with his arms crossed? He doesn't look happy to me!"

Why Decks Differ

Why do some cards feature illustrations that differ dramatically from assigned, traditional meanings?

Badly designed decks

Some Tarot decks are hastily produced promotional items. People who know little to nothing about Tarot design these decks. For example: a deck packaged with a perfume sample featured the Eiffel Tower on the Tower card simply because the creators mistakenly thought any picture of a Tower would be appropriate.

Differences in underlying systems or traditions

Not all decks are based on the same astrological or numerological systems. Decks from different countries reflect different traditions of interpretation. For example: the Universal Tarot reflects a tradition that associates the Six of Swords with travel. The Tarot of the Master, though, based on a different set of assumptions, associates this card with courage and valor.

Differences in emphasis

A dramatically different illustration may emphasize a different aspect of a familiar meaning. For example: someone who associates 'travel' with the Six of Swords may be very comfortable with the illustration for this card in the Universal Tarot. But upon seeing the same card from the Tarot of the 78 Doors, the Reader may ask, "What does a young man surfing the Internet have to do with travel?" Only upon reflection might the Reader notice the maps and masks on the wall and conclude, "Ah! He's researching vacation destinations!" or "Travel is seen as a metaphor, and browsing the internet is just another form of travel."

Fom left to right - The Magician of the Tarot of Marseille and the Tarot Liber T. Decks belonging to different traditions express the same cards with very noticeable differences.

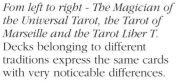

The Magician from the Happy Tarot. Detail. Some cards may depict similar scenes, and yet convey totally different feelings

Different purposes

The purpose of the Universal Tarot is to reinterpret a specific set of designs by an occultist named Arthur Edward Waite and first illustrated by an artist named Pamela Colman Smith. By contrast, the Tarot of the Elves is designed to explore how familiar Tarot themes may be expressed in original stories. Both decks are Tarot decks but they have been designed with different goals in mind. The parallel cards in these decks appear at first glance to have very little in common.

The World from Tarot of the Elves, designed by Mark McElroy, artwork by Davide Corsi.
The Tarot of the Elves cards do not follow traditional iconography. They depend on the narrative logic based on the Hero's Journey. The World Card represents the culmination of the story, as the young Prince returns home to his father.

Dealing with Differences

A Reader who encounters a radically different illustration on a familiar card, has at least five options:

Ignore the difference

Many Readers keep a set of familiar meanings and are reluctant to part with them. They ignore the conflict between the illustration and the assigned meaning if they encounter a radically different version of the card. This speeds the reading process but may confuse Querents who notice the difference between the apparent meaning of the card (based on the illustration) and the meaning the Reader assigns to it. Also, all the benefits of the Intuitive Reading will be lost. In this case, a good suggestion is to choose a deck whose illustrations are more in tune with the *Mental Deck* of the Reader.

Reconcile the difference

Some Readers try to reconcile the difference between a surprising illustration and their preferred interpretation of it. They may study the new card, searching for parallels between the illustration and their expectations. They may decide the two different versions aren't so different after all. This solution usually provides excellent results, but may be time consuming. When the difference between the decks is very strong, the reconciled meaning may feel too forced.

Blend the meanings

The Reader may choose to blend meanings, suggesting, for example, that the Six of Swords in the Tarot of the Master calls for "courageous travel" or hints at a "journey toward courage."
This solution requires a bit of experience from the Reader, but it's very effective. The blending of two meanings often gives a very clear interpretation.

Consult a reference

The Reader may always read the booklet packaged with the deck, consult a companion guide, search the web, ask other people using the deck, or ask the designer, "Why did you choose this illustration for this card?"

This solution may not work every time. However, when it does work, it offers an exceptionally useful and different point of view. This can be truly enlightening and lead to a meaningful experience with the cards and add to your personal philosophy.

Embrace the difference

Many Readers, citing an obligation to honor the unique voice of each deck, set familiar interpretations aside. They embrace new meanings wholeheartedly. This process enables the Reader to see the Tarot from a radically different perspective and enriches the library of memorized meanings the Reader uses.

Embracing what is different is an opportunity fro growth.

USING GENDER AND AGE

Some esotericists pursued the goal of blending masculine and feminine energies. They believed that doing so presents the perfect integration of all aspects of the soul. Using this point of view, you can see why the World card is often viewed as a hermaphrodite. To blend and combine both the masculine and feminine sides of the soul is to bring balance and harmony to life.

Among the many techniques a Reader acquires over the years, one of the most valuable is the ability to use the gender and age pictured on the cards to imbue cards with meaning. This technique can be used with any tarot deck at any time.

We don't embrace stereotypes in life, nor should we. Stereotyping locks and belittles our world. But when working within the structure of Tarot, a bit of stereotyping goes a long way in bringing readings to life. You will find plenty of masculine/feminine stereotypes with court cards but gender can be used with every card in the deck. Stereotypes, as a rule, have one very obvious value: they can be easily shared and communicated. As the work of the Reader is not just to interpret the cards, but to find a way to communicate with the Querent, this kind of technique can really be effective.

Stereotypes, especially gender stereotypes, are a double edged sword. They can help you communicate a basic concept in a fast and effective way, but they can also oversimplify, mislead and offend.

Feminine and Masculine

Suits

The four Suits of Tarot contain a masculine and feminine structure. Can you determine which suits are masculine and which are feminine just by looking at them? Pull four suits from the deck and examine. Guess which are masculine and feminine. If you assumed the sharp, phallic and outwardly pointed suits of Swords and Wands are masculine you were right. If you assumed the soft, receptive and receiving suits of Cups and Pentacles are feminine you are correct.

Yin and Yang Tarot Style

The typical understanding of masculinity as it applies to Tarot may come down to the actual physiology of the human body. Masculine suits are male in their external qualities, phallic and protruding. Thay have *Yang* attributes in common. Yang cards relate to extroversion, action, direction and a "taking the bull by the horns." Approach comparing and contrasting this with the feminine suits, we can understand them to be nurturing, soft, compassionate and receptive. Feminine Suits can be called *Yin*.

A Sword or Wand can be placed within a Cup or soft earthy Pentacle. We look to the elements themselves and note that Water and Earth are soft, malleable and receptive while Air and Fire forcefully shape the world.

Yang and masculine

Wands and Swords are considered Yang and masculine Suits. Their symbol has a phallic, pointed shape.

Yin and feminine

Cups and Pentacles are considered Ying and feminine Suits. Their symbol has a round womb-like shape.

Male and Female Characters

Looking past the Suits to the actual characters on the cards, pictorial depictions depend on the choice of the artist and author. Characters, just like Suits, carry masculinity and femininity. A woman implies the ability to take care of others, nurturing and healing, along with other ideals of the feminine. In contrast, male figures are attributed with the ability to command, determination, vitality and linear thinking.

But what should you do when these characters appear in a reading? Remember each Tarot card represents aspects of humanity, regardless of gender. The Magician does not always imply a literal man and the High Priestess does not always represent a literal woman. As you gain confidence you will read with clarity. You will discover when the cards are talking about other people or about you.

Reading the Age of an Arcana

You can read the age of any character on the cards just as you read gender. You observe young figures, such as the child on Waite's Sun card and you may make the logical conclusion. Youthful figures represent modern attitudes, optimism and enthusiasm. These qualities can belong to anyone, regardless of age. For instance the Sun card in a love reading may refer to the attitude and feelings of the Querent after reuniting with a long lost childhood love. This brings optimism, hope and a feeling of growth to their life. Conversely, older figures represent rich, ripe experience and worldview.

It is also helpful to play with your own ideas of gender and age when reflecting upon the cards. Strength is typically depicted as a woman holding a lion. What would happen to the card, and your interpretation, if it were an old man holding the lion? What if a child controlled the lion? How would that change the meaning if the card? What if the Knight of Pentacles became a scantily clad woman on a horse? How would this change your feelings about the cards and what it means?

Age is not about outward beauty and make-up. Age is a natural evolution of the character of every human being.

An old blind woman is the Hermit in the Manga Tarot.
In this deck all the conventional gender of the cards have been reversed, so that Arcana traditionally depicted as male appear as female, and the other way round.

Who Do They Represent?

At first, simply assume all cards refer to the Querent or to your own state of mind. Do not become caught up attempting to decipher if the characters are the Querent or people in their life. As you gain experience, you will slowly find yourself being drawn to certain cards as they stick out in readings as other people. Trust your instincts when it comes to whom the cards are referring to.

Age in a Reading

Scan the spread for male and female figures and the ages represented. This tells us something about the reading. Does the situation look balanced or is there a lot of masculine or feminine energy involved? Are there many children or young people in the spread? Perhaps that indicates that the people involved are behaving childishly and need to "grow up" in order to come to an agreement. A good interpretation depends on paying attention to the qualities symbolized and not just the literal images.

464

MEDITATING WITH TAROT

Tarot is an extraordinary tool for meditation. One can reach a state of inner calmness, explore a card's interior and discover new and exciting qualities that cannot be learned of any other way. You may enter the card as if it were a window into another world. Reaching a state of calmness and serenity, you can immerse yourself in the scenario described by the Arcanum.

Recent studies of meditation show it has positive benefits, reduces stress, frees your mind, offers a feeling of relaxation and psychological wellbeing. To meditate using the Arcanum, the Reader should focus on the images on the cards. The process of meditation can be achieved through ten stages.

You can meditate everywhere.

Ten Stages to Meditation

1 Choose a quiet place where you will not be disturbed. Turn off all electronic equipment. While it is not necessary, you may use any of the suggestions in the ritual chapter, candles, incense or music to help bring you to a relaxed and peaceful state. Some people shy away from using aids as they feel they must learn to reach a meditative state in any environment without candles, incense or music. These elements are, however, a tremendous help to facilitate the onset of meditation.

2 Sit down comfortably and focus on your breathing. Focus on release and relaxation with every exhale. Breathe while taking whatever time you need to reach deep calm. Clear your mind. Freeing the mind from thought is important. Thoughts will likely come rushing in. Simply request they go away or gently push them aside. By the same token, any external noise you hear does not distract you but helps you fall deeper into relaxation.

3 While in a state of equilibrium, begin to shuffle your deck. Should the mind wander, these thoughts can be put aside and returned to at a later time. Conduct this process calmly and serenely. This activity is to help you become more and more aware of your inner world.

4 Select a single card from the deck.

Meditation can make you feel small, and at the same time perfectly connected to the Universe.

5 Do not fret if you select an unfamiliar card. The purpose of this exercise is to explore. Take as much time as you need to absorb the images of the card. How does it make you feel? What it looks like? Do you enjoy what you see? Does it remind you of anything? Take your time.

6 When you are ready, close your eyes and remain silent. You must now mentally reconstruct your card with as much detail as possible. It may happen that you add new details, things that are not actually present in the card. This is normal, useful and positive. Do not judge yourself!

7 Recreating the card in your mind, you may now proceed to expand upon this image. Use your senses to explore the world of the card. What are the sounds that you hear? Is there music within the card? What is the temperature or the weather? What scent and smells prevail in the card? Are the characters on the card speaking? What do they say? Are they reacting to something? What are they doing?

8 Your mind, relaxed and focused, should now make a request of the card. Express a desire to communicate with the card. Ask with an open heart and mind, "What can you show me?" or ask, "Do you have a message for me?"

9 Pay the greatest attention at this moment. This is what you will carry with you back to the "real" world. Sometimes, characters will speak to you. Other times you will feel overcome with emotion. Sometimes nothing happens. If this occurs, do not feel frustrated but happily accept the silence and continue to observe it.

10 Having acknowledged and accepted your experience, it is time to slowly and gently come back to the physical world around you. To exit the world of the card, it is useful to imagine the card's borders. Imagine the threshold of the card, thereby returning to your regular everyday world.

Acclimation

Feel yourself completely back in the material world. The world of the card is safely behind you. Take three deep purifying breathes and slowly open your eyes. Take your time, peacefully and gradually. There is no rush. At this point, you may analyze the session and the results obtained. Interpret the Arcanum and the feelings experienced during the meditation, just as if performing a normal reading. Be sure to record your experience in your Tarot journal. Meditations, like dreams, are easily forgotten over time.

Meditation is not about excaping the material world. It's about cherishing it, without being confined by it.

TAROT FOR EXPRESSION

Tarot can be used for more than just questions. Tarot can be used to express people, personalities and issues in your life. You may often find expression through a card when words seem to desert you. You can use cards to express the essence of a situation and therefore find a new form of symbolic expression. For instance, with a card a day practice, it is likely you will quickly find defining cards that appear again and again. These cards will likely describe your situation/challenge at the moment. It is important to record these observations in your Tarot journal.

Themes

Cards often point out the current themes in your life. Say you are a fiction writer. Since the start of a new novel, you find the Emperor appearing again and again in your daily practice. The Emperor can be understood as sticking to your writing routines, overcoming troublesome emotion rising up, moving ahead and being productive. He is also a sign that you really know what you are doing. Conversely, you are torn between two lovers and do not know which way to turn. Who to choose? What to do? The Hermit appears regularly in your practice as a reminder to take time out for yourself. Step away from your lovers to figure out what is the best course of action. Cards describe recurring themes and situations while also offering guidance on how to deal with it.

The theme for the Ten of Pentacles is family. But also age and generations.

Who do you know who best exemplifies the qualities of Temperance in your life? If this card were one of your friends/family/acquaintances, who would it be? Ask yourself similar questions, on any Arcana.

People

You can use cards to express what you are sensing from the people in your life. Say you are head over heels in love with your girlfriend. She is mysterious and unpredictable and you express her as the Moon card. Unfortunately, she has a super critical best friend who gives you the evil eye every chance she gets. Feeling her hypercritical attitude, you can't help but feel like the Justice card is peering at you in her presence.

One person becomes many to others who encounter them. Use your mother for example. Let's say she is a nurse. To her patients, she is embodied by The Star card (full of healing energy) as she tends to their needs. To her husband or lover she might be The Queen of Wands (sexy, confident woman). In her own mother's eyes she will always be a Page of Cups (youthful, open and curious girl). To you she is mom and embodied by The Empress card (nurturing, earth mother). To her best friend she is the Ace of Cups (always there, open and supportive), and to a woman who is jealous, she is the Devil. Do you see how a person embodies many cards at once?

Exercise

List the roles you play for all the people in your life. Use your contact list in your phone or email if you need help. Once you have your list of close acquaintances, friends and family, look through the cards to discover those that best describe the qualities you exude to these people.
Once you list how you function for others, make a list of what card attributes your friends and family carry for you.

470

INTRODUCING HISTORY

Tarot decks are drenched in mystery and lore. It is the very reason many are drawn to the cards. How the cards evolved, why they are laced with secrecy, and the manner in which they evolved is a fascinating area of study. While Tarot history contains many missing fragments, we can examine deck evolution, artwork, the culture, and personalities of people who have passed Tarot along to us.

Tarot history evolved from the historical fabric covering Western Europe. It requires the student to jump into the tail end of the Middle Ages and meet courtly characters of the Renaissance. The Tarot student must mingle with magicians, freemasons, and the secret society brethren of the last 300 years. They must travel to the 60's hippie subculture that ushered in the free loving Age of Aquarius that brought its own revolution to Tarot.

Caesar's Triumph. Etching by Andriaen Collaert, XVI century. The origin of the Chariot iconography.

It all began in the Renaissance

Tarot history - like a flowing river - continues to grow and evolve, even now.
The Tarot of tomorrow will be different from the Tarot of today.

The oldest Tarot cards were hand painted art objects crafted by the contemporaries of Leonardo da Vinci for wealthy Italian nobles. Tarot was played as a tavern game before becoming the paraphernalia of the fortune-teller. Famous occultists such as Levi, Papus, Waite and Crowley did not even write or work exclusively with Tarot. Their Tarot work was often conducted within a larger esoteric framework of which Tarot was only a piece.

Fortunetelling, soothsaying, and predicting the future are a practice as old as humanity itself. A vast gap exists between Tarot as a cultural artifact (the way cards have been used by the general public), and the gentlemen who first published books and papers regarding Tarot theory. Early mandates and material on the subject of Tarot made use of intricate esoteric systems. However, the wise women and grandmothers who 'read cards' at their kitchen table used vastly different folk systems. Sadly, these were not recorded.

Tarot moved through history like on a river. From Italy, to France and Paris (below), then to England and finally to the United States.

History offers little to no published work of the "wise women" who read Tarot or even read regular playing cards in private. We can assume most lessons were passed orally between teacher and student. Sadly, history belongs to those who write and record it. We can only follow the paper trail of those who connected Tarot to grand esoteric theories and those who published books and decks. All other information fades away into the shadows.

What does this mean?

Two things. First, the story and evolution of Tarot reading is largely untold. Only certain perspectives were put forth. Secondly, the history of Tarot continues to evolve and change with each and every Tarot reading and usage. You are affecting the future of Tarot. And like a flowing river, the Tarot arts will change, adapt, and grow as humanity does.

While Tarot History can be read in books, it may be easier to see it as a sequence of important milestones, divided in to a few major periods, marking the evolution of Tarot.

The following information refers to what is - so far - historically proven. There are also many other theories, some of which say that Tarot is much older than the Renaissance. Those theories, while having been supported by many esoterists through the ages, never found any form of historical confirmation.

Samson and the Lion, xilography by Virgil Solis, XVI century. Early iconography for the Strength card. It contains the same meaning, spiritual strength prevails over brute strength.

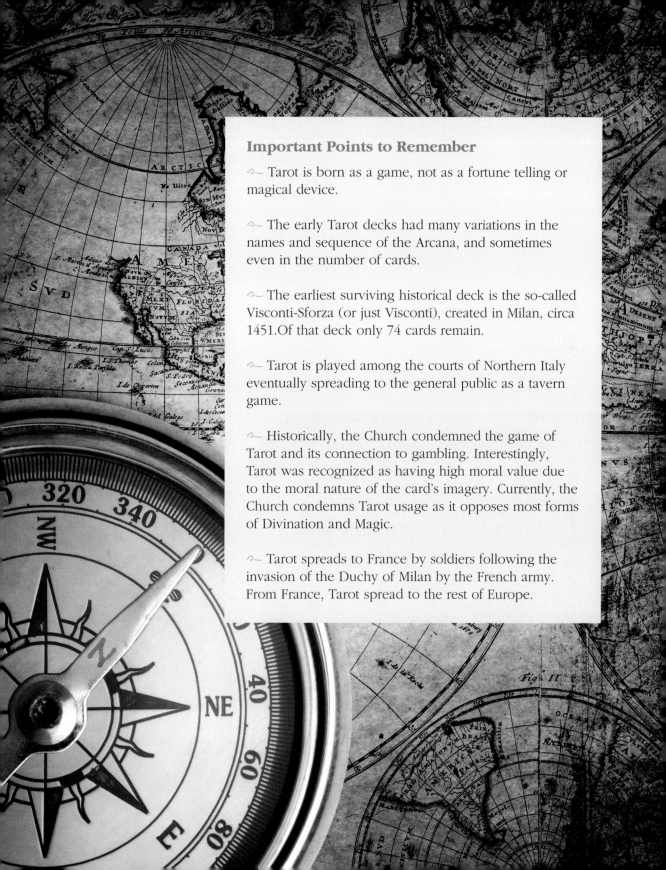

Important Points to Remember

➣— Tarot is born as a game, not as a fortune telling or magical device.

➣— The early Tarot decks had many variations in the names and sequence of the Arcana, and sometimes even in the number of cards.

➣— The earliest surviving historical deck is the so-called Visconti-Sforza (or just Visconti), created in Milan, circa 1451. Of that deck only 74 cards remain.

➣— Tarot is played among the courts of Northern Italy eventually spreading to the general public as a tavern game.

➣— Historically, the Church condemned the game of Tarot and its connection to gambling. Interestingly, Tarot was recognized as having high moral value due to the moral nature of the card's imagery. Currently, the Church condemns Tarot usage as it opposes most forms of Divination and Magic.

➣— Tarot spreads to France by soldiers following the invasion of the Duchy of Milan by the French army. From France, Tarot spread to the rest of Europe.

The Milestones of Tarot's History

circa 1440	Tarot is born in Northern Italy, probably in Milan or Ferrara.
1440 - 1500	Tarot is played in the Renaissance Courts.
1500 - 1650	Tarot is played in taverns for gambling and as a game of change and ability.
1650 - 1750	The Marseille Tarot iconographic model spreads all over Europe.
1750 - 1900	Tarot is used for Divination and is studied and changed by occultists.
1900 - 1910	The modern meanings of Tarot are codified within the Hermetic Order of the Golden Dawn. In 1909 the deck later known as Rider Waite Tarot, Waite Smith Tarot or RWS is first published.
1970 - today	Tarot spreads to general use all over the world. Thanks to intuitive readings, everyone can now read Tarot, and literally thousands of new decks are created.

Front of Schifanoia Palace, in Ferrara, Italy. XV century. Inside the building there are several frescos depicting astrological and Tarot symbolism.

Esoteric Tarot Milestones

1770	Etteilla publishes the first Tarot book about Divination: *A Way to Entertain Yourself with a Deck of Cards*.
1855-1856	Eliphas Levi connects Tarot with Kabbalah.
1870	Jean-Baptiste Pitos, under the pseudonym of Paul Christian, publishes the *Histoire de la Magie*, where Tarot is connected to ancient Egyptian religion.
1888	The Hermetic Order of the Golden Dawn is formed.
1889	Papus (Gérard Encausse) publishes the book *Le Tarot des Bohémiens*, expanding on Levi's theories.
1889	Oswald Wirth, inspired by De Guaita, publishes a deck of 22 Major Arcana incorporating new Masonic and Kabbalistic symbology. The deck is later published in color in 1927.
1909	Arthur Edward Waite publishes *The Pictorial Key to the Tarot* along with a deck illustrated by Pamela Colman Smith. Usually the publication date is noted as 1910, as the book and deck were first released in December 1909.
1938-1942	Lady Frieda Harris paints the Thoth Tarot following Aleister Crowley's instructions.

Ancient Astronomical clock in Prague.

On the next page:
The manufacturing process of
making Tarot with wooden printing
blocks, hand coloring and hand
cutting of card sheets. Illustration
from the Diderot-D'Alambert
Encyclopedia (Paris 1770).

In the 20th century, Tarot
transformed from an esoteric
construct and to a metaphysical
device connected to spirituality and
psychology.

Modern Tarot Milestones

1971	The Rider Waite Smith deck is published again, by U.S. Games systems, in Stanford, U.S.A.
1987	Pietro Alligo founds Lo Scarabeo, a publishing house in Turin (Italy), which will create many of the most important and innovative Tarot decks over the next twenty years.
1991	Llewellyn Worldwide (USA) publishes the Robin Wood Tarot, a pivotal deck, replacing most of Tarot Christian symbolism with Pagan and Wiccan symbolism.
1995	Indian philosopher Osho (Bhagwan Shree Rajneesh) combines Zen and Buddhist mysticism with Tarot in the Osho Zen Tarot.
1970 - today	Especially in the United States, but also in England, Italy and many other countries, new scholars and Tarot experts contribute to the evolution and understanding of Tarot. Among the most influential names we can find Mary K. Greer, Rachel Pollack, Barbara Moore, Mark McElroy, Marcus Katz and Tali Goodwin. Each of them and many many others contributed to Tarot growth.

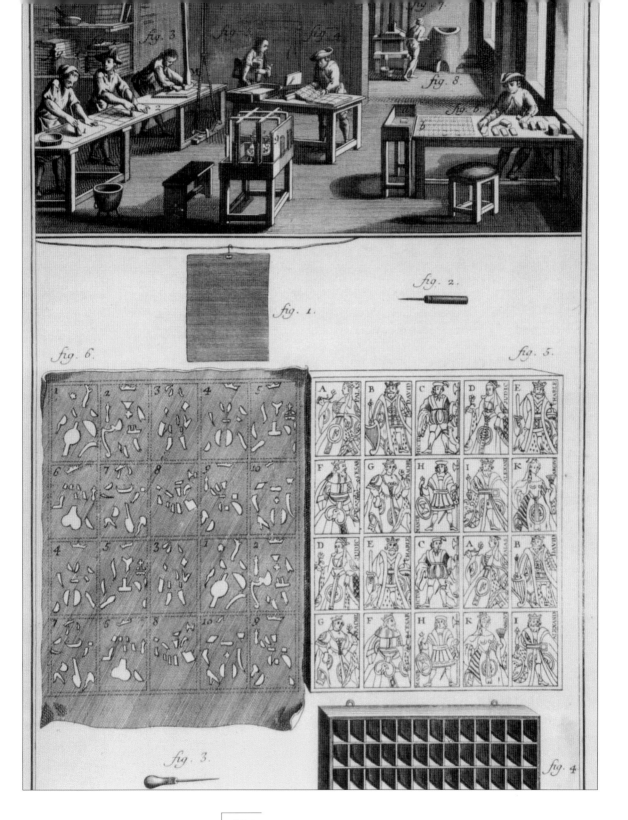

fig. 3

fig. 4

fig. 2.

fig. 1.

fig. 6.

fig. 5.

fig. 7

fig. 8.

fig. 6.

fig. 3.

fig. 4.

Tarot History Timeline

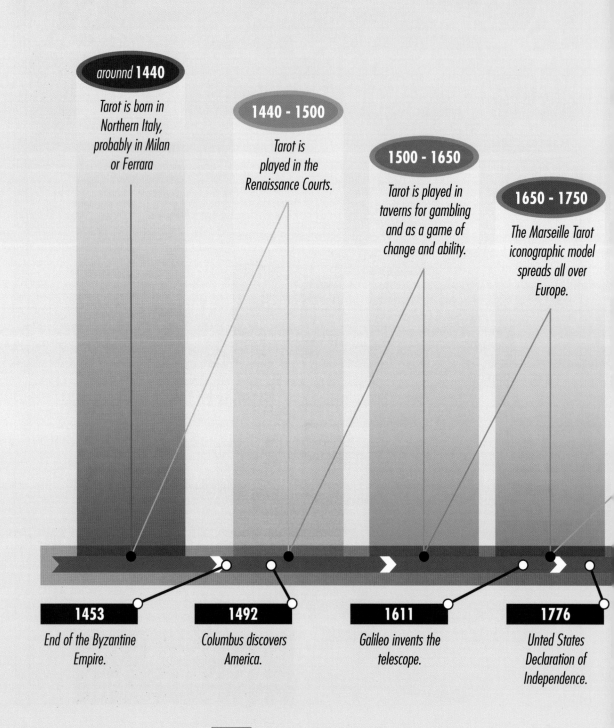

arounnd **1440**

Tarot is born in Northern Italy, probably in Milan or Ferrara

1440 - 1500

Tarot is played in the Renaissance Courts.

1500 - 1650

Tarot is played in taverns for gambling and as a game of change and ability.

1650 - 1750

The Marseille Tarot iconographic model spreads all over Europe.

1453

End of the Byzantine Empire.

1492

Columbus discovers America.

1611

Galileo invents the telescope.

1776

Unted States Declaration of Independence.

Important Points to Remember

∾ Tarot originates in Italy, moves to France, and then to England.

∾ Tarot scholarship splits into two schools of thought; the French School (Levi, Papus, and Wirth) and the English School (Mathers, Waite, and Crowley).

∾ These two schools are still reflected in the modern traditional meanings and interpretations. The French School influenced the Major Arcana's meanings while the English School influenced the Minor Arcana's meanings.

1750 - 1900

Proper Tarot Divination begins and is studied and transformed by occultists.

1900 - 1910

The modern meanings of Tarot are codified witthin the Hermetic Order of the Golden Dawn. In 1909 the deck later known as Rider Waite Tarot, Waite Smith Tarot or RWS is first published.

1970 - today

Tarot spreads to general use all over the world. Thanks to intuitive readings everyone can now read Tarot, and literally thousands of new decks are created.

1789

Beginning of the French Revolution.

1863

Emancipation Proclamation abolishes slavery in the United States.

1914

Beginning of the First World War.

1939

Beginning of the Second World War.

1969

Neil Armstrong is the first person to walk on the Moon.

483

Esoteric Tarot Timeline

1770

Etteilla publishes the first Tarot book about Divination: A Way to Entertain Yourself with a Deck of Cards.

1855 - 1856

Eliphas Levi connects Tarot with Cabala.

1870

Jean-Baptiste Pitos, under the pseudonym of Paul Christian, publishes the Histoire de la Magie, where Tarot is conencted to ancient Egyptian religion.

1888

The Hermetic Order of the Golden Dawn is formed.

1889

Papus (Gérard Encausse) publishes the book Le Tarot des Bohémiens, expanding on Levi's theories.

1889

Oswald Wirth, inspired by De Guaita, publishes a deck of 22 Major Arcana incorporating new Masonic and Cabalistic symbology. The deck is later published in color in 1927.

1768

The Royal Academy is founded in London.

1851

The New York Times is founded in New York.

1865

Lewis Carroll publishes Alice in Wonderland.

1876

The Ring of the Nibelungen, by Richard Wagner, is first performed at Bayreuth.

1891

Oscar Wilde publishes the Picture of Dorian Grey.

1905

Albert Einstein publishes the Theory of Relativity.

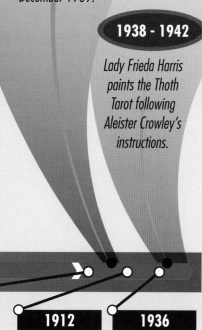

1909

Arthur Edward Waite publishes The Pictorial Key to the Tarot along with a deck illustrated by Pamela Colman Smith. Usually the publication date is noted as 1910, as the book and deck were first released in December 1909.

1938 - 1942

Lady Frieda Harris paints the Thoth Tarot following Aleister Crowley's instructions.

1912

The Pravda is first published in St. Petersburg.

1936

Charlie Chaplin stars in Modern Times.

Innovations of the French School

◦— Tarot transforms from a game and fortune telling device into a magical and spiritual information system.

◦— Tarot is linked to Western esoteric disciplines including Astrology, Alchemy, and Kabbalah.

◦— Tarot symbolism becomes a journey and understanding of life and living.

◦— The most important names in the French school are Court de Gebelin, Etteilla, Paul Christian, Eliphas Levi, Papus, and Wirth.

Innovations of the English School

◦— The Minor Arcana are encoded with meanings and given an esoteric name

◦— The minor Arcana starts to be fully illustrated in decks, creating the basis for intuitive reading.

◦— Strength and Justice are switched in the sequence of the Arcana. Cabbalistic correlations of the Major Arcana are altered, incidentally making Tarot finally gender balanced.

◦— Many Tarot secrets, previously reserved for initiates of esoteric societies only, are now made public.

◦— The English school includes innovations of all members of the Golden Dawn including; William Westcott, Samuel Mathers, Kenneth Mackenzie, Arthur Waite, Pamela Coleman Smith, and Aleister Crowley.

Modern Tarot Timeline

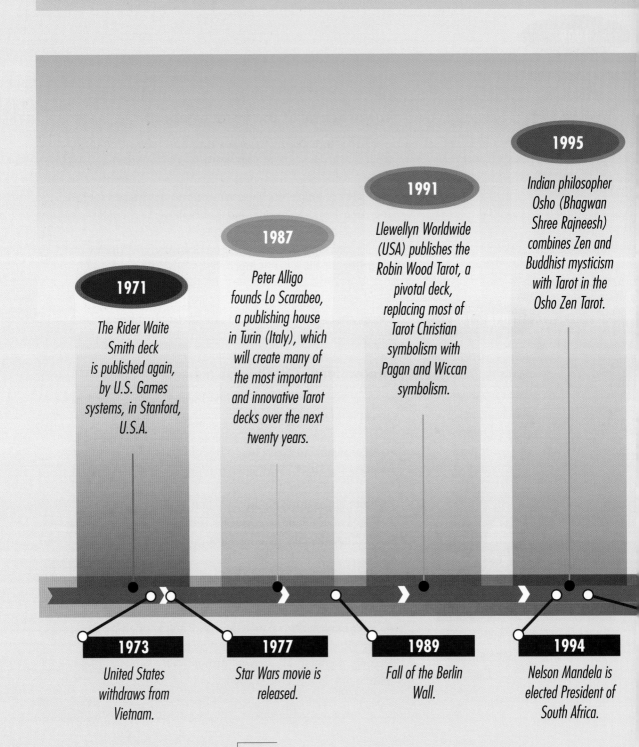

1971

The Rider Waite Smith deck is published again, by U.S. Games systems, in Stanford, U.S.A.

1987

Peter Alligo founds Lo Scarabeo, a publishing house in Turin (Italy), which will create many of the most important and innovative Tarot decks over the next twenty years.

1991

Llewellyn Worldwide (USA) publishes the Robin Wood Tarot, a pivotal deck, replacing most of Tarot Christian symbolism with Pagan and Wiccan symbolism.

1995

Indian philosopher Osho (Bhagwan Shree Rajneesh) combines Zen and Buddhist mysticism with Tarot in the Osho Zen Tarot.

1973

United States withdraws from Vietnam.

1977

Star Wars movie is released.

1989

Fall of the Berlin Wall.

1994

Nelson Mandela is elected President of South Africa.

Tarot experts from the United States, England, Italy and many other countries contribute to the evolution and understanding of Tarot. Forerunners in the field and influential authors and scholars include Mary K. Greer, Rachel Pollack, Robert Place, Barbara Moore, Mark Mc Elroy, Marcus Katz and Tali Goodwin. They, along with others, contribute to ongoing Tarot evolution.

1997

Hong Kong returns to China.

Important Points to Remember

‿ Tarot modern for favors intuitive reading. This paves the way subjective vision and a personal interpretation of the Arcana.

‿ Tarot cards, alongside New Age philosophy, evolved to become a tool of spiritual and psychological awareness.

‿ Explosion of Tarot decks published, different themes, different art, and literally thousands of decks.

‿ Development of Intuitive and Narrative Reading.

‿ People read Tarot for themselves.

‿ Modern Tarot Readers use more than one deck.

‿ Tarot is not only used to predict the future but also as a learning device and to help the person grow in the best way possible.

‿ Most Tarot Readers agree that Tarot books include important guidelines and basic definitions but ultimately, each person develops a personal style, technique, and practice.

‿ There is no one great, absolute truth to Tarot. Tarot is what the Reader makes of it.

‿ The cards are not containers of truth but mirrors and windows to a higher truth that every person can access through sensitivity and intuition.

1451

1770

1889

Visconti Tarot

Etteilla Tarot

Wirth Tarot

Only 74 cards out of 78 remain. The deck was laminated by engraved gold plates.

A card from the French carto-mancer Etteilla, published in Paris, 1870.

As published in color, in 1927.

1909

Waite-Smith Tarot

Also known as Rider-Waite Tarot.

1942

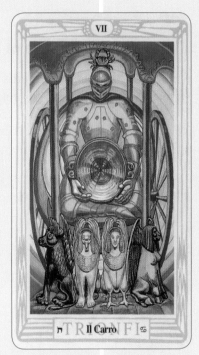

Thoth Tarot

Created by Aleister Crowley and painted by Lady Frieda Harris.

2013

Illuminati Tarot

A modern Tarot representation of intuition.

EARLY TAROT HISTORY

When people discuss early Tarot history, the are usually reffering to the time period before Tarot was used for proper divination, and before it was picked up by the esotericists and scholars of high magic.

Many people assume Tarot ceased to be used as a game, however, in Italy, France and Spain, the game of Tarot was still played regularly throughout the 20th century.

The Visconti Sforza Deck

Early hand-painted Tarot cards are extremely rare and no set has survived completely intact. The Visconti-Sforza Tarot cards are the most complete 15th century deck we have. It is our oldest trace of Tarot. Three early Tarot card packs are attributed to the Italian painter, illuminator, and miniaturist, Bonifacio Bembo.

Strength, Justice and the World from the Visconti Tarot.

490

Historians generally agree the Visconti Sforza deck was
painted for Francesco Sforza. This deck was created amidst
a struggle for power. Sforza, a military commander, married
the wealthy and powerful Bianca Maria Visconti. Bianca's
family ruled Milan and Bianca's father, Filippo Maria Visconti,
was the ruling Duke of Milan. The Visconti Sforza deck was
created to celebrate their marriage and the merger of these
two families.

Sforza, hungry for power and prestige, waited to be named
Duke when his father-in-law died. However, when his
father-in-law passed away Francesco Sforza was not named
Duke. With the full support of his wife Bianca, he had to
use his full military power and might to claim Milan as his
own. In the end, Sforza's strategy worked and he seized the
Dukedom.

Heraldry of the Visconti and Sforza families on the Sforza Castle in Milan.

Sforza knew it was important to maintain the continuity of Visconti rule. He combined his own heraldic devices and symbols with those of the Visconti's. Many of these symbols appear on the Visconti Sforza deck. The symbol of three linked rings, a Sforza symbol appears on many Visconti cards. Laurel and palm leaves, a Visconti symbol, appear on the Emperor and Empress card. The Visconti motto "a bon droyt" meaning "with good right" also appears on many cards.

Four cards, two Majors and two Minors, are missing from the Visconti-Sforza pack. This includes the Devil and Tower cards. The Visconti Major Arcana is not numbered. Historians do not know if these cards were included in the original deck. The Knight of Pentacles and the Three of Swords have also disappeared.

The deck is the work of painter Bonifacio Bembo with the exception of six Major Arcana cards. These six cards: Fortitude, Temperance, the Star, the Moon, the Sun and the World

were obviously painted by a different artist. Not only is there a difference in the painter's artistic ability but these six cards also retain a subtle difference. The characters are all painted standing at the precipice of a cliff.

Historians know of no fortune telling interpretations or meanings for Tarot before 1760. Tarot was used as a card game. Decks were commissioned for families of Italian nobility and only in later years Tarot spread to the general public as a tavern gambling game with rules a bit similar to modern Bridge. Even if the Visconti Sforza decks is the earliest deck we have (almost) complete, the earliest known mention of Tarot deck comes from Ferrara, Italy circa 1442.

After the Visconti-Sforza deck, Tarot evolved. Deck differentiations occurred based on where the game was played. As in regional cooking where the same dish takes on different regional flavors and nuances, so did Tarot deck designs. Tarot retained the essential structure of the Major and Minor Arcana but card designs and symbols differed from region to region.

493

Tarot cards were found across all of northern Italy by the end of the 15th century. Ferrara, Bologna and Milan were the three great centers of the game. Wealthy Italian nobility commissioned famous artists to create Tarot decks like the Visconti Sforza deck. Each card was hand painted, inlaid with gold on sturdy card stock and stood as its own work of art.

While Noble cards were treasured, playing cards for the general public were created from wood block stamps. Flimsy sheets of paper were stamped, colored, and cut. Public cards were ephemeral, easily destroyed, and intended to be discarded. This is the reason so few cards constructed prior to the 18th century remain.

The Tarocchi Players. Casa Borromeo, Milan, 1440
Despite the name by which the painting has become known, there is no actual proof that the cards used were Tarot, and not conventional playing cards of that time.

494

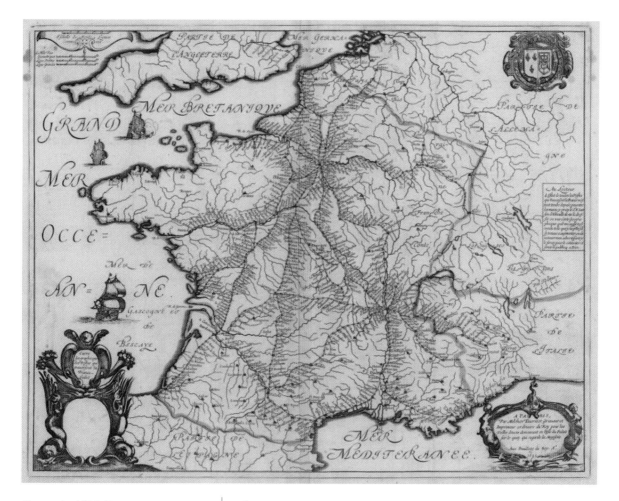

France in 1632. Post routes map, by Nicolas Sanson

The Printing Dynasties

Tarot, as a card game, spread through all of Europe by the 18th and 19th century. The card producer's most successful model came from France in the early 18th century. This model was called Marseille and it became the standard iconographic Tarot model. The French Marseille Tarot became a point of reference for manufacturers and for card players.

The master printers, a cross between artists and craftsmen, were driven to produce their Tarot cards for mostly commercial (not esoteric) reasons. Their impact on the history of the Tarot was extraordinary.

Great Printing Families

The Marseillaise model changed very little since its inception in terms of iconography and in card numeration. Printer's signatures and printing year were usually found on the Two of Pentacles and the Two of Cups. This information was compared to tax registers and a list of a list of hundreds of printers from the 18th and 19th century became known.

The Marseille model

The iconographic model of the Marseille Tarot was constantly maintained throughout the ages.

The Lovers from a deck by Claude Rochias (beginning of 19th century, Switzerland), and The Hanged Man from the Tarot of Jean Dodal (circa 1720, Lyon).

Important printers (and their years of activity) include:
- Arnoux (Marseille, 1790-1829)
- Benoit (Strasbourg, 1751-1803)
- Conver (Marseille, 1760-1890)
- Fautrier (Marseille, 1753-1793)
- Grimaud (Paris, 1748-1950)
- Madeni (Dijon, 1700-1795)
- Tourcaty (Marseille, 1701-1809).

The name of Marseille refers only to the iconographic template, not the actual place the cards were printed. Also, there are many different Marseille decks, with small variations in design, symbolism and colors.

Switzerland's printers include:
- Burdel (Freiburg, 1751-1850)
- Rochias (Neuchatel, around 1775-1850
- Shaer (Mumliswil, around 1730-1896).

These artisans passed the secrets of their trade from generation to generation. The Marseille manufacturers extended beyond the region of Marseille to the southeast region of France, Switzerland, northern Italy, and Belgium. The name of Marseille refers only to the style of cards created, not the Marseille region specifically.

Important Differences

Many printers substituted The High Priestess with Juno and The Hierophant with Jupiter in the second half of the 18th century. This switch may have been the result of religious difficulties between Catholics and Protestants.

During the French Revolution, the new regime ordered the elimination of the King and Queen from the Tarot deck.

Changed cards

Among the cards that were most often changed in the Marseille decks, where those of political or religious significance.

Juno replaced the High Priestess in the Tarot of Jean Jerger (beginning of 19th century, Besancon). In the Tarot of Adam De Hautot (around 1740, Rouen) the High Priestess is replaced by Captain Fracassa.

497

The Devil, Tarot by Jean-Baptiste Galler (1780 ca., Bruxelles)
This card is an example of a variation from the Marseille model. The iconography takes inspiration from the Bolognese Tarot.
It is proof that the design of Tarot cards, even in the 18th century, was not set in stone, but open to many different interpretations and ideas.

It was decided the King and Queen should be replaced with the new heads of society. Nevertheless, at the beginning of the 19th century the original model returned. Only some printers modified the production: some imitated the German printers, who were making themselves known in central Europe with an extraordinary variety of Tarot. Cartomatic decks such as Book of Thoth, the Sybille and Lenormand cards were in vogue.

Production Techniques

The commercial success of the Marseille Tarot created a demand for the cards. The French economy was strong in the 1700's. Artisan techniques improved. These new techniques allowed for the production of more decks with better quality at a lower cost.

The printing began with engraving work. The engraver stenciled figures on hardwood or sheets of copper. Using this stencil, the figures were printed in black. Once the sheets were dry, a screen was placed on top. The first color was hand-painted on. This was left to dry and then another screen with another color was painted over.

Generally, four colors were used; red, yellow, green, and brown. Tonalities varied with each manufacturer. The sheets were cut, the cards collected into a full deck, and covered in wrapping.

Italian Printers were considered to produce the highest quality cards. They used a longer, more costly procedure. Each card was glued to a small page and the borders brought around the card to reinforce the edges.

The End of an Era

Tarot had already undergone a profound transformation during the second half of the 19th century. Tarot no longer thrived under the exclusive domain of gaming. They were at the center of a renewed interest in esotericism.

Printing processes were revolutionized by new industrial technologies. The precious engraved stencils of master

Nicolas Conver, 1760
The printer name and the date of printing could often be found in the 2 of Pentacles.

paper producers, handed down over the generations had lost their value. Still, the work of these artist craftsmen was fundamental in defining the codification of the iconography of the Tarot. Their work, to this day, was irreplaceable for the spread and conservation of Tarot in Europe.

LE·BATELEUR

Focus on the Marseille Tarot

The Marseilles Tarot remains the most important reference point for Mediterranean countries such as Italy, Spain, and France. In the rest of the world, and in particular in Anglo-Saxon countries, Tarot enthusiasts appear to have set aside the Marseille, considering them a historic curiosity. Yet no other Tarot model presents the Reader with two equally vital aspects: common, simple, humble, and familiar symbols and a mysterious and spiritual aspect.

A timeless deck

Modern occultists believe that the images engraved in wood three or more centuries ago are outdated, even funny or grotesque, in their representation of personalities. An un-illustrated Minor Arcana presents an obvious obstacle to Tarot reading techniques based on intuition and visual associations. Other occultists, while recognizing these criticisms of the Marseille Tarot, succumb to their fascination and maintain that these cards have unique characteristics that have disappeared in successive decks.

Marseilles personalities, do not carry the idealized qualities of beauty, grace, and youth as many modern decks have. The aesthetic aspect may be compromised but the deck gains the possibility of separating the interpretation of the meanings from cultural aspects or social prejudices. The images, in their simplicity, possess an abstract strength much greater than many decks realized in the past decades. The Marseille is therefore considered "An archetype of the Tarot." Many esoterics and cartomancers see a distillation of all magic knowledge: a more efficacious synthesis and above all one closer to tradition than any other Tarot model.

LE·PENDU

A modern Reader tries not to choose a single type of Tarot deck for her journey, because each deck, each family retain their own value. The Marseille Tarot are considered an excellent deck for beginners. This may be due to the fact they extract the meaning of Tarot from context and structure rather than images. The absence of images in the Minor Arcana forces the Reader to consider the structure of the deck and internalize their own knowledge, bringing them into a timeless dimension and outside the epoch of these Tarot.

The First Marseilles Tarot

Historians claim that the ancestor of the Marseilles Tarot is found in the Tarot defined "proto-marseilles," produced in Paris in the second half of the 1600's. Many state that the first Marseilles deck was printed by Francois Chasson. Chasson worked in Marseille between 1734 and 1736. It is difficult to precisely establish the origin of this deck because all relevant historical documents contradict each other.

The name of the printer and the production date, 1C72 (interpretable only as 1672) appear on the Two of Pentacles. There is no reference to the place where it was published, while on the body of The Chariot and at the bottom of the Two of Chalices, the monogram GS can be seen. This could be a reference to the engraver, master printer Guillaume Sellon, who lived in Marseille from 1676 to 1715. One of the possible hypotheses is that Chasson, in 1734, used the stencil created by Sellon more than sixty years earlier.

The Marseilles family of Tarot, can be divided into three categories: philological reproductions, restored editions and new realizations. The philological reproductions consist in a faithful reprinting of the original decks. These reprints contain the imperfections and defects that 1700's Tarot possessed, including the effects of their wear and tear over time.

A modern interpretation of the Marseille Judgment, from the Le Millenaire Tarot of Marseille by Christopher Butler.

The restored editions attempt to reproduce the 1700's Marseilles decks as they were or as they would have appeared if modern printing techniques had been available. The restorations make the colors clear and defined, complete the outlines, and cancel the effects of wear and tear on the cards.

The new realizations instead re-propose the Marseilles model with modifications, colorations, modern, and innovative elements. Often these decks, such as the Marseilles Tarot presented in this collection, are used more frequently In one deck, they manage to unite all the strengths of the Marseilles.

Esoteric Tarot

The evolution of Tarot from the second half of the 18th century to the Second World War was marked by the influence of many scholars and occultists, beginning in France and then continuing in England. Even today the French School (still referencing to the Marseille Tarot model) and the English School (taking as main reference the Rider Waite Smith deck) are the two main traditions of Tarot.

Esoteric Evolution and Tarot

The Pyramids at Giza, in Egypt
According to many French esoterists, Tarot originated in ancient Egypt. However no historical fact supports this theory, and it was, most likely, a fabrication intended to make Tarot appear more magical and interesting.

The key to understanding the evolution of Tarot's esoteric usage lay in taking a quick survey of the schools of thought and history giving way to esoteric thinking. While by no means a comprehensive survey of esotericism, this jumping off point provides a basis of understanding from which to launch a personal esoteric inquiry of Tarot.

Mystery Schools

Mystery Schools or 'The Mysteries' of the ancient world belonged to Greece. The Mysteries were a recognized public institution in the ancient world. They were a major influence up until the 16th and 17th centuries. It is hard modern minds to grasp exactly what a Mystery School was. Depart from a modern rational, scientific minded nature and think of what life was like five hundred years ago. The modern mind thinks of a world that is seen, felt and measured.

Hermes Trismegistus
Hermes Trismegistus - the Thrice Great - may be a representation of the syncretic combination of the Greek god Hermes and the Egyptian god Thoth. He is the purported author of the Hermetic Corpus, a series of sacred texts that are the basis of Hermeticism.

The ancient mind believed the universe was not limited to purely physical phenomena. Vast, non-material realms were recognized and considered part of the normal world. The Gods operated in these non-material realms. These non-material realms were thought to bear a direct impact on the world of ordinary experience.

Mystery schools provided knowledge of non-material realms to their members. This knowledge was imparted to initiates in a series of advancements through grades, instructions, and elaborate rituals. Their symbolic structure was meant to codify principles as well as communicate them. These realms can be likened to dreams, the creative imagination, or even the space you enter when you meditate into a Tarot card.

Members also learned of the natural laws that operated within them. Though their existence was recognized, Mystery School work was usually done in seclusion. While the laws were considered to be of divine origin, the work itself was not considered religious.

Greek mystery schools brought initiates into a hidden world that could only be experienced. You couldn't read about it, you couldn't be told about it. The only way to learn was to experience it through the series of rites. These rites induced the transformation of personal consciousness. This transformation awakened energies and abilities within the body. The two most important Western Mystery Schools were the Dionysian, worship of food and wine, and Eleusinian, celebrating the myth of Demeter.

A statue of Hermes, in Stuttgart, Germany.

Below:
The Caduceus, symbol of Hermes

On the next page:
Demeter celebrating the return of Persephone. Painting by Frederic Leighton, 1891

Mystery Schools vs. Secret Societies

While both organizations usually included initiations and ceremonies, a mystery school typically guides individuals through a series of rites inducing the transformation of consciousness. Secret Societies sometimes offered this. Secret societies more often operated as a social club or fraternity.

Secret Societies

A secret society is an organization, known or unknown, whose rituals, objectives, and meetings are considered secret. A mystery school teaches there is a hidden world that can only be experienced, not taught.

First Mystery Schools and Societies

Ancient Greece contained numerous mystery schools from which secret societies grew. The Greek word was *myein*, meaning to close, a direct reference to the closing of the eyes and mouth to receive secrets. The initiate was called *mystagos* and the leader was called the *hierophant*.

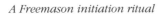

A Freemason initiation ritual

Three original cards from three decks created by the Visconti family.
The Emperor of the Tarot by Filippo Maria Visconti (left) probably depicts the Holy Roman Emperor Sigismund.
The Visconti-Sforza deck (center) is the one that almost totally survived to these days.
On the Ace of Swords of the Tarot by Filippo Maria Visconti, is possible to read the family motto: "A bon droyt" "by good right".

Cults were allowed to exist as long as they demonstrated they were religious in nature.

These cults held initiation ceremonies that mimicked death and resurrection. These same initiatory rites can be found cross culturally from Native American Indians to New Guinea tribes who send their teenage boys into the jungle for manhood initiations. The death and resurrection process transforms the initiate.

This same transformation is revealed in Tarot when the Major Arcana is viewed through the lens of the Hero's Journey. The Fool greets and moves through each card of the Major Arcana just like an initiate moves through rituals and rites.

Middle Age and Renaissance

The Middle Ages was filled with alliances and fraternities of all sorts, from trade guilds like the Freemasons, to secret fighting orders such as the Knights Templar.

The Renaissance in the 15th Century brings with it a period of relative stability. The Renaissance is distinguished from the Middle Ages in intellectual and cultural terms, and was a blossoming period for the arts and architecture. Italy is considered the birthplace of the Renaissance and where we also discover our oldest Tarot cards.

Italian Power

Italy was in a unique situation during the Middle Ages. There was no country called "Italy" but a geographic area that stretched from Venice and Milan in the north to Naples and Sicily in the south. The cities were known as "city-states" and helped to keep Italy fragmented. Italy's boot shape, and geographic location, south and east of Europe, gave it unique access to Europe, Africa and the Middle East. Feudalism never dominated Italy like it did the rest of Europe. Trade continued to flow through Italy. Merchants from all over the

Florence, Venice, Genoa, Milan were among the most powerful cities in 16th century Europe. In their courts, art and culture flourished as never before.

world conducted business in Italian cities. New languages and ideas flourished as trade and money flowed into Italy.

The wars of the Middle Ages were expensive for the Kings, Princes, and Popes who waged them. Italy found itself in a superior situation. Italian merchants enjoyed so much trade and plenty of individuals had money to loan for wars. This gave rise to the powerful Italian banking families, including the famous Medici's family of Florence.

These wealthy banking families employed artists who enjoyed "rock star " status. Patrons commissioned artists to create portraits, paintings, sculptures, and buildings. The wealthy Visconti-Sforza's family of Milan employed Leonardo da Vinci, famous in his time. The Visconti-Sforza's are the same family who commissioned the world's oldest surviving tarot deck.

The trial of Galileo in 1633 was one of the most important episodes of the Scientific Revolution.

Scientific Revolution

The Scientific Revolution occurred in Europe during the 16th and 17th centuries. It paved the way for new scientific thought. The most important and radical idea was that the universe operated according to a system of rational and quantifiable laws. The Scientific Revolution removed the earth from the center of the universe and it permanently changed the way Europeans thought about the world around them. This new thinking fostered the Enlightenment, an intellectual movement that came together in the mid 18th century and its core mission was educating the public.

Enlightenment

The goal of The Enlightenment was to free Europeans from superstitions, dogmas, and false medieval ideas. Enlighten-

510

ment thinkers believed they could replace magic and occult thinking with reason, experimentation, and scientific method. This "cultural intelligentsia" sought to educate the "upper crust" of society. The Enlightenment's unofficial headquarters was in France. Intellectuals met in salons and spread their ideas by word of mouth, with numerous publications, letters, and encyclopedias. The Enlightenment influenced luminaries such as Benjamin Franklin and Thomas Jefferson and played a major role in the American and French Revolution.

Hermeticism

Hermeticism is a set of religious and philosophical writings attributed to the famous Egyptian figure Hermes Trismegistus (translated as thrice great, or his name three times repeated). Hermes is often referred to as the Egyptian god Thoth and the Greek god Hermes.

Mercury-Thoth, inventor of Astronomy. Etching by Antoine Lousi Romanet, from Histoire de Mercure in "Monde primitif analisé et comparé avec le monde moderne", by Antoine Court de Gebelin.

Depending on the historian you speak to, it is suggested that Hermes Trismegistus wrote between 40 and 40,000 books. How could one person do this? Hermeticists wrote Hermetical texts but didn't sign it with their own name. They signed it with the name Hermes. They were expanding on his ideas or believed themselves to be channeling Hermes as they wrote.

Subjects of Hermeticism included; Astronomy, Math, Geometry, Alchemy, Spirituality, Philosophy, and Magic. According to legend, Hermetic writings turned up everywhere in the ancient world and influencied many religions. The bulk of his work was destroyed in the great fire of Alexandria in 48 BC. These lost volumes transformed Hermes into an even more mythological and magical creature. Sadly, there is no concrete proof any of this is actually true.

In the 15th century the Gutenberg printing press was created. Books and pamphlets became easier and cheaper to mass-produce. As a result, literacy spread across Europe. Works attributed to Hermes Trismegistus were snapped up by the public and widely circulated. Many secret societies

The Death Card of the Waite-Smith deck.
The Mystic Rose on the banner is a symbol that derives from Rosicrucian symbolism.

Rosicrucian symbol: Joachim Frizius, Summum bonum quod est verum magiae, cabalae, alchymiae verae fratrum Rosae Crucis verorum, Frankfurt, 1629

On the previous page:
Secret, etching by Pierre Philippe Choffard.
Before the discovery of the Rosetta Stone, Egypt was considered the land of secret and magic.

desired an ancient pedigree. Hermeticism was born in ancient Egypt so many societies hopped onto the Hermetic bandwagon. The Rosicrucians were the first organized group to set up their secret society around the core of Hermetic beliefs.

Six general qualities define Hermeticism:
1. The world is a living being.
2. The imagination has true value.
3. Correspondence or "as above, so below."
4. The belief in transmutation.
5. The perennial philosophy.
6. Spiritual truth is gained through initiation.

The Rosicrucians

Rosicrucians were essentially Christian in their belief systems but were influenced by Hermetic writings, ancient philosophy, and Eastern mysticism. Their symbol is a cross with a white rose in the center.

This symbol contains a slew of meanings including budding spiritual growth, life and death, while the cross represents the quartering of the world into Four Alchemical Elements, Earth, Air, Fire, and Water. To Alchemists, Mystics, and Spiritualists this is the secret symbol of immortality.

Solar and Planetary system. Etching, painted by hand by Johann Baptist Homann. In the XVII century Astrology was considered a science.

The Rosicrucian legend comes from published accounts of the group's German founder, Christian Rosenkreutz. Rosenkreutz was supposedly born in 1378 and raised in a monastery until he travelled to the East in search of spiritual and mystical knowledge. Here, he studied with masters of the occult arts. Rosenkreutz came back to Europe and begin meeting with a group whose ultimate goal was to assemble knowledge of the world into a universal message in preparation of the Final Judgment of God. Rosenkreutz died in 1484.

Between 1614 and 1616, three mysterious pamphlets were circulated. These pamphlets were attributed to Rosenkreutz but, in truth, it the greatest publicity stunt of the 17th century. The pamphlets were actually the brainchild of a Lutheran minister, Johann Valantin Andreae. He and a small circle of friends hatched a plan to invent an organization that would reform social life through new learning. It would provoke a new search for the secrets of life, nature, and the universe. This organization became the Rosicrucian societies.

The back of the Initiatory Tarot of the Golden Dawn.
The esoteric references are a combination of Rosicrucian and Kabbalistic symbology. For example, the Rose at the center of the cross has been replaced by the Tree of Life, and by the 22 Hebrew letters, arranged however as the petals of a rose.

Andreae's pamphlets, "Fama Fraternitatis," "Confessio," and "Chemical Marriage of Christian Rosenkreutz," outlined a worldwide organization of practitioners of the occult, who had supposedly survived the centuries by hiding out. Here was true secret society with an agenda of bettering the world using long lost, ancient knowledge and strange, mysterious rituals. Truthfully, there was no real organization to join. Regardless, Rosicrucian societies popped up all over Europe in response to these pamphlets.

The Enlightenment insisted on scientific answers to religious questions. Rosicrusianism was balanced perfectly between superstition and science. It combined Science, Religion, Alchemy, Magic, Egyptian mysticism, Jewish Mysticism, and Christianity. However, as scientific methods improved, the allure of Rosicrusianism died out with a few exceptions in France. In the mid 19th Century, Eliphas Levi would bring back strong interest in Rosicruciansim with his series of books about Transcendental Magic.

Quick Kabbalah

The Kabbalah (or Cabala, Kabala, Cabbalah, all spellings are relevant) is central to Rosicrucian lore. The Reader will find reference to Kabbalah in nearly every Western secret society. Kabbalah is a branch of Jewish study that mystically describes the origins and operations of the universe. For centuries, Kabbalah was passed down to adepts orally. The male student had to be over the age of 40 to receive it. A 13th Century Rabbi Bahya ben Asher is credited with the first written examination of Kabbalah. Christianity and Islam would have their own variations of Kabbalah.

Kabbalah, with Astrology and Alchemy, is the pillar of the western magical tradition

On the next page:
*The Freemason symbol, with the
Square and the Compass.
On the side: Freemason's cerimo-
nial sword*

The central image of Kabbalah is the "Tree of Life," which
has ten branches connected by twenty-two paths. The
numbers and images between Tarot and Kabbalah merged
beautifully when esotericists decided to combine them.
Tarot's Minors have ten numbers and there are ten branches
on the Tree of Life. The twenty-two paths on the Tree connect to Major Arcana's twenty-two cards. In typical Cabalistic
understanding, the twenty two-paths are connected to the
twenty-two letters of the Hebrew alphabet. This provides
additional meaning to the cards.

*Diagram of the Kabbalistic Tree of
Life, in the version devised by A.
Crowley.*

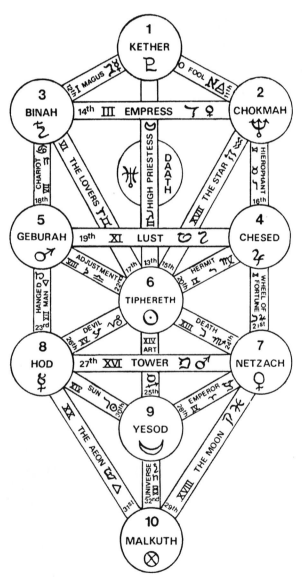

Traditionally, it is thought one can't truly understand Kabbalah without an understanding of the Hebrew language. To a Kabbalahlist, the Hebrew language is Holy. When God communicated the first five books of what is considered The Old Testament, he did so in a certain code. To crack the code is to discover the mysterious secrets of life and the universe.

Freemasonry

Whisper the word Freemasonry and various images are conjured. Are Freemasons a dangerous secret society or a group of drunken, silly men? What is Freemasonry and why are so many conspiracy theories and romantic notions attached to them? How are they connected to Tarot and why do we find their symbols in important Tarot decks?

Freemasonry is a fraternal organization. Fraternal organizations, stemming from the Lain *frater* meaning "brother" are

Eight of Pentacles of the Waite Smith Tarot.
The card is full of Freemason symbols, like the apron, the bench and the hammer. However the symbology is blended in the card in a way not to became obvious.

brotherhoods, which are essentially, secret societies. There are two types of Masonic organizations, "Speculative" and "Operative." It is important to understand the difference between the two. Operative Masons were architects and the actual builders and stone workers. They organized themselves into the guild of Masonry in medieval times, perhaps even earlier. These were the men who built grand European cathedrals and architectural wonders that stand today.

As these stone workers organized into trade guilds, they used secret signs and rituals to safeguard their profession. It was important to safeguard oneself in Feudal society. Because a Mason held a trade and because of their highly specialized skill, they were able to move freely through Feudal society. A Mason was not tied to the land and beholden to the King ruling that land as most of the European population was. This afforded a certain freedom to Feudal masons that was not afforded to the average surf. Feudal masons had the unique ability to travel to where the work was.

Speculative Masonry is what comprises modern Masonic lodges. Speculative Masonry evolved in the late 16th century, creating a path of spiritual and moral development based on the preexisting signs and rituals used in Operative Masonry. Speculative Masonry is comprised of people who practice and belong to Masonic lodges but who are not actual builders, architects or stone workers.

Why and how did a path of spiritual and moral development spring from a group of architects and builders? No one can say with absolute certainty. It probably had something to do with the fact that Masons were charged with creating the 'sacred space' of the medieval world, as they were erecting the grand European cathedrals. Spiritual principles must have been applied in building these "houses of God."

The split into Speculative Masonry did not create the first esoteric ideas about Masonry. In fact, Operative Masonry included a belief in the divine nature of Geometry and Mathematics Masonry itself may even have roots in Sufi mysticism. Certainly it is an exciting and extraordinary to realize the very people who built the great cathedrals, chapels, churches, temples and mosques used ideas of Sacred Geometry in their construction of sacred space. Sacred Geometry is a blanket term used by archeologists, anthropologists and geometricians to encompass religious, philosophical, and spiritual beliefs that have sprung up around geometry in various cultures and was also used by Masons.

A brief examination of Sacred Geometry leads to understanding how the contemplation of outer space i.e. buildings and structures, leads one to the desire to study one's inner space. The esoteric and mystic study of Tarot can be viewed as the desire to unravel one's inner space or spiritual space through the architecture of Tarot's 78-card structure.

Diagram: an example of Sacred Geometry.

The Golden Dawn

The stranglehold of religion and magic seemingly became less to the modern mind and the public at large. Yet, something extraordinary, even shocking, happened in the 19th Century. Populations in Europe and America begin to par-

519

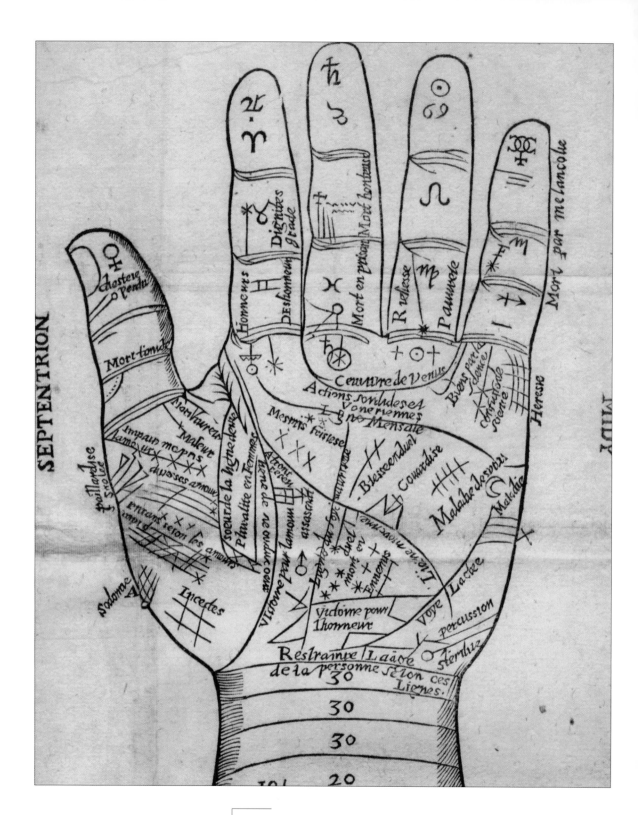

take in rituals that were essentially magical but they did not recognize them as such. Masonry exploded with popularity, trade unions, and specialized groups began adopting "mason like" rituals. People participated in these rituals, lodges, and secret societies but viewed these societies as social and charitable, not magical. This explains the proliferation of famous Freemasons at the turn of the 20th century with names such as John Jacob Astor, Winston Churchill, Sir Arthur Conan Doyle, J. Edgar Hoover, Harry Houdini, all seven Ringling Brothers, Theodore Roosevelt, just to name a few.

Why did Freemasonry have such a significant impact on the history of Tarot? Until Masonic ideas exploded, most ritual Magicians and Alchemists worked from old grimoires. They performed lengthy and solitary procedures to evoke their powers. With Masonry came a systematized structure of ritual and initiation. Grades and rites were laid out. Esotericists could bring a group of people together and apply any magical system to the Masonic structure.

Three high-ranking Freemasons came together in London, 1888, to form the Hermetic Order of the Golden Dawn. Out of this group, the most influential modern Tarot deck was born.

TAROT'S FOREFATHERS

The occult writers and thinkers who contributed to Tarot's evolution all share striking similarities. Most of these personalities displayed an early interest in a spiritual path of life springing from traditional organized religion. Most were heavily involved in spiritual life from a young age. Many of these occult thinkers began as ordained ministers or belonged to Christian orders before branching into the esoteric world. Almost every esoteric Tarot influencer changed their given names and adopted new names at some point of their lives. Historic Tarot scholars all shared strong ties and affiliations with secret societies, Masonry, and Rosicruciansim.

Lodge Plan, etching from a XVIII century book.
It's possible to clearly see the Jakin and Boaz column (see the High Priestess card). Eliphas Levi was the first to combine the work of the Masonic Lodges with the symbolism of Tarot.

PLAN DE LA LOGE

POUR LA RECEPTION D'UN APPRENTIF-COMPAGNON,

Tel qu'il a été publié à Paris, mais inexact.

1. Colonne Jakin.
2. Colonne Boaz.
3. Les 7 marches pour monter au Temple.
4. Pavé Mosaïque.
5. Fenêtre d'Occident.
6. Planche à tracer, pour les Maitres.
7. Etoile flamboyante.
8. Fenêtre du Midi.
9. Perpendiculaire, ou Aplomb.
10. Fenêtre d'Orient.
11. Niveau.
12. Pierre brute.
13. Equerre.
14. Pierre cubique à pointe.
15. Houpe dentelée.
A. Place du Grand-Maitre.
B. Place du premier Surveillant.
C. Place du second Surveillant.
D. Autel.
E. Tabouret.
F. G. H. Les trois Lumières.

Tarot's Occult Beginnings

Court de Gebelin
1725 – 1784
*Freemason, Intellectual,
Scholar of Ancient
Mythology*

Court de Gebelin

All of Tarot's occult associations appear to begin in Paris with a single, well educated, highly political man, Court de Gebelin. For highly educated France, the mysteries of ancient Egypt became a fashionable subject involving every layer of society, from bourgeois salons to esoteric associations. Napoleon's conquests had brought many Egyptian artifacts to Europe. The Rosetta Stone had not been discovered and undeciphered hieroglyphs appeared magical and fascinating to the public. Gebelin's claim that Tarot was an ancient Egypt artifact was the right myth at the right time. His theories on Tarot would catch on like wildfire. The occultists who followed would expand Gebelin's work. His work still influences modern Tarot but sadly, Gebelin's theories were based on intuitive guesswork, not on fact.

Court de Gebelin: portrait

A. COURT DE GÉBELIN.
NÉ A NIMES EN 1725, MORT A PARIS EN 1784.

Gebelin was born in Nimes, France in 1725. He was the only son of Antoine Court, a French Protestant reformer and pastor. Gebelin would eventually take on his grandmother's name and become Antione Court de Gebelin. No doubt influenced by his father, Gebelin studied theology in Lausanne, Switzerland. He became an ordained Protestant pastor in 1754.

Gebelin left the clergy after his father's death. Wanting to devote his life to literary pursuits, he moves to Paris to be close to the books he would need. Gebelin zealously em-

Frontespice of Monde Primitif, by Antoine Court de Gebelin.

MONDE PRIMITIF,
ANALYSÉ ET COMPARÉ
AVEC LE MONDE MODERNE,
CONSIDÉRÉ
DANS LES ORIGINES GRECQUES;
OU
DICTIONNAIRE
ÉTYMOLOGIQUE
DE LA LANGUE GRECQUE,
PRÉCEDÉ DE RECHERCHES ET DE NOUVELLES VUES SUR L'ORIGINE DES GRECS ET DE LEUR LANGUE.

PAR M. COURT DE GEBELIN,
DE DIVERSES ACADÉMIES, CENSEUR ROYAL.

A PARIS,

Chez { l'Auteur, rue Poupée, Maison de M. Boucher, Secrétaire du Roi.
VALLEYRE l'aîné, Imprimeur-Libraire, rue de la vieille Bouclerie.
SORIN, Libraire, rue Saint Jacques.
DURAND, Neveu, rue Galande.

M. DCC. LXXXII.
AVEC APPROBATION ET PRIVILÉGE DU ROI.

524

The Rosetta Stone allowed Jean-François Champollion to start the translation of Egyptian language in 1822.

braces Freemasonry and becomes the Secretary of Neuf Seurs Lodge, a famous Parisian Masonic lodge. Neuf Seurs refers to the nine muses and its membership included Benjamin Franklin, founding father of the Unites States and Voltaire, French writer, philosopher and historian. In fact, it is Benjamin Franklin and Court de Gebelin who are the conductors for Voltaire's initiation into the lodge. How interesting that at the beginning of Tarot's occult influence, Court de Gebelin is residing in the same intellectual melting pot with the very minds who influence the French and American Revolution!

Gebelin is a fierce intellectual, a linguist, and an ardent scholar of ancient mythology. He believes in the theory of a "Golden Age," a mythical time in which the arts and sciences are handed to man by the gods. This concept of a pre-existing golden time/era is a common myth spanning across many cultures. Studying religion from the point of linguistics, he believes he will detect a common pattern

525

within language. He believes these patterns will lead scholars directly back to this "Golden Age."

Gebelin also wants to decipher Egyptian hieroglyphics, which he believes will explain all existing mythology. He believes symbols reveal the underlying truth. Gebelin was not wrong in his assumptions. Psychiatrist Carl Jung would later describe the archetypal myth that resides in the collective unconscious. Joseph Campbell eloquently expresses the fact that mythic similarities cross all cultural boundaries. It is far this very reason that Tarot endures today as a cultural artifact, crossing nations, cultures, and philosophies. It is not surprising that Gebelin made the connection between hieroglyphs and Tarot, as they both communicate via visual iconography.

Gebelin's contribution to Tarot came as part work of a much larger framework. Tarot was only one of the many things Gebelin wrote about. Gebelin undertakes twenty years of research and between 1775 to 1784, he sells a subscription series to his observations "Monde primitif, analyse et compare avec le monde moderne, or "The Primitive World, Analyzed and Compared to the Modern World." This encyclopedic work of anthropological linguistics is intended to comprise thirty volumes. Gebelin completes only nine volumes before his death. Volume eight of his encyclopedia contains his famous 60-page essay on Tarot. This volume includes an additional thirty page essay on Tarot by a mysterious author who signed his work as M. Le C de M. The mystery writer is later identified by historians as Louis-Raphael-Lucrece de Fayolle, comte de Mellet, the governor of Maine and Perche.

Gebelin sells over one thousand subscriptions to "Monde Primitiffe," including one hundred to the Royal family of France. In fact, the Royals are so impressed by Gebelin, they appoint him as a royal censor. Royal censors in 18th Century France regarded themselves not as book banners but as the guides of the literary traffic of the Enlightenment. They served as cultural intermediaries who bore the responsibility of progressive thought. They held the power to pre-approve or reject all publications in France. How ironic Gebelin himself would be in the position of rejecting texts when ev-

erything he wrote about Tarot was intuitively invented, made up, and based on no factual evidence.

Even more interesting, a relatively unknown man of meager means named Etteilla tries to publish a book on Tarot while Gebelin is a royal censor. Etteilla's Tarot book is continually rejected by censors until after Court de Gebelin dies. Was Gebelin trying to repress other thoughts and ideas about Tarot that were not his own? Did he steal Tarot ideas from Etteilla? It is likely and possible but cannot be proved.

Gebelin teases his readers in his tarot essay. What would they think if an ancient book of Egypt was hiding right under their noses? Hidden in plain sight? What would they think if they were to discover that the secrets of ancient Egypt have survived the ravages of time, the fires of antiquity and the ignorance of man? He claims that this Egyptian book has survived. It has been hidden within the game of Tarot.

Gebelin explains how he discovered Tarot quite by accident. He had visted Madame la C. D'H, who had just arrived from Germany. He finds her among friends, playing the game of Tarot. Although he has heard of Tarot as a child, he admits knowing nothing of the game. Looking at the Tarot cards in a mystical vision, he immediately recognizes the allegories of the pictures. He declares Tarot Egyptian, flipping each card, he explains exactly what they mean.

It becomes clear to him that Tarot is the Egyptian Book of Thoth. The Egyptian Book of Thoth is a book of magical secrets written by Thoth, the Egyptian God of Wisdom. The holder of this book would know how to communicate with animals, cast great spells, and most importantly, communicate with the Gods themselves. Gebelin claims the Egyptians funneled their most prized and useful knowledge into the game of Tarot and then hid it in the most covert place of all in plain sight!

Gebelin claims proof of his theory by examination of the deck. His ascertainments are based entirely on conjecture and no actual fact. He explains the four suits represent four states or four orders of Egyptian political society; Swords

528

The Egyptian God Thoth had the head of an Ibis.

On previous page:
ancient hieroglyphics on an
Egyptian column.

being sovereigns and military nobility, Cups the clergy and priesthood, Wands being agriculture, and Pentacles being trade/commerce. The number seven was sacred to Egyptians and Gebelin claims variations of the number seven, make up the deck. Each minor suit is twice seven. The Majors (excluding the Fool numbered zero) equal 21, three times seven, and the entire deck totals 77 if we do not count The Fool, numbered zero.

Gebelin's etymological dictionary of the French language, states the word Tarot is derived from an Egyptian source. He claims that Tar means "way, path" and the word Ro means "king, royal," therefore the Tarot displays the "Royal Path of the Human Life." He stated this as fact again in volume eight's tarot essay. His theory of Tarot's origin is incorrect. Truthfully, Tarot's French name was originally Tarraux and is derived from the older Italian name of the deck, Tarocchi. For nearly two centuries, his followers and admirers expanded upon his ideas and continued to develop his theories even though they are based on pure speculation. Author and famed Tarot artist Robert Place points out one simple fact. Paper was not available in ancient Egypt. Therefore it is impossible that playing cards would have existed.

529

Tarot's Creation Myth

Jean-Baptiste Alliette Etteilla

1738 – 1791

Astrologer, Europe's First Celebrity Tarot Reader, Alchemist

Etteilla in his studio. Print from 1804.

Jean-Baptiste Alliette – Etteilla

Etteilla is often referred to as Europe's first professional Tarot reader. It is perhaps more fitting to call Etteilla Europe's first Tarot celebrity. He expanded upon Court de Gebelin Egyptian origin theories and he organized a unified system of meanings with the cards. He created the first esoteric deck and went on to become the most famous fortuneteller of his time. He called himself Le Celebre Etteilla or "Etteilla, The Great Diviner" and installed himself at the Hotel de Crillon on Rue de la Verrerie in Paris, one of the oldest luxury hotels in the world. It was the same hotel where, in 1778, Benjamin Franklin signed the Treaty of Alliance with France: Franco American Treaty.

Before Etteilla came along, diviners used regular playing cards or techniques such as palmistry or tealeaf reading for their clients. Etteilla's Tarot system placed the card's meanings in a rational and orderly system that anyone could understand. His success was also due to how he brought the general public into an esoteric culture usually reserved for elite intellectuals. These were the same group of people who sought to have their cards read. He garnered a massive following who paid him for astrological readings, card readings, custom made talismans, classes and spiritual counseling. He is also credited for creating the word *"cartomancy."* Etteilla's interpretations of the Minor Arcana are what many modern meanings are still based on.

Little is known about Etteilla's early life except that he was the son of a food caterer/wine merchant and born in Paris in 1738. His birth name was Jean-Baptise Alliette and he later changed his last name by spelling it backwards. Historians note that his writing style suggests a very modest education. He married Jeanne Vattier at age 25 and separated from her six years later while working as a seed merchant. His career in seeds failed to grow. Etteilla reinvented himself as dealer of art prints, an author, and eventually, a fortuneteller.

Etteilla published his first book in 1770, "Etteilla, ou maniere de se recreer avec un jeu de cartes," or "Etteilla, Or a Way to Entertain Yourself with a Deck of Cards." This book explained how to use regular (non-Tarot) playing cards for divination. It was successful and reprinted a number of times under different titles. Historians have no way to verify if Etteilla created this system by himself or if he used a pre-determined system of folk magic. By his own admission, Etteilla claimed to have learned card reading from an Italian teacher. His system utilizes the same process modern Tarotists use. He had the Reader deal the cards into a spread and then interpret them with a pre-assigned set of meanings. Etteilla was the first to write a book on how to do this.

Etteilla's book on regular playing card divination included Tarot on its list of divination tools. The publication of his book pre-dates Gebelin's volume eight of "Monde Primitif." This proves Tarot was known in Paris before Gebelin "discovered" it. It is interesting to note that in 1782 Etteilla attempted to pass his Tarot manuscript through the royal censors and he is denied. In 1785, after Court de Gebelin's death, his manuscript made it past the censors and he published, "A Way to Entertain Oneself with a Pack of Cards Called Tarots."

His book was a success and went into its second printing the following year. What made his book special was that he assigned broad themes to a series of cards, setting the stage for our modern card practice. He also assigned specific physical traits to selected cards. He even offered upright and reversed meanings. Etteilla also included instructions on how to combine Tarot with astrology, another first.

Just like Gebelin, Etteilla claimed that Tarot was the work of ancient Egyptians. He went even further by inventing the first creation myth about Tarot. Etteilla claimed that Tarot was composed by 17 great magicians, descendants of Mercury-Thoth, at the Temple of Fire, near Memphis, exactly 1,828 years after the Creation, or 171 years after the Great Flood. This made Tarot 2,125 year old when his book was published. Etteilla did not provide one scrap of historically supported evidence.

In 1788 Etteilla published the very first Tarot deck designed specifically for esoteric purposes including divination. Up until this point, all decks, including the Tarot de Marseille, were designed for gaming. Etteilla's deck was a success and in many respects, was the Rider Waite Smith deck of its time. The deck is designed with 22 Major Arcana and 56 Minor Arcana. He reinterprets the Major Arcana. Etteilla wanted to restore Egyptian elements. He reordered the Majors, providing them with a new iconography and new names. Part of his desire to do this sprang from his belief that the first seven Trumps should depict the creation myth. In addition, he assigned zodiac signs and the four Elements to selected cards. He was also the first person to place captions on both the Majors and Minors.

Towards the end of his life, Etteilla used his knowledge of Astrology, Tarot and other occult sciences to earn a living from his books, Readings and teaching students. He trained a new generation of card readers who, in turn developed and spread his methods and deck. In 1788, exactly one hundred years before the formation of the Golden Dawn, he founded the first organization devoted to the study of Tarot, "The Societe des Interpretes du Livre de Thot," or "Society Interpreters of the Book of Thoth." Three years later, at age fifty-three, he died.

Homme blond.
Nº 20. Remarquable.
R. 21. Abus.
E.....Cloître.
4 Rois. Grand Honneur.
3 Rois. Consultation.
2 R... Petit Conseil.
4 Rois. Célérité.
3 R... Commerce.
2 R... Projets.
Homme chatain blond.
Nº 10. Luteur.
R. 21. Abus.
E.... Cloître.

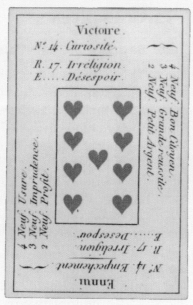

Victoire.
Nº 14. Curiosité.
R. 17. Irréligion.
E..... Désespoir.
4 Neuf. Bon Citoyen.
3 Neuf. Grande remarte.
2 Neuf. Petit Argent.
4 Neuf. Usure.
3 Neuf. Imprudence.
2 Neuf. Profit.
Ennui.
Nº 14. Empêchement.
R. 17. Irréligion.
E. Désespoir.

Femme brune.
Nº 24. Commerage.
R. 7. Désunion.
E..... Injustice.
4 Dames. Grand Pourparler.
3 D...... Trompere de femme.
2 D...... Amie.
4 Dames. Mauvaise société.
3 D...... Gourmandise.
2 D...... Ouvrier Ouvrage.
Femme chataigne brune.
Nº 24. Épouse.
R. 7. Désunion.
E. Injustice.

Militaire.
Nº 4. Fierté.
R. 27. Généalogie.
E.......On nous attend.
4 Valets. Maladie contagieuse.
3 V...... Dispute.
2 V...... Inquiétude.
4 Valets. Privation.
3 V....... Paresse.
2 V....... Société.
Domestique.
Nº 4. Parent.
R. 27. Généalogie.
E. On vous attend.

Un Homme.
Nº 2. Fidélité.
R. 29. Voleur.
E.... Or sur vous.
4 Rois. Grand Honneur.
3 Rois. Consultation.
2 Rois. Petit Conseil.
4 Rois. Célérité.
3 Rois. Commerce.
2 Rois. Projets.
Un Homme.
Nº 2. Père.
R. 29. Voleur.
E. Or sur vous.

Homme de robe.
Nº 17. Science.
R. 14. Irréligion.
E. Innocent dans les fers.
4 Rois. Grand Honneur.
3 R... Consultation.
2 R... Petit Conseil.
4 Rois. Célérité.
3 R... Commerce.
2 R... Projets.
Homme veuf.
Nº 17. Foiblesse.
R. 14. Irréligion.
E. Innocent dans les fers.

Cards from the deck called Petit Etteilla, stencil-painted etchings. The Petit Etteilla, published by B.P.Grimaud in Paris in 1895, was a cartomancy game of 32 cards. It was created by Etteilla and first published in 1791.

Tarot Evolves

Jean-Baptiste Pitois – Paul Christian

Jean-Baptiste Pitois
Paul Christian
1811 – 1877
Librarian, Scholar,
Prolific Author

Paul Christian was a shockingly prolific author, journalist, editor, and translator who wrote under many assumed names. He picked up where Etteilla left off, expanding upon the creation myth of Tarot.

Christian was born in the Vosges district of France at Remiremont on May 15th 1811 under the name of Jean-Baptiste Pitois. He later changed his name to Paul Christian. Christian's family intended for him to become a priest. He had a religious upbringing with the community of the *Clercs de la Chapelle Royale*. In 1828 he was novice in the Order of Trappist Monks under the name of Dom Marie-Bernard. Trappist monks are cloistered contemplative monks. While not always taking a vow of silence, Trappist monks generally speak only

Paul Christian: portrait

534

when spoken to and idle talk is strongly discouraged. Contemplative silence is the preferred order of the day. Christian gave up religious life but the religious influence remained with him.

Christian's publishing career began with his close friend Charles Nodier, curator of the Paris Arsenal Library. Christian is also the nephew of publisher and bookseller Pitios-Levrault who later published his nephew's translations. Christian became the Librarian at the Ministry of Public Education. He was given the arduous task of sorting these texts. His first year of work began with a redistribution of spare and uncatalogued library books and found the job delightful. His discoveries included books on supernatural, magical, and philosophic subjects.

Christian picks up where Etteilla left off. He forges evidence to connect Tarot to ancient Egyptian mystery cults and refers to Tarot as Arcana, as secrets. Occultists from this point on call Tarot's fifth suit the Major Arcana and the pip cards the Minor Arcana.

In book two of his "The History of Magic" Christian describes an initiation ceremony for the ancient Egyptian mysteries taking place inside the Great Sphinx and Great Pyramid. He describes how the initiate faces horrific life threatening ordeals and descends a seventy-eight rung ladder. This ladder leads to a room with twenty-two mystical paintings containing secret doctrines. Each doctrine is related to an ancient letter and number. He does not mention the word Tarot but there is no doubt he is referring to the keys of Tarot. He claims to have found this information on in the book "On the Mysteries," written by the fourth-century Neo-Platonist, Iamblichus. But no such description exists. Paul Christian simply made this story up. Future occult writers would expand upon this theory. One need only to read a few pages of Christian's extraordinarily seductive writing to understand why readers would want to take his words at face value and consider them as truth.

Tarot at the Center of Occult Science

Eliphas Levi
1810 – 1875
*Ordained Deacon,
Freemason,
Martinist Order,
Ceremonial Magician*

Eliphas Levi

Neither contemporary metaphysical traditions nor the practice of Tarot would ever be the same again after Eliphas Levi emerged in the second half of the 19th century. Levi placed Tarot at the *center* of all occult sciences. As a result, all occultism and esotericism can be placed in relation to one another through Tarot. Tarot was the common ground upon which many different philosophies intermingled.

Levi was born in Paris, in 1810, under the name Alphonse Louis Constant and was a simple shoemaker's son. Levi had a Roman Catholic education and was ordained as a deacon at seminary of St. Sulpice in 1835. Levi displayed an early fascination with the occult and was eventually expelled. His reasons for expulsion are unclear but speculations include the fact that Levi's doctrines were at odds with the church, he carried radical political views, or simply he had difficulty maintaining his vow of celibacy.

Alphonse Louis Constant, alias Eliphas Levi. Photography.

DOGME ET RITUEL

DE LA

HAUTE MAGIE

PAR

ÉLIPHAS LÉVI

Auteur de l'Histoire de la magie et de la Clef des grands mystères

DEUXIÈME ÉDITION TRÈS AUGMENTÉE

Avec 24 Figures

TOME SECOND

Rituel

PARIS

GERMER BAILLIÈRE, LIBRAIRE-ÉDITEUR
RUE DE L'ÉCOLE-DE-MÉDECINE, 17

LONDRES   NEW-YORK
Hippolyte Baillière, Regent street, 219.   Hipp. Baillière brothers, 440, Broadway.
MADRID, C. BAILLY-BAILLIÈRE, PLAZA DEL PRINCIPE ALFONSO, 16.

1861

Frontespice of the second volume of Dogme and Rituel de l'Haute Magie (Dogma and Ritual of High Magic), the most important work by Levi.

Free from the constraints of the Roman Catholic church Levi began writing two radical socialist books. These get him thrown into Paris prison for two brief sentences against the Church. Levi enters French Freemasonry in 1846 and a Martinist Order in 1850. Polish Cabbalist Hoene Wronski had a large influence on Levi. Levi changed his French birth name from Alphonse Louis Constant to the magical name Hebrew name, Eliphas Levi.

Two years later, in 1855, Levi published his first and most important esoteric work, "Dogma and Ritual of High Magic." Levi tried to reconcile his magical doctrines with the Catholic religion, but he always regarded magic as the pure expression of spirituality, which put man in direct contact with the Divine. He believed magic also overcame divisions between various religions. Levi's work marks the final transition of Renaissance magic and medieval tradition into the groundwork for modern esotericism.

An image from Dogma and Ritual of High Magic, illustrating the relationship between the words ROTA and TARO.

Levi was born in the Age of Enlightenment, which used scientific reason and logic to gain insight to the human condition. Levi examined his esoteric works with the experimental attitude of science. He considered all esoteric experience phenomena to be studied and experimented with in order to discover the universal laws that governed them.

From this point of view, Astrology, Alchemy or Kabbalah were no longer confined to irrational superstition but defined as "Occult Sciences." This term, coined by Levi, also applied to dark magic like Necromancy magic involving communication with the dead for the purposes of divination. At its finest expression, it is a scared spiritual art attempting to bridge the realms of the living and the dead. "Occult Sciences" also apply to Demonology, a branch of theology relating to superhuman beings that are not gods. Levi, like any scientist was not going to evade these issues but face them with the spirit of scientific impartiality.

Levi's theories on Tarot are contained in his first and most important esoteric works, the two volumes, "The Dogme et Ritual de la Haute Magie," and "Dogma and Ritual of High Magic," (Paris, 1855-56). Levi suggested the meanings of

538

the Arcana are connected to the 22 letters of the Hebrew alphabet. Levi believed the 22 letter Hebrew alphabet were not the only way to use and understand the Arcana. Levi considered Tarot as "The most perfect instrument of divination," an oracle that can answer all questions. Above all, he considered the Tarot "Key" to all ancient religious dogma. He considered Tarot to be the symbolic synthesis of all earthly and supernatural knowledge.

Levi's theories had tremendous impact on the esoteric scholars who followed. Frenchman Gerard "Papus" Encause built upon Levi's ideas. Englishman Samuel Liddell Mathers did the same, creating two distinct currents, the French and Anglo Saxon schools of Tarot. Levi was a profound influence on the Golden Dawn who incorporated Levi's rituals. Aleister Crowley was born on the day Levi passed away and claimed to be Levi reincarnated.

An image from Dogma and Ritual of High Magic, illustrating Levi's theory on magic.

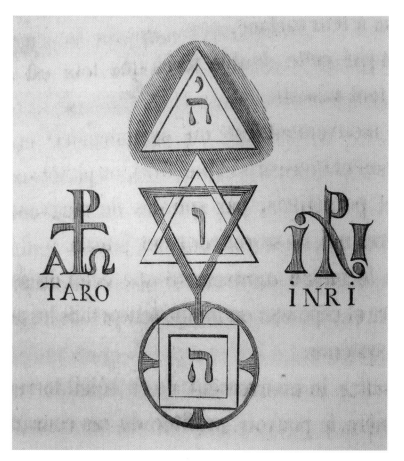

Ushering Tarot into the XX Century

Gérard Encausse – Papus
1865 – 1916
Writer, Esotericist, Doctor, Hypnotist

Gérard Encausse – Papus

Papus keeps Tarot momentum moving forward by forging a deep connection between Tarot and Kabbalah, the two largest Western magical traditions.

Gerard Anaclet Vincent Encausse, was born in La Coruna, Spain in 1865. His family relocated to Paris when he was two years old. Papus entered medical school in 1885 and received his doctorate in medicine in 1894. He affiliated himself with the Martinist Order in 1882 and founds the Order Kabbalah of the Rosicrucians with Stanislas De Guaita and Josephin Peladan. Traveling to England, France, Germany, and Russia, he meets with other great masters of the occult.

In 1889, at the age of 24, Papus writes a massively complicated book on Tarot. "Le Tarot des bohemiens:le plus ancien livre du monde," or "Tarot of the Gypsies: The Most Ancient Book in the World," otherwise known as "Tarot of the Bohemians."

Géranrd Encausse, alias Papus. Photography.

Papus, Tarot and the Kabbalah

After the studies of Papus, Tarot decks started to associate Arcana with Hebrew letter. According to Papus, Aleph, the first letter, is associated with the Magician (Arcanum number I), while Tau, the last letter, is associated with the World.

Papus associations were later changed by the English school, as Aleph was associated with the Fool (Arcanum number 0).

Aleph

Tau

The Magician of the Contemplative Tarot, by Adriano Buldrini.
The card follows Papus' Kabbalistic associations.

Papus believed Tarot to be a repository of ancient esoteric wisdom and a tool for divination. He goes so far as to call Tarot "The Bible of Bibles." He stated, " Yes; the game of cards called the Tarot, which the Gypsies possess, is the Bible of Bibles . . . Thus whilst the Freemason, an intelligent and virtuous man, has lost tradition; whilst the priest, also intelligent and virtuous, has lost his esotericism; the Gypsy, although both ignorant and vicious, has given us the key which enables us to explain all the symbolism of the ages."

Papus asserts Tarot is handed down from the ancient Egyptians. He claims that Tarot contains a detailed, systematic exposition of Kabbalah, Astrology, Numerology, Theogony (the study of the creation of a god), Androgony (study of the creation of man), and Cosmogony (study of the creation of the universe). Oswald Wirth illustrates his book.

Papus believes, like Levi, that magic can be expressed with the same language and precision as the rational sciences. He believes the metaphysical and spiritual could be measured in the physical world and was scientifically observable. He describes the meaning of the 22 Major Arcana by relating it to the 22 letters of the Hebrew alphabet. While attributing

the meanings of the letters from the Kabbalah, he establishes new interpretations for each card.

Papus created a new philosophy born from letters and symbols. The French Tarot represented the tendrils that link God, man, and the universe together. Papus used four-letter acronyms, Kabbalah, and its connection to Tarot. He believed the most important symbols were IHVH, INRI, and ROTA.

IHVH means Yahweh and is the so-called Tetragrammaton. INRI is the Sacred Name of God, the acronym for the phrase that was written on the cross of Jesus. Nazarenus Rex means Iudeorum, Jesus of Nazareth, King of the Jews. Those same letters could be interpreted with the alchemical motto Igne Nature Renovatur Integra: for through fire, nature is fully renewed. Finally, the word ROTA, the wheel of existence, readable as TARO (Tarot) often appears on the Wheel of Fortune. The same word, written another way may indicate TORA, the Jewish Law.

Papus argued that those who knew and understood these acronyms also understood Masonic, Cabalistic science, Catholic symbolism, and esotericism. Papus believed in the relationship between the 22 letters of the Hebrew alphabet and thought that Tarot described the "Doctrine of the Cosmic Wheel." This wheel reflected the fall of souls in the material world and their subsequent ascent to the divine world. He believed Tarot was the symbolic key that allowed a virtuous man to return to Paradise.

Papus divided the Major Arcana into different groups:

- **Cards I – VII** are defined as Theogony or "Divine Origin."
- **Cards VII – XIII** are defined as Androgony, "Human Origins."
- **Cards XIII – XIX** are defined as Cosmogony, "Cosmic Genesis."
- **Cards XIX, XX, and 0** are defined as the moment of "Spiritual Rebirth."
- **Card XXI**, the World, is defined as the symbol of the entire Universe.

Papus believed the cards also marked Adam and Eve's stages of expulsion from the Garden of Eden. Man could retrace these steps in an attempt to recover Divine Grace.

Papus was called to the army front as a front office doctor at the outbreak of World War 1. He suffered lung issues and became very ill. He died at the Hospital Charity in Paris, surrounded by friends and disciples.

Tarot's Symbolist

Oswald Wirth

1860 – 1943

Symbolist, Author, Free-mason, Healer

Oswald Wirth

Oswald Wirth was most famous for his work with the Marseille Tarot and he specialized in symbolism. His massive study of symbol and meaning continue to guide modern scholars of esotericism.

Joseph Paul Oswald Wirth was born in the alpine village of Brienz, Switzerland in 1860. Wirth's father was a painter. Wirth would learn techniques from his father that he would later apply to the illustrations of his many books. He studied at a Benedictine monastery in Sarmen and at age 19, he was sent to London where he worked as a business accountant. In 1882 he returned to France to serve in the military. In 1884, Wirth eagerly embraced Freemasonry and quickly obtained the degree of Master Mason. In 1886, he returned to civilian life, attempting to resume his existence as an accountant. Wirth found himself drawn to the exercise of "magnetizing," the modern equivalent of "healing."

Oswald Wirth. Photography.

The Empress, the Emperor and the Hyerophant from the Tarot of Wirth, 1927.

An auspicious friendship blossomed between Wirth and aristocrat Count Stanislas De Guaita. De Guaita was suffering from incurable pain and invited Wirth to his Paris home hoping Wirth can heal him. De Guaita is a passionate lover of esoteric philosophy and the two immediately formed a bond. De Guaita encourages Wirth to join the Order of the Kabbalah Rosicrucians. This brotherhood had been formed to promote the study of High Magic while combating the evils of rampant materialism.

De Guaita conceived of a new Tarot deck in 1880 that was "strictly complete and properly designed." Under De Guaita's direction, Wirth restores "the 22 Arcana of Tarot to their hieroglyphic purity," fulfilling the earlier idea of Eliphas Levi. Wirth completed the deck in 1889 and it was printed in a limited edition of 350 decks. The deck accompanied Papus's book *Le Tarot des Bohemians*, which appeared the same year.

His book "Le Tarot des Imagiers du Moyen Age" was important to Tarot history but not the only important work

545

of Wirth's life. Wirth devoted more time and work to Freemasonry. He would become one of the greatest populizers of Masonic thought thanks to his many books on the subject. He died in 1943 in Monterrico-sur-Blourde, a small village south of Poitiers where he fled as a refugee after the Nazi invasion.

Rosicrucian symbol in use in the Kabbalistic Order of the Rose+Cross, of which both De Guaita and Wirth were prominent members.

The English Masters

**Kenneth Mackenzie
William Wynn Westcott
Samuel Liddell Mathers**
*Founders of the Hermetic
Order of the Golden
Dawn*

Kenneth Mackenzie, William Wynn Westcott, Samuel Liddell Mathers

The leading English pioneers of esoteric Tarot studies were members of the Societas Rosicrucian in Anglia. Their ideas, initially linked to the French School, took an autonomous turn. These ideas were instrumental in the modern development of Tarot.

An enormous esoteric revolution took place in early 20th century England. It was a result of numerous movements. It included many people whose work is fundamental in understanding the evolution of Tarot. Brits were the first teachers to merge the ideas of French fortune-tellers and occultists and create a cultural basis that would revolutionize Tarot.

In England, the first people to receive and understand these esoteric ideas are Kenneth Mackenzie, William Wynn Westcott, and Samuel Liddell Mathers. These gentlemen were all members of the Societas Rosicrucian in Anglie. Out of the three men, only Kenneth Mackenzie (1833-1886) personally met with Levi. On a trip in 1861, Mackenzie was instructed to "Work with Tarot." Despite preferring a method derived partially from Etteilla and partially from an unidentified

*From left to right:
William W. Westcott, photography;
Samuel L. Mathers, photography*

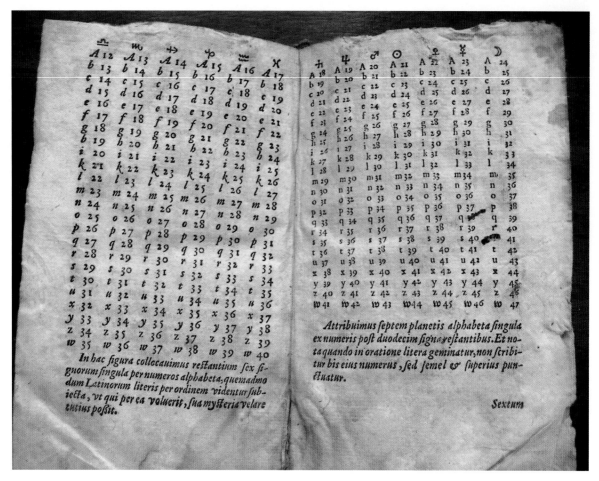

Pages from Trithemius' Steganography (1500 ca.).

This book allegedly had inspired first Levi and then Mackenzie. On the borders on a copy of this book, Levi had written many notes that later were gathered by the Golden Dawn.

On the next page: portrait of Trithemius.

Italian method, Mackenzie gathered enough notes and information to create a work titled, "The Game of Tarot and Archaeological Considered Symbolically, Illustrated with 78 Arcana." It was never published.

William Wynn Westcott (1848-1925) published, "The Magical Ritual of Sanctum Regnum, Rituals of the Holy Magic Kingdom," but attributed the authorship to Levi. He felt this gave it more weight. Westcott had a book he claimed had once belong to Levi by Johannes Steganographic Trithemius von Heidelberg (1462 - 1516), a Renaissance magician and student of cryptography. He claimed his copy of the book was full of notes by Levi on self-initiation magic and it was all based on the 22 Major Arcana.

548

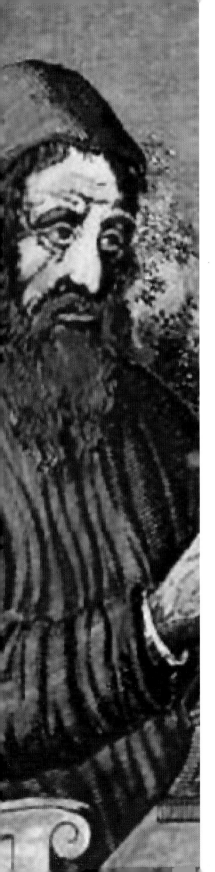

Tarot Divination Transforms Into Tarot Magic

Despite its limited distribution, Westcott's book, "The Magical Ritual," marked a pivotal moment. This was the official transition from Tarot for divination into Tarot for proper magic.

"The Magic of The Untied Holy Ritual" (London, 1896), was Westcott's treaty on Tarot. It was not very successful. In fact, Readers found his incomplete text difficult unless they already possessed knowledge of Alchemy and Astrology. What remains of importance is the book's instructions for the use of Tarot as a veritable manual of self-initiation for ritual magic.

Westcott's initiation procedure follows the numerical order of the Majors from the Magician to the World. The public's lack of interest was, perhaps, due to the time the book was published. At the turn of the century, many esoteric and Masonic brotherhoods were linked to the idea of collective ritual magic. This was regulated by a precise hierarchy and was performed in groups. Westcott's book described a solitary, individual self-initiation.

Formation of the Golden Dawn

London's Hermetic Order of the Golden Dawn had the most profound affect on the modern understanding of Tarot. The Golden Dawn was devoted to the study of occult arts and founded in 1888 by William Wynn Westcott, MacGregor Mathers, and William K. Woodman. The temple, located in an upscale London suburb, included poet William Butler Yeats, author Bram Stoker, playwright August Strindberg, artist Edward Munch, magus Aleister Crowley, actress Florence, Arthur Edward Waite, and Pamela Coleman Smith.

The Golden Dawn's mysterious origins began with the discovery of an "ancient" ciphered manuscript. William Woodman discovered this manuscript in a London Bookshop and brought it straight to Westcott. Westcott recognized the code as one used by an Alchemist in the 16th century. The cipher revealed plans for a secret occult society that admitted both men and women. Most fraternal societies of the day excluded women. The cipher even included the name, the Hermetic Order of the Golden Dawn, referring to the 17th century Rosicruscian ideal of a new spiritually enlightened age. The title spoke of the occult goal of "seeking the light," This goal is sometimes represented as the image of the alchemical sunrise.

There would be ten numbered grades, like the Freemasons but these grades were connected with the sephiroth of the Cabalistic "Tree of Life." The initiate progressing through the grades of the Golden Dawn would be progressing through the "Tree of Life."

One of the symbols of the Societas Rosicruciana in Anglia (S.R.I.A.)

Mathers and Westcott managed to organize a vast array of occult materials. They synthesized it into a teachable system. An initiate of the Golden Dawn studied Alchemy, Astrology, Kabbalah, Enochian magic, basic magical concepts and signs, the "Egyptian" writings of Hermes Trismegistus, and Tarot. Several pages of the cipher dealt with Tarot and its attributes. The group used all of this knowledge to conduct rituals that helped them to astral travel, meet deities, connect to other levels of reality and effect change on a non physical reality. They were truly a modern Mystery School who acknowledged alternate planes of existence. They believed that by working in these areas, they could transform their physical reality.

The Golden Dawn eventually fell apart due to conflicting personalities, politics, and splintering factions. At least half a dozen groups exist today, each claiming to be real descendents of the Golden Dawn. The Golden Dawn's mark on Tarot evolution was extraordinary. Not only did the group have a unique way of working with the cards, each member was required to create their own deck. The Golden Dawn system of Tarot attributions did many things including switching the Strength and Justice card for astrological purposes. Golden Dawn members Arthur Edward Waite and Pamela Coleman Smith created the Rider Waite deck, the most used deck in tarot history. Aleister Crowley and Frieda Harris created the famous Thoth deck.

The Rider Waite Smith Deck

Arthur Edward Waite

Arthur Edward Waite was born on October 2nd, 1857, in Brooklyn, to Emma Lovell and Charles Waite, a captain in the US Navy. Following the death of her husband, Emma returned to England. Waite's mother found spiritual support from the Roman Catholic Church and young Arthur received a strict Catholic upbringing. He served as an altar boy and embraced the idea of becoming a priest. His poor health and mental depression soon did away with such aspirations. Waite fell into deep despondency following the death of his sister Federica. He even abandoned the idea of entering uni-

Pamela Colman Smith and Arthur Edward Waite.

On the next page:
Detail of the Sun card from the
Waite-Smith tarot, edition of
December 1909.
This card was later subject to many
small modifications, and it can be
used to recognize the edition of a
deck. For instance, in later editions
the sunflower on the right has
black dots as same as the others.

versity. While Waite entertained thoughts of suicide, he never neglected his service to the church. In 1877, he wrote articles in defense of the Catholic faith, which criticised upper levels of the clergy. At age 20, Waite had many questions about the nature of religious life.

One of Waite's favorite hobbies included the reading of weekly stories. These stories of pirates, horror, and police investigations were called "Penny Dreadfuls." Though his mother banned Waite from reading them, Waite continued to be enchanted and inspired. Waite began writing fiction and poetry. He published his first story in 1878, "Tom Trueheart," in the periodical, "The Idler." He also devoted himself to the writing of poetry.

Waite began conducting research on magic and esotericism at The British Library. His latent interest in the occult was provoked by a discovery in 1878 of a Spiritualist newspaper. The Spiritualist movement claimed to prove life after death through communication with the spirit world. The pessimism he'd felt after his sister's death was availed. He immersed himself in Spiritualist literature, contacted various groups, and began participating in séances with the most famous mediums of London. Séances were all the rage in England and the US at this moment in history. Sisters Kate and Margaret Fox had created an alphabet code to decipher the rapping's of a spirit living in their house. Spiritualism exploded over the next few years.

Waite found himself influenced by Madame Blavatsky's seminal work "Isis Unveiled," published in 1877. Blavatsky was the founder of the Theosophical Society and Waite became close with many of its members, including Alfred P. Sinnett (1840-1921), a great populizer of Theosophy. Waite began to devote himself to the study of magic and found himself particularly drawn to Levi. Though Levi's works had yet to be translated into English, they exerted considerable influence on the Theosophical movement.

Waite considered Levi, "The most brilliant, most original interpreter of the most fascinating occult philosophy of the West." Despite his enthusiasm toward Levi, Waite was not

uncritical toward the French occultist. Waite condemned Levi's historical inaccuracies and inadequate translations of Latin. Waite published an article in the Theosophical Light in 1886, called "Eliphas Levi and the Antiquity of the Tarot." His article highlighted the mistakes made by Levi in dating the oldest Tarot.

According to Waite, the genius of Levi was that he attempted "To establish a harmony between religion and science and was able to reconcile the physical and spiritual forces, the balance of which is life and immortality." Above all, Waite admired "his beautiful moral philosophy" and "the great Arcanum of will power, which includes a word, the whole story, and the mystery of magic." Nevertheless, Levi offered no enlightenment to those seeking a way to God. Waite said, "He was a transcendentalist, not a mystic."

While conducting research at The British Library, Waite acquired knowledge of occult history and practices. In the 80's, he dedicated himself to the study of Alchemy. Levi asserted that "The writings of the Alchemists contain a doctrine of physical and spiritual evolution which is their main foundation, the philosophy was applied in laboratory practice." But Waite did not believe that Alchemists truly sought to produce silver and gold. He believed their work was similar to the operations and rituals of ancient Greek Mysteries Schools, "The conscious and the hypostatic union of the intellectual soul with the divinity and his participation in the life of God." According to Waite, "The Alchemists, like other mystics, were in possession of a secret theory of universal evolution that was applicable in every realm of thought and nature..." Waite applied this theory pictorially using the symbol of the snake consuming his own tail in the Magician card.

Waite progressively developed works that were published between 1888 and 1896. Later, his interest in the occult turned to other branches of esotericism. He inherited Levi's theory that the Masonic, Alchemical, and Rosicrucian symbolism, Ceremonial Magic, Kabbalah, the legend of the Holy Grail and the Tarot, would be attributed to a secret doctrine that had been kept alive over the centuries within a narrow, elite group of initiates.

554

Waite believed this tradition was "perpetrated by the institutions and mysterious cryptic literature," but by virtue of mystical tendencies, these institutions served to spread "Immemorial knowledge concerning man's way back the way he came and that using a method of internal life … that the followers must prepare to enter the 'Holy Assembly,' a secret church that can only be known within themselves as a spiritual experience". The search for the 'true guardians" of this tradition is one of Waite's dominant literary themes.

Pamela Colman Smith

Pamela Colman Smith
1878 – 1951
*Illustrator, Painter of
Rider Waite Deck, Intuitive,
Golden Dawn Member*

Corrine Pamela Colman Smith was born on February 16th, 1878 in London, to an artistic family. The first ten years of Pamela's life were spent in England where her family ran with a theater crowd. Her family then moved to St. Andrew's, Jamaica where her mother died in 1896. Pamela grew close to her Jamaican nurse and was heavily influenced by Jamaican folk culture. Pamela lived on the tropical island for several years before enrolling as an art student at the Pratt Institute in Brooklyn, NY. Her grandfather had been the first elected mayor of Brooklyn. Pamela left school and in 1899. She illustrated and published four books. She toured with the famed Lyceum Theater Company in 1899 and when her father passed away, she returned to London with the Lyceum.

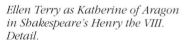

Ellen Terry as Katherine of Aragon in Shakespeare's Henry the VIII. Detail.
Ellen was the person that gave Pamela the nickname Pixie.

Pamela formed close ties to Bram Stoker and Henry Irving. Stoker was the author of Dracula and the business manager of the Lyceum Theater for 27 years. She referred to Stoker as Uncle Bramy and she even illustrated Stoker's last novel, "The Lair of the White Worm." Henry Irving ran the Lyceum and was the most famous actor of his day.

Her close-knit theater family also included a deep friendship with famed actress, Ellen Terry, who gave Pamela the nickname, "Pixie." Ellen Terry was inspiration for many cards in Pamela's Tarot deck.

Pamela was a gifted painter with a high degree of synesthesia, a neurologically based condition where one sense opens a cognitive pathway to a second sense. When Pamela listened to music, she also literally saw the music.

Pamela joined the Hermetic Order of the Golden Dawn in 1901. Her name and fate was sealed with Tarot history when Waite called upon her to illustrate his deck of Tarot cards. Waite held her in great esteem and thought she possessed "enormous mental qualities." Waite intended a Tarot deck for mass consumption, with occult overtones, but without giving away any Golden Dawn secrets. Following Waite's instructions, Pamela completed over 80 tarot cards. The Rider Company published the deck in 1909.

The innovation of her Tarot deck and the reason it became the best selling, most copied Tarot deck in the world, was that Pamela designed simple to understand, symbolic, yet mysterious, images for the Minor Arcana. Illustrated Minors opened the deck up for intuitive reading. She must have had access to the ancient Sola Busca cards, the only other deck known to contain an illustrated Minor Arcana. There are many similarities. She took literal liberties with the Three of Swords and Ten of Wands.

The last 35 years of Pamela's life remain largely untold. She passed away on September 18th, 1951 in Bude, Cornwall. She never knew the impact that her tarot cards were to have on the public.

Lady Areballa.
Illustration by Pamela Colman Smith for Bram Stoker's novel "The Lair of the White Worm".

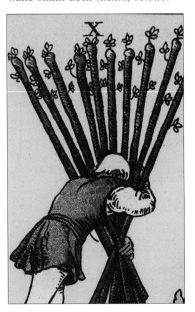

The Ten of Swords from the XVI Century Sola-Busca Tarot, inspired Pamela for the Ten of Wands of the Waite-Smith deck *(detail, below)*.

Waite and Smith's Tarot Collaboration

No one could have predicted the success of The Rider Waite Smith Tarot Deck, also known as Rider Waite Deck. Arthur Edward Waite, a leading British occultist and Pamela Smith, an intuitive illustrator, collaborated to create this deck. Published in 1909, it would revolutionize the way Tarot was used by the public.

Tarot, at the turn of the 20th century, would have likely remained hidden, appreciated only by a few historical and esoteric scholars, had it not been for the Waite and Smith collaboration. Certainly, Tarot would have remained unknown among the general population. The Waite Smith deck is a milestone due to its unprecedented innovation. Pamela Coleman Smith illustrated the Minor Arcana.

While Smith designed the images, Waite was using the divinatory meanings from the Golden Dawn's "Liber T," the text used to educate Golden Dawn initiates on Tarot. Smith executed these meanings in a beautiful and understandable fashion. The abstraction of Minors, which had existed in decks such as the Marseilles Tarot, was now recognizable to anyone who looked. Smith's paintings were of extraordinary impact. Finally, ordinary people, not just occultists or members of esoteric societies, were able to use Tarot.

Waite kept with the surface meaning of the 78 cards and never entered the depths of the "Secret Doctrine" from which it was inspired. However, reading Waite's other esoteric works, one can decipher what Waite meant by "Secret Doctrine." Tarot was a representation of universal ideas using universal symbols. The Major Arcana represented the journey through which one discovers a higher, deeper, evocative, spiritual truth. It is impossible to verbally communicate this truth. This truth lies in the sanctuary of the soul residing in each individual.

Almost every Tarot deck created and published since the Rider Waite Smith deck follow the Waite-Smith Tarot and their interpretation of the Minor Arcana. These decks are referred to as a "Rider Waite Clones." The technique of "Intuitive Reading" Tarot was born with Waite. Waite suggested a beginner interpret the cards using only the image and later with meanings assigned to them.

Thoth Tarot

Aleister Crowley
1875 – 1947
Wickedest Man in the World, Ceremonial Magician, Mystic, Occultist

Aleister Crowley

No discussion of the occult would be complete were it not to mention Aleister Crowley. Crowley was an occultist, mystic, ceremonial magician, and mountaineer who developed an infamous reputation for himself at the turn of the century. Born to repressive parents who were members of a strict Christian sect called the Plymouth Brethren, Crowley rebelled in a stellar manner. He lived up to his reputation as "the wickedest man alive." Some regarded him as a maverick and visionary, clever and amusing, while others deplored his behavior. He died a heroin addict and was reputedly cruel to humans and animals.

Crowley indulged in every type of psychoactive substance he could find, practiced sex magic and staged public performances of magic where he would spike the audience's drinks with hallucinatory drugs while charging an absurdly high amount of money for tickets. He was tossed out the Alpine climbing

Alesiter Crowley. Photography. In this photo from the 1900, he was wearing the ritual attire of the Golden Dawn.

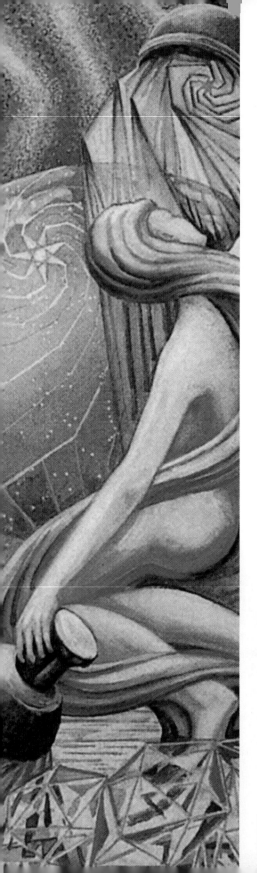

Club for not following rules. Crowley created an abbey of sexual and drug induced debauchery in Palermo, Sicily until Mussolini threw him out of the country.

Initiated into the Golden Dawn on November 18th, 1898, Crowley quickly rose within the ranks. He disliked poet W. B. Yeats because Yeats was not supportive of Crowley's own poetry. Crowley also disliked Arthur Waite and wrote searing critiques of Waite's work. He even invented satirical pieces aimed at Waite, including a piece called, "Wisdom While You Waite," and a mock obituary called "Dead Waite." Crowley left the Golden Dawn just two years after joining it.

An incredible collaboration was born when Crowley met surrealist painter, Frieda Harris. Harris was the wife of the British Parliament member, Percy Harris. Allegedly, Lady Harris was not very interested in the magic rituals but she was fascinated by the esoteric culture that Crowley drenched himself in. Lady Harris had already been associated with the Theosophical Society for years and bore a close association with the Freemasons even though she was female. Harris painted three large panels for an English Mason society. They were the three degrees of initiation; Apprentice, Fellow, and Master.

Crowley and Harris undertook the task of creating a new Tarot deck. Their deck of cards would integrate Magic, Kabbala, Science, Mathematics, Philosophy, and Anthropology. The project, supposed to last a few months, became a five-year project. Lady Harris found herself continually interpreting sketches provided by Crowley and integrating new suggestions and ideas. Crowley continually added new ideas. He would place additions on to cards, even ones he already approved. Several cards were redesigned. Despite these ongoing thoughts and corrections or perhaps because of this constant evolution, the final result was exceptional in every single way. The Thoth tarot would take its place in the lexicon of influential decks, altering Tarot's landscape forever.

The first source of inspiration for the Thoth deck came from the "Liber T." The "Liber T" was a book containing the instructions and symbols reserved for adepts of the Golden Dawn, where Crowley was a member of for two years.

On the previous page, detail of the illustration for the Star of the Thoth Tarot.

Crowley wanted to move further. He envisioned that each figure on the card be, "A pictorial representation of the natural forces as they were conceived by the ancients according to conventional symbolism." In fact, the Book of Thoth would be much more. Each card is mixed with the symbols of different traditions from Gnosticism to Buddhism to Taoism. This was combined with references from the literature of the Holy Grail, Astrology, Kabbalah, and Alchemy. Sometimes, inextricable symbols are hidden within geometry and the colors of each Arcanum. Lady Harris masterfully completed the job of integrating these forms of complex, expressive power. In doing so, she displayed awesome grace and dexterity. The cards radiate with striking animal-like intensity and power.

Completed in 1942, it was accompanied by the "The Book of Thoth," written by Crowley under the pseudonym Master Therion. Only two hundred copies were published. In 1977, US Games would properly publish the deck in collaboration with Samuel Weiser.

Despite Frieda's eclectic interests, she led a secluded life, nurturing her spirituality in eastern forms. In fact, the last days of her life were spent in far off Srinagar, Kashmir in northern India.

The World, called Universe, and the Queen of Pentacles, called Queen of Disks, from the Thoth Tarot, Italian edition.

New Tarot Renaissance

A new Tarot Renaissance blossomed in North America in the 1970's. The cultural openness of the United States and Canada, born in the hippie culture of the 1960's, paved a new chapter in Tarot evolution. The first milestone was the publication of the Rider Waite Tarot deck, which hit the American market in 1971. The Rider Waite Tarot and its successor decks (like the Universal Tarot) remain the modern references for Tarot iconography. However, out of one beautiful seed, many different trees sprouted. The New Age movement created a cultural base for Tarot to become accepted and welcomed by society at large.

New Age is a broad cultural movement encouraging people to give more attention to spiritual awareness, while not being framed in any specific religion context.

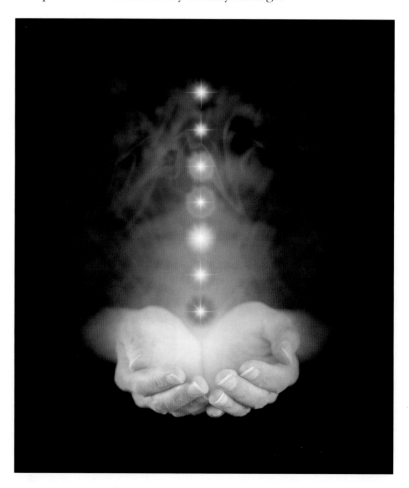

Tarot Arrives in America

Smith, Waite, and Crowley were busy moving Tarot into the next century while a man named **Paul Foster Case** conducted landmark work with American Tarot. Case had become fascinated with Tarot in 1901. He was the Praemonstrator General (Supreme Chief) of the Golden Dawn for The Unites States and Canada at the time. When Case resigned from the Golden Dawn, he created Builders of the Adytum. Commonly called BOTA, it offers Tarot lessons via mail correspondence. Case also created a BOTA deck. The BOTA deck is unique because students color their own cards. Although students are instructed on which colors to use, their artistic involvement with the cards fosters great attachment and attention to the cards. The BOTA deck was developed in the 1920s and is similar to the Waite Smith deck, although Case displays direct, unhidden esoteric symbols on his cards.

History of the New Age

The term New Age is used to identify the movement in Western culture that developed in the second half of the 20th century. Its draws on both Eastern and Western spiritual and metaphysical traditions, then infuses them with self-help and motivational psychology, holistic health, parapsychology, consciousness research, and quantum physics. New Age thought aims to create spirituality without borders or specific dogmas.

Progressive globalization brought Eastern mystical practices like Buddhism, Zen, and Feng Shui to Western lives. New Age is an umbrella terms that contains a complex set of philosophies and beliefs. New Age philosophy includes elements and influences from the oldest religions and spiritual practices, combined with ideas of modern science, psychology, and ecology. Strong influences include: Spiritualism, Buddhism, Hermeticism, Hinduism, Shamanism, Sufism, Taoism, Neo-Paganism, and Wicca.

The term New Age is a reference to the astrological Age of Aquarius. According to astrological thinking, the world has entered a new era dominated by the sign of Aquarius. The term New Age is freely used and can be applied in many contexts. It can refer to religious movements but also to design, musical, and literary styles.

New Age Zodiac Signs

New Age philosophy brought Tarot into modern times as a device for touching deeper aspects of reality. Great occultists in the 19th century were convinced that Tarot was the key to "high magic." Modern people still believe that Tarot is connected to magic but in a different way because the very definition of modern magic has changed. Tarot has undergone a transformation along with magical thought because Tarot is always used in a way that reflects the culture and people who use it.

Tarot's connection to magic is not based on superstition. It stems from recognizing Tarot's connection to personal intuition and subjective experience. The New Age generally understands magic as the path of energies and forces that

564

do not belong to matter and rationality. New Age "magic" becomes a way to recover a natural vision of the world, a way to approach and examine the unknown, to explore spirituality, to deepen personal beliefs, and merge with the sacred and divine.

Tarot to Know Yourself

The antiquated idea of a fortuneteller who predicts your future, the notion you are a slave to fate, and carry a predetermined destiny, is dear to novels and cinema but has little to do with a modern Tarot practice. Modern Tarot includes using the cards as a conduit for individual spiritual vision and using the Arcana as catalysts for energy and ultimately personal growth. This is the main reason people use Tarot today and the reason most people read the cards for themselves.

As people read the cards for themselves, they communicate with their higher, deeper, or spiritual self through the cards. Spirituality is a complex and personal issue. Most modern practitioners use Tarot as a tool for spirit growth. Even though many Readers work with clients in an empowering way, this does not dismiss the fact that there are large portions of the population who believe

Socrates said it around 400 B.C.

that Tarot professionals also work in areas of folk magic, sorcery, and witchcraft. While these beliefs and operations do exist, most modern Tarot books, decks, and communities operate under the umbrella of a modern New Age spirituality. This spirituality places responsibility solely in the client's hands and is concerned with personal growth.

Tarot Publishers Now

Tarot Returns To Europe

Just as Tarot was born in Italy during the Renaissance, the first modern publisher of Tarot was also Italian. While the late 60's brought hippies, drug culture, and innovations in rock music, a man named Vito Arienti brought innovation to Tarot. Arienti founded a publishing house named Solleone. Solleone published limited editions and antique decks. Each deck was a unique work of art and a collector's item.

Osvaldo Menegazzi published the Fantastic Voyage Tarot in 1974. Modern publishers were creating decks for an audience of collectors and art lovers. The public's thirst for the New Age was great and publishers stepped up to give them what they wanted.

Lo Scarabeo carved a unique path in the Tarot world. Lo Scarabeo (The Scarab) was founded in Turin in 1987 by graphic artist and collector, Pietro Alligo. Unlike houses who publish on multiple New Age topics, Lo Scarabeo enjoys the luxury of concentrating exclusively on Tarot. Their creative team focuses on the preservation of traditional Tarot decks as well as the innovative production of new decks. New decks are inspired and gathered from the world's finest artists. As a result, Lo Scarabeo has published over 100 Tarot decks and is acclaimed for their originality and quality.

Spanish publisher Fournier created the first known artistic deck while the Praguese Art Studio Magic Realist Press has created some of the most original decks of the latest years. The German company, Isis-Urania, contributes strongly to the diffusion of the Rider Waite deck in Europe.

Osvaldo Menegazzi in his craft shop in Milan: a true temple to Tarot and craftmanship.

American Production

Three publishers were fundamental in bringing Tarot to the American public: Samuel Weiser, Stuart Kaplan, and Carl Weschcke.

Born from a bookstore in New York City, Samuel Weiser founded Weiser Books in 1957. Weiser made it his mission to translate, publish, and bring European and Eastern works of the occult, magic, and metaphysics to American audiences. Weiser was a pioneer of New Age culture.

Stuart Kaplan, collector and scholar, founded U.S. Games System in 1971. He brought the Rider Waite Tarot, Tarot's biggest influence on American Tarot reading, to the public. The Rider Waite deck was a resounding success. Today, US Games is the largest Tarot publishing company in the world with over 300 decks in its collection. Kaplan also wrote extensively on the subject of Tarot including the massive four-volume work, The Encyclopedia of Tarot. These books, published in 1978, 1986, 1990, and 2006 offered a comprehensive list of all existing Tarot decks at the time of publication.

In the previous page:
America had the greatest cultural influence in the second half of the XX century.

567

The wall at Lo Scarabeo, with a clock for local time, one for US time in Minneapolis and one for Australian time in Melbourne.

Carl Weschcke founded Llewellyn Worldwide in 1964. Llewellyn became the largest independent publisher of mind, body, and spirit books. Llewellyn is truly at the forefront of holistic and metaphysical books and resources including Tarot. Among the most important decks published by Llewellyn, are the Robin Wood Tarot, the Gilded Tarot, the Shadowscapes Tarot, and the Steampunk Tarot.

Schiffer Books and Tarot Media Company have recently emerged and created a platform to widely distribute new Tarot authors and artists.

Changes in printing technology and social media have created the same wave of change in Tarot publishing as in the greater publishing world. No longer do artists and writer need solely rely on professional publishing houses. Many individuals create and distribute their own works. This has resulted in an explosion of new Tarot decks. It is really a new Tarot Renaissance.

It will be exciting to discover what new innovations will come to Tarot as technology evolves and moves forward. Perhaps in the not so distant future, we will have the pleasure of walking into a virtual Tarot card or enjoy a Tarot augmented reality. Will this replace a deck of paper cards and single burning candle? Only time will tell …

ADDITIONAL CONTENT

The following section of Tarot Fundamentals would not have been possible without the contribution of our Kickstarter backers.

We would like to use this space to send our personal thanks to the 1,000+ people who backed this book on Kickstarter. If you're one of them, please accept our gratitude. If you're not, please consider backing the next book, Tarot Experience, in 2016.

In any case, we hope you enjoy these bonus chapters.

Major Arcana Advice

with Lunea Weatherstone

Tarot whispers, speaks and conveys messages to anyone who observes and listens. It is the very art of listening to the cards' advice and input that creates a passionate, lifelong practice. However, for a beginner, lost in the myriad of card meanings, listening to the voice of the cards can be tough.

Luckily, Lunea Weatherstone has already performed the first step for you. In this article, Lunea articulates the advice each of the twenty-two Major Arcana has for the new Tarot Reader. New Readers are well advised to take out their Tarot decks along with this essay. Examine each Arcana's image individually as Lunea shares the guidance they offer a new Reader.

Tarot and Social Media

with Marcus Katz and Tali Goodwin

Technology, the Internet and social media are a uniting factor for every niche community in the world. From cat lovers to vampire fanatics, the Internet has provided a place where passions can be shared and explored. Tarot is no different. Tarot Readers who were once without colleagues, fellow readers or perhaps even secretly practiced Tarot while living in conservative communities are now connected through the Internet.

Marcus Katz and Tali Goodwin have successfully utilized technology in their creation of the Tarosophy Tarot Association, Tarot Professionals and other platforms and forums. In his essay, Marcus explains how the Tarot Reader can use social media to their very best advantage.

Talking Tarot

with Richard Webster

Reading a Tarot card is fairly straightforward. Flip a card and receive an answer. But how can Readers keep the process fresh for themselves after they've flipped the Ace of Pentacles for the hundredth time? What's a Reader to do when they look at a card and blank out, receiving nothing?

Richard offers up a fabulous technique. It is appropriate for a new or continuing Reader. Use Richard's technique as a fun exercise, to add spark and or as a potential lifesaver when a reading is heading toward a dead end. Best of all, Richard's technique is an eloquent reminder that when the Reader trusts herself to become immersed in the cards, she can cultivate all the information she could ever need.

Truth About Tarot

with Barbara Moore

Truth is a funny thing. The nature of truth has preoccupied influential philosophers since classical antiquity. Is truth absolute or is it relative? Is it universal or is it local? Does the truth depend on reported fact or personal emotional reality? Can a thing be totally true or totally false? And how in the world do we discover the real truth about an object as mysterious and beguiling as Tarot?

Barbara Moore knows precisely how to cultivate truth. She poses questions. Questions that only the Reader can answer. Read Barbara's article carefully. Do your best to answer each and every question Barbara poses. Answering Barbara's question will make for salient entries and thought provoking exercises in your Tarot journal. Doing so, you'll arrive closer to the truth about Tarot than you ever thought possible.

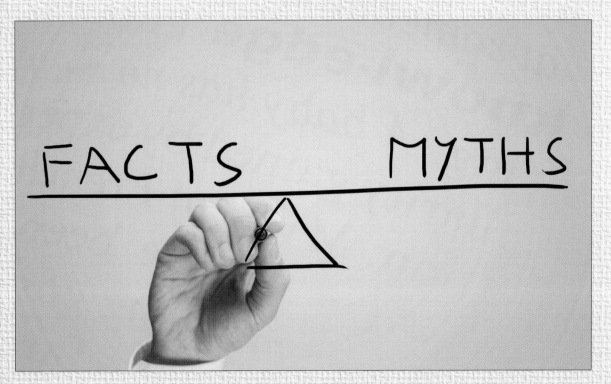

Tarot Glossary

with Sasha Graham

Tarot glossaries are an invaluable addition to understanding and using this book and other Tarot books. A glossary is a list of terms in a specialized subject, field, or area of usage and their definitions. It will help the Reader understand any unusual words and expressions related to the world of Tarot.

Special thanks for this Glossary are also due to Marcus Katz and Tali Goodwin who first suggested its need and contributed the first material for its creation.

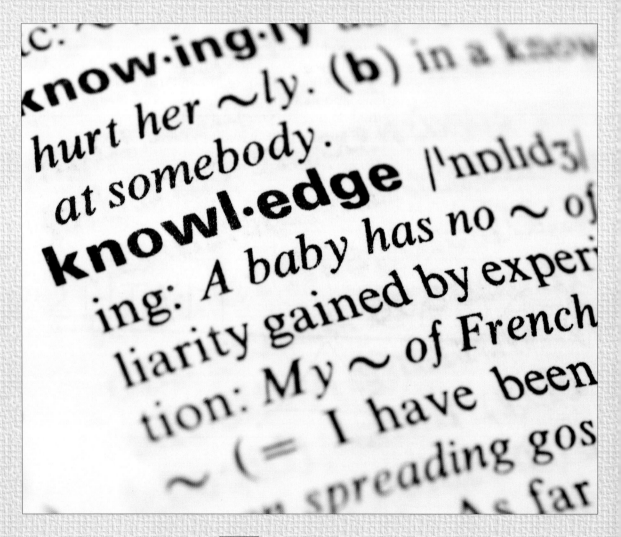

Lunaea Weatherstone

Is an author, teacher, priestess and Tarot counselor. She is a contributor to Llewellyn's Magical Almanac, created the *Wicca Oracle*, *Astrological Oracle decks* and created *The Mystical Cats Tarot* and *The Victorian Fairy Taro*t and is the author of *Tending Brigid's Flame*. Lunea resides in Portland, Oregon.

MAJOR ARCANA ADVICE

When you're a newcomer to Tarot, the sheer amount of information available can be overwhelming. Hundreds – thousands – of books, articles, websites, forums, and tutorials clamor for your attention. So let's go straight to the source: the Major Arcana itself. These 22 personas and archetypes have definite opinions on how to work with Tarot, and frankly, they think it's about time we asked them. Over to you, Majors! Tell the new Reader what they need to know.

The Fool

There is a Zen concept called beginner's mind, in which you set aside any preconceptions, prejudices, and desires to fully experience the moment and learn from it. Everything is fresh and wondrous when you choose to see it that way. As you explore Tarot, embrace beginner's mind. Abandon your expectations. Welcome new ideas and explore as a child would. Turn over each card with an open mind and an eagerness to learn.

The Magician

The most important ingredient in magic is belief, and the same goes for Tarot. Like any magical tool, Tarot is an extension of yourself. The cards are not the magic, and you are not the magic – the cards and the Reader work together symbiotically. If you don't believe you can read the cards, the magical exchange occurring between you and the cards will falter and fizzle. Believe in your abilities; don't second-guess yourself. Open up to the magic that is Tarot.

The High Priestess

Wisdom can come in flashes of insight or through unhurried contemplation, and so it is with Tarot. Sometimes you will look at a card and receive a clear and perhaps unexpected message. Other times you will gaze upon the cards and see connections and symbols gradually weaving themselves into meaning before your eyes. Always remember that deep wisdom lives within you, and Tarot is a conduit, a connecting device, to access that wisdom.

The Empress

Be patient and kind to yourself as you are learning about Tarot. Nurture your emerging skills as a gardener tends a young plant or a mother tends her child. Enjoy the growth process! Don't be frustrated if you can't move as quickly as you'd like – you are just taking your first steps along this path. Take it as an opportunity to slow down and luxuriate in the visual delights of your cards. Drink in the images and colors. Let Tarot's beauty nourish your spirit.

The Emperor

Supportive friends make excellent practice subjects as you are learning Tarot, but be sure to set your boundaries. It's fine to say no when someone asks you for a reading – not only when you're a new Reader but throughout your Tarot career. Don't feel obliged to sort out everyone's problems by consulting the cards. Expand into doing readings for others when you are ready, not before. Wait until you feel confident and in control.

The Hierophant

Dogma and fundamentalism are rife in the Tarot world, and there are plenty of Tarot folk who will be more than happy to tell you what you're doing wrong. Fortunately, there are also many good teachers who encourage independent thinking about Tarot. Seek out experts, whether in person or through books, who can help you build a solid foundation of established Tarot lore. Learn the basics, but don't stop there. Always bring your own vision to the table.

The Lovers

Choosing a new Tarot deck is like any other meaningful relationship – your choice must be guided by your heart. A deck will call to you with its beauty or theme or symbols, some combination of qualities that says, "Yes! We understand each other." Sometimes that initial connection doesn't hold true over the long term. That's fine. Tarot doesn't demand fidelity. Some Readers stay with the same deck for life, while others are polyamorous, even combining more than one deck in a single reading. Tarot love is free love.

The Chariot

Books and decks that promise to teach you all about Tarot in the wink of an eye can give you some quick satisfaction, but it's weak compared to the feeling of having earned your laurels. No Tarot card can be adequately summed up in a few keywords. Keywords are signposts along the journey, not the journey itself. Don't dumb down by accepting shallow interpretations. Do the work! You are up to the challenge. Focus on your goal and move forward with confidence.

Strength

It's tempting to jump right in and try complicated multi-card spreads – and then feel defeated when you don't understand what you're seeing. Tarot can seem like a giant beast, too big for you to conquer. Here's a secret: you don't need to conquer it, you just need to tame it. Seventy–eight of anything is hard to take in all at once, much less images with layer upon layer of meaning. Pick just one card and come to know it well. Make it your ally. When you're ready, pick another card.

The Hermit

In your exploration of Tarot, there is a time for seeking the guidance of others and a time for setting other people's ideas aside. This is especially important if you find yourself getting confused by Tarot practitioners who have conflicting ideas. It can be tempting to pose your questions on social media, but the likelihood of finding clarity is slim. It is far more likely that you will emerge from the cacophony more bewildered than before. At such times, quietly withdraw from the Tarot community until you can hear your own inner voice.

Wheel of Fortune

One thing most Readers have in common is a desire to move the reading in a positive direction. No one likes to give bad news, and even the most negative cards are never completely without redeeming virtues. Take care not to go too far – it's fine to spin your interpretation toward the positive, but don't sugarcoat it. Bad things do happen, and you're asking the cards for the truth, after all. A Tarot reading isn't likely to change anyone's fate, but it can offer good advice on how best to deal with it. Always try to end your readings on an upswing.

Justice

Define your own system
of ethical beliefs about
Tarot and then strive to be
impeccable in its practice.
Begin by asking yourself
questions such as: Is it
okay to do a Tarot reading
about someone else without
their knowledge? What are
my responsibilities toward
people I do readings for? Do
I always need to tell what I
see in the cards, especially if
it's frightening? What is my
position on confidentiality?
Think about how you would
like to be treated by other
Tarot readers and at least
match that degree of integrity. If possible, exceed it.

The Hanged Man

As a new Reader, one of the first things to decide is whether you will use reversals or not. When a card comes up reversed, you have the choice of reading the reversed meaning or simply turning it upright and going on as usual. Working with reversals can provide an extra dimension of understanding, but it can also trivialize the card's meaning by just flipping it on its head – what was good is now bad and vice versa. One you choose how you will handle reversals, be consistent. The cards need to know how you plan to read them so the proper cards appear in your reading.

Death

It is a little cosmic joke that newcomers to Tarot will inevitably draw the scariest cards right off the bat and probably keep on drawing them for a while. This is your chance to work through any inclination you might have to drop these cards like a hot potato and thus deny their usefulness and importance in a reading. Cards like Death hold powerful messages and should not be watered down. Welcome the cards that teach about life's biggest challenges.

Temperance

In the art of Alchemy, materials are combined to see how they react with each other. You can apply the same principles to Tarot. Experiment by combining divination tools to reveal additional insights – for instance, pull a rune or oracle card to go with each Tarot card. Or try using two decks rather than one – choose randomly from the first deck, then find those same cards in the second deck and compare the symbols. By this process, your knowledge about each individual element will expand.

The Devil

Tarot rules can bind you in doubt and worry about doing it the "right" way. Some people say you should never buy a deck but only accept one as a gift. Some people say you should never read the cards for yourself. Don't limit your own potential by handing over your power to other people's rules. Do you want to buy a deck? Buy it! Do the cards speak to you about your own life? Listen! Break the chains of bondage to any system of Tarot that doesn't feel right on a gut level.

The Tower

Not everyone who begins to study Tarot sticks with it. Whether it's due to frustration or burnout or just plain old boredom, if you find yourself buying book after book hoping to find that spark again, or collecting deck after deck to find the one that's just right, don't hesitate to just knock the whole thing down. Put your cards away. Pack up the books. Create some empty space for a new interest to come in – or a renewed interest in Tarot.

The Star

A deck of Tarot cards is more than just pictures printed on paper. Tarot gives you access to the collective consciousness through symbols both ancient and modern. Look beyond the everyday questions that complicate your life for cosmic patterns that determine the human experience. Get your ego out of the way and let your higher self choose cards that tell you what you need to know right here, right now. Expand into universal understanding.

The Moon

Divination is not logical. Whatever complex systems of esoteric philosophy are applied to Tarot, in the end it still comes down to intuition. Multiple meanings are possible for every symbol on every card, and you can become confused and lose the thread unless you trust your perceptions. As you would with a dream, let your interpretation of a reading meander along mystical, moonlit paths. When you take your cards out of the box, take your imagination out too.

The Sun

Getting to know your Tarot deck gets easier the more you work with it – and play with it! Tarot is a serious counseling tool, a powerful form of divination, and it's also really, really fun. You might even want to get a special deck that is only for fun, for when you want to play Tarot games or use the cards as a storytelling helper. At such times, don't worry about the interpretations being "correct," just enjoy the shiny happy moment. Playfulness and humor keep your relationship with Tarot full of life and ever-growing.

Judgment

Many new Tarot enthusiasts rush to consult the cards about every little thing, from a casual conversation to the best choice for lunch, or even about the outcome of an upcoming TV show. This has been made easier through the use of Tarot apps that bring your favorite decks right to your omnipresent phone. Use your good judgment and respect the wisdom of the Tarot. Know when to ask and when to stop asking.

The World

The Tarot world is vast. It can be reassuring to recognize that you will never know all there is to know. There's no test at the end because there is no end. But you will find milestones along the way that give a sense of wholeness, such as the first time you do a reading for someone else or the sudden realization that you don't need (or want!) to check the book. At least once a month, go through the entire deck one card at a time. Greet them, appreciate them. Honor what you know and what you have yet to learn. When you can truly see each card, and see the big picture, you are well on your way to becoming an excellent Tarot reader.

Marcus Katz

Has been working with and teaching Tarot for over thirty years. He co-founded the Tarosophy Tarot Association, the world's largest professional Tarot Association, with Tali Goodwin in 2009. His first book, *Tarosophy*, was called a "major contribution" to Tarot by Rachel Pollack. He co-authored *Around the Tarot in 78 Days* with Tali and it won the COVR Award in 2013. He also co-authored *Secrets of the Waite-Smith Tarot* with Tali. He lives in the Lake District with his wife, fellow author and editor, Brina, and magician's cat, Alex.

Tali Goodwin

Has researched and written about the Tarot for many years. She co-founded the Tarosophy Tarot Association, the world's largest professional Tarot Association, with Marcus Katz in 2009. Tali is credited with bringing the long-hidden Waite-Trinick Tarot to publication in *Abiding in the Sanctuary*. She has co-authored innovative teaching books such as *Tarot Flip*, *Tarot Life*, and others which are regularly in the top ten best-selling tarot books on Kindle. Her book, co-authored with Marcus, *Secrets of the Waite-Smith Tarot* has been described as "astonishing" by Mary K. Greer. She lives in the Lake District with her partner, leading Astrologer and author Lyn Birkbeck, and dog, Rufus Oakapple.

TAROT & SOCIAL MEDIA

The game of Tarot and playing cards has always been a social activity. Whilst we can play solitaire with cards, the enjoyment of cards often comes from playing in company, with friends, family, or even as a professional gambler. However, in the case of cartomantic Tarot, many who are attracted to the cards are often solitary and introspective. The development of social media - online and connected platforms where individuals can share discussions and material – has been extremely influential on Tarot.

In the earliest days of online systems, alternative discussion groups were founded on bulletin board systems and on the Usenet system, which transferred posts and threads through email to subscribers of specific groups. These were arranged in a hierarchy, so the main Tarot discussion group was alt.tarot, and there was also a mailing discussion group list called tarot-l. Some users congregated to discuss magick and Tarot on private Compuserve and AOL groups and in The Well, an early online social media system.

The Tarot online communities started out from mailing lists.

Forums, such as Tarotforum.net, were the natural evolutions of Tarot mailing lists.

These systems were difficult, text-based and largely unmoderated, leading to many groups erupting in flamewars and splitting off into separate and rival groups. In the beginning, they were only open to quite technical and dedicated users, so everyone had a strong opinion and were free to voice it. As the internet developed, these groups and systems became redundant, being replaced by several large forum systems. In turn, these static forum systems became increasingly obsolete with the rise of the latest social media platforms such as Facebook. As time goes on, we are increasingly seeing a trend to mobile and instantly interactive platforms and applications. The isolated Tarot reader now has access to the online world of Tarot discussion.

Facebook

Facebook is composed of Pages and Groups in addition to personal walls. There are several larger groups for the discussion of Tarot on Facebook and other social media platforms, and each has its own characteristics and rules of conduct. Explore several groups to find which – if any – suit your requirements.

Here are some questions by which you can check out different groups:

1. Is the group moderated? Does it have one person, or an accountable team? This will influence how you might be treated within the group and the general nature of postings. An unmoderated group will often be short-lived or flooded with adverts and posts you might find boring or offensive.

2. Does the group have a clear set of posting policies? Whilst these are not mandatory online, they help give a clear guideline and encourage fair use of the group for the benefit of all participants. If you do not agree with the guidelines, it can quickly inform your decision to stay or leave the group.

3. Is the group associated with a particular organization, school, business, or individual? This will likely influence the ethos of the group, the types of postings, and the interests of people in the group.

4. How active is the group? Is it full of adverts and self-promotion? This tends to come from the moderation level and policy, but sometimes a more active group can become unmoderated and begin to get flooded with adverts and self-promotion.

5. What atmosphere does the group generally encourage? You can observe any group and get a feeling for the overall nature of the postings and responses. These might be very diverse in a large group, with no overall theme, but you might see some groups are very tolerant of beginners, some are more geared to robust and considered arguments, and others are general. Some may come across as quite serious; others might have a crazed sense of humour. Whilst groups are composed of many individuals, they often take on a character themselves.

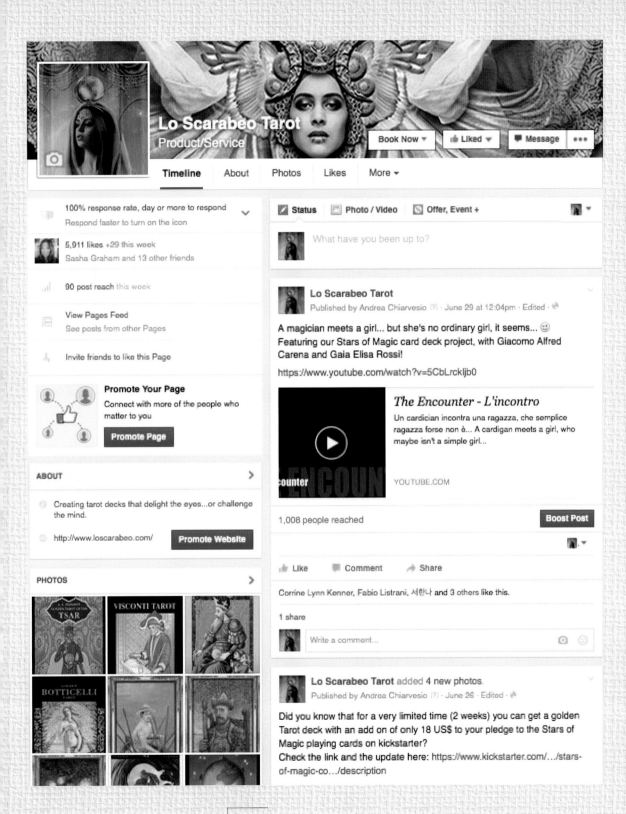

Twitter

Twitter is an instant messaging tool, which has exploded in popular awareness. It is also extremely useful for asking quick Tarot questions to a large group of your followers or rapidly sharing an offer, news, or an event. It can be connected to other social media platforms, so a Facebook or email update can be automatically tweeted, letting people know that new activity has taken place.

Twitter is a medium not yet widely used by the Tarot community.

Youtube

There are thousands of videos on Tarot on Youtube, with an equally wide variation in quality and content. It can be confusing to watch several suggested Tarot videos together, as individuals may offer conflicting and contradictory advice.

As ever, we must take information with caution, and test it out for our own use.

Youtube offers many Tarot reviews, information, Spreads and Readings, of many different qualities.

A smartphone is a gateway not just to social media, but also to many Tarot Apps.

Pinterest/Tumblr/Instagram

As Tarot is an entirely visual medium, it is of no surprise that sites which encourage image sharing are full of Tarot to explore. These sites are often connected (as are many) with other social networks, allowing content producers to rapidly share their material, promotions, and information in a visual manner. A typical Pinterest producer or board (compilation of other "pins") will include Spreads, sample cards from decks in development or for sale, infographics, "top ten" type hints, tables of correspondence and keywords with graphics, and much more.

Blogs

Whilst there are many great Tarot blogs out there, a major problem is that they are time-consuming to create and often offer little in the way of return for their creators. They are best produced alongside other forms of communication and platforms, in support of a commercial website for example. So it is difficult to recommend any particular blog as often they become archived or left fallow for long periods of time.

New Networks: Tsu

During the time of writing and publication, several new networks have been launched although these have been met with varying success. A platform such as Tsu adopted a new model from existing systems by sharing advertising revenue with content providers, although early reports from Tarot individuals who migrated their time and resource to several new networks have been mixed.

Tarot blogs contain a huge amount of opportunities as people can follow their favorite authors, Readers or reviewers.

Crowdfunding Platforms

Whilst not strictly social in terms of their interaction, there are several further platforms for networking and utilizing the connectivity and numbers afforded by the internet. These are crowd-funding platforms such as Kickstarter and Indigogo. At present, over 15 new decks are in production or have been funded through Kickstarter, and a similar number on Indigogo. There are also Tarot photography, gallery, and book projects, and new approaches including interactive installations, and mobile phone applications. In funding, sharing, and otherwise supporting these projects, you can learn more about Tarot, be involved in the creation of new material, and network with those who share your passion.

Platforms like Kickstarter make possible the impossible. Volumes like the present one would have been never published without the support of Kickstarter.

Richard Webster

Is the author of over seventy-five titles on New Age subjects that have been translated into thirty-one languages and sold over eleven million copies.

His titles include: *Playing Card Divination for Beginners, The Encyclopedia of Superstitions, Spirit and Dream Animals, Spirit Guides and Angel Guardians, Creative Visualization for Beginners* and *You Can Read Palms*. Richard resides in New Zealand with his wife, three children and five grandchildren.

THE TALKING TAROT

When reading the cards, I frequently enjoy a conversation with the people and other images that appear on the cards. I'll silently ask the image a number of questions, pausing for a reply after each one. The responses appear as thoughts in my mind. If I'm reading the cards for someone else, I may or may not tell the sitter what I'm doing. As far as he or she is concerned, I'm simply reading the cards.

Some of the cards show just one person, and I'll enjoy a conversation with that person. However, many of the cards give me a number of possible images to speak with. Inside the Lovers, for instance, I might be able to speak with the man, woman, angel, or even the snake, if it appears in the deck I'm using. The Nine of Pentacles could give me a choice of the lady, the bird on her hand, and even the tiny snail in the foreground. The Wheel of Fortune provides several images I can talk with: Anubis, Bull, Snake, Eagle, Lion, Angel, and the Sphinx.

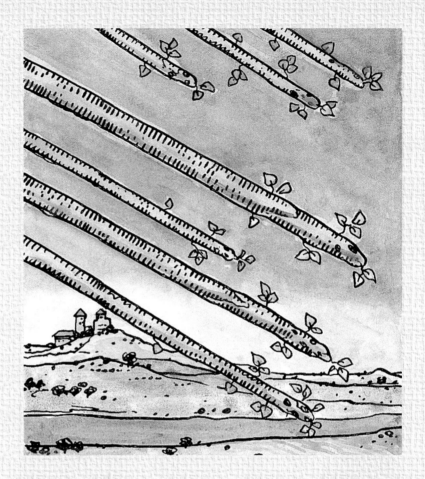

The person I speak with doesn't need to be alive. If the Death card appears, I might ask the dead king for his insights into my clients' problems. The fact that he's passed over sometimes provides a valuable point of view that helps him answer my questions.

Some of the cards show no figures. The Aces of the four suits usually show a hand holding a representation of the suit. In this situation, I speak to the person whose hand I see on the card. In many decks, the Minor Arcana cards are not illustrated with pictures, and show the number of wands, cups, pentacles or swords represented by the card. When this occurs, I speak with whoever was responsible for arranging the objects on the card. The Eight of Wands in the Waite and Universal Tarot decks show the eight wands in the foreground, with a large house in the background. When necessary, I talk to the owner of this house.

My conversation with the images depends on the situation. Usually, I ask questions that relate to my sitter's concern. Recently, I gave a reading for a woman in her middle forties. She was concerned that she and her husband were drifting apart. I dealt three cards, revealing the Two of Swords, the Six of Cups, and The Lovers. This looked positive, but I was able to gain more information by asking a series of questions. The Two of Swords usually indicates a disagreement, or a parting of the ways. However, when I asked the blindfolded lady on the card questions about the future of the relationship, she told me that the couple were blind, and were jointly responsible for the decline of the relationship.

Most of the time, Tarot refers to metaphorical or spiritual blindness, rather than literal one. Obviously, "most of the time" does not mean "always".

2 of Swords, interpreted as disagreement.

6 of Cups, interpreted as happy times in the past.

Lovers, interpreted as an happy ending to be built through careful choices.

My sitter reluctantly agreed that this was the case. The Six of Cups is a sign that the sitter is remembering happy times in the past. I asked the little girl in the card if the couple had a future together. "Yes," she replied. "As long as they listen to each other more." My sitter agreed that her husband seldom listened to what she had to say, but added that she always listened to him. The final card, The Lovers, initially appeared to indicate a perfect outcome. However, this card can indicate change, and a choice that's not easy to make. I decided to ask the angel in this card if the couple would be happy long term. "Yes," was the reply. "However, the two people involved will need to use their intuition, as well as their hearts and minds, to resolve the situation." These added insights enabled me to help the sitter understand that both people in the relationship needed to improve their listening skills, and that with love and mutual understanding, the relationship could become better and stronger than it had ever been in the past.

615

Sometimes the answers I receive are surprising, and don't appear to relate to the reading I'm giving. Several years ago, a client asked me if the overseas trip she and a friend were about to embark on would be successful and enjoyable. I asked the hard-working man on the Eight of Pentacles about this, and he made a comment about my client's teeth. After hearing this, my client admitted she was having problems with her teeth, but had put off making an appointment with her dentist as she couldn't afford to pay for the trip as well as dental treatment. I asked further questions, and the man stressed how important it was that she visit her dentist. She made an appointment, and found that her teeth needed a great deal of work. Her dentist made arrangements for her to pay him over a period of time, which meant she was able to receive the treatment she needed, and also take the trip. If she'd ignored this advice, she may have experienced toothache and other problems while on vacation.

In cases of relationship, and other, problems, I sometimes ask my clients to choose a card to represent them, and another card to indicate the person they're having problems with. They select an image from each card and allow them to have a conversation. This provides interesting insights into the problem, as well as possible ways to resolve it.

Over the last few years I've asked some of my clients to talk to the images on the cards. Most people are receptive to this idea, and enjoy their conversations with the image they choose. However, not everyone is comfortable doing this, and I tend to use it mainly with repeat clients and people who obviously enjoy being actively involved with their reading.

I like to ask questions from people and animals, but you can also ask questions of anything you see in the card. You might speak to a specific wand, sword, cup or pentacle, for instance, or maybe choose a wall, tree, cloud, mountain, star, or flag.

Fortunately, it's simple to practice this technique. All you need do is ask questions every time you create a spread, for yourself or others, and wait for a response. With practice, you'll receive answers to your questions almost instantly. This will increase the amount of information you can supply, and make your readings even more useful for the people you read for.

Conversation is the road to intuition.

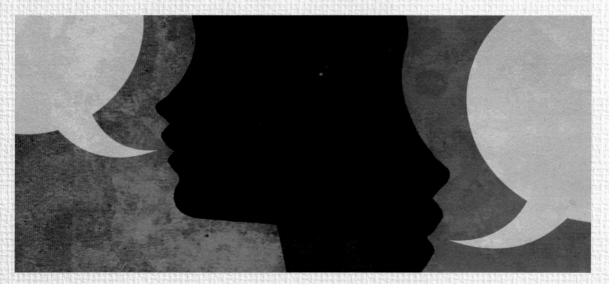

Barbara Moore

In the early 1990s, at a party, someone put a Tarot deck in Barbara's hands.

She's held on tight ever since. Tarot provides just enough structure so that we don't get lost as we explore the mysteries, plumb our dark corners, and find our paths in the dark woods. Barbara has been reading and writing for as long as she can remember. She's published a number of books on tarot, including *Tarot for Beginners*, *Tarot Spreads*, *The Steampunk Tarot*, *The Gilded Tarot*, *The Mystic Dreamer*, and *Tarot of the Hidden Realm*. Writing is solitary work and is relieved by teaching Tarot at conferences around the world. Barbara also loves working with clients, using the Tarot to provide guidance and insight.

TAROT TRUTH

The truth about Tarot is this: in the end, it means whatever you say it means.

The truth about Tarot is this: in the end, it means whatever you say it means. Meaning is what Tarot is all about, isn't it? We spend years and pages and so many words just to say what a certain card means. This makes perfect sense because symbols, which Tarot images are all very complex symbols, are rich and deep. We can peel layers off The Empress, for example, all day long and still not have plumbed her depths. These symbols carry echoes from the past. They are also voices from our wiser, intuitive selves, beckoning us toward the future. They are mirrors that show us ourselves, as we are in this moment. In order to get the most out of them, we study them intensely. But learning what the cards mean is only part of the process of learning to read the cards.

Tarot can be seen as a mirror that shows us ourselves.

Learning Tarot requires self-reflection and self-knowledge.

How Does it Work?

Perhaps it is even more important, as a first step, that we understand the truth about how Tarot works. As with the card meanings themselves, this answer will vary from person to person. There is always debate about whether we can predict the future with the cards. There is always debate about where the answers come from. There is always debate about whether you should let someone touch your cards. I think we can end a lot of this debate right now. It will require self-reflection and self-knowledge on your part. Maybe that's not as sexy as interpreting the complicated undercurrents of The Devil or the mysterious secrets of The High Priestess, but I believe the questions that follow are a few of the questions that everyone should ask before they even begin learning the cards. The answers to the questions will shape how and even why you use the cards. They will determine what kinds of readings you do. Tarot is symbolic from top to bottom and this means that everything you do with the cards should be symbolic in some way, reflecting and representing your deepest truths.

I believe the questions that follow are a few of the questions that everyone should ask before they even begin learning the cards.

The answers to the questions will shape how and even why you use the cards. They will determine what kinds of readings you do.

Can Tarot Predict the Future?

Before you answer that question, you must ask yourself if you believe that the future can be predicted. Are events, our actions, and choices pre-determined? If so, who or what has determined them? If the future is predictable, to what extent? Is it important that the future be predictable? Is it spiritually necessary or useful to know the future? You might even push this further and ask yourself, if the future can be predicted, does it follow that it should be predicted?

Fate and Free Will.

Where Do the Answers Come From?

I think this is a very important question because the useful-ness of answers depends on the source. For example, asking your five-year-old what the best snack is you might get a different answer than from asking a nutritionist. Does it make a difference if the answer comes from your subconscious, your higher self, or a Divine being? I think so. Understanding where you think the answers come from can help you develop practices to becoming a better vehicle for the an-swers. For example, if you think that the answers come from a Higher Being, you may begin your readings with a prayer. If you think they come from the other person's Higher Self, you may begin you readings with an invitation to the Higher Self to be present and perhaps even ask if it wishes to be involved…and have a plan in place in case it doesn't. If you believe that the answers come from your own mind as a result of interpreting the symbols, then you would improve yourself as a channel by learning as much about the symbols as possible.

Some questions cannot be answered by a book, but only by yourself and your beliefs.

Energy can be subjective and magical.

Who Touches the Cards?

Should you let anyone touch your cards? Or a related question: does the querent have to shuffle the cards for a reading to "work"? This ties in with your beliefs about how the Tarot works. If the answers, for example, come from a Higher Being, then it is not necessary for the querent to touch the cards for any energetic reason (however, you may still wish to have the querent shuffle in order to engage them more fully in the experience). If you believe that the answers come from the querent's Higher Self, then you may decide that having the querent shuffle is a way to activate or involve that Higher Self.

623

Purpose of the Reading?

Another question is: what is the purpose of a Tarot reading? The short answer is probably the same for everyone: to get answers! But the nature of the answers will vary depending on your belief system and intent. Someone with a more psychological bent is probably looking for insight into how they really feel about a situation. They are looking for understanding of themselves and through that knowledge hope to figure out how to act. When you read the cards, what are you hoping to accomplish? What sort of answer are you looking for or expecting? Are you looking for a prediction about the future, a description of the underlying energies of a situation, or advice about what to do?

Why you read cards and how, depends on you.

624

Does Tarot Tell the Truth?

There's a difference between knowing the path and walking the path.

This last question is one that I find fascinating. Does the Tarot always tell the truth? I've heard people say that yes, the cards always tell the truth but that the Reader may interpret them incorrectly. But I wonder, let us suppose that the cards are a way for Spirit to communicate with us and guide for our own highest good. And here's my thing. I don't think that Spirit is an answer machine that pops out answers like a gum ball machine. I don't know if Spirit always tells us the "truth." Instead, I wonder if Spirit tells us what we need to know in order to have the life experience (and learn the lessons) we are meant to learn. This is, after all, what happened in the movie The Matrix, when the Oracle told Neo that he wasn't The One (and we should all take our deepest spiritual teachings from movies, right?).

After it became apparent that Neo was, in fact, the One, Neo tried to argue with Morpheus about it.

Neo: Morpheus. The Oracle, she told me I'm...

Morpheus: She told you exactly what you needed to hear, that's all. Neo, sooner or later you're going to realize, just as I did, there's a difference between knowing the path and walking the path.

When you hold the cards in your hand, you hold a hologram of the universe. It is vast. It is infinite. To let its truth resonate with your truth, read it through the lens of your understanding.

I'm still chewing on this, though, and I hope you do, too. Tarot is, on all levels, a continuous adventure into ourselves, life, and the universe. It opens up our hearts, spirits, and minds to new things and also provides a structure to help organize all those experiences. This is, more than readings, more than specific answers, the most amazing aspect of Tarot.

When you hold the cards in your hand, you hold a hologram of the universe. It is vast. It is infinite. To let its truth resonate with your truth, read it through the lens of your understanding.

Ace: The first card in the sequence one to ten. The Tarot card bearing only one symbol, usually seen as the highest or lowest in value of the deck.

Age of Aquarius: The New Age Movement of the 1960's and 1970's.

Alchemy: A historic tradition, partly the basis of modern chemistry and medicine, concerned with the transmutation of elements often expressed in Symbols and metaphors. Several Tarot decks are entirely based on or incorporate alchemical concepts.

Antiquity: The ancient past, especially referring to the time period before the middle Ages.

Augury: The art of ranking a set of possibilities.

Arcana: The Latin word for 'secrets' or 'mysteries.' It is used to indicate the Tarot cards (singular: Arcanum)

Archetype: A fundamental pattern of thought or an original universal pattern that manifests across time and space, such as the Mother, Father, Hero, Wise One, etc. These archetypes are reflected in the Tarot, particularly the Major Arcana.

Art Decks: Tarot decks carrying particular artistic styles and art. Art decks offer new emotional and intuitive insights using visual expression.

Astrology: The practice of divination by observation of astronomical events, such as the placement of the Sun in the twelve signs of the zodiac. Each Tarot card is assigned an astrological association.

Balance of the Spread: Examines the relationship between Majors, Minors, suits and numbers. This system establishes the tone of the reading and the cards are read as a single connected unit. The Reader can point out what is dominant and what is missing. The Reader suggests a course of action that re-establishes balance.

Card of the Day: A daily practice where a Reader pulls a random card from the deck in the morning, and interprets it. The card is often revisited in the evening to see how it informed the day's events or how it correlated.

Cartomancy: The practice of making a divination by any form of cards, including Tarot.

Cartomancer: A person who performs acts of divination and readings from Tarot, playing or oracle cards.

Celtic Cross (Spread): A ten-card spread first published by A. E. Waite in 1909. One of the most popular Tarot spreads in use.

Ceremonial Magic: Referred to as high magic or learned magic refers to complex and complicated rituals of magic of Hermeticism and Western esotericism.

Cipher: A code. A secret or covert way of writing.

Clearing Ritual: A ritual performed to cleanse the energy of a Tarot deck or a space or both.

Client: Usually refers to a paying Querent or sitter who is having a professional reading.

Crystal Cleanse: The energetic cleansing of a Tarot deck using crystals and gemstones.

Codified: To arrange in a systematic code, plan or formula.

Commission: In regard to art and/or Tarot decks, it is to give the order, authorization, or to purchase the production of a specific piece of art or Tarot deck.

Consecration: An action done to establish a relationship and bond with new deck of Tarot cards. The opening and blessing of a deck is important whether the deck is new or second hand.

Consistency: In a reading, consistency means to choose a system in advance and stick to it for the duration of the reading. This includes the spread, use of reversals and adhering to a chosen ritual (if one is chosen).

Correspondence: The concept of making similarities between objects or concepts based on their attributes or qualities. In Tarot this is often done between systems, such as Astrology or Cabbala.

Court Cards: The 16 cards in a Tarot deck assigned to court figures, usually King, Queen, Knight and Page, in each suit.

Court Card Ranking: A system of utilizing multiple Courts Cards of the same rank that appear in a spread. This gives the Reader additional information and advice. For example, multiple Kings suggest imposing limits while multiple Pages suggest having more fun and loosening up.

Cultural Artifact: Anything created by humans providing information about the culture and people that created it. Tarot decks are cultural artifacts.

Cultural Decks: Tarot decks utilizing the symbolism and themes from various cultures around the world.

Cups: One of the four suits, associated with the element of Water and the quality of emotion. Also called Chalices.

Deck: A complete set of cards.

Deck collecting: Collecting numerous Tarot decks for personal use or ownership.

Dionysian: Relating to the god Dionysus.

Divination: The practice of gaining insight through esoteric methods, including cartomancy, astrology, ritual, scrying, etc.

Elements: The four classic elements of Earth, Air, Water and Fire, corresponding to the suits of Pentacles, Swords, Cups and Wands.

Encode: To convert into a code.

Dogma, dogmatic: A set of principles applied and set as absolute truth by an authority.

Eleusinian Mysteries: Annual ancient Greek initiation ceremonies honoring the cult of Demeter and Persephone based at Eleusis.

English School: Tarot scholarship taking place in England at the turn of the 20th Century. The English school influenced the Minor Arcana's meanings (Key players: Mathers, Waite, and Crowley).

Enlightenment: An intellectual movement of the 17th and 18th centuries in Europe emphasizing reason and individualism over tradition and superstition.

Ephemeral: Lasting for a brief period of time.

Esoteric, Esotericism: Hidden or secret teachings usually relating to the relationship between human beings and the universe.

Esotericist: An individual who works specifically with hidden knowledge, secret teachings or mystical philosophies.

Esoteric Arts: Tarot, Astrology, Numerology, Magic, Kabbalah, Path working, Shamanic Journeying, etc.

Esoteric Decks: Decks created by history's most influential occultists as well as metaphysical decks developed by modern mystery schools.

Essential Meanings: Found inside Tarot Fundamentals, these are two words for each card that contain the card's core truth. Used to unlock the meaning of a card and open the door to understanding.

Feudalism: A dominant social system found in medieval Europe between the 9th and 15th centuries whereby land and was held by nobility in exchange for labor.

Fortune Telling: The practice or act of foretelling future events.

Free association: Tarot images become a point of departure in which the symbols on the card make way for a free association of new ideas and fresh meanings.

Freemason: A member of the fraternal order of Freemasonry.

French Revolution: The French uprising lasting from 1789 - 1799. It ended the thousand-year rule of the monarchy and resulted in France becoming a republic.

French School: Tarot scholarship taking place in France at the turn of the 20th Century. The French school influenced the Major Arcana's meanings (Key players: Levi, Papus, and Wirth).

Fully Illustrated Deck: A Tarot deck whose Major and Minor Arcana are illustrated as opposed to "Majors Only Decks" that only contain an illustrated Major Arcana.

Full Moon Cleanse: Energetic powering of a Tarot deck achieved by placing Tarot cards in a pool of moonlight. Leave them to absorb the lunar rays all night.

Four Cardinal Virtues: The four virtues recognized in classical antiquity as Prudence, Temperance, Fortitude, and Justice.

Golden Dawn: A hermetic order of students founded in 1888, which developed on the western esoteric initiatory system. The order taught Tarot in a synthesis also including Astrology, Cabbala and Alchemy. Full title: Hermetic Order of the Golden Dawn.

Grimoire: Often used in reference to witchcraft, a hand written book of personally recorded spells and/or magic including the use/creation of spells, talismans, charms, divinations, etc. A Tarot Grimoire can be fashioned as a personal divinatory textbook.

Hermes Trismegistus, Hermes: The archetypal combination of the Egyptian god Thoth and the Greek Hermes. God of writing, magic, astrology, alchemy and knowledge. Many magical books and texts were attributed to Hermes.

Hermeticism: A set of religious and philosophical traditions based on the writings attributed to Hermes Trismegistus.

Historical Decks: Reproductions, reconstructions, or reinterpretations of the great Tarot decks of the past.

Iconography: The images, symbols or pictorial material that relates to a particular topic. The imagery or symbolism of a work of art.

Illustrated Minors: A deck in which the Minor Arcana is fully illustrated with scenes depicting the card's meaning as opposed to a "Majors Only" deck in which the Minors are represented with only symbols of their suit.

Initiation ritual: A systematized rite of passage into a group or society. It often infers a "rebirth" and is seen in organized religion via baptisms, confirmations or bat mitzvahs, in the profane world via graduation ceremonies or rites inside secret societies and fraternal organizations when a member is accepted into the fold.

Interpretation: The process of explaining the meaning of a card(s).

Intuition: Any means of gaining knowledge without direct and conscious reasoning.

Intuition Building: Activities and exercises performed purposefully to strengthen the intuition as one would strengthen any muscle in the body.

Intuitive Reading: A subjective interpretation of the cards by acting and reading on impulse. It captures the emotional essence of the cards.

Golden Age: A mythical time in which the arts and sciences are handed to man by the gods or a time when peace reigned abundant on earth.

Grades: In regard to secret societies, grades are the ranks or degrees of accomplishment through which a member passes.

Gutenberg Printing Press: The printing press, created by Johannes Gutenberg circa 1440, leading to the mass production of books. Regarded as the most important event of the modern world leading to mass literacy, the Renaissance, the Enlightenment and Scientific Revolution.

Hebrew Alphabet: Twenty-two Hebrew letters used in the Hebrew language, which can also be connected to the twenty-two cards of the Major Arcana.

Heraldic Devices: Coats of arms and symbols conveying genealogy, rank and power.

Hero's Journey: A narrative and archetypal pattern which repeats cross-culturally, based on the work of scholar Joseph Campbell. The Hero's Journey may be seen in the context of the progression through the Major Arcana.

Journal: A handwritten or electronic record of readings, keywords, spreads, notes, thoughts, etc. made by a Reader.

Journey, Earthly: The material world and encountered personalities (Fool, Magician, High Priestess, Empress, Emperor, Hierophant, Lovers, Chariot).

Journey, Heavenly: Communing with the divine and ultimate transcendence (Devil, Tower, Star, Moon, Sun, Judgment, World).

Journey, Spiritual: The spiritual world enlightenment and great personal truth (Strength, Hermit, Wheel, Justice, Hanged Man, Death, Temperance).

Kabbalah (or Cabala, Kabala, Cabbala): A Jewish system of mysticism associated with Tarot.

Keywords: Two words used to immerse the Reader in the meaning of the card.

Lenormand cards: A deck of 36 cards used for divination that bears the name although has little connection with the famous 19th century Parisian fortune-teller Mlle. Marie Anne Lenormand. Not a Tarot deck.

Magic(k): Influencing the course of events using mysterious or supernatural forces. In general terms, any act that cannot be explained by something other than esoteric systems. Tarot can be used as a tool for magic, including use in spells, mandalas, path working or ritual.

Majors Only Decks: Tarot deck of only 22 cards, containing the Major Arcana but not Court and Numerals cards. Used mainly as beginner decks or as travelling decks.

Marseille: A style of Tarot originating in Southern France. It refers only to the iconographic template, not the actual place the cards were printed. There are many varieties of Marseille decks, with small variations in design, symbolism and colors.

Medium, Channeler: An individual who communicates with spirits, those who are dead or who have "passed over" and those who are of supernatural origin.

Mental Deck: An individual's mental idea and invisible connection with his/her deck. It carries all of the Reader's associations with the cards. A library of associations, expectations, insights and memories the Reader carries in regard to the Tarot deck.

Metaphysical Decks: Tarot decks that channel intuitive insights and enhance the exploration of personal, psychological and spiritual dimensions.

Middle Ages: A period of European history between the fall of the Roman Empire (the fall of Classical Antiquity) and the Italian Renaissance, circa 1000 – 1453.

Minor Arcana: The Ace to Ten of each of the four suits and associated with daily events.

Mystery School: Mystery religions, sacred mysteries or mysteries were recognized public institutions in the ancient world. They provided knowledge of non-material realms to their members via initiation and rituals.

Mystic: An individual who seeks to transcend ordinary human knowledge via direct communication with the divine, intuition, spiritual ecstasy or nature.

New Age: A broad non-religious movement characterized by alternative spiritual and philosophical beliefs and practices beginning in the West circa 1970's.

Negative Cards: Tarot cards appearing frightening or uncomfortable for the Reader, Querent or viewer. Also see Spooky Cards.

Noble cards: Hand painted Tarot cards of exceptional artists commissioned by wealthy European families. Noble cards were considered art objects and differed from the flimsy paper playing cards used by the general public.

Numerology: The study and association of occult significance of numbers.

Occultist: An individual who studies and works with the occult sciences.

Occult Science: The study and systematic research into occult practices, including Numerology, Astrology, Divination, Spiritualism, ESP, Kabbalah, etc.

Omens: Indication of future events based on a seen event or unusual occurrence.

Operative Freemason: The builders, architects and stone workers who organized themselves into the guild of Freemasonry in medieval Europe.

Oracle: A person who communicates prophetic messages from a divine source. Derived from the Latin oraculum and orare 'to speak.' Can also be a response or message given by an oracle.

Palmistry: The practice of determining someone's character or destiny as seen by examining outward features of the hand, fingers and palm.

Path of Cups: The maturity of emotion through intuition and sensibility as seen in the numeric progression of the suit of Cups in a Tarot deck.

Path of Pentacles: The maturity of material concerns through physical experience and economic administration as seen in the numeric progression of the suit of Pentacles in a Tarot deck.

Path of Swords: The maturity of intellect through communication and adversity as seen in the numeric progression of the suit of Swords in a Tarot deck.

Path of Wands: The maturity of desire through passion and creative expression as seen in the numeric progression of the suit of Wands in a Tarot deck.

Pentacles: One of the four suits, associated with the element of Earth and the quality of reality. Also called Coins.

Psychic: A person who receives information that cannot be explained by rational, logical means. Communication and ideas transmitted beyond means of the known senses.

Physical Persona: Used in relation to a Court Card, these are the physical traits assigned to each Court Card through history. Also the typical occupations suiting each Court Card's personality type.

Pope Joan: The popular legend of a female who reigned as pope for a few years during the middle ages. Her story is connected to the High Priestess card who is called the Papess in early historical decks.

Practice: (Noun) A habit or customary operation or exercise. For example, an active Tarot Practice means working with Tarot on a regular basis. Sometimes refers to a profession or occupation.

Printing Dynasties: The master printers, a cross between artists and craftsmen, who were driven to produce their Tarot cards for mostly commercial (not esoteric) reasons.

Querent: A term used for a person receiving a reading. Also called Client or Sitter.

Reader: The person who interprets the cards.

Reading: The whole activity of using Tarot cards in divination, comprising of ritual, shuffle, spread and interpretation.

Reading Record: Captures the date and time of the reading, cards received, their orientation, if the Reader reads reversals, interpretation notes, and any other impressions.

Renaissance: Period of European history from the 14th – 17th century in marking a great revival of art, literature and learning and the transition from medieval to the modern world.

Rider Waite Tarot, Waite Smith Tarot or RWS: Tarot deck conceived by Arthur Edward Waite and illustrated by Pamela Coleman Smith, published in 1910. The first deck since the Sola Busca deck to illustrate the Minor Arcana. The Rider Waite deck paved the way for modern Intuitive Tarot Reading.

Ritual: Any form of repeated activity usually conducted prior or following a reading. A ritual can include lighting a candle, spoken words, or simply tapping the deck on the table.

Roles: In Tarot Fundamentals it is the way a particular suit operates, i.e. masculine/feminine, rational/intuitive, etc.

Rosetta Stone: A stone discovered in 1799 near Rosetta, Egypt whose inscriptions made it possible to decipher ancient Egyptian hieroglyphics.

Rosicrucians: 17th and 18th century secret society devoted to the study of metaphysical, mystical and alchemical lore.

Sacred Geometry: The geometry used in the construction and design of religious structures such as churches, temples and mosques and for sacred spaces such as meditative labyrinths, holy wells, contemplative gardens, etc.

Scientific Revolution: The emergence of modern science in which mathematics, biology, chemistry and physics transformed views of reality, society and nature, 1550 – 1700.

Séance: A gathering of people where they attempt to make contact with the dead, usually by using an individual working as a medium.

Secret society: An organization of people who swear an oath of secrecy regarding their activities.

Shuffle: Any means of re-arranging the cards prior to a reading. A Shuffle may be done on the table or in the hands of the Reader, or by the Client or Querent, or by both.

Sister Manfreda: Possible inspiration and source for the Visconti Papess (High Priestess) card as put forth by historian Gertrude Moakley.

Smudging: The act of burning of herbs and creating ritualized smoke for emotional, psychic and spiritual cleansing and purification.

Sunlight Cleanse: Energetic cleanse of the deck with solar energy by placing the deck in the light of the sun for an entire day. Especially effective on the Summer Solstice, the longest day of the year.

Sortilege: Divination based on the rolling of dice, casting of lots, sticks or stones, beans, coins or any group of items.

Soothsaying: The act of foretelling future events.

Soul Themes: Working with your own or a Querent's spirituality leading to probing examinations of core beliefs and values.

Speculative Freemason: Freemasons who practice and belong to Masonic lodges but who are not actual builders, architects or stone workers.

Spiritualist Movement, Spiritualism, Spiritualists: A movement that began in the United States in the 1840's. It held that spirits of the dead could communicate with the living and that active communication was possible. Led to the formalized Spiritualist Church and Spiritualists who are its active membership.

Spontaneous Divination: Free form divination where an answer is derived from a random object.

Spooky Cards: Cards which are sometimes viewed as scary or dark cards, including, the Tower, Death, Devil, Five of Pentacles, Three of Swords, Nine of Swords and Ten of Swords. Also see Negative Cards.

Suit: A Tarot deck is arranged in four sets; Pentacles, Swords, Cups, Wands.

Superstition: A belief, custom, notion or idea that ominous significance exists in a particular occurrence or circumstance. Examples include: an upside down horseshoe brings good luck or a black cat crossing your path signifies bad luck. Also known as old wives' tales or urban legends.

Swords: One of the four suits, associated with the element of Air and with the quality of the mind.

Sybille Cards: Illustrated European fortune-telling cards based on folk traditions pre-dating the esoteric use of Tarot cards. Size and suit vary according to the region in which produced.

Symbolist: A person who uses and actively works with symbols and/or symbolism either professionally or in personal life.

Symbol, Symbolism: An object or happening that is used to represent something other than what it basically or literally is. For example: A metal crown: symbolic of royalty and power. A collapsing tower; symbolic of sudden institutional change.

Symbolic Reading: Creates a symbolic alphabet allowing a rational interpretation for each Arcana.

Synesthesia: "Union of the senses," a neurologically based condition where one sense opens a cognitive pathway to a second sense. A Synesthetic might "taste" colors or "see" music. Pamela Coleman Smith, the artist who painted the Rider Waite Smith deck, was Synesthetic.

Synthesis: The moment at which the Reader sums up all of the cards in a reading.

Tarot: Any deck conforming to the structure of seventy-eight cards utilizing four suits, twenty-two Major Arcana, fifty Minor Arcana and sixteen Court Cards.

Tarot Usage: The varieties of ways in which Tarot is used; i.e., personal readings, professional readings, inspiration, as art objects, as entertainment, fortune telling, etc.

Theosophical Society: An organization created in New York City, co-founded by occultist and mystic Madame Helena Petrovna Blavatsky to investigate the nature of the universe and understand humanity's place within it.

Theosophy: Meaning "Divine Wisdom," it is the teachings, traditions and notions put forth by the Theosophical Society that refers to the direct knowledge experienced by mystics, yogis and sages. This wisdom reflects the inner enlightenment and the basis of the mystical side of many religions and philosophies.

Thoth: A God of ancient Egypt. The scribe of the Gods and credited with the invention of the alphabet.

Three Card Spread: Popular Tarot spread where the past, present and future is indicated by each of the three cards.

Tree of Life: The central illustration of Cabala, most usually expressed as ten concentric circles or a matrix of ten circles connected by twenty-two paths, symbolic of the Hebrew letters.

Trump (verb): To outrank another card or to "Triumph" over it.

Thoth Tarot Deck: Tarot deck created by Aleister Crowley and painted by Lady Frieda Harris. Crowley referred to this deck as the Book of Thoth.

Traditional Interpretation: The meaning of each Tarot card as found historically in Tarot books.

Triumphal Processions: Popular European Renaissance parades. Costumed actors portrayed authorities (Emperors and Popes), Christian virtues (including Strength and Justice), life events (like Death and Resurrection) and even heavenly bodies (including the Stars, the Sun and the Moon).

Twenty-two paths: Usually refers to the Tree of Life and the paths between the ten circles, which are associated with the Major Arcana.

Visconti-Sforza Deck: The oldest known Tarot deck in existence, 15th century.

Visualization: The practice of using imagination to experience a card or enter into the scene of a card and explore it interactively.

Voice of the Deck: Each deck has a unique voice. It is a combination of its structure, theme, titles, keywords, illustrations and symbolic vocabulary.

Wands: One of the four suits associated with the element of Fire and relating to the quality of Passion.

White Cloth Cleanse: Deck cleaning technique in which the deck is wrapped in a white cloth for twelve to twenty-four hours.

Woodcuts: Relief printing technique used for printing ancient cards. A design was created and carved into a block of wood. The wood is placed in ink and used to stamp sheets of paper, which were later colored and cut. Process can also be used to apply different colors to a card.

THANKS

SPECIAL THANKS TO:

Sasha Graham is the first person we would like to thank. Her editing and compiling work has been crucial to make Tarot Fundamentals a book we, Lo Scarabeo, are proud of.

Our authors and contributors are next. A huge thank you to **Barbara Moore, Mark McElroy, Marcus Katz, Tali Goodwin, Giordano Berti, Richard Webster**, whose experience and knowledge is distilled through the pages of this book and will be further explored in the following ones.

A special place on this thank you list goes to our chief editor *Riccardo Minetti*. This book would simply not have been possible without his dedication, passion and professionalism.

The graphic project of Tarot Fundamentals, was created by *Santo Alligo* and became real thanks to the efforts of *Alessandro Starrantino* and *Manfredi Toraldo*. The cover is a kind concession by *Erik C Dunne*, and he too deserves an enormous thank you from us all. We also would like to thank collectively all the artists that worked for Lo Scarabeo during these years: their work now allows us to access an almost endless gallery of amazing illustrations, and several of those are enriching this book.

The successfully crowdfunded campaign on Kickstarter was coordinated by *Andrea Chiarvesio*, who would also like to thank *Elspeth Christie* for her help with proofreading.
Of course, none of the above would have been possible if *Mario Pignatiello* and *Pietro Alligo* had not founded Lo Scarabeo 28 years ago, made it grow and turned it in the successful international company it is now. Their vision and capacity to believe in new projects is the cornerstone of every new Lo Scarabeo project such as this one.

We also would like to thanks all our Kickstarter supporters, one by one.

Let's start with our *Special contributors list*

Alda Elvarsdottir	Colleen Setchell
Andrew Duncan	Cynthia Rose King
Angelo Nasios	Dana M Ferrera Burns
Ann-Marie J Lorde	Danielle Trujillo
Anthony J Farrugia	Danny de Hoyos
Backer Name	David Menning
Barbara Paterson	David Sacks
Bill Good	Diana D'Emeraude
Brandon Woolard	Donna A Wayne
Brenda Zack	Donna Mazzoni
Brian Watson	Dr. Zei
Carla Jadôt	Dyan Langdon
Carol Roche	Edna M. Garcia
Caroline Dufault	Elizabeth M. Sanchez
Carrie E. Newman	Elizabeth Rose Anderson
Carrie Paris/CarrieParis.com	Emmy Moon
Catherine Lavender	Evalyne Hall
Cheryl Ryder	Francisca E. Roele
Christopher Godwin	Gail Conley
Cindy Joy Trew	Guiomar Rebelo

Hannah Cross
Jamerria Martin
Jane E. Powell
Janis Garan
Jason Colmer
Jennifer Sansfacon
Jezebel (Gipsy) London
Joanna Jakes
Jon Hudson
Julia Hesse
Justine Mathers & Corrine Yakovlevich
Kari J. Wegg
Kay McBee
Lee Howard
Loren Levenstein
Lorenza Montes Fong
Lynette J Asmar
Maggie Grevenow
Marie Suk
Mark Miller
Markus Uhl
Martha Lebrón-Dykeman
Mary A. D'Alba
Mary Ann Baughan
Maryann Troche
Matt Rifley
Maximilian Wong, Duan Hong
Mellissa Wood
Michael L. Perkins
Michelle Gruben
Mrs. Shannon C. Gorton
Ms Adrienne Baker
Ms. Leigh Strother-Vien

Naha Armády
Nina Heggelund
Nora Linderman
Patricia A. Duplantis
Peter Stuart
Polly Taskey
Priscilla Lhacer
Rev. Ronald G. Cosseboom
Reverend Terrie Brookins
Robb (Nurkas DeWulf) Z
Robert F. Carty
Rodney W Carter
Ronald Mittlebeeler
Ryan Grant
Sam Boblenz and Audra Irvine
Sheila Lynn Masson
Shellee Moon LaCombe
Sherry Warner
Shivi Krishna
Stefan Spelkens
Stephanie S Tino
Steven R. Morrill - CasaTarot.com
Sue Wilhite
SuEllen Shepard
The Fool's Dog
The Tarot School
Theresa Reed, The Tarot Lady
Thorn Mooney
TouTarot
Tung Nguyen LT
Tze-Wen Chao
Zhivko Juzevski

Thank You

We would also like to extend our thanks to all our other Kickstarter backers:

78 tarot, Abby Gordon, Adrianne Dawkins, Adrienn Faklya-Schmitz, Adrienne Ritenburgh, Aimee Kanemori, Aja Martinez, Alaina Barrow, Alessandro Magnani, Alex Indigo, Alex Lambert, Alex Luna, Alex Randall, Alexa Gulliford, Alexandre Valois, Alexei Treiger, Alicia Carr, Alicia Kork, Alicia Vidal, Alison Harville , Alison Holden, Allison Grant, Allison Grier, Allison Riley, Alyssa De Leon, Amanda Davey, Amanda Keiser, Amaril Andras, Amarin Astarte , Ambra Chiavarotti, Amy Castonguay, Amy Robertson, Ana Patricia Ocegueda Azpeitia, Ana Vitoria, Anastasia Haysler, Andrea Haddad, Andrea Io, Andrea Nagel, Andreas Henriksson , Andres Miller, Andrew Barker, Andrew Conneely III, Andrew Duckworth, Andrew Harris, Andrew Rinella, Angel Leigh McCoy, Angela Carrillo, Angela Mondor, Angela Paul, Angela Pennacchini, Angela Tan, Angelica Casimira, Ann Coghlan, Ann Houghton, Ann Marie Baumann, Ann Tupek, Anna Manzo, Annik Boyer, Anthony Farrugia, Antonia Vogel, Apryl Green, Arthur Wu, Ashley Oppon, Ashley Peake , Athena Halverson, Audra l Linder, Aurora Díaz, Austin Zalewski, Avalon Cameron, Axel Liljencrantz, Barbara Belder, Barry Bailey , Ben Jones , Benjamin Russell, Beth Maiden 'Empress', Betty Hackney, Beverley Williams, Bill Gimbel, Bob Hardy, Bogdan Manolache, Bonnie Cehovet, Bonnie Shiff, Boyd Stephenson, Braid Kopling, Brandy Latshaw, Brian Anderson, Brian Atkinson, Brian Bailey, Brian Madsen , Brian Sun, Brighid Gale, Britta Carlson, Bruno Boulanger, Bruno Monteiro, Bryan Grayson, Bryce Bartlett, Caleb Campbell, Camilla Venezuela, Cara Terry, Carla Alexandra Duarte Roda, Carla Costa e Silva, Carmen Quinones, Carmen Waterman, Carol Johns, Carole Webb, Carolina Mayle, Carolyn Ayres, Casey Ernest, Casper Rojahn, Cassia Regina da Silva, Cath Evans, Catherine Swidzinski, Catherine Chandler, Catherine Currie, Catherine Leja, Cathy Brown, Charles Olbert, Charlotte venkatraman, Chelse Rhea Williams, Cheryl Burney, Cheryl Fox, Cheryl Turtlemoon Millsom, Cheryll Maze, Chetan Jain, Chris Chaney, Chris Ness, Chris Schweda, Chris Whittington, Christian Widmer, christina harland, Christina Herrera , Christina Quick, Christine McPhee, Christine Smith, Christoph Sackl, Christopher Troutman, Cindy Corbett, Claire Simons, Colin, Colin Robertson, Cori Ander, Corwin Briscoe, Cosette Paneque, Cyndee Todgham Cherniak, Cynthia Arrington, Cynthia King, Cynthia Schaum, D. Kelly, Dan Lendzian, Dani Marie Kice, Daniel Dabrowski, Daniel Gagnon, Daniel John, Daniel Siedler, Daniela Maffei, Daniele Nigris, Danielle Lean Zhi Jiun, Danielle Shipman, Dara Doolittle, Dave Warden, David Eichler, David Kees, Nicole de Lan ge, David Koch, David Widstrom, Debbie Crabb, Debbie Freeman, Debbie MacLeod, Debbie Smith, Deborah Ashe, Deborah Camenzuli, Deborah Cortlandt, Deborah Ketchen, Deepra Smith , Deirdre Carter, Denali White, Denise Chagas, Denise Young, Dennis Ng, Denny Yan, Derek Guder, Desiree Horsey, Devin Kreuger, Devon Bouffard, Diana Chin, Diana Pantoja, Diane Rae, Diane Wilkes, Dianne DeMarco, Dirk M. Weger, Dirk-Jan van Gerwen, Dogukan Ozyurt, Dominique De La Cruz, Don DeCoster, Donald Ingrao, Donna Collins, Donna Fraser, Donna M. LaSota, Doug Taylor, Douglas Thornsjo, Dylan Fogle, E Bordeaux, Eben Mishkin, Edward Markland, Elaine Honeywood, Eliana Davidson, Elijah Egnor, Elise Kress, Elisha Riley, Elizabeth Fedoruk, Elizabeth Kitrel, Elizabeth Paniagua, Elizabeth Sceneay, Elizabeth Tuckwood, Elizabeth Welke, Elizabeth Will, Elle Jacobs, Elly Cockcroft, Elspeth Christie, Emilia Georgieva, Emiliano Zanini , Emily, Emily Jiggins, Emily Shiffer, Emily Smith, Emma Levine, Eric Gold, Eric Wagner, Erica Bercegeay, Erica True, Erik Berglund, Ernest lessenger, Ethony Dawn, Fanny Verrier, Felipe Shimabukuro Kai, Filipe Santos, Finbarr Farragher, Fiona Mellish, Forrest Borie , Fran Marley, Francesca Hedrick, Francken Carine, Frank Waters, Frank Zepp, Fritz Hintringer Bakke, Gabriele B. Hefer, Gabriella Busuttil, Gabriella Ripoll, Gabrielle English, Gaelen Hudson, Gail Johnson, Gale Hamby, Gareth Thomas, Gary Halstead, Gavin Pugh, Geneve Mingl, George Cooper, Gerald Kuick, Giancarlo Kind Shmid, Gilbert Lugo, Gillian Paterson, Gloria Bardell, Glynn Ryland, Graham Pedersen, Greg Robinson, Grey Townsend, Grundkoetter Klaus-Peter, Guinevere Jones, Hadley Fitzgerald, Haley McLoughlin, Heather Brown, Heather Flores, Heather Hank, Heather Matthews, Heidi Kim, Helder Lavigne, Helen Crumpbolt, Helen Edwards, Helen Garside, Helene enström, Henrietta Niclasen , Hilary Wood Lecoy, Hillary Kellum, Hillary Mueri, Hiroyuki Ihara, Holly Pickett, Hunter Wilcox, Ian O'Beirne,, Ieva Melgalve, Ilbel Ramirez, Iliana Adler, Inbal Meron , Irene Castellani, Irina Shukurova, Jacob Walker, Jacqueline Caci , Jacqui Diamond, James Shultz, Jami N. Riley, Jan Davies, Jana Stange , Jane Davis, Jane Morris, Jane Westover, Janet Welsh, Janine Hall, Jasmine White, Jason Gazee , Jason L. Corlett, Jay Zastrow, Jaymi Elford, Jeanine Southall, Jeanne DiLeo, Jeannine Jordan, Jeff Tressler, Jenna Matlin, Jennifer Carmen, Jennifer Colesellhill, Jennifer Harper, Jennifer McDonald, Jennifer Oad, Jennifer Pol, Jennifer Prickett, Jennifer Routson, Jennifer Wares, Jennifer Wyatt, Jenny Cartledge, Jenny Gavelin, Jeremy Baker, Jeremy C. Smith, Jeremy Voranath, Jeri Unselt, Jesamyn Angelica, Jesse Rouse, Jessica Brown, Jessica Daly, Jessica McMeans, Jessica Painter, Jessica Radigue, Jessica Snyder, Jessica Welke, Jesterdev, Jill Ackiron- Moses, Jill Pitts, Jill Sophia Fein, Jillian Studholme, Jo Lister, Joan Sargent, Joanne Howitz, Johanna Hermann, John Biffle, John Coombs, John Lambert, John Marron, John Stewart Muller, Joled Kob, Jolene Vineyard, Jonathan Bocknek, Jonathan Fesik, Jonathan Pearson, Jonathan Saiz, Jason Grubl & Andi Todaro, Jordan Crick, Joseph Parris, Joshua Clarke, Joshua leon, Jousseaume Audrey, Joy Vernon, JT Fischer, Judi Jurist, Judi McInally, Judy Baker, Julia Allen, Julia Consterdine , Julia Gothe, Julie Black, Julie Hughes, Julie Wescott, Justine Jones, Justine Pong, Kaitlyn Cinnamond, Kali McNeil, Karen Borusiewicz, Karen Buebler, Karen Larson, Karen Leymarie , Karen McIsaac, Karen Sealey, Karen Shelley, Karen Tritton, Kari Jamison, Karie-Anne Getta, Karmun Khoo, Kat Chaluisant, Kate Scott, Kate Thomas, Katherine Forrester, Kathleen Anderson, Kathleen Purmal, Kathy Ayres, Kathy squires, Katie MacAlister, Katrin Tomasdottir, Kayla Lacotta, Kaylene Glass, Kelley Jabr, Kelly black, Kelly Gerlach, Kelly Murray, Kelly ringle, Kelly Turnbull, Kenneth Thronberry, Kerrianne Hancock, Kevin Burr, Kevin Leijten, Kiki Dombrowski, Kim Davies, Kim Franklin, Kim Huggens, Kim Methven, Kim Nguyen, Kim Tompkins, Kim Weaver, Kimberly McKinney, Kimly Do, KIpton Lade, Kirstie Maylor, Kirsty Crosby, Kirsty Skidmore, Kit O'Shell, Konstantinos Bragkatzis, Kori Hamm, Kris Trower, Krista Humphrey, Kristen Jett, Kristie Stevens, Kritsada Poolwan, Krysta Gibson, Kurt Johnson, Lady Pipera, laetitia wurtz, Lafayette

Michael, Lara Baruca, Larry Cosmos, Laura Figueroa, Laura Fletcher, Laura Miller, Laura Osborne, Laura Trittipoe, Laura Whitaker, Lauren Fein, Lauren Granillo, Laurie MacNider, Lawrence Dudzik, Lea Roselli, Leagh Waugh, Lee Van Sant , Leeon Pezok, Leonie Woudstra, Lester Tan, Liberté Angéliaume, Lilly Ibelo, Lily Greer, Linda Bean, Linda Gavin-Morand, Linda Lancaster, Linda Satchell, Linda Slack, Lisa Anderson, Lisa Douglas, Lisa Lavoie, Lisa Lloyd, Lisa Sciamanda, Lisa Webb, Lisa Wysocki, Lisette Anderson, Lola Dechant, Lonnie Scott, Loreen Muzik, Lorena O'Grady, Lori Buschbaum, Lori Hahn, Lori Owens, Lotten Heldtander, Louise Johnson, Luca Mordazzi, Luis Penn, Luke Martin, Luna Valentine, Lynn Gray, Lynn Lemyre, Maggie Elliott, Mai Huong Nguyen, Mandy Gray, Margaret Devlin, Margaret Garland, Margaret Morton, Maria Fernandez, Maria Gilson, Maria Jerrard, Maria torres, Marian Mc Quinn, Mário António Portela, Marisa McCall, Marjie Ho, Mark Franklin, Mark Harnois, Mark Hughes, Mark Rapp, Markus Pfeil, Marsha Fortney, Martha McCulloch, Martin Audrey, Martin Payne, Mary A. Black, Mary K. Greer, Mary Mannix, Matt Suter, Matthew House, Matthew McNally, Maurice C Cherry, Max Haskvitz, Meddy Mills, Meg Petz, Megan Congdon, Megan Harris, Megan Weber, Meghan Drake, Melani Weber, Melanie Climis, Melissa, Melissa Goss, Melissa Page, Melissia Selwyn, Meri Hoopingarner, Merlion Sqyqc, Mette Markert, Michael Itzo, Michael Surbrook, Michael Vermilye, Michel Lampo, Michelle Armbrust, Michelle Kennedy, Michelle Riggs, Mike Hernandez, Mike Lin, Mitchell Osborn, MJ Foley, Mj Willard, MM Meleen, Moira Payne, Monika Antonelli, Monika Stojs, Morten Agerfeldt, Mr. Lee, Mrs Gemma Daniels, Mrs M Quinnell, Mrs Michelle Thompson, Mrs Sarah L Robinson, Mrs Sarah Russell, Ms Jaimie Pattison, My Huynh Thi Hanh Nghia, Nadine Roberts, Nancy Booth, Nancy DePoe, Nancy Hutchins, Nancy Matus, Nancy Siwik, Nancy Stewart, Natalie Dawes, Natalie Martinez, Natasha Dyson-Lee, Neal Reynolds, Nedre Carter, Ng Ka Yung, Nicholas Blackwell , Nicholas Weaver-Weinberg, Nico Mara-McKay, Nicole Henninger, Nicole White, Paige Connell, Pam Fulton, Pamela J Goodwin, Pamela Koster, Pamela L. Johnson, Pamela Steele, Pamella Marschall, Patricia Brown, Patrick Martin, Patrik Askert, Patti Newell, Paul Hughes, Paul Miller, Paul Nagy, Paul Rostance, Paula Tague, Pauline Bonnet, Peter Brownell, Peter White, Phil Crawley, Phil Deason , Phillip Licata, Pierre Blanchet, Pip Winstone, Preston Ward, Quek JiaJin, Rachael Hammond, Rachael Nicholas-Mark, Racheal Adams, Rachel A. Reznik, Rachel Droessler, Rachel Harris, Rachel Howell, Rachel Jones, Rachel Kitcher , Rachel Maynard, Rae Douglass, Rae McFarron, Rafael Soto, Raimonds Lellis, Rebecca Ballou, Regina McDaniel, Rhonda Jackson, Richard Hussey, Richard Naxton, Richard Olinger, Richard Spinello, Rin Revell, Ritesh Aswaney, Rob Harper, Rob Steinberger, Robert Harris, Robert R Narmore Jr, Robert Zupko, Roberto Arteaga, Robin Gilman, Robin Milgate, Robyn Wescombe, Rodolphe Duhil, Rodrigo Santacruz, Roger Hyttinen, Roger Shepherd, Roland Volz, Rolin D Jenkins, Rommy Driks, Ronald Kanagy, Rosemary McCreery, Rosemary Wisniewski, Ross O'Donoghue, Roxann Chalfant , Ruediger Pfeiffer, Rukesh Patel, Ryan Lyons, Ryan Tice, Sabine Peters, Sabrina Fatale, Sally, Sally Hill, Sam Kong, Sandi Oswalt, Sandie McDonnell, Sandra Beecher, Sandra Gregory   , Sandra Grünwald, Sandra Moran, Sara Bender, Sara Dziarmaga, Sarah Aylward, Sarah Barry, Sarah Brown, Sarah Connell, Sarah Ferguson, Sarah Gledhill, Sarah Helena Bedeschi de Camargo, Sarah K Spiers, Sarah kral, Sarah Lewis, Sarah Underwood, Sasha Albertini, Satu Väänänen, Scott A Williams, Scott Barnes, Scott Mudd, Sean Mackey, Sebastian Harris-Nielsen, Serena Carter, Shane Coineandubh, Shanna Adams, Shannon Burton, Sharon Davidson, Sharon Groff, Sharon Merlier, Sharrye Deer, Sheila Fontaine, Shelby Fullington, Shelly Tannehill, Siovhan Frey-Ortega, Snædís Guðmundsdóttir, Sonya Hicks, Sophia Vassilagoris, Sophie Castède, Sophie Prior, Spiritual Garden, Stefania Dragomir, Stephanie Coffin, Stephanie Henkel, Stephanie Prinz, Stephen Davison, Stephen Roesch, Steve Gladstone, Steve Salmon, Steven Long, Steven McGee, Steven White, sue smith, Surasak Boonyachai, Susan Adami, Susan Anderson, Susan Ann Collins, Susan Brackley, Susan Dulak, Susan Goodwin, Susanne Hochreuther, Susanne Vreugdenburg , Suzanne Flynn, Suzi Petito, Suzie Wright, Sven Hendrieckx, Sylvain Poirier, Sylvia Patricia Betts, Sylvia Vallotton, T Susan Chang, T.Y Hoang, Tabitha Wiegers, Taisha Forster, Tamera Robinson , Tammy Mobr, Tammy Patterson, Tana Knox, Tara Colligan, Tara Kelly, Tara Winstanley, Tarek von Bergmann, Tasha Erker, Teerawut Ananthana, Teresa Sutton, Teri Iosbaker Vermillion, Tesie Price, Theresa Charlton, Therese Downer, Therese Porter, Therese Totten, Tia Jackson, Tia Lam, Tiago Tempera, Tiffany Fitzpatrick , Tiina Childress-Khurana, Tim Jones, Tina Georgitsis, Titova Irina Igorevna, Tom Majski, Tomas Koulak, Toni Carmine Salerno, Toni Dafeldecker, Torsten Berger, Tracey Fearn, Traci Whitehead, Tracy Diss, Tracy Timmerman , Trevor Donnelly, Trish Vidal, Vanelli Feitoza, Vanessa Baudichon Domingues, Veronica Duncan, Vickey Milligan, Victoria Jones, Vidya Gopalakrishna, Vyolet Wylde, Wai Ling Wong, Wallis Doerge, Wayne Nicholson, Wendy Blake, Wesley de Souza, William Andrews, William Doggett, William Fontaine Jr, William McCracken, William S. Habdas, Wim Driessens, Yannick Plourde, Yasmin Eaton, Zantiago Echeverri, Zhu Wenming,

Sasha Graham would like tanks also:
Barbara Moore, Bill and Isabella Brady, Brock Lady, Juniper Lusk, Mom, Riccardo Minetti

Names are listed in alphabetical order by first name. Some backers did not replied to our post-campaign survey so we had to list them under their account name on kickstarter. We do apologize in advance for misspellings or if you are a backer and you don't find your name in this list.